W9-BYB-890

INTERNATIONAL RELATIONS OF THE MIDDLE EAST

INTERNATIONAL RELATIONS OF THE MIDDLE EAST

LOUISE FAWCETT

OXFORD

UNIVERSITY PRESS

OXFORD
UNIVERSITY PRESS

Great Clarendon Street, Oxford OX2 6DP
Oxford University Press is a department of the University of Oxford.
It furthers the University's objective of excellence in research, scholarship,
and education by publishing worldwide in
Oxford New York

Auckland Bangkok Buenos Aires Cape Town Chennai
Dar es Salaam Delhi Hong Kong Istanbul Karachi Kolkata
Kuala Lumpur Madrid Melbourne Mexico City Mumbai Nairobi
São Paulo Shanghai Taipei Tokyo Toronto

Oxford is a registered trade mark of Oxford University Press
in the UK and in certain other countries

Published in the United States
by Oxford University Press Inc., New York

© editorial material and arrangement Louise Fawcett 2005
© individual chapters the several contributors 2005

The moral rights of the author have been asserted
Database right Oxford University Press (maker)

First published 2005

Reprinted 2005

All rights reserved. No part of this publication may be reproduced,
stored in a retrieval system, or transmitted, in any form or by any means,
without the prior permission in writing of Oxford University Press,
or as expressly permitted by law, or under terms agreed with the appropriate
reprographics rights organization. Enquiries concerning reproduction
outside the scope of the above should be sent to the Rights Department,
Oxford University Press, at the address above

You must not circulate this book in any other binding or cover
and you must impose this same condition on any acquirer

British Library Cataloguing in Publication Data

Data available

ISBN - 13: 978-0-19-926963-1

ISBN - 10: 0-19-926963-7

3 5 7 9 10 8 6 4

Typeset by Newgen Imaging Systems (P) Ltd., Chennai, India
Printed in Great Britain
on acid-free paper by
Ashford Colour Press Ltd. Gosport, Hants.

Contents

Acknowledgements

Discussions over the nature and contents of this volume started in the summer of 2001. I have since benefited greatly from the help and advice of many colleagues both in Oxford and elsewhere. From Oxford University Press, Angela Griffin, Sue Dempsey, Helen Adams, Ruth Anderson and Nicola Rainbow have all, in different ways, either helped to get the project started, keep it moving, or to see it through to completion.

Many Oxford University colleagues have been enormously helpful. Some are contributors themselves, others have suggested names, still others have helped to host and chair a parallel seminar series under the auspices of the Middle East Centre at St Antony's College in the Michaelmas Term of 2002, which saw lively discussions of some of the papers and issues discussed in the volume. The Middle East Centre has been a source of support and encouragement from start to finish. I am particularly grateful to its director Eugene Rogan, but also to Avi Shlaim and Philip Robins for all their help and advice. Elizabeth Anderson also deserves special thanks for her organizational input. Outside the Centre, the seminar series also received the support of the Department of Politics and International Relations. Aby Bidwell, Fellows' Secretary at my own College, St Catherine's, has been a great help in collating and printing out material.

Other individuals upon whose advice I have depended include Fred Halliday, James Piscatori, Yezid Sayigh, and the different contributors themselves, all of whom have responded patiently and generously to my repeated requests for guidance.

I have benefited from helpful and detailed comments from two different sets of outside readers, all of whom provided extremely useful feedback at different stages in the production of the volume. It remains for me to say that the responsibility for any errors is mine alone.

A final and very big note of thanks is due to my family: Eduardo, Beatriz, Carlos, Claudia and Francisco, who have put up with my long working hours and grumbles—particularly during the final stages of the production of this book!

Note on Contributors

Louise Fawcett is Fellow and Tutor in Politics at St Catherine's College Oxford. She is the author of *Iran and the Cold War*.

F. Gregory Gause, III is an Associate Professor of Political Science at the University of Vermont, and author of *Oil Monarchies*.

Clement Henry is Professor of Government at the University of Texas at Austin. He is co-author (with Robert Springborg) of *Globalization and the Politics of Development in the Middle East*.

Ray Hinnebusch is Professor of International Relations and Middle East politics at the University of St. Andrews, Scotland. He is the author of *International Politics of the Middle East*.

Rosemary Hollis is Head of the Middle East Programme at the Royal Institute of International Affairs (Chatham House) in London. She has recently written 'The US Role: Helpful or Harmful?', in Lawrence Potter & Gary Sick, eds., *Unfinished Business: Iran, Iraq and the Aftermath of War*.

Michael C. Hudson is Seif Ghobash Professor of Arab Studies and Professor of International Relations at Georgetown University. He is editor of *Middle East Dilemmas. The Politics and Economics of Arab Integration*.

Bahgat Korany is Professor at the Universities of Cairo and Montreal. He is co-editor of *The Many Faces of National Security in the Arab World*.

Giacomo Luciani is Professor of Political Economy at European University Institute and Professorial Lecturer in Middle Eastern Studies at Johns Hopkins University Bologna Center. He is the editor of *The Arab State*.

Richard Norton is Professor in the Departments of Anthropology and International Relations at Boston University. He is the editor of *Civil Society in the Middle East* (2 vols).

Dr. Eugene Rogan lectures in the modern history of the Middle East in the University of Oxford and is a Fellow of St Antony's College. He is the author of *Frontiers of the State in the Late Ottoman Empire*.

Professor Avi Shlaim is a Fellow of St Antony's College and a Professor of International Relations at the University of Oxford. He is the author *The Iron Wall: Israel and the Arab World*.

Peter Sluglett is Professor of Middle Eastern History at the University of Utah, Salt Lake City. He is co-author of *Iraq since 1958: from Revolution to Dictatorship*.

Charles D. Smith is Professor of Middle East History in the Department of Near Eastern Studies, University of Arizona. He is the author of *Palestine and the Arab–Israel Conflict*.

Janice Gross Stein is Belzberg Professor of Conflict Management and Director of the Munk Centre for International Studies at the University of Toronto. She is a Fellow of the Trudeau Foundation. Her most recent book is *The Cult of Efficiency*.

Introduction

Louise Fawcett

The Book and the Title

This book aims to provide the reader with a comprehensive, yet accessible guide for understanding the International Relations of the Middle East in the last century. Few parts of the world have been quite so buffeted by conflict and war; few parts of the world so much written about and debated in recent times, while at the same time remaining so subject to misunderstanding and stereotype. As one scholar wrote, reflecting on the legacy of fifty years of academic study of the region: 'Middle Eastern political processes defy observation, discourage generalization and resist explanation' (Bill 1996: 503). This volume is designed to improve our understanding of the Middle East by contemplating its International Relations in broad terms.

These two subject areas, International Relations and Middle East politics, are highly interdependent, as even a cursory survey of major works shows. No book on the Middle East can afford to ignore the way that external forces have shaped the development of the region's politics, economics and societies, or indeed how the region itself has contributed to frame and shape the global environment. Similarly, no International Relations text can afford to ignore the rich case studies that the Middle East has supplied, and how they illuminate different theories and concepts of the discipline. It is a surprising feature of the literature, that despite advances in recent years, relatively little work has been done to bring these subject areas closer together. While other regions of the world appear to have been more susceptible to such exercises, Middle East Studies and International Relations continue to stand apart in an uneasy and often unfamiliar relationship (Tessler et al. 1999).

This volume aims to help fill the vacuum, to move beyond some well-rehearsed arguments of *exceptionalism* that have been commonly applied to the Middle East, and to offer an integrated approach in which some key ideas and concepts in International Relations and some key themes of Middle East Studies are brought together and discussed in systematic way.

Though at first sight unproblematic, and not the first, nor certainly the last book to bear a similar title, a word of explanation is still in order (Brown, L. C. 1984; Ismael 1986; Hinnebusch 2003; Halliday 2004). The Middle East is a term which has slipped into popular use since the Second World War, and though there remain divergences over its extension, both as whether it should be narrower, to exclude African Arab States west of Egypt, or broader to include (among others) the Muslim republics of Central Asia, a compromise definition is usually favoured. The region is now commonly understood to include the Arab States of West Asia and North Africa— members of the Arab League—and Iran, Turkey and Israel. This is the region which will be considered here. Ungainly though it is, enjoying no obvious continental reach, or geographical tidiness, it possesses certain distinctive 'systemic' properties and unifying characteristics (Gause 1999).

International Relations, for its part, is an evolving and often imprecise term to describe a still imprecise social science. Once more narrowly limited to the study and analysis of relations between states, recent International Relations scholarship has moved fully into the non-state domain: it now stretches well beyond the concept of the state and its relations with other states, to cover a broader range of interactions between peoples and societies—'the web of transnational politics' (Frankel 1988).

This expansive, and expanding notion of international relations is useful for this book in many ways. Much of the volume is concerned, of course, with the mechanisms and institutions of formal inter-state relations, but also with less formal interactions and patterns of behaviour which operate above and below the level of states. These seem especially pertinent to the Middle East: for regional scholars, and historians in particular, the non-state domain has often been the normal, if you like default position.

To illustrate this, for sizeable parts of the twentieth century the idea of Arabism and or Islam were held as consistuting important elements in the International Relations of the region. Tribal and religious identity both preceded, and transcended state boundaries in shaping regional behaviour (Khoury and Kostiner 1990). At the beginning of the twenty-first century, though some states looked stronger than before, these forces have remained salient. One transnational force of particular note has been the startling manifestations of terrorism, reflected in networks of extremist Islamist groups, operating across state boundaries. Such groups and their actions both challenge and erode the fragile legitimacy of many states, while making them subjects for intervention. The charge that Afghanistan and Iraq had encouraged such networks, contributed to the US-led interventions in 2002 and 2003 respectively.

The transnational or subnational case should not be overstated. Despite its contested, and at times fluid properties, the states system in the Middle East has proved

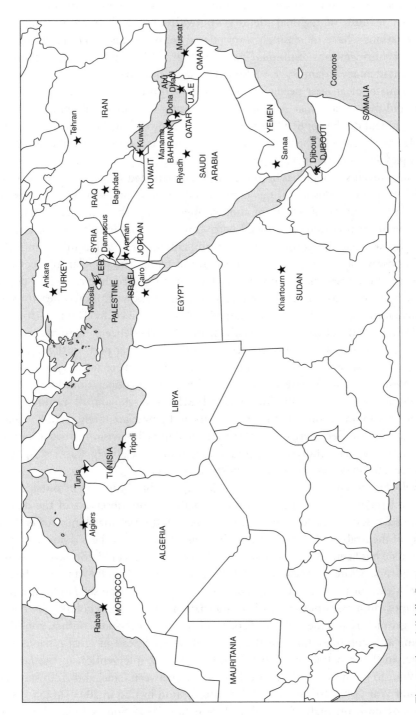

The modern Middle East

remarkable for its survival and durability, and it is the contention of some that the older features of regional identity—notwithstanding their recent and violent manifestations—have increasingly surrendered to, or at least conditioned by more powerful considerations of *raison d'etat*. Pan-Arabism has undoubtedly declined as a dominant ideology (Ajami 1978/9). Still, it remains clear that a state-centric approach is inadequate, or at least needs balancing with a throrough consideration of other actors and movements that compete with states for authority and popular support. This argument can be applied to any region, but it is worth making for the case of the Middle East, because of the way in which it is singled out for the special relations that its peoples and societies have enjoyed.

Strong currents of regional homogeneity have persisted in a variety of forms, and are reflected in the book's subtitle: 'conflict and cooperation', which in turn requires some clarification. While the term conflict appears unproblematic, cooperation for some might seem curious as applied here. Conflict is the default state of affairs in International Relations, cooperation is a realm entered only with caution, and where certain observable criteria and conditions are in place. The popular and persistent perception of the region, and one which has pervaded academic as well as popular circles, is to see the Middle East as a region of conflict and war. It provides, for some, an illustration of the international state of nature described by Thomas Hobbes, a world which, in the absence of a Leviathan, sees the prevalence of anarchy, greed and power struggle. It is an 'unfinished' region, not unlike other parts of the developing world, with weak states and weak regional institutions, where territory and borders are contested, and inter-state war persists. The kinds of cooperation, identified and parsimoniously explained by International Relations scholars, of rational actors seeking maximum payoffs in terms of security and power are rarely seen. Yet against this vision of disorder, there is a contrasting and compelling vision of order, one long familiar to regional scholars: of peoples cohabiting a relatively seamless space, of tolerance and diversity—cultural, linguistic and religious.

Until quite recently, this difference of perception has been one of outsiders and insiders. Insiders—that is to say—scholars of the region, observers of the detail of Middle East politics, have long been impressed by the ties that bind. An enduring feature of the Arab world, and one that differentiates it from others is how the failure of one state has been seen as the failure of all. This remark could not have been made about Europe before the Second World War; nor could it be said to apply in the same way to Africa, or to other parts of Asia. In this sense pan-Arabism *has* been unique. What most impresses outsiders—like International Relations scholars, observers of the bigger picture—is the persistence of conflict. Even inter-state conflict, considered by some as becoming a thing of the past, still rears its head in most obvious form: whether in the Iran-Iraq war (1980–88); Israel's 1982 intervention in the Lebanese Civil War, to say nothing of the previous clashes between Israel and Arab states; the first Gulf War (1990–91); or the US-led intervention in Iraq in 2003 (Maoz 1997).

Perhaps unsurprisingly, for leading International Relations scholars like Steven Walt or Joseph Nye, the Middle East has provided the ideal case study of how states conduct themselves in international anarchy, a term commonly used to describe the unregulated nature of the international system (Walt 1987; Nye 2000).

Those who are insiders and outsiders—and this includes a number of contributors to this volume—have found themselves obliged to wear 'two hats' as Avi Shlaim once eloquently expressed it. Middle Eastern hats are exchanged with International Relations hats to suit different fora and publics. This book represents an effort to bring closer together two hitherto divergent perspectives: to substitute the two hats for one.

To be fair, this outsider view has already started to change. There are some fine contributions to the debate that are both International Relations friendly and region sensitive contributing to a 'modest renaissance' in integrating theory and area expertise (Nonneham 2001). This book continues and develops this trend by demonstrating that the International Relations of the Middle East is incomprehensible without first appreciating the regional and domestic frame within which states operate, and second the juxtaposition of patterns of cooperation alongside persistent conflict. Understanding these relationships provides in turn important clues both to understanding patterns of war and peace, as well as the continuing story of state-building in the region.

Organisation of the Volume

The organisation of a volume such as this one presents a number of challenges. There are, of course, alternative routes to accessing and interpreting the International Relations of the Middle East, or indeed of any region. These, in turn, reflect the eclectic origins and mixture that is the study of International Relations itself. One could start with a history of societies and peoples, or the regional economy (Hourani 1991; Richards and Waterbury 1996). One could focus on the patterns and practices of foreign policy or diplomacy (Brecher 1972; Korany and Dessouki 1991; Hinnebusch and Ehteshami 2002; Brown, L. C. 2003). One could opt for the single-issue approach, to include case studies of great power relations with a particular state or group of states, or analyses of individual crises (Gerges 1994; Sela 1998). Finally there is the growing trend, already noted, towards bringing core International Relations themes to the Middle East in discussions of the role of identity, security, globalisation, regionalism, resources and power (Telhami 1990; Korany, Noble and Byrnen 1993; Barnett 1998; Hudson 1999; Henry and Springborg 2001; Yergin 1991).

All such approaches have their uses in illuminating different aspects of the International Relations of the region. Since this book is deliberately designed to reach a wide student public from different disciplines, as well as to draw on the strengths of individual authors, the aim has been to include a range of perspectives, rather than favour any single approach, or indeed to try to apply a set of uniform questions across the different chapters of the volume.

With the above in mind, the book is divided into three Parts as follows:

1. An opening Part that offers a **broad historical overview** of the twentieth century. History provides one vital and enduring point of entry into understanding the International Politics of any region. 'All history is contemporary history', as one historian of the early twentieth century famously observed (Croce 1941: 19). Further the historian's eye for detail and analysis can tell us much of what we need to know about the present by egaging us, in E. H. Carr's words, with 'an unending dialogue' with the past (Carr 1961: 30)

2. The central Part of the book considers some **key themes of International Relations and Political Economy** and applies them to the Middle East. Here, topics such as oil, globalisation, the role of ideas and identity, democratisation, the management of regional and external relations, and patterns of war and peace—themes that are universal to the study of International Relations and International Political Economy—are examined and deployed with particular reference to regional experience. In this Part different authors explore a variety of International Relations based-approaches and assess their relative usefulness in understanding the region and its interactions with the rest of the world.

3. The final Part looks at some case studies, considering **both region specific conflicts and situations, and the role of external actors** in shaping the international relations of the region. Included here are the Arab-Israel conflict, and attempts at its resolution, the different Gulf Wars and the policies of both the United States and the European powers in shaping the region.

Though far from exhaustive, and highly interdependent, each Part provides a set of discrete yet interconnected insights. In offering this menu for choice, the volume aims at a broad readership among students of the Middle East Studies, International Relations and International Political Economy. The different chapters are intended to stand alone for those who wish to focus on a particular historical period, event or theme, but can be read together, and thus provide the possibility of acquiring a solid, well rounded perspective on any given question.

There are the obvious pitfalls of overlap, repetition and exclusion. The selection of chapters for a book which proposes to offer an International Relations of the Middle East is necessarily a subjective process, and a number of factors need to be considered. Following current fashion might suggest a different choice. In a world where the state, for some, has become an outmoded concept, where security may be viewed through a different lens, as suggested by the United Nations Secretary General Kofi Annan in outlining his concept of 'human security', the subject might be approached in an entirely different way. Here, rather than fashion, the relative weight or salience of topics *over time* must be a guide. One question asked in the organisation of the volume is which are the topics and issues that students of International Relations and Middle East Studies commonly seek to address? If we contemplate the contemporary International Relations of the region, we find that issues of war and peace, relations with external powers, the processes of economic and political liberalisation and the politics of identity and alliance formation, all feature prominently. This book tackles such questions while acknowledging that the questions themselves may change, or already be changing. A book on International Relations of the Middle East written in 2050 may read very differently: just consider the differences between a book written on the International Relations of Europe in the 1930s and a book written on the International Relations of Europe today.

Within these constraints, the different chapters in the three Parts of the book offer a balance between Middle Eastern and International Relations perspectives. The authors all do this in a slightly different way, reflecting their own interests and preferences. There has not been attempt to turn area specialists into International Relations scholars, or *vice versa*, an exercise which would run the risk of being both artificial and superficial. Rather, in locating their chapters within the broad remit of the *International Relations of the Middle East* and considering different axes of conflict and cooperation: a theme that runs through all the chapters of the volume, there is an invitation to each author to play to his or her respective strengths, but with an eye to developing a theme or idea that is intelligible to both disciplines. The result is a blend, which aims to bring them a little closer together. Each chapter in its own way contributes to a broader understanding of the patterns of relations between Middle Eastern states and societies and other states and societies at different moments and different levels.

Chapter outlines

Part 1: Historical overview

In Part 1, **Chapter 1** by Eugene Rogan starts with the origins of the Middle East states system, or the entry of these states into the broader international system. This chapter provides essential background material on the emergence of the modern Middle East into the twentieth century international system. In presenting his analysis, Rogan is influenced by the ideas of the 'English School' of International Relations, inspired by Hedley Bull and others for whom International Relations can be best understood in terms of the concept of an 'International Society', still anarchical in the sense described above, but one in which certain shared norms, values and practices develop and which states find in their interests to nurture and preserve (Bull 1977). The emergence of the Middle East sees some states entering and participating in this society. Against this backdrop however, we saw also the elements of resistance and revolt where the state system failed to meet the needs of different peoples, and became synonymous with oppression and inequality, the consequences of which still reverberate today, not only in the Middle East but in different parts of the developing world.

Chapter 2 tells the story of the Cold War in the region. Here the evidence of which factors drove regional developments has been contested by International Relations and regional scholars alike. In the historiography of the Cold War, traditional interpretations of its origins attribute much to external agency, and in these respects are linked to the dominant realist, or state-centric, paradigm in International Relations. US policy is seen as a reaction to the Soviet threat—and vice versa—and moulded accordingly in balance of power and containment terms. More recent, or so-called 'post-revisionist' accounts place more importance on the role of domestic actors or regional agency in shaping events. In Peter Sluglett's account, the persuasive power of realism holds important explanatory power. Though mindful of the regional frame, he is attracted to the thesis that the politics of power and influence, embedded (then) in the structure of the bipolar system determines in large measure the behaviour of its parts. The Middle East in the Cold War was thus very susceptible to superpower influence and pressures, and he demonstrates this in a case study of Iraq, by illustrating how the mind-set of politicians and intellectuals of the time was powerfully shaped by the politics and corresponding ideologies of the USSR and the US, with lasting consequences for the region.

   Chapter 3 and the last in this Part, deals with the post-Cold War era. As in the previous two chapters the major events and developments are in place, but there is also the move from historical narrative and analysis, to an introduction of the themes and issues that dominate the contemporary International Relations of the Middle East. The chapter thus provides an effective bridge or link between the first, second and third sections. In his own words, Korany is helping us to sort our our 'post-Cold War conceptual lenses'. In doing so he looks at questions of oil, patterns of war and peace, the phenomenon of globalisation and the contours of religio-politics, all themes which are then picked up in later chapters. Of particular interest is Korany's presentation of the events of the 1990s, after diplomatic breakthroughs in the Arab-Israel conflict at Madrid (1991) and Oslo (1993), as heralding the real possibility of a durable peace dividend, a move away from the cycle of violence and conflict towards broad regional cooperation and successful international engagement.

Part 2: Themes in International Relations and political economy

In the second Part some key themes of International Relations and International Political Economy are addressed. The opening two chapters by Giacomo Luciani and Clement Henry respectively, pick up on two of the conceptual lenses supplied by Bahgat Korany: oil and globalisation. In these we are exposed to the central dilemmas of the region's political economy and how this interfaces with the broader inter-national political economy.

   In **Chapter 4** Luciani tackles the inescapable and omnipresent question of oil. If oil is at the centre of the debate about the domestic politics of the region, it is also at the centre of the debate about its international relations. Here Luciani demonstrates the compelling links between oil and the consolidation and evolution of the modern state system, yet finds that while outside powers have invariably used oil in their calcu-lations of Middle East policy, it has figured less prominently in the foreign policies of Arab states, whose concerns remain of a more parochial kind. As regards domestic politics, the rentier model developed by Luciani demonstrates how oil has conditioned outcomes in both oil-rich and oil-poor states, arresting the prospects for reform and renewal that have characterised other regions. In this respect oil matters because it both helps to determines the regional balance of power, and the behaviour of external powers towards the region.

Clement Henry, in **Chapter 5**, looks at the political economy of the region through a different lens, one in which oil plays a central part in what he calls the 'clash of globalisations' currently waging in the Middle East and elsewhere. The Middle East, in his analysis, is becoming the principal battleground for contending visions of new global order, a point that is picked up in different ways in other chapters in the volume. This is not a clash of civilisations thesis, as suggested by Samuel Huntington, which pits Islam against the West, but one which see the current global vision of the United States, ranged against the 'multilateral proponents of globalisation'. Middle East states, while setting the scene for this conflict, also have to contend with the actions and consequences of their radical internal oppositions. The chapter includes a discussion of the antecedents and consequences of different facets of globalisation and the different coping mechanisms employed by Middle Eastern states.

In **Chapter 6** we move from considerations of economic liberalisation to related questions of political reform. Richard Norton's chapter, in analysing the problematic of democratisation, which he aptly calls the 'puzzle of political reform', also finds the region trapped in some way outside global trends. He avoids the term exceptionalism, but the fact remains that the Arab world in particular has been deficient in respect to democratisation, and here as in other chapters the political economy of states, the persistence of conflict, the nature of incumbent regimes and ambiguity over the relationship between democracy and Islam are highlighted. This relationship is not necessarily a contradictory one. Norton points out how much Islamic discourse is marked by participation and diversity, not by rigidity and intolerance. Further, civil society is vibrant in many states across the region. Responses from the West to political reform have been hitherto lukewarm with stability being privileged over democracy, though this may be changing. The evidence from the region is that peoples do want better government, even if they remain unclear as to what type of government that may be. From an International Relations perspective, this question is central, because of the much debated relationship between stable democracies and peace.

Chapter 7 by Ray Hinnebusch offers a clear yet critical exposition on the explanatory power and limitations of identity in understanding the region. An appreciation of the role of ideas and identity has already found its way into mainstream International Relations scholarship in the work of the 'constructivist' school. The Middle East, through the work of Michael Barnett and others, has already made an important contribution to this debate. Their importance is demonstrable, and Hinnebusch shows how when Arabism declines, Islam occupies a similar transnational or supranational space. But he is also cautious of attributing too much to ideas alone, noting how the 'material' bases of identity alongside other factors, determine the regional order and relative durability of the states system. Both Arabism and Islam have been captured by states and their leaders, taking on distinct national forms; their impact is conditioned by the ever present domestic and external constraints that limit its explanatory power.

Identity also plays an important part in **Chapter 8** by Louise Fawcett which offers an overview of the changing dynamics of cooperation and alliance making in the region. The idea and practice of regionalism, broadly interpreted, are examined alongside International Relations approaches which focus on the role of ideas as well as domestic and external agency in explaining different efforts to build consensus and cooperation around core issues. In considering the history of different efforts at cooperation in comparative perspective, the chapter demonstrates the poor fit between traditional International Relations-type concerns and regional realities. Domestic, regional and international level factors combine to explain the region's poor record hitherto in terms of successful regime or institution building, though some important precedents point the way to some alternative regional futures.

Chapter 9, by Janice Stein, the last chapter in this Part, offers a tightly focused analysis of the region's ongoing security dilemma. In offering her perspective on the dynamics of war and peace in the region she examines the obstacles to any long term settlement of regional conflict, obstacles which need to be adressed before the Middle East can move forward to embrace a new broader security agenda. Drawing on the case studies provided by the Arab-Israel wars, she exposes some the deficiencies of realist analysis when applied to what some have seen as the most realist of conflicts. Strategies of deterrence, based on superior military power, have repeatedly failed to prevent war where deep seated grievances remain. Domestic pressures and constraints, as much as military balances, have determined decisions to go to war in the region, and will continue to do so unless a new contracts are formed between peoples and governments.

Part 3: Key issues and actors

While Janice Stein's chapter uses International Relations tools to analyse the nature of the region's central security dilemmas, the first two chapters in this section deal directly with what has been the most central and contentious issue in the International Relations of the modern Middle East: the Arab-Israel conflict, and attempts at its pacification and resolution. The lessons here for International Relations scholars are many. In **Chapter 10**, by Charles Smith, the different aspects of the conflict—military, political and economic—are explored. In line with other chapters and themes already set out, he demonstrates how both realism, and the contours of identity politics inform the position of different states. Even the high point of the conflict, the 1967 war, is as much about Arab identity as it is about the struggle with Israel. Curiously, while Arab policies have become increasingly realist, the debate in Israel is still centrally about the contested identity of the Jewish state. Many of the themes introduced here are familiar ones to observers of the region and flow naturally from those developed by other chapters.

Against this backdrop we turn to **Chapter 11** by Avi Shlaim which covers the landmark series of negotiations in the early 1990s, culminating in the Oslo Accords (1993), which marked the first sustained effort at peaceful resolution of the conflict. These events, which dominated the regional panorama and captured international imagination, are considered in some detail, for they assist in our understanding not only of the nature and direction of Middle East politics, but also the positioning of those politics within the broader international order, outlined during the first Bush presidency. At first it seems that the Accords, in reconciling the two major parties to the conflict, the Israelis and the Palestinians, was indeed a demonstration of an emerging and more liberally-founded international order (possibilities that are explored in Korany's chapter). Yet the fragile bases of this order, in the Middle East and elsewhere, were soon exposed. Domestic politics, as Avi Shlaim explains, provide part of the answer: given Israel's dominance in the regional balance of power, the only way keep the peace momentum alive was through sustained international intervention. When this faltered, for reasons that are also explored in Michael Hudson's chapter on the policies of the United States, the opportunity was lost. Like the end of the Cold War itself, the promise of a new international order in the Middle East was shallow and ephemeral and contingent on the influence of dominant regional and extra-regional actors.

The Gulf states have had little more success in overcoming their own security dilemmas, as Gregory Gause demonstrates in **Chapter 12**. In looking at the shifting dynamics of International Politics in this crucial region, he examines the policies of two major players: Iraq and Saudi Arabia as well as the process of growing US involvement. In regard to the former, in line with other chapters, the classical realist tool, the balance of power, can only partly explain the positioning of states. The domestic frame and its (positive and negative) interaction with transnational influences as well as external actors is crucial to understanding the different frames within which local actors operate: whether revolutionary Iran, Saddam Hussein's Iraq or the Gulf monarchies. Given that regime security still drives states in their foreign policies, the need to cope with internal and external threats is compelling. Outside actors are important in as much as they supply or help to combat such threats. Gause uses the case of Iraq in particular to demonstrate how such threats were a determinant to action, but also notes the difficulties encountered by the Saudis in balancing the need for US support with powerful transnational and internal forces which push in the opposite direction.

Chapter 13 by Michael Hudson pursues some of these themes in his study of US policy towards the region, starting with a review of its origins and development over the past century. Interwoven into this analysis—and an implicit critique of realism—is the crucial and interdependent relationship between different domestic constituencies in the US, and the conduct of its foreign policy a relationship which in its present phase has led to the so-called neo-conservative revolution. History though, as Michael Hudson points out, tells a different story. At first the US was a state which managed to avoid the stigma of great power politics which were identified with the two major rivals in the region (Britain and Russia). And despite the obvious geopolitical constraints colouring the attitudes and policies of different administrations during the Cold War, the US proved to be the major mediator in many of the different conflicts that occurred, a pattern that was reinforced at the end of the Cold War. The current interventionist trend in US foreign policy, with roots in new alliances forged in goverment and society, looks rather different. It presupposes the ability to construct a new regional security architecture around a reformed Iraqi state. The success or failure of such a project will depend upon not only the regional environment, notoriously hostile to external meddling, but on the delicate balance of domestic forces within the US itself.

Chapter 14, by Rosemary Hollis, and the last of the volume, explores the evolution and development of European approaches to the Middle East. A central question here is how relevant is, or can Europe be as an actor in influencing patterns of politics and development in the Middle East? Why is it that Europe, economic giant that it is, remains a political pygmy in a region of such profound historical and contemporary interest? (Roberson 1998) Realism would point to the relative irrelevance of institutions like the European Union. Yet, medium powers, if Europe can be understood thus, can influence outcomes in International Relations, and there are Middle Eastern states that have looked to Europe to supply this balancing effect, both in normative, but also in policy terms. This potential has been demonstrated in the Euro-Mediterranean Partnership Programme initated in 1995 which may yet provide a cornerstone for further developments in regional cooperation. The problem for Europe, as Rosemary Hollis demonstrates, is not merely the result of difficulties on the ground, or differences with the US, real though these are, but tensions within the European Union itself, in terms of articulating a common position or policy.

A Concluding Note

This volume does not offer a conclusion. Each chapter, in different ways, provides its own. Still, the European note is an appropriate one to end a volume whose sub-title is conflict and cooperation. If there is one region in the world where deep division and rivalry has been overcome, and meaningful cooperation made possible, it is Europe. In this regard Europe can be regarded both as a model of how its own cooperative experience might be applied elsewhere, and as one possible source of a set of policies and programmes which might yet help the region overcome its own conflicts.

As this introduction has demonstrated, the focus of the volume has been deliberately expansive and all encompassing, with the underlying aim of relating 'global and regional themes of the times to an analysis of the Middle East' (Halliday 2002: 2). One theme that links all chapters is that if the language of the Middle East has remained somehow exotic and unfamiliar to International Relations scholars, the language of International Relations has also—until quite recently—remained rather opaque to students of the region. The evidence so far is that rather more has been done to remedy this on the Middle Eastern, than on the International Relations side (Korany 1999). The authors of the chapters have, in different ways, demonstrated the difficulties with existing scholarship in terms of bringing the two disciplines together, but each in their own way opened room for dialogue. Sustaining this dialogue and building on it further can only help to advance the project of bringing International Relations to the Middle East.

Two theoretical strands—realism and constructivism—are subject to particular scrutiny in the volume, and found helpful, alongside domestic level approaches, in explaining the different aspects of the International Politics of the region. As the above discussion has made clear however, this book does not propose to offer a definitive analysis, or any single route to understanding the International Relations of the region. Rather, it aims to expose to the reader to a variety of perspectives and approaches, familiar to International Relations and Middle East scholars alike, to make better sense of the complexity of region, and its broader interactions with the international system.

PART 1

HISTORICAL OVERVIEW

1

The Emergence of the Middle East into the Modern State System

Eugene L. Rogan

OVERVIEW

The modern states of the Arab Middle East emerged from the collapse of the Ottoman Empire and the post-World War I settlement. The fall of the Ottoman Empire left the Turks and Arabs ready for statehood, though unprepared for dealing with the international system. The experience of Ottoman reforms had left an important legacy of statecraft in the Arab world. While the Arab people were thus prepared for statehood in 1919, they had little prior experience of diplomacy. In Ottoman times, relations with the European Powers had been mediated through Istanbul. Moreover, the Arab lands constituted provinces of a common state, rather than distinct states with their own national boundaries, and thus had no experience of dealing with other Arab communities as foreign states. The Arabs had no say in the post-war partition of their lands under League of Nations auspices, distributed among the victorious Powers as a new form of colonial state known as mandates. Nationalist movements emerged within the confines of these new states in opposition to colonial rule. This legacy would leave the Arab world struggling between a widely-held ideal of Arab unity and a reality of nation-state nationalism reinforced by nationalist struggles for independence. The Arab states post independence were divided by factionalism and infighting. These divisions were apparent in the first issue to test the independent Arab state system—the Palestine crisis (1947–49). The new states of the Middle East have proven remarkably stable, though in their genesis lay the foundations for many of the conflicts that subsequently have troubled the region.

Introduction: The Arab Entry to International Relations

The Arab world made its entry to International Relations at the Versailles Peace Conference following the First World War. Prior to the War, the Arab lands of North Africa had been colonised by France, Italy and Britain, while the majority of the Asian Arab lands had been under Ottoman rule. The Arab delegations, newly independent of the defeated Ottoman Empire, came to Versailles to seek those essential attributes of independent statehood: juridical equality with other states, and absolute sovereignty (Bull and Watson 1984: 23). They faced two major impediments. To start, there was no consensus among the Arabs on the post-war state structure they sought. While some delegations came to present demands for discrete national states like Egypt or Lebanon, others pursued a broader vision of Arab statehood. The Arab delegations were thus working at cross purposes. The Europeans posed the second impediment to Arab ambitions. As Hedley Bull asserted, 'non-European states entered an originally European club of states as and when they measured up to the criteria of admission laid down by the founder members' (Bull and Watson 1984: 123). The Arabs faced real disparities of structural power in negotiating with the Europeans, who harboured imperial interests in the Eastern Mediterranean and whose soldiers still occupied Egypt, Palestine, Syria and Iraq.

The dilemma the Arab delegations to Versailles faced was common to all newcomers to the international order. Admission to international society was conditional on recognition of sovereignty, and 'states do not have sovereignty apart from recognition of it by others' (Bull 1984: 122). The entry of many Asian and African states to international society would face the same constraints (Clapham 1996; Bull and Watson 1984). The very institutions governing the workings of international society in 1919 were little changed from the previous century. The governance of the system was in the hands of the Great Powers, who played a decisive role in codifying the norms of the system in a set of regulatory rules of war and peace known as international law. The Powers met and applied international law to resolve conflicts through congresses such as Versailles. Outside periods of conflict, relations between states were maintained through diplomatic missions (Watson 1984: 24–5, 27).

Almost without exception, the new states of Asia, Africa and the Middle East were alien to the institutions of the European system of international relations. Those

North African states already under European colonial rule before the outbreak of World War I had surrendered control of their foreign relations to their colonial masters. Those Arab territories that had formerly been part of the Ottoman Empire had never known formal relations with outside powers, as the Empire's foreign relations were conducted through the imperial capital, Istanbul. Indeed, the Ottomans themselves were relatively recent entrants to the European system of diplomacy.

Ottoman Diplomacy

The Ottoman Empire was a nineteenth-century newcomer to the European state system. Up to the reign of Sultan Selim III (1789–1807), Ottoman relations with Europe were based on a unilateral system whereby European ambassadors were received by the Porte but no Ottoman permanent missions sent to European capitals. Ottoman ambassadors were dispatched infrequently, for specific missions, and returned to Istanbul, often with extraordinary stories of the alien culture they had encountered (Itzkowitz 1970; Gocek 1987). European states conducted their relations with the Ottomans through trade companies such as the English Levant Company (established 1581). European merchants resident in Ottoman domains enjoyed extraterritorial rights to be judged by their own nation's laws, as set out in a series of bilateral treaties known as the Capitulations.[1] The Capitulations were drafted when the Ottomans were the dominant Mediterranean power and saw little need for more formal relations with Christian Europe. Selim III's first experiment of reciprocal diplomacy, establishing embassies in London, Vienna, Berlin and Paris in the 1790s, was most remarkable for its bad timing: the French Revolution and Napoleonic wars were low points in the European state system.

It was only when Europe began to intervene in Ottoman affairs to prevent the fall of the Sultan's government that the Ottomans were assimilated into the European state system. The two Egyptian crises (1831–32 and 1839–40) led the European powers to enter Ottoman domains to contain the ambitions of Egyptian governor Mehmet Ali Pasha—and each other. The London Convention of 1840, resolving the Second Egyptian Crisis, marked the Ottoman entry to continental European politics. It was the first European convention signed by Ottoman diplomats on behalf of the Sultan. What is more, British Prime Minister Lord Palmerston drafted a secret 'self denying protocol' adopted by Britain, Austria, Prussia and Russia, pledging that no power would seek territorial or commercial gains in Ottoman domains to the exclusion of any other Power (Hurewitz 1975: 271–5).

The Ottomans formally joined the Concert of Europe in 1856 when they signed the Treaty of Paris marking the end of the Crimean War, along with Britain, France, Austria, Prussia, Russia and Sardinia. The Ottomans were entering a system whose rules they had no say in drafting and of whose terms they had at best an incomplete knowledge. The Ottoman Foreign Ministry was established only in 1836.

In the course of the nineteenth century, permanent embassies were opened in European capitals, and Istanbul received ambassadors from the Great Powers, whose residences still grace the European quarters of Istanbul. Diplomacy in Ottoman domains was thus almost exclusively confined to the imperial capital. While European consuls were posted to key provincial cities such as Jerusalem, Beirut, Damascus and Aleppo, their interaction was with Ottoman governors, mediated through Istanbul. Local Arab Muslims had little or no contact with these foreign dignitaries, and no experience of the international system.

By 1878, Palmerston's 1840 'self-denying protocol' had lapsed. The Ottoman Empire had declared bankruptcy to its European creditors (1875). Battles with Bulgarian nationalists seeking independence from Ottoman rule had been reported in the European press in terms of atrocity and led to a disastrous war with Russia in 1877–78. Utterly defeated, the Ottomans were forced to accept enormous territorial losses. Britain claimed Cyprus as a colony; Britain and Germany gave France the nod to occupy Tunisia; and in the Treaty of Berlin, the Ottomans were forced to cede some two fifths of their territory, mostly in the Balkans. In 1882, Britain occupied Egypt, still officially Ottoman territory. The European Powers had embarked on the dismemberment of the Ottoman Empire that would reach its climax in the secret agreements concluded in the course of the First World War.

Yet in the last quarter of the nineteenth century, the collapse of the Ottoman Empire was far from inevitable. Despite Ottoman territorial losses to European states and Balkan nationalist movements, reforms proceeded apace in the institutions of state-craft. The influence of these reforms would prove an enduring legacy in Arab lands.

An Ottoman Legacy of Statehood

It was the common wisdom of the peacemakers at Versailles that the Arabs had no experience of statecraft when, following the collapse of the Ottoman Empire in the World War I, they first emerged among the community of nations. The exceptions were those North African countries that had developed instruments of statehood, all of which were under direct colonial rule in 1919: Morocco, the oldest formal Arab state, became a French protectorate in 1912; Tunisia had been under French rule and Egypt under British rule since the 1880s. Algeria, the first Arab territory to come under European colonial rule (1830), was assimilated to metropolitan France and never had the chance to develop autonomous instruments of rule to the same extent as the other North African states.

When speaking of the Arabs, the victors at Versailles were referring to the Arab provinces of the Ottoman Empire. The Arab lands formally under Ottoman rule in 1914 were Yemen, the Red Sea province of the Hijaz, Greater Syria (comprised of the modern states of Syria, Lebanon, Jordan and Israel/Palestine) and Iraq. Tenuous Ottoman claims to the Najd region of central Arabia, and the Persian Gulf shaikhdoms stretching to Qatar, had lapsed by 1913 (Anscombe 1997). Britain and France, intent on adding these territories to their colonial possessions as spoils of war, claimed that the newly liberated Arab lands were not ready for independence, but would first require a period of tutelage in statecraft.

While none of these lands comprised a state in their own right, each had enjoyed extensive exposure to Ottoman instruments of state, particularly since the period of reforms in the second half of the nineteenth century. The Ottoman reforms, known as the Tanzimat (1839–76), were in small part designed to preclude European pretexts to intervene in Ottoman affairs. Arguably, the chief aim of the reforms was to make for a more viable Ottoman state and to consolidate Istanbul's hold over its Asian provinces as nationalist movements led to the progressive secession of the Balkan provinces.

Much of the literature on the Tanzimat has focused on issues of minority rights, and the equality the reforms established between Muslims and non-Muslims. This was a measure taken by the Ottomans to prevent the European Powers from exploiting minority issues to intervene in Ottoman domestic affairs. However, the Tanzimat as a reform process was far more significant in the realm of domestic governance and financial regularity. Seen in this light, the milestones of the Tanzimat were not the major policy pronouncements made by the Sultan (the reform decrees of 1839 and 1856, and the Constitution of 1876) so much as the 1858 Land Law, the 1864 Provincial Governance Law and the promulgation of the civil law code known as the *Mecelle* (1870–76). These were the measures that brought rational bureaucracy, fiscal regularity, a consistent rule of law and growing contact between Ottoman subjects and their government. What is more, the era of reforms did not end in 1876 but continued across the reign of Sultan Abdülhamid II (1876–1909), dubbed by one author as 'the culmination of the Tanzimat'. As Stanford Shaw argued: 'Every aspect of the Ottoman system was included [in Abdülhamid II's reform agenda]—the military, the central administration, the provinces, the law courts, finance, the economy, public works, education, fine arts, and the administration' (Shaw and Shaw 1978: 221). The reforms in this sense extended from 1839 through the first decade of the twentieth century.

Arguably, the Arab provinces of the Ottoman Empire were initiated in statecraft in the last quarter of the nineteenth century, and the first two decades of the twentieth. This education involved direct knowledge of and contact with the government bureaucracy, and a subordination to the 'rule of books' through the census, land registration, the tax office and military conscription. Arab Ottomans came to know the complexity of government, at both the provincial and imperial levels. The Arabs also had their first experiences of elected office at this time, both at the provincial level to town and regional councils, as well as to the Imperial Parliament, in 1876 and again after 1908. A consistent rule of law was applied and enforced by police and gendarmes in the countryside and by courts in the towns.

What is more, residents of the Arab provinces came to associate certain benefits with the exercise of statecraft. The extension of the rule of law brought a new degree of security, particularly in the countryside. The rapid expansion of the primary and secondary school system in the provinces broadened literacy and witnessed a growing number of locals entering the civil service—in the Arab provinces as well as in Turkish Anatolia (Findley 1989; Somel 2001). A clear sense of 'citizenship', with attendant rights and responsibilities, appears in correspondence written by Ottoman subjects to Ottoman officialdom. Arabs in the provinces found a political voice assertive of individual rights, property rights, constitutional law, justice and humanitarianism in their telegraph communications with Ottoman officialdom (Rogan 1998: 123–6).

It is striking how the victorious European Powers shaped the Arab state system in the image of Ottoman provincial government. After the 1864 Provincial Reform Law, Ottoman provincial capitals were the focus of extensive investment and construction. Government buildings (administrative offices, courthouses, barracks), communications infrastructure (post, telegraph, roads, trams and railways), commercial and residential quarters underwent rapid development in the latter nineteenth century. Provincial capitals such as Jerusalem, Beirut, Damascus and Baghdad were easily adapted to make national capitals in the mandates of Palestine, Lebanon, Syria and Iraq.

Taken together, these aspects of late Ottoman rule constitute a legacy of 'stateness' that had prepared the Arab people for some degree of self rule by 1919 (Rogan 1999). To some extent this was acknowledged in the Covenant of the League of Nations:

Certain communities formerly belonging to the Turkish Empire have reached a stage of development where their existence as independent nations can be provisionally recognized subject to the rendering of administrative advice and assistance by a Mandatory until such time as they are able to stand alone. The wishes of these communities must be a principal consideration in the selection of the Mandatory. (Art. 22)

Given their more advanced state of development than the other mandated territories, in Central and South-Western Africa, as well as in the Pacific Islands, the Arab lands were designated type A mandates, i.e. proto-states in need of interim tutelage in preparation for independent statehood. However, this was not to be. For the whole of the interwar years, all Arab states bar Iraq remained under de facto British or French colonial rule. The origins of this colonial division date back to the time of the First World War.

Wartime Plans for the Partition of the Middle East

In the course of the First World War, Britain took the lead in three distinct negotiations for the post-war disposition of the Arab lands.

Between July 1915 and March 1916, the British High Commissioner for Egypt Sir Henry McMahon and the Sharif of Mecca, Hussein ibn Ali of the Hashemite family, negotiated the terms for an Arab revolt against Ottoman rule. In exchange for opening this internal front against the Ottomans, Sharif Hussein sought British support for an enormous Arab Kingdom stretching from Mersin and Adana (in modern Turkey) to Persia in the north, to the Persian Gulf, the Indian Ocean, the Red Sea and the Mediterranean, excluding the British colony of Aden. McMahon responded in his famous letter of 24 October 1915 with British acceptance of these boundaries, with the sole exclusion of the 'two districts of Mersina and Alexandretta and portions of Syria lying to the west of the districts of Damascus, Homs, Hama and Aleppo' and those areas in Mesopotamia of strategic interest to Great Britain (Hurewitz 1979: 50). With these assurances, Sharif Hussein initiated the Arab Revolt of T. E. Lawrence fame in July 1916.

While Britain's representatives in Cairo were negotiating with Sharif Hussein, the British Foreign Office initiated negotiations with the French Ministry of Foreign Affairs to agree a post-war partition of Ottoman domains. The agreement, known by the names of its British and French authors, Sir Mark Sykes and Charles François Georges-Picot, was approved on 4 February 1916 and gained Russian support in March 1916 in exchange for Anglo-French agreement to Russian territorial demands in Eastern Anatolia. According to this agreement, France would establish an administration in those areas Sir Henry McMahon had excluded from the Arab Kingdom—the 'two districts of Mersina and Alexandretta and portions of Syria lying to the west of the districts of Damascus, Homs, Hama and Aleppo'—while Britain would establish an administration in Mesopotamia. The inland territories between these areas were to be divided into British and French spheres of influence, with Palestine internationalised to prevent disagreement between British, French and Russian claims to the Holy Lands (Hurewitz 1979: 60–4).

Finally, on 2 November 1917, the British government gave formal support to the aspirations of the World Zionist Organization to establish a Jewish national home in Palestine. The Balfour Declaration, transmitted in a letter from Foreign Minister Arthur James Balfour to Lord Rothschild, confirmed Britain's support for 'the establishment in Palestine of a national home for the Jewish people' (Hurewitz 1979: 106). The Balfour Declaration contradicted both the pledge to Sharif Hussein and the Sykes-Picot Agreement, and further complicated the post-war settlement at Versailles.

Upon the fall of Damascus and the subsequent Ottoman retreat from the Arab lands in September 1918, Britain found itself in sole possession of the Arab Middle East. Now faced with a post-Ottoman reality, Britain had to square conflicting interests with wartime pledges to its Entente allies. This difficult task was left to the negotiations at Versailles.

The Post-war Settlement (1919–22)

Two features of the post-war settlement are apparent: The weak bargaining position of the Arab delegates to Versailles, and the duplicity of the Great Powers. For Britain and France, the colonies and territories of the vanquished German, Austrian and

Ottoman empires were seen as spoils of war. The United States, somewhat naively, espoused a much more liberal view of a new world order, set out by President Woodrow Wilson in Fourteen Points in his famous address to a joint session of Congress on 8 January 1918. Wilson spoke to the aspirations of Arab political ēlites in his twelfth point:

The Turkish portion of the present Ottoman Empire should be assured a secure sovereignty, but the other nationalities which are now under Turkish rule should be assured an undoubted security of life and an absolutely unmolested opportunity of autonomous development.

The Arab delegates to Versailles were early proponents of President Wilson's vision. However, they would prove no more successful than President Wilson himself in imposing a new order on old world diplomacy, a complex science in which they had little understanding and less experience.

The Arabs in Versailles

A number of delegations from former Ottoman domains sought the opportunity to press their claims before the victorious Entente Powers for recognition. The Greeks pressed for territory in Anatolia. Armenians presented their case for statehood. The Hashemites, in de facto control of Geographic Syria (roughly corresponding to modern Syria, Lebanon and Jordan) and the Hijaz, sought to secure the Arab Kingdom promised them by the Hussein-McMahon correspondence. The Zionist movement was active to uphold the Balfour promise of a Jewish national home in Palestine. And in Egypt, the British refusal to permit a delegation to go to Paris to present Egyptian claims for independence prompted a nationwide uprising in 1919 that led to a reversal of policy and the dispatch of an Egyptian delegation to Paris. In some regards the Paris Peace Conference marked the entry of the Middle East as a region into the prevailing system of International Relations. The experiences of the Arab delegations revealed the disadvantages of having their relations with the European state system mediated through Istanbul for the length of Ottoman rule.

Egypt and the Wafd

The nationalist movement in Egypt had been gaining momentum in the early years of the twentieth century. Under British occupation since 1882, Egypt had already developed the institutions of independent statehood. The monarchy could trace its origins back a century to the appointment of Mehmet Ali Pasha as governor of the Ottoman province of Egypt in 1805. The Pasha was to rule Egypt for forty-three years and set the province on a path to autonomy. His descendants had ruled the country ever since. The *khedives*, as the rulers of Egypt came to be designated, governed in consultation with a cabinet of ministers whose portfolios conformed to formal government divisions (e.g. foreign affairs, finance, education, health). There was even a proto-parliament, known as the Chamber of Delegates, that met regularly between November 1866 and March 1882 (Schölch: 1981). Occupation came as a result of financial and political crises starting with the Egyptian bankruptcy in 1876 and ending with a military-led revolt against European control and Khedive Tawfiq, believed by many in Egypt to be himself under excessive European control (Owen 1981).

By the end of the nineteenth century, nationalist parties were formed, their views aired in a range of newspapers. Their main agenda was to end the British occupation. Such nationalist activity was contained during the long years of the First World War. Egypt was formally separated from the Ottoman Empire in November 1914 following the Ottoman entry into the war on Germany's side, and declared a British protectorate. The Khedive was now designated a Sultan, raising expectations of independence in the aftermath of war. When the victorious Entente Powers began to plan for a peace conference in 1918, Egyptian nationalists again mobilised. There is some dispute over who first proposed to send a delegation (in Arabic, *wafd*) to represent Egypt's claims, though the men who called on the British High Commissioner, Sir Reginald Wingate, were associated with the Ummah Party. Headed by Sa'd Zaghlul, a former judge and minister of education, the delegation was rebuffed. The Egyptian public responded with petitions and growing anger. When the British authorities arrested and exiled Zaghlul and his supporters to Malta, a mass uprising followed. The 'Revolution of 1919' rendered Egypt ungovernable, and the British were forced to recall Zaghlul from exile and arrange for him to address the delegates at the Versailles peace conference.

Egyptian nationalists were to return from Versailles empty handed. On the day Zaghlul and his party arrived in Paris, the American delegation issued a statement recognising Britain's protectorate over Egypt. Egyptian hopes pinned on Woodrow Wilson's support, raised by his Fourteen Points, were dashed. Zaghlul and his colleagues, no stranger to European politics, had learned that colonised people could only change imperial politics through domestic disorder. The Egyptian delegation returned to alternate periods of political disorder and negotiations with the British, leading up to the 1922 Treaty ending the protectorate, if preserving British influence over Egypt.

The Hashemite Arab Kingdom

Following the Ottoman retreat from Damascus in 1918, Amir Faisal (crowned King of Syria in March, 1920) found himself de facto ruler of Syria which, at that time, had no recognised boundaries or formal government. Faisal sought to consolidate his position in Syria at the Versailles Peace Conference. The greatest threat to his position came from Britain's other wartime promises. Faisal came to terms with the Balfour Declaration and signed an agreement with Zionist leader Chaim Weizmann in January 1919 conceding Palestine to the Zionist movement on condition that his demands for an Arab Kingdom be otherwise accepted by the Powers (Laqueur and Rubin 1985: 19–20). Faisal first learned of the Sykes–Picot Agreement when the

Bolsheviks published the secret treaties of the Tsarist government in 1918, at the height of the Arab Revolt. While Faisal saw no alternative to continuing with the Revolt, the threat of French rule hung over his new state and he held few cards to improve his position at Versailles.

Faisal presented the Supreme Council of the Paris Peace Conference with a memorandum setting out Arab aspirations in January, 1919. Faisal appeared before the Supreme Council, accompanied by T. E. Lawrence, the following month (6 February). In his memo, Faisal wrote that 'the aim of the Arab nationalist movements . . . is to unite the Arabs eventually into one nation.' He based his claim on Arab ethnic and linguistic unity, on the alleged aspirations of pre-war Arab nationalist parties in Syria and Mesopotamia and on Arab service to the Allies' war effort. He acknowledged that the different Arab lands were 'very different economically and socially' and that it would be impossible to integrate them into a single state immediately. He sought immediate and full independence for Greater Syria (including Lebanon, Syria and Transjordan) and the western Arabian province of Hijaz; accepted foreign intervention in Palestine to mediate between Jewish and Arab demands, and in Mesopotamia, where Britain had declared its interest in oil fields; and declared the Yemen and the central Arabian province of Najd outside the scope of the Arab Kingdom. Yet he maintained a commitment to 'an eventual union of these areas under one sovereign government.' He concluded:

In our opinion, if our independence be conceded and our local competence established, the natural influences of race, language, and interest will soon draw us into one people . . . To achieve this [the Great Powers] must lay aside the thought of individual profits, and of their old jealousies. In a word, we ask you not to force your whole civilisation upon us, but to help us to pick out what serves us from your experience. In return we can offer you little but gratitude. (Hurewitz 1979: 130–2)

As subsequent events would prove, it was not realistic to expect Britain and France to act in so disinterested a fashion.

A second set of claims were made in the name of the Syrian people by the chairman of the Central Syrian Committee, Shukri Ghanim. Ghanim's recommendations were diametrically opposed to Amir Faisal's. Stressing Syria's lack of preparation for self rule and need for foreign assistance, Ghanim asked the Council of Ten to place Syria under the tutelage of France for reasons of alleged historic attachment, demonstrated capacity to reconcile Muslims and Christians and, perhaps most improbably, its lack of imperialist interest in the region. It would later be revealed that Shukri Ghanim was a French citizen who had been away from Syria for thirty-five years (Helmreich 1974: 54–5). Indeed, France sought by all means to undermine Hashemite claims to Syria and to keep to the spirit of the Sykes-Picot disposition of Arab territory.

Faced with divergent claims on behalf of the Syrian people, with disagreement between Britain and France over the future of the Arab lands and American disapproval of the secret wartime agreements as a whole, the United States proposed to dispatch a commission of enquiry to establish the wishes of the Syrian people, and gained British and French agreement. Faisal was delighted, writing to President Wilson in March 1919 to express his gratitude for granting the Arabs the opportunity to express 'their own purposes and ideals for their national future' (Howard 1963: 35).

The King–Crane Commission

President Wilson named Oberlin College President Henry Churchill King and Chicago businessman Charles R. Crane to serve as commissioners. Wilson 'felt these two men were particularly qualified to go to Syria because they knew nothing about it' (Howard 1963: 37). Knowledge here was conflated with interest, and Wilson sought men of integrity with no prior interests in the region. In fact, both men had extensive knowledge of the Middle East, King as a scholar of Biblical history and Crane through his travels in Ottoman lands, dating back to 1878. When the British and French withdrew from the commission, the Americans set out for Syria in May 1919 with instructions to meet with local representatives and report back on the aspirations of the Arab peoples in Syria, Iraq and Palestine. The commission arrived in Jaffa on 10 June and spent six weeks touring Syria and Palestine. They held meetings in over forty towns and rural centres, and collected over 1,800 petitions. As James Gelvin has argued, 'while the entente powers had charged the commission with a simple fact-finding mission, its presence in Syria catalysed a mobilization of the Syrian population that was unprecedented in scope' (Gelvin 1998: 35). The local Arab government distributed sermons to be read in Friday prayers in Syrian mosques, political and cultural associations were enlisted to prepare petitions for the commission and the headmen of villages and town quarters were mobilised to encourage an enthusiastic response to the commission.

In August 1919 the commission withdrew to Istanbul where King and Crane drafted their report, which was delivered to the American delegation in Paris at the end of the month. The report went no further. There is no evidence that it was ever consulted by the British or French, and it was only made public in 1922, well after the post-war settlements had been signed. Yet their report serves as a yardstick to measure the gulf that separated Arab claims of self determination made to the commissioners from the mandate system they received.

King and Crane summarised their findings after five weeks of collecting testimony. While noting explicit Syrian preference for full independence, they recommended a fixed term mandate under American or, as second choice, British authority (but explicitly ruling out French administration) leading to full independence. Syria, including Palestine, should be established as a single monarchy under Faisal's rule, with Lebanon given extensive autonomy within the Syrian state. They called for major restrictions in Zionist settlement in Palestine, noting that 'more than 72 per cent—1,350 in all—of all the petitions in the whole of Syria were directed against the Zionist program' (Hurewitz 1979: 196). In Iraq, they called for another unified monarchy under British mandate. In essence, the recommendations of the

King–Crane Commission overturned the Balfour Declaration and Sykes–Picot Agreement. It is no wonder that the British and French chose to ignore the document and proceed with a modified partition plan.

San Remo and the mandate system

By the time Britain and France reached the peace conference, the Sykes–Picot Agreement had been overtaken by events. Most importantly, the Bolshevik Revolution had led to the withdrawal of Russia's claims on Ottoman territory. The Soviets, preoccupied with securing their state against outside menace and internal challenge, would not play a major role in Arab affairs through the interwar period.

The British position had changed in many ways since 1916 as well. For one, its armies had occupied Syria and Iraq, which gave it a better sense of its strategic imperatives and an improved bargaining position to assure them. Two areas in particular were to come under revision: the northern Iraqi region of Mosul, allotted to the French sphere of influence, and Palestine, which was to come under international control. These were important points of difference and they needed formal agreement.

The premiers and foreign ministers of Britain, France and Italy, and two delegates from Japan, met in San Remo in April 1920 to agree the partition of the Arab lands. They were not alone. As Lord Curzon complained: 'Syrians, Zionists, Armenians . . . They take rooms in the same hotel as we are in and they dog our footsteps wherever we go' (Nevakivi 1969: 242). The lobbyists did not manage to influence events, as the decisions on the Arab lands had largely been negotiated and agreed between Britain and France months beforehand. France was to obtain mandates over Lebanon and Syria, spelling the end of Faisal's Arab Kingdom in Damascus. In return, France conceded its claims to northern Iraq (though Mosul would not be formally conceded to the Iraq mandate until 1925) and acknowledged Britain's rule over Palestine, including the lands east of the River Jordan stretching to Iraq that would later be made into a separate mandate of Transjordan. The British and French established a boundaries commission to agree the frontiers between their respective territories. When the League of Nations sanctioned the decisions taken at San Remo on 24 July 1922, the boundaries of the mandates had already been agreed between Britain and France.

Britain had, with some modification, met its commitments to both the Sykes–Picot Agreement and the Balfour Declaration. Only the promises to the Hashemites had been disregarded. At the end of 1920, Britain called Faisal, the deposed King of Syria, to London to gain Hashemite acceptance of the San Remo division of the Middle East. In return, Britain would place its new mandates under the sons of Sharif Hussein. This plan came to be known as the 'sharifian solution', both a way to partially redeem Britain's promises to its wartime allies and 'an interlocking political grid whereby pressure on one state could win obedience in another' (Wilson 1987: 49; Paris 2003). The Sharifian solution was made policy by Colonial Secretary Winston Churchill in the Cairo Conference in March 1921.

Churchill and the Hashemites

The two territories conceded to Britain at San Remo were Iraq and Palestine. Given these were mandates rather than traditional colonies, Britain needed to devise governments for the new states. Iraq was the first item on the agenda at the Cairo Conference, and it was quickly agreed to place Faisal on the throne in Baghdad. A mechanism still needed to be found to gain Iraqi public acceptance of Britain's choice, though this was left to Britain's colonial agents on the ground. A referendum was held and Faisal confirmed as King of Iraq in August 1921.

The next item on the agenda was Palestine—or rather those lands to the east of the River Jordan stretching to the Iraqi frontier that had been claimed by Britain as part of Palestine. Faisal's brother, the Hashemite Amir Abdullah, had ridden with a group of supporters from the Hijaz to the Transjordanian town of Ma'an in a bid to reclaim Damascus from the French. While no one had any illusions that Amir Abdullah might succeed in this aim, they saw his presence in Amman as threatening to destabilise the new borders between the French and British mandates. Churchill and a delegation from the Cairo Conference proceeded to Jerusalem and met with Abdullah. They struck an agreement with Amir Abdullah, who agreed to serve as provisional ruler over Transjordan for a six month probationary period. He was given a stipend of £5,000 and assigned to contain both anti-French and anti-Zionist activity. Churchill held out the prospect of a throne in Damascus if Abdullah proved his merits to the French—a prospect that must have looked as improbable at the time as it does in hindsight. Yet with Iraq, Transjordan, and the Hijaz under Hashemite rulers,[2] Churchill could claim to have gone as far as he could to redeem Britain's pledges to Sharif Hussein and his sons (Paris 2003).

As for Palestine itself, Britain chose to rule the mandate directly under a High Commissioner and to develop the structures of statehood in cooperation with the Arab and Jewish communities. Neither the cooperation nor the structures were forthcoming as Palestine came to be the arena of two rival nationalist movements, Zionist and Palestinian.

The Colonial Framework

In the four years following the Ottoman retreat from Arab lands, the map of the modern Middle East was drawn. The failure of the Arab parties to attain their national aims at Versailles revealed the weakness of their bargaining position when challenging European imperial interests. Given this somewhat compromised genesis, it is all the more remarkable how enduring the borders of the Middle East have proved.

The Middle East that emerged from the post-war negotiations was almost exclusively an Anglo-French preserve. Algeria was a full French colony, Morocco and

Tunisia protectorates, and Syria and Lebanon were held as League of Nations mandates. Egypt gained nominal independence in 1922 but continued to be under British influence through a restrictive treaty. Sudan was held as a 'condominium' ruled jointly by Britain and Egypt. Aden, or South Yemen, was a British colony, Palestine, Transjordan and Iraq were held as mandates, and Britain's interests in the Persian Gulf were upheld through treaty arrangements with the ruling families in Kuwait, Bahrain, Qatar and the shaikhdoms known as the Trucial States for the anti-piracy treaties, or 'truces' signed between them and Britain. Muscat and Oman were similarly under informal British control. Libya, an Italian colony since 1911, was an exception to this Anglo-French division of the region.

Three states in what is now called the Middle East escaped some form of colonial rule. Turkish nationalists rallied around General Mustafa Kemal (later known as Atatürk) in opposing the draconian terms of the Paris Peace Conference, culminating in the Treaty of Sevres (August 1920) that reduced the Ottoman Empire to a rump state combining parts of northern and western Anatolia with Istanbul as its capital. The Turkish War of Independence (1921–22) resulted in the Republic of Turkey, whose sovereignty and independence were recognised in the Treaty of Lausanne (24 July 1923). In the aftermath of the First World War, Iran was occupied by both British and Soviet forces. British attempts to establish a protectorate by treaty (1919) were stoutly resisted by a proto-nationalist movement. In 1921, the commander of the Iranian Cossack Brigade, Reza Khan, led a coup that brought down the Qajar dynasty and gave rise to the Pahlevi state that would rule Iran until the Islamic Revolution in 1979. And in Arabia, the forces of Abdul Aziz Al Saud (known in the West as ibn Saud) succeeded in uniting the Arabian peninsula from the Persian Gulf to the Hijaz Province on the Red Sea by 1924. Britain recognised Abdul Aziz as King of the Hejaz and Nejd in 1927, and in 1932 the kingdom was renamed Saudi Arabia. These three nation states pursued their own development independent of European political domination, though in the case of Iran, British influence remained profound.

For the rest of the Middle East, the interwar years were a period of national self-definition within the boundaries of the new states, and a battle for self-determination against the colonial powers. In this, the Middle East shares a common experience with those parts of Asia and Africa that emerged into the community of nations through European imperialism in the interwar years. The difference in the Middle East was the enduring appeal of a supranational identity based on a range of greater Arab nations transcending the colonial boundaries. There was the Hashemite vision of an Arab Kingdom combining the Arabian Peninsula, Greater Syria and Iraq. Others saw Egypt as an integral part of the greater Arab state. Others yet saw the whole of the Middle East and North Africa, stretching right to Morocco, as part of a common Arab Islamic nation. The enduring legitimacy enjoyed by the vision of the greater Arab Nation was to prove to the detriment of inter-state relations in the Arab world. Those who put their own narrow nation state interests before those of the ideal 'Arab Nation' were deemed collaborators in a European agenda of 'divide and rule'.

Yet, as was to be expected, the nationalist leaderships and the confrontations they endured with the colonial powers gave rise to vested interests within states.

'French' North Africa and Libya

The French colonial possessions in North Africa experienced limited nationalist agitation in the interwar years and only gained their independence in the 1950s and 1960s. This had the effect of limiting the involvement of North African states in the international relations of the Middle East more generally. Algeria, the first Arab state to be occupied by a European colonial power (1830), was the last to gain independence, after a violent war spanning the years 1954–62 that claimed over one million lives. Morocco and Tunisia were protectorates rather than formal colonies, and were ruled by France through their own monarchies. Given their own institutions of state, and a much smaller French colonial settler community, both Tunisia and Morocco achieved their independence earlier, with far less confrontation. Morocco's King Muhmmad V wrote demanding independence of France in 1952. His exile gave rise to an armed resistance movement that forced a French reversal and recognition of Moroccan independence on 2 March 1956 (Pennell 2000). Tunisia initiated autonomy talks with France in 1955, achieved independence as a monarchy in 1956 and declared a republic in 1957. As for Libya, following the execution of Omar al-Mukhtar in 1932, Italian rule went unchallenged until the British occupation in 1942–43. The United Nations oversaw Libya's independence as a monarchy in 1951 (Anderson 1986).

Morocco, Algeria and Tunisia, and to a lesser extent Libya, were bound by similar colonial histories and the timing of their independence. This has marked North Africa as a distinct sub unit of the broader Arab world known as the Mahgreb. Though members of the Arab League, the Mahgreb states, along with Egypt, are active in the Organisation of African Unity. These four states are also marked by a special relationship with the European Mediterranean—especially Spain, France and Italy. While tensions between Mahgreb states have been pronounced—between Morocco and Algeria in particular—there have been numerous attempts to create a union of Mahgreb states, given their common interests and geographic proximity. Yet these very differences have set the Mahgreb apart from the rest of the Arab world, hinged to some extent by the keystone Arab state, Egypt.

Egypt and the Sudan

Following the nationwide disturbances of 1919, the British sought to normalise relations with Egypt in such a way as to preserve their strategic interests while giving the semblance of independence. The result was a treaty replacing the protectorate with a nominally independent monarchy bound to Britain by a treaty. The 1922 Treaty recognised Egypt's independence while preserving four areas under British control: The security of imperial communications in Egypt (primarily the Suez

Canal); the defence of Egypt against outside aggression (assuring Britain base rights for its military); the protection of foreign interests and minorities (as enshrined in the extraterritorial rights of the Capitulations); and the Sudan. These limits on Egyptian independence were sufficiently intrusive as to prevent Egypt's admission to the League of Nations, and were an enduring source of nationalist grievance.

The interwar years have been termed Egypt's 'liberal age' (Hourani 1962; Botman 1998), an era of party politics and parliamentary elections. Britain continued to dominate Egyptian politics by playing the monarchy and the parliament against each other. The most popular party by far was the Wafd, founded by Sa'd Zaghlul. In every free election, the Wafd won by landslide majorities. By the late 1930s, the death of King Fuad and accession of his son Faruq, combined with the return of the Wafd to power under the premiership of Mustafa al-Nahhas, set in motion renewed negotiations with the British authorities. On 26 August 1936, a new Anglo-Egyptian treaty was signed. The twenty-year treaty was essentially a defence pact that recognised Egypt's sovereignty as an independent state and paved the way for Egyptian admission to the League, in 1937. Egypt could now establish embassies and consulates for the first time. In return, the Egyptians permitted Britain to station a maximum of 10,000 troops in the Suez Canal zone during peacetime, and guaranteed Britain base rights to protect its imperial lines of communications in emergency. The treaty also preserved the status quo in the Sudan, which would remain under Anglo-Egyptian rule until 1953 and only gained independence in 1956.

The mandates

Unlike the other colonial arrangements, Britain and France were held accountable by the League of Nations for their rule in the mandates. They were required to submit annual reports to the League secretariat outlining their progress in establishing the institutions of statehood deemed prerequisite for national independence. In theory at least the mandates were meant to be tutorial exercises in self-rule rather than out and out colonial rule. The experience varied widely from country to country, though in each case the combination of colonial state formation and nationalist agitation for independence set in motion the evolution of nation states from the former provinces of the Ottoman Empire.

Iraq and Transjordan

In every regard, Iraq was deemed the role-model mandate. Through an admittedly rigged referendum, King Faisal I was installed at the head of a government composed of many Arab nationalists who had fought in the Arab Revolt in World War I. In close alliance with Britain, the institutions of statehood were established, including a constitution, cabinet government and elected parliament. Oil and agricultural resources combined to endow Iraq with a viable economy. Yet the majority of Iraqis resented the British presence deeply. A nationwide revolt broke out in 1920 similar to anti-British riots in Egypt in 1919. Popular opposition to the British presence continued through the 1920s and encouraged the British to reconsider their position in Iraq. The initial treaty of alliance of October 1922 imposed the sort of limits on Iraq's sovereignty that precluded admission to the League, as had been the case in Egypt. Persistent nationalist agitation, and domestic British opposition to paying for unproductive colonies, led to the drafting of a treaty of alliance in 1930 that allowed for the termination of the mandate. Britain supported Iraq's application to the League of Nations and, in 1932, Iraq's sovereignty was recognised with membership of the League. As in the Egyptian treaty of 1936, Britain retained base rights in Iraq, transit facilities for its military and preferential relations in diplomatic and military spheres. These restrictions notwithstanding, Iraq's emergence into the community of independent states was the envy of the Arab world (Tripp 2000).

The only other Arab state to negotiate the end of its mandate was Transjordan, though its mandate outlived the League itself. The long duration of the mandate reflects the low level of opposition to what was in fact a very light British presence. Amir Abdullah secured his rule over the Transjordan and was maintained on a modest British subsidy. The main objective of Abdullah's politics was the aggrandisement of his modest state. His first target was Damascus, and he enjoyed close ties with some Syrian nationalists, such as Dr Abd al-Rahman Shahbandar, as well as with Druze leaders in southern Syria. Both the French mandate authorities and the majority of Syrian nationalists opposed Abdullah's 'Greater Syria' plans. Abdullah also looked to Palestine for access to the Mediterranean. His quick acceptance of partition plans for Palestine when first pronounced in 1937 led to widespread Arab criticism of Abdullah (Wilson 1987). Abdullah, whose introduction to international diplomacy came through representing his father Sharif Hussein in his wartime negotiations with Sir Henry McMahon, developed extensive experience of international relations through his long rule (1921–51) and close ties to Britain. He was one of the most active leaders in inter-Arab relations and had the most exchange with the Jewish Executive in Palestine (Shlaim 1988). However, his first attempt at negotiating the end of the mandate in 1946 led to so partial an independence that the United States refused to recognise the state and blocked Transjordan's entry to the new United Nations (Dann 1984). It was not until 1948, when Britain and Transjordan signed a treaty less restrictive of its sovereignty that Transjordan gained American recognition—and not until 1955 that the country was admitted to the United Nations.

Palestine

If Iraq was the most successful British mandate and Transjordan the easiest, Palestine was to prove the most unsuccessful and difficult of British colonial possessions in the Middle East. The origins of the problem may be traced to the contradictions inherent in the Balfour Declaration. Arguably, there was no mechanism for Britain to establish a Jewish national home without disadvantage to the rights of the indigenous Palestinian Arabs. The mandate structure and the Jewish nationalist ideology of Zionism gave rise to an active Palestinian nationalist movement demanding full sovereignty over all of

Palestine, an end to Jewish immigration and an end to the British mandate that provided the framework for the Jewish national home. Palestinian resistance to the mandate and refusal to participate in its institutions prevented the building of any enduring state structure. On the other hand, the Yishuv, as the Jewish community in Palestine was called, cooperated fully with the British and initiated a process of state-building, establishing a trade union movement, a modified cabinet government, even its own military. With their close links to the World Zionist Organisation, the Jewish Executive enjoyed a degree of experience in negotiations with European powers that the Palestinians would never match. In essence, the Palestinians could only force changes in British policy through confrontation. Riots, economic boycott and an all-out armed revolt lasting nearly three years (1936–39) produced commissions of enquiry, a raft of white papers and finally in 1939 a programme of reduced Jewish immigration and the promise of independence in a decade. The terms of the 1939 White Paper were rejected by the Zionists, and between 1945 and 1947 radical Jewish groups engaged in a terror campaign against the British authorities in Palestine. Britain conceded defeat in 1947 and referred the Palestine problem to the United Nations for resolution. The UN voted for the partition of Palestine into Jewish and Arab areas, setting off a war that raged within Palestine through the spring of 1948 and, following the British withdrawal on 14 May, exploded into the first Arab–Israeli war (Segev 2000).

Syria and Lebanon

The French created very different mandates in Syria and Lebanon. In Lebanon they merged the highlands of Mount Lebanon with the coastal plain from Tyre to Tripoli and the Biqa Valley stretching between the Lebanon and Anti-Lebanon Mountain chains to create the state of Grand Liban, or Greater Lebanon. The aim was to create the largest territorial expanse while preserving a Christian majority. While this plan was opposed by Sunni Muslims and Druzes, the colonial power enjoyed the ardent support of their Maronite allies and the tacit agreement of other Christian communities. Greater Lebanon was established by decree of General Henri Gouraud, commander-in-chief of French forces in the Levant and High Commissioner, and declared an anomalous 'independent State under French Mandate' (Salibi 1977: 164). After six years under French military governors, the Lebanese Republic was founded in 1926 with an elected chamber of deputies, an appointed senate, a constitution and president selected by the two chambers. There were of course nationalists who opposed the great influence the French mandate authority exercised over the nominally independent Lebanon, symbolised by the original national flag which imposed a Lebanese cedar on the French tricolour. While the Lebanese enjoyed autonomy in domestic affairs, France assumed full responsibility for Lebanon's foreign relations and defence. Over the 1920s and 1930s, the institutions of the Lebanese state came increasingly into conflict with the mandatory power and sought fuller independence. A range of nationalists movements pulled Lebanon in different directions, some calling for Lebanon to be reattached to Syria while others sought the end of the mandate and full independence.

The French enjoyed virtually no indigenous support in their Syrian mandate. The French sent a military force to drive out King Faisal and his supporters and occupy Damascus. The French engaged a small force of irregulars at Khan Maysalun on 24 July 1920, entered Damascus the following day and asked Faisal to leave on 27 July. This blatant disregard of Syrian self determination for colonial ends blighted Franco-Syrian relations from the start. Subsequent French efforts to break Syria into four smaller units based around Damascus, Aleppo and two minority statelets for the Alawites and Druzes, provoked fierce opposition for the clear attempt at divide and rule. In July 1925, the Druze launched a proto-nationalist revolt against French administrative measures that spread to Damascus and the rest of Syria that raged for two years. Peace was only restored when the territorial integrity of Syria was respected. These events consolidated nationalist forces fragmented by the years of fighting the French into what came to be known as the National Bloc, who sought to attain Syrian independence through negotiations (Khoury 1987).

The end of the mandates in Syria and Lebanon followed similar trajectories. France sought to curtail nationalist dissent with treaties granting independence to both states in 1936. Modelled on the Anglo-Iraqi Treaty of 1930, the Syrian treaty was widely accepted while the treaty proved very controversial in Lebanon, provoking clashes between its advocates and its detractors. Neither instrument was ratified by the French Chamber by the outbreak of war in 1939. The mandates looked slated for termination in 1941 with the Allied occupation and the Free French declaration of the independence of Syria and Lebanon. In practice, though, the French sought to preserve their authority. The Lebanese were the first to achieve independence. General elections were held in Lebanon in the summer of 1943. The new Chamber elected Bishara Khuri president, and purged all French prerogatives of the mandate from the Constitution. French efforts to arrest Khuri and his government and reassert their prerogatives provoked nationwide resistance and a reversal of policy that led to full Lebanese independence. In Syria too independence was initiated through constitutional reform, and by 1944 both Syria and Lebanon gained international recognition. By declaring war on Germany in 1945, both Syria and Lebanon were invited to the founding conference of the United Nations. However, France retained forces in both Syria and Lebanon and sought preferential treaties before withdrawing. It was only after Syria and Lebanon brought UN pressure to bear that France withdrew its troops from Syria (April 1946) and Lebanon (December 1946), and both countries could claim full independence.

The colonial experience: an assessment

These brief historical overviews demonstrate that, while each Middle Eastern state had a distinct interwar encounter with imperialism, the colonial experience left certain common legacies. The post-war settlement created a number of new states. Within their new, European-drawn boundaries, a process of state formation was initiated under strict imperial control. The new states were insulated from foreign affairs by their colonial masters. Politics were overwhelmingly domestic, and domestic politics were dominated by the search for national independence. The struggle for independence created vested interests in the individual nation states that conflicted with popular notions of a greater Arab nation. By the time independence was achieved, in nearly all cases in the aftermath of the Second World War, the newly emergent states of the Middle East were hardly better integrated to the prevailing system of international diplomacy than they had been at the end of the First World War. Relations between Arab states were fraught with rivalries and factionalism that undermined regional organisations like the Arab League and the Arabs were ineffectual in such international arenas as the United Nations and in great power diplomacy. These weaknesses were apparent in the Arab handling of the Palestine Crisis of 1947–49.

The Arab States and the Palestine Crisis

Following the Second World War, Britain found its position in Palestine increasingly untenable. Armed conflict with Jewish groups and demoralising terror attacks placed a burden on British armed forces when the shattered post-war economy could least bear it. In the end, Foreign Secretary Ernest Bevin referred the Palestine question to the UN for resolution.

The UN resolved in November 1947 to partition Palestine into two states. The six Arab members of the United Nations (Egypt, Lebanon, Saudi Arabia and Syria were founding members of the UN; Iraq joined in December 1945 and Yemen in 1947) all opposed partition, but had no impact on the debate within the General Assembly. They failed to build a coalition of nations to support Arab claims to Palestine and were outmanoeuvred by the Jewish Agency. The final vote in the General Assembly was thirty-three to thirteen, giving the necessary two third majority to ensure the passing of the Partition Resolution (Hurewitz 1976: 301).

While one might make allowances for the difficulties the Arab states encountered in going against policies advocated by such great powers as Britain and America, they were hardly more accomplished in inter-Arab diplomacy, as witnessed by the ineffectual actions of the Arab League. The Arab states were deeply divided and distrustful of one another. King Faruq of Egypt and King Abdul Aziz ibn Saud of Saudi Arabia sought to contain the Hashemite kings of Iraq and Transjordan. King Abdullah of Transjordan and the leader of the Arab Higher Committee of Palestine, Hajj Amin al-Husseini, loathed each other. The President of Syria, Shukri al-Quwwatly, feared King Abdullah's ambitions in Syria (Rogan and Shlaim 2001). The Arab League engaged in a series of fruitless summits to address the growing crisis in Palestine across 1947 and 1948.

The incongruous territories allotted to the Jewish and Arab states were not acceptable to either party (although the Yishuv formally accepted the terms of the UN resolution), and the partition resolution gave rise to a civil conflict in Palestine in which Jewish forces occupied several Palestinian cities in the autumn of 1947 and spring of 1948 (most notably Tiberias, Safad, Haifa and Jaffa). Even when war was inevitable, the Arab League only decided two days before the end of the mandate in May 1948 to dispatch the armies of Egypt, Iraq, Syria and Lebanon into Palestine, along with Transjordan's Arab Legion. This last-minute invasion involved a fraction of the national armies involved—only 10,000 Egyptian soldiers, 3,000 Syrians, 3,000 Iraqis and 1,000 Lebanese, in addition to the 4,500 Transjordanians—well below the forces necessary to achieve a strategic advantage over Jewish forces. King Abdullah was named commander-in-chief of the Arab forces, but each nation's army operated under its own commanders without any overall coordination.

Immediately following the termination of the mandate and the withdrawal of British troops from Palestine on 14 May 1948, Israel declared its statehood. The armies of Syria, Lebanon, Iraq, Transjordan and Egypt invaded Palestine to engage the Jewish forces. Between 15 May 1948 and the end of hostilities on 7 January 1949, the State of Israel contained or defeated all of the Arab armies and expanded its boundaries to embrace 78 per cent of the Palestine Mandate. The military defeat in Palestine reflected both a failure by the newly emergent Arab states in international diplomacy and the legacies of the colonial experience. In effect, the nationalist leaders who oversaw the transition to independence within the boundaries of the colonial states fell at their first hurdle when they failed to live up to their rhetoric and save Arab Palestine from the Zionist threat (Rogan and Shlaim 2001). The Arab defeat in Palestine was to plague the international relations of the region down to the present.

Conclusion

The Palestine crisis brought to light Arab weaknesses in the international arena and in regional affairs that were a legacy of the way in which the colonial powers shaped the emergence of the modern Middle East. It was also a harbinger of the problems that would plague the region for decades to come.

Coming out of the Ottoman experience, the Arabs aspired to national independence. Promises of a new order of international relations, set out by American President Wilson in his Fourteen Points, generated expectations of national self-determination. Instead, the Arabs found themselves denied any say in the disposition of their lands and under British or French colonial rule. Within the parameters of these new states, again, shaped without the consent of those governed, Arab politics were primarily focused on gaining independence from colonial rule. The new Arab states had little or no exposure to the international order so long as their colonial masters oversaw their foreign affairs. This extended to inter-Arab affairs, often divided between those states under British versus those under French rule. Thus divided, domestic interests prevailed over broader Arab interests in a way that allowed the colonial powers, and later even the young state of Israel, to play the Arab states against each other.

The manner in which the Middle East was shaped in the interwar years produced a number of stable states that have, with time, established themselves in the community of nations. It also gave rise to enduring problems that have troubled the region and the international order. The most obvious example was in Palestine, where the rival national claims have made the Arab–Israeli conflict an enduring feature of the international relations of the Middle East. French efforts to create the largest possible state for their Maronite clients in Lebanon, and the sectarian system they helped shape to govern the many religious communities that fell within its boundaries, laid the foundations for one of the most violent civil wars in the Arab world (1975–91). Yet it is Iraq that has proved the most unsettling to the international system. The decision to create a state of the three Ottoman provinces of Mosul, Baghdad and Basra laid to rest promises of a state that would have served as a homeland to the Kurdish people. Instead, the Kurds distributed between Turkey, Iran, Iraq and Syria have known periods of intense nationalist agitation and civil war. Noteworthy examples were the PKK insurgency in Eastern Turkey of the 1980s and 1990s and the numerous Kurdish uprisings in Iraq, repressed with increasing brutality by the Ba'thi regime, including the use of gas against the villagers of Halabcha. Yet it was Iraq's claims to territories formerly associated with the Ottoman province of Basra in the modern state of Kuwait (1937, 1961 and 1990) that have provoked the greatest wars to rock the region. Saddam Hussein's invasion of Kuwait on 2 August 1990 divided the Arab world and led to war in 1991, twelve years of sanctions, and a second war in 2003. The emergence of the state system in the Middle East is thus a history of both the creation of stable states and of destabilising conflicts.

Further Reading

BROWN, L.C., *International Politics and the Middle East: Old Rules, Dangerous Game* (Princeton, NJ: Princeton University Press, 1984). An excellent study that traces the evolution of the nineteenth century 'Eastern Question' into the troubled Arab state system of the twentieth century.

FROMKIN, D., *A Peace to End All Peace: Creating the Modern Middle East, 1914–1922* (London: Penguin, 2000). This book discusses the formative period of World War I and the Versailles Treaty in shaping the Arab state system.

HUREWITZ, J.C., *The Middle East and North Africa in World Politics* (New Haven: Yale University Press, 1975–79). A two-volume compilation, that comprises the best collection of documents on the diplomacy of the Middle East. The first volume covers the four centuries spanning 1535–1914, and the second the years 1914–1945.

HOURANI, A., *A History of the Arab Peoples* (London: Faber, 2002). A magesterial study, among the best general histories of the Middle East in the twentieth century. See especially Parts IV and V.

YAPP, M.E., *The Making of the Modern Near East, 1792–1923* and *The Near East since the First World War* (London and New York: Longman, 1987–91). A highly recommended two-volume history.

Notes

1. The first treaty of capitulation was drafted in 1352 with Genoa, followed by similar treaties with Venice and Florence. In 1535 a commercial treaty was negotiated between France and the Porte, and a formal negotiated capitulation concluded in 1569, followed by similar instruments with England (1580) (Hurewitz 1975: 1–10).

2. Sharif Hussein assumed the kingship of the 'Arab Countries' in 1916 though was only recognised by Britain as King of the Hijaz. He abdicated in favour of his son Ali in 1924, who ruled until the Saudi conquest of Hijaz in 1925.

2

The Cold War in the Middle East

Peter Sluglett

OVERVIEW

This chapter attempts to examine the effects of the Cold War upon the states of the Middle East. Although clearly not so profoundly affected as other parts of the world in terms of loss of life and revolutionary upheaval, it is clear that the lack of democracy and the distorted political development in the Middle East is in great part a consequence of its involvement in the interstices of Soviet and American foreign policy. After a brief discussion of early manifestations of USSR/US rivalry in Greece, Turkey and Iran at the beginning of the Cold War, Iraq is used as a case study of the changing nature of the relations between a Middle Eastern state and both superpowers from the 1940s until the collapse of the Soviet Union. Considerable attention is devoted to the ways in which various Iraqi regimes were able to manipulate the two super-powers throughout the period. A final section attempts to assess the overall effects of the Cold War on the region as a whole.

Introduction

It seems something of a truism, but, apparently, a truism not universally accepted, that the Cold War had deep, lasting and traumatic effects upon the Middle East.

Thus, Halliday considers: 'For all its participation in a global process, and the inflaming of inter-state conflict, the Cold War itself had a limited impact on the Middle East; in many ways, and despite its proximity to the USSR, the Middle East was less affected than other parts of the Third World'. Specifically, there were no significant pro-Soviet revolutionary movements, and the casualties in the Arab–Israeli conflict between 1947 and 1989 (about 150,000 Arabs and 11,800 Israelis), were very much lower than those in wars elsewhere; compare the casualties in Korea (4 million) or Vietnam (2–3 million) (Halliday 1997: 16). However, apart from prolonging the region's *de facto* colonial status, it seems clear that the constant struggle for influence waged by the United States and the Soviet Union effectively polarised and/or anaesthetised political life in most Middle Eastern countries, encouraged the rise of military or military-backed regimes, and generally served to stunt or distort the growth of indigenous political institutions. In addition, the regional clients of the superpowers made generous contributions to the destabilisation of the region by attempting to involve their patrons in the various local conflicts in which they were engaged.

Of course, much the same might be said for many other regions of the non-Western world, and it is undeniable that a number of 'intrinsic' or specific factors, including the presence and development of oil in much of the Middle East, and the perceived need by the rest of the world for unfettered access to it, as well as complex local issues such as the Palestine conflict and the invention and growth of political Islam, all would have had, and of course did have, their separate and cumulative effects on the political and socioeconomic development of the region, Cold War or no Cold War. Thus the end of the Cold War has had virtually no impact on the Arab–Israeli conflict, at least not in the direction of facilitating a solution or settlement, which, it was sometimes alleged, was being prevented by superpower rivalry.

It is also not helpful to exaggerate the extent to which each superpower—especially the United States, whose influence was usually stronger since it had more and often better quality inducements to offer—was able to control the actions, or force the obedience, of its local clients. Thus, both the US and the Soviet Union were unable to prevent Israel and Egypt going to war in 1967 (Tibi 1998: 65); in 1980, Iraq did not inform the Soviet Union of its intention to invade Iran until the invasion had taken place (which resulted in an immediate stoppage of Soviet arms deliveries). As I have already suggested, the amount of manipulation exercised by such individuals as Gamal Abd al-Nasser, Hafiz al-Asad, Saddam Hussein and others should not be under-estimated; the phenomenon of the tail wagging the dog is very much in evidence over these decades. It now seems very obvious (as historians can say with hindsight—presumably it was not so clear at the time) that local actors could and frequently did take advantage of superpower rivalry to play the US and the USSR off against each other for their own or their country's benefit. Particularly given this latter consideration, it is important not to subscribe, as many in the region do, to a culture of 'victimhood', the notion that peoples and governments are merely the playthings of immeasurably stronger international forces, a notion which, if accepted, denies any agency to local peoples, governments and states.[1]

The Immediate Origins of the Cold War

It is not difficult to see why, or how, almost immediately after the Second World War, the struggle for control or influence over the Middle East became sharply contested between the United States and the Soviet Union. (While the example, and occasionally the influence, of China was certainly important in the Middle East, China's regional role is more significant in terms of the Sino–Soviet conflict than of the wider struggle between 'East' and 'West' being conducted by the Soviet Union and the United States.) Among many important areas of contention, or perhaps more accurately of anxiety, were, first, the desires of the superpowers to gain strategic advantage in the region, second, the fact that the region contained some two thirds of the world's oil reserves in a context where oil was becoming increasingly vital to the economy of the Western world, and third, the fact that, in a novel way which made it quite distinct from previous power struggles, the Cold War represented an *ideological conflict* between two very different political, social and economic systems. As Stalin observed to Tito and Djilas: 'This war [the Second World War] is not as in the past; whoever occupies a territory also imposes on it his own social system . . .' (Kuniholm 1980: 117).

In terms of what might be called traditional strategic considerations, the former Soviet Union shared a common frontier with two Middle Eastern states, Turkey and Iran (or three, if Afghanistan is included), and in the case of Iran, a particularly long one. Given that more or less overt hostility between the two powers surfaced soon after, even sometimes before, the end of the Second World War, it did not take long for the Soviet Union to see itself facing actual or potential threats from its southern neighbours, while its southern neighbours were equally quick to see actual or potential threats from the north. At the risk of stating the obvious, an important difference in the situations of the two superpowers before the development of long range or intercontinental ballistic missiles in the 1960s, was that while an invasion of the Soviet Union could be launched, or threatened, from Iran or Turkey, the Soviet Union had no comparable access to the United States from the territory of any of the latter's neighbours. At the same time, while the United States would have to send troops half way across the world to assist its friends and allies in Iran or Turkey, it was rather easier for the Soviet Union to, for example, train and supply Greek guerrillas from Bulgaria and Yugoslavia (see the map in Kuniholm 1980: 403) or to support and or encourage potentially friendly autonomist movements in Iranian Azerbaijan and Kurdistan (Fawcett 1992; Sluglett 1986).

The conflicts in Azerbaijan, Kurdistan and Greece were among the earliest manifestations of Cold War activity in the Middle East, and were the result of the coincidence of a number of different factors. In Greece, for example, to simplify a complex reality, the communists had gained a fair sized following by the mid-1940s as a result of their leadership of the resistance to the German occupation after the Allied evacuation in April 1941. However, they were fiercely opposed to the American plan of supporting the return of the exiled king, to which, to complicate matters further, the British were equally opposed. By the end of 1944 the Soviet Union was also becoming keenly interested in the situation in the Balkans; Bulgaria and Rumania were occupied by Soviet troops in September and October, at more or less the same moment that the Soviet Union was pressing Tehran for oil concessions in north-western Iran. Between the end of the war in Europe in May 1945 and early 1947 the Greek communists, like the Iranian 'autonomists' a little earlier, sought to capitalise on a combination of their own gathering strength, the Soviet connection and Britain's declared intention to withdraw its occupation forces.

Faced with this situation, of an armed leftist movement with powerful external support, coupled with the imminent prospect of British withdrawal—reflecting Britain's economic prostration after the war rather than a 'positive' political choice— (Louis 1984: 11–15) and with parallel (if not quite so alarming) developments in Turkey, the United States announced the Truman Doctrine, which promised American assistance specifically to both Greece and Turkey, in February/March 1947. Truman's speech has an oddly familiar ring:

One of the primary objectives of the foreign policy of the United States is the creation of conditions in which we and other nations will be able to work out a way of life free from coercion . . . We shall not realise our objectives, however, unless we are willing to help free peoples to maintain their free institutions and national integrity against *aggressive movements that seek to impose upon them totalitarian regimes* (my italics). This is no more than a frank recognition that totalitarian regimes imposed on free peoples, by direct or indirect aggression, undermine the foundations of internal peace and hence the security of the United States.[2]

The situation in northern Iran, which flared up at much the same time, was at least equally if not more complicated. Briefly, many Azeris and Kurds either sought autonomy for their area(s), or, more modestly, a genuine reform of the machinery of central government in Tehran, which would eventually trickle down to the provinces.[3] Such aspirations had been encouraged by the course of the Bolshevik Revolution, the Jangali movement in neighbouring Gilan, on the southwestern shore of the Caspian, between 1915 and 1921, the short-lived Soviet Socialist Republic of Iran (Chaqueiri 1995; Kuniholm 1980: 132) and also, especially among the Iranian Kurds, by the more repressive aspects of some of Reza Shah's centralising policies in the 1920s and 1930s.

In August 1941, as a result of the change in the international constellation of forces after the German invasion of Russia, British and Soviet forces entered and occupied Iran. The British remained south of a line south of an imaginary line connecting Hamadan, Tehran and Mashad (roughly 35 degrees North), while Soviet forces occupied northern Iran, eventually controlling about one-sixth of the total land area, but, in Azerbaijan alone, about a quarter of the population of Iran. At least initially, neither of these incursions was rapturously received by the local populations. The two new allies were no strangers to the area, having interfered in Iran's internal affairs continuously and generally quite blatantly since the early nineteenth century.

However, on this occasion, perhaps not entirely to Britain's liking, a new political situation had come into being.

The nature of the alliance between the Western democracies and the USSR meant that the occupation of Iran ushered in a sudden flowering of political freedom, which not only benefitted organised political groups, especially the Tudeh Party, but also paved the way for the appearance of a relatively free press and the formation of labour unions and professional associations. However, Britain controlled the government in Tehran (Kuniholm 1980: 155); in addition, most of the government officials as well much of the wealthier element among the population quickly left the north for the British zone in the south when the Russians came (Fawcett 1990: 201–21). Initially things changed little when the United States entered the war after Pearl Harbor, but in time, British apprehensions of what might turn out to be the 'true nature' of Stalin's future policies were communicated to the Americans. The result of this, in December 1943, was the joint *Allied Declaration Regarding Iran* (signed by Churchill, Roosevelt and Stalin), which guaranteed, *inter alia*, Iran's future sovereignty and territorial integrity (Kuniholm 1980: 167).

However, some two years later, a few months after the war ended, events in the north seemed to be proceeding somewhat at variance with the *Declaration*. While most Azeris and Kurds probably had not initially regarded the Soviet occupation as a possible means of freeing themselves from the control of Tehran, it seems that after four years of it, that is by the time of the provincial elections in November and December 1945, a number of politicians in both regions had decided that autonomy within Iran, with Soviet support, was both practicable and desirable. Accordingly, a Kurdish autonomous republic and an Azeri autonomous government were declared soon after the provincial elections, which looked, or were represented as looking, somewhat threatening from London, Washington and Tehran.

In spite of these apparently alarming developments, it soon became clear that there were great limitations on the Soviet Union's freedom of manoeuvre. In addition— and here is a theme which recurs over and over again—there were also clear limits to the risks the Soviet Union would take in any confrontation with the United States. In spite of threats and cajolery, it proved impossible for the Russians to wrest the oil concession that they wanted out of the Iranian *majlis* in 1944, and after a relatively brief bluster (they were supposed to have left by March 1946) Soviet troops were withdrawn by the middle of May 1946 (Louis 1984: 62). After this, the Soviet Union had virtually no leverage in Azerbaijan and Kurdistan, nor, indeed, in the rest of the country. The three Tudeh cabinet ministers (for health, education and trade and industry) who had been appointed to the government of Ahmad Qavam in August 1946 were dismissed by November. In December 1946, Iranian troops marched into Tabriz and Mahabad and the two autonomous entities came to an abrupt end.

It is not entirely clear what the Soviet Union's objectives were in Iran; it certainly wanted an oil concession in the areas around the Caspian, and a friendly local government on the other side of the border. No significant oil deposits have ever been found in northern Iran, although it is possible that the Soviet Union was angling for a share of the AIOC concession further south. On the other hand, it seems far-fetched to imagine that the Soviet Union actually wanted, or thought it would be permitted, to **annex** northwestern Iran (Rubin 1981: 31). Given the political constellation in the region at the time, the Soviet Union's support for minorities in Iran probably raised warning flags for other governments with sizeable minority communities such as Iraq and Turkey, although both states were already so firmly anti-Soviet in outlook at the time that this probably only served to confirm already deeply held suspicions (Carrère d'Encausse 1975: 12). In many ways, these two sets of incidents, in Greece and Turkey and in Iran, were emblematic of later developments in the Cold War in the Middle East, in the sense that, on the one hand, the Soviet Union wanted to take whatever fairly limited measures it could to assure the safety of its frontiers, while the United States found itself equally obliged to defend 'free peoples' wherever it judged that their freedom was being threatened. I will return to the matter of these 'perceptions' later on.

Oil in the Middle East

One obvious lesson of the Second World War was that the future oil needs of the West were going to be met increasingly from the oil production, and from the huge oil reserves, of the Arab world and Iran. In chronological order, Iran had been exporting oil since 1913, Iraq since 1928, Bahrain since 1932, Saudi Arabia since 1938, and Kuwait since 1946, although this had all been on a fairly limited scale. Demand had risen enormously in the course of the war, and oil rapidly became a major strategic factor in the region.[4] By the mid to late 1940s, US oil companies controlled at least 42 per cent of Middle Eastern oil, as well as, of course, having majority interests in companies nearer home (in Mexico and Venezuela and in the US itself). In the 1950s, 1960s and 1970s, the Middle East became the principal source of oil for Western Europe and Japan, aided in time by new discoveries and exports from Algeria, Libya, Qatar and the Trucial States.[5]

The Soviet Union hardly participated here, importing only insignificant quantities of Middle Eastern crude (although, in a different context, Soviet technical assistance and sales guarantees were crucial preconditions for the nationalisation of Iraqi oil in 1972 (Farouk-Sluglett and Sluglett 2001: 123–6, 145–8). While much was made, and still occasionally is made, of the potential damage to the world economy which could be effected by a potential hostile group of 'revolutionaries'—or more recently (and equally implausibly) 'terrorists'—gaining control of one or more Middle Eastern oilfields, the history of the last few decades has shown such fears to have been largely groundless. It cannot easily be assumed that the deterrent effect of strong links with the US has played a significant role. Thus, even the most eccentric or 'extreme' regimes which came to power in the region (in Libya in 1969, in Iran ten years later) did not take long to direct their oil exports towards the exactly same markets as those favoured by their 'reactionary' or 'amoral' predecessors. Similarly, although it certainly caused a major price hike, the oil embargo which began in October 1973 had almost ceased to function by the spring of 1974 (Stork 1975: 210–56). Thus, to play the counter-factual card, if a group opposed to the Al Saud had come to power in the 1970s or 1980s, and seized the oil fields, it is difficult, given the monocultural nature of the Saudi economy, not to imagine that they would sooner or later have begun to sell their country's oil to their country's former customers.

Hence, it is difficult to pin point the true role played by oil during the Cold War. Like many other features of this period, it was something of a chimera, to be evoked in passionate discussions of American and European 'vital interests', or as an excuse for supporting this or that more or less undemocratic regime, but in reality it never functioned as a contentious issue between East and West. Even oil nationalisation, a heady rallying cry for countries eager to control their own economies, degenerated into a damp squib, given the despotic nature of most Middle Eastern governments. In the first place, the economic independence of individual states was a thing of the past by the 1970s, and secondly, much of the money so gained went into the pockets, not of the toiling masses of the country concerned, but into those of the more or less unscrupulous cliques in charge, whether in Iran, Iraq, Libya or Saudi Arabia. Only the first of these moves, the nationalisation of Iranian oil in May 1951, was carried out by a more or less democratically elected government, and it was of course frustrated by Britain's resolute refusal to countenance it.[6]

A Clash of Ideologies

The role played by the Soviet Union after its entry into the war on the Allied side in June 1941 was vital, probably decisive, in the Allies winning the struggle against the Axis. One consequence was that it quickly became necessary for Britain and its allies to present their new partner in a favourable light, partly to show their appreciation, and partly to rally support from the broad left and the labour movement throughout the world. In consequence, Middle Eastern Communist and leftist parties enjoyed a few years of relative freedom before being pushed firmly back into the closet (or the prison cells) in the late 1940s and 1950s. I have already mentioned some of the consequences of this in Greece and Iran in the 1940s, but this period of respite also allowed the Iraqi Communist Party to lead the clandestine opposition to the *ancien régime* in the late 1940s and early 1950s, and permitted Communists to rise to the leadership of almost all the principal labour unions (Farouk-Sluglett and Sluglett 1983).

There can be no doubt that ideology played an important role in defining the nature of the competition between the two powers for the hearts and minds of Middle Eastern regimes, and, although in different ways, of Middle Eastern peoples. In 1945, with the exception of Afghanistan, Iran, (Saudi) Arabia, Turkey and

(North) Yemen, the whole of the Middle East and North Africa either had been, or was still, under various forms of British, French or Italian colonial control, at least since the end of the First World War. Even the territories just mentioned had been subjected to economic or other kinds of pressure by the European powers. Thus Iran, though never actually colonised, had been fought over by Britain and Russia for economic and strategic reasons well into the twentieth century. Initially, of course, with the process of decolonisation under way after 1945, both the United States and the Soviet Union (which was at pains to dissociate itself from its Tsarist past) could point to their clean hands, their lack of colonial-imperial involvement in the region.

In the context of the process of decolonisation in particular, there was a certain degree of ambiguity in the attitude of the United States, which took several episodes to resolve. Thus, the United States was very publicly opposed to Britain over Palestine and, over Iranian oil nationalisation, did little to discourage the Egyptian revolution in 1952, and in spite of having less than cordial relations with Abd al-Nasser after his decision to buy arms from the Soviet Union in 1955, showed itself both firm and single-minded in its opposition to the tripartite invasion of Egypt by Britain, France and Israel in November 1956. Of course, things gradually became less confusing as Britain's withdrawal from the region increased in momentum. Indeed, by January 1968 Dean Rusk described himself as 'profoundly dismayed' at the prospect of Britain's military withdrawal from Southeast Asia and the Middle East, which he considered 'a catastrophic loss to human society' [sic].[7]

In broad terms, the United States offered its own vision of modernity, initially that of a disinterested senior partner which could offer assistance, both in terms of goods and 'advice' to young nations struggling to become members of the 'free world', which was emerging after the devastation of the Second World War. 'Communism'—and this was long before the extent of the excesses of Stalinism was fully known—was represented as the incarnation of evil totalitarian forces, bent on world conquest, and in particular as inimical to the spirit of free enterprise, an activity considered on the western side of the Atlantic as one of the most vital expressions of the human spirit. On the other side of the ideological divide, the Soviet Union, parts of which were at least as backward as much of the Middle East in the 1940s and 1950s, offered an alternative vision, of an egalitarian society where class divisions had been, or were being, abolished, and where a benevolent state would look after the interests of its citizens from the cradle to the grave. Both visions of the world, and of the future, had their partisans and adherents in the Middle East. At this stage, of course, few people from the region had had the chance to study either system at first hand.

As has been noted in the context of Iran and Greece, it became apparent soon after the end of the Second World War that the depleted financial and military resources of Britain, and France would not permit them to resume the paramountcy that they had enjoyed in the region in the inter-war years, and that, in addition, something of a power vacuum would be created by their departure and indeed by any major reduction in their regional role. France's departure from Lebanon and Syria in 1945 and 1946 was both more or less final and fairly abrupt, although the decolonisation of

North Africa, particularly Algeria, was to take longer and to be extremely painful and costly. As far as Palestine was concerned, the Labour cabinet first wanted to cling on, and then, seeing it that it would get no support from the United States for the creation of a binational state, decided at the end of 1946 that it would make better sense to refer the matter to the United Nations (Louis 1986). Similarly, the increasingly anachronistic nature of Britain's position in Egypt (and a few years later, but in much the same way, in Iraq), the narrowness and isolation of the clique that supported the continuation of the British connection and the relentless forward march of nationalist or anti-colonial movements, meant that the question became when, rather than if, Britain would depart. Into the vacuum thus created stepped, in different ways and at different times, the United States and the Soviet Union.

Naturally, the role of ideology, and the relative appeal of the Soviet Union and the West, changed quite dramatically as the Cold War unfolded. In the first place, the two powers took some time to define their respective roles. For one thing, after the events in Greece and Iran which have just been described, the Soviet Union went into a period of relative isolation (not only, of course, in the Middle East), from which it only began to emerge after the death of Stalin in 1953. The only major exception to this was the Soviet Union's hasty recognition of Israel as an independent Jewish state in May 1948, on the well-known but still rather extraordinary grounds that Israel, founded on what the Soviet Union believed to be 'socialist principles', provided a 'last chance to destabilise the Middle East from within' (Carrère d' Encausse 1975: 14–15).

Throughout the Cold War, this action on the part of the Soviet Union always remained one of the choicest of the many big sticks which their local rivals were to use time and again to beat the Middle Eastern communist parties. Apart from this, and the episodes already discussed, Stalin's main concern, both before and after the Second World War, was the internal reconstruction of the Soviet state (the doctrine of 'socialism in one country'), and Soviet foreign policy was directed to that end. Given the situation in 1945, the subjugation of the states of Eastern Europe can be understood in terms of the pursuit of that goal. A further important factor, which became a serious challenge to much of the received thinking in the Soviet Union, was that even in the early 1950s, and even to the most diehard partisans of political correctness in Moscow, it was becoming uncomfortably clear that the imminence of the 'crisis of capitalism', on which a great deal of Soviet thinking had been predicated, was a product of wishful thinking in the Kremlin, and had very little foundation in fact.

In the late 1940s, the East/West conflict was symbolised by the Berlin blockade and the Korean War: after the early incidents which have been described, it was some time before the Middle East developed into an arena of conflict. In fact, Soviet interest in the Third World in general remained fairly subdued until the death of Stalin in March 1953, and its main concern outside its own borders was assuring the 'stability' of the states of Eastern Europe. For its part the United States was fairly active in organising the defence of the 'Free World', with the creation of NATO (of which Turkey became a member in 1952). In 1955 the United States created (though it did not join) the Baghdad Pact, which brought Britain and the so-called

'Northern Tier' states—Iran, Iraq, Pakistan and Turkey—into an anti-Soviet alliance. The Soviet Union was somewhat slower to take action in the region, and in fact the formal embrace of the Warsaw Pact (May 1955) never extended beyond the Soviet Union's allies in Eastern Europe.

The relationships of the two great powers with the states of the Middle East were quite complex and nuanced in nature, and cannot simply be written off as an imperialist or neo-imperialist. They also changed markedly over time, especially as the limitations on the freedom of manoeuvre of the Soviet Union and the eastern European countries became increasingly apparent in the late 1970s and 1980s. To some extent they can be described as 'patron/client' relations (Osterhammel 1997: 115–17), with the peculiarity that the clients (in the Middle East and elsewhere in the third world) were able to switch patrons, and often to have more than one patron at once, in the case of both poor and rich countries—Egypt and Iraq, for instance.

One of the most remarkable aspects of the Cold War in the Middle East was the speed with which the various Middle Eastern states acquired the ability to play one superpower off against another. This meant that relations were often competitive, especially in terms of the provision of goods and services. An obvious example here was the willingness of the Soviet Union to finance the Aswan Dam when the United States would no longer support the project because Egypt had bought or ordered arms from the Soviet Union. Bargaining over arms supplies was a major point of leverage, since the United States would not supply the kinds of arms to the Arab states that might enable them to defeat Israel. It took some time for it to become clear that the Soviet Union would not do so either, and those years of uncertainty marked the heyday of 'Arab-Soviet friendship'.

Elements of a Case Study: Iraq, the Soviet Union and the United States, 1945–90

Iraq's changing and complex relations with the superpowers offer an interesting example of the extent to which the Middle Eastern tail was so often able to wag the superpower dog. As has already been mentioned, the decision of the Soviet Union to join the Allied side in 1941 ushered in a brief but important period of political freedom for the left in both Iran and Iraq. However, since Iraq had defied Britain in the 'thirty days war' of April–May 1941, the liberalising effects of Soviet membership of the alliance did not become apparent until after Nuri al-Said's resignation from the premiership in June 1944. One of the major, if indirect, beneficiaries of this relaxation in the political climate was the Iraqi Communist Party, which had been founded in 1934. Although its numbers were small it was able to wield considerable influence, especially among workers in the modern industrial sector (Basra port, the Iraq Petroleum Company, the Iraqi railways) and among 'intellectuals'. Between late 1944 and the spring of 1946, sixteen labour unions, twelve of which were controlled by the Communist Party, were given licences, as were a number of political parties. However, the enforced resignation of Tawfiq al-Suwaydi's ministry (as a result of pressure from the Regent and Nuri al-Said) at the end of May 1946 brought this brief period of political freedom to an end.

A number of British officials and some British ministers in London had come to realise that 'with the old gang in power this country cannot help to progress very far' (Quoted Louis 1984: 309). Nevertheless, there were limits to the amount of pressure which Britain, and behind it the United States, was prepared to bring to bear on Iraqi governments immediately after the war. Given his very close ties with Britain, the débâcle in Palestine was evidently a serious embarrassment for Nuri al-Said, especially since it came close on the heels of the hostile atmosphere created by the Iraqi government's botched attempt to renegotiate the Anglo-Iraqi Treaty at Portsmouth in January 1948. Yet, with a combination of ruthlessness and repression, and the rapid rise in oil revenues in the late 1940s and early 1950s (from ID 2.3 million in 1946 to 13.3 million in 1951 and 84.4 million in 1955), the *ancien régime* was able to put off what seemed to many observers as the inevitable for another ten years.

The Baghdad pact was effectively an eastward extension of NATO, representing an attempt on the part of the United States to create an anti-Soviet alliance of states bordering, or close to, the Soviet Union. At this stage the Soviet Union was slowly emerging out of the post-war isolation which Stalin (who died in March 1953) had imposed upon it, and was beginning to make its first cautious forays into the politics of the Middle East. Early in 1955, in the wake of an audacious Israeli raid on Gaza, Egypt had asked the United States for arms and had been rebuffed. In April–May 1955, Nasser, Sukarno and Tito formulated the doctrine of 'positive neutralism' (neither East nor West) at the Bandung conference. In September, Czechoslovakia, acting on behalf of the Soviet Union, announced that it would sell arms to Egypt (and later to Syria). This greatly enhanced the Soviet Union's image and popularity in both countries as well as in Iraq, although under the conditions then prevailing in Iraq listeners to eastern European radio stations faced the prospect of hefty fines or prison sentences if caught.

At this stage, the main objective of the Iraqi opposition (which was composed of a wide gamut of largely incompatible elements) was to become truly independent of Britain and to set up a national government. Although there was no mistaking the US hand behind the Baghdad pact, anti-American feeling in Iraq was probably secondary to anti-British feeling, since the British presence, British bases and the regime's obvious dependence on Britain were daily realities. Hostility to Britain increased with the tripartite invasion of Egypt in November 1956, an episode which transformed Nasser from an Egyptian to an Arab political figure with almost irresistible appeal. It is not clear how far Iraqis understood the extent to which United States intervention had been crucial in bringing the Suez crisis so swiftly to an end.[8] Thus, while it, became increasingly obvious over the ensuing months that the United States was alarmed by the possible consequences for the rest of the region of Nasser's 'victory', it had not managed to damage its reputation irrevocably in the eyes of all anti-British Iraqis by the time of the Iraqi Revolution of July 1958.

The Eisenhower administration's responses to Suez, the attempt to build up King Saud of Saudi Arabia as a counterweight to Nasser, and the pledge to come to the aid of nations threatened by 'International Communism' (the Eisenhower doctrine) had little immediate impact on Iraq (Kunz 2002). The Iraqi public's imagination had been much more excited by the announcement of the setting up of the United Arab Republic of Egypt and Syria in February 1958 (Sluglett 2002). However, the declaration would set alarm bells ringing in Washington: the Iraq Petroleum Company's pipelines to the Mediterranean crossed Syria, and, by the spring of 1958 the UAR was threatening Lebanon—or so the US' friends in the Lebanese government were alleging (Kunz 2002: 88).

As I have shown elsewhere (Sluglett 2002), it is most unlikely that there was any direct involvement of either Egypt or the Soviet Union in the Iraqi revolution of 1958. Of course, both countries welcomed the change of regime in Baghdad, especially early indications that the country would tilt in the direction of 'Arabism', or 'positive neutralism', or both. But for all his talk of Arab unity, Nasser was actually quite wary of extending his remit further across the Middle East. The UAR had been the Syrian Ba'th's idea rather than Nasser's, and the pressure for post-revolutionary Iraq to join the UAR came, again, from Arab nationalist groupings in Iraq, not from Cairo.

As for the Soviet Union, the notion gradually developed in the Kremlin and its think tanks in the late 1950s and early 1960s that national liberation movements which pursued the 'non-capitalist road' when they came to power could be considered worthy allies and partners. However desirable it might be that they should immediately choose the 'socialist road', few newly independent states either did so or showed any particular desire to do so—Cuba was the exception. This explains the complex and uncertain relations between the Soviet Union and, say, Egypt, or Iraq, or Syria, throughout the Cold War. The military regimes which seized power in the Middle East in the 1950s and 1960s were nationalist and anti-imperialist, and sought, and generally achieved, independence for their countries, but they were not, however Western analysts might choose to portray them, socialist or communist. Indeed, for the most part they were highly suspicious of and hostile to socialism and communism and of those who espoused such ideas locally. At the same time, while the Soviet Union was keen to intervene in, and exert influence upon, regional conflicts, it would not do so to the extent of seriously endangering or threatening its generally status-quo-upholding relationship with the West. Soviet military planners also knew that in the event of a military confrontation they would not be equipped to challenge American superiority.

These limitations on Soviet power, and greater or lesser degrees of local understanding of them, explains much of the *now hot/now cold* relationship between the Soviet Union and the Arab states. The West would not give the Arab states weapons which might result in them gaining military superiority; the Soviet Union would not either, but it did supply, generally on rather easy terms, the kind of bread and butter military hardware that the Arab states could roll out for their publics on army day or national independence day.[9] In brief, Iraq and the Soviet Union went through something of a honeymoon period for much of the first twenty years of the republic (until the late 1970s), especially after the (fairly early) souring of the Soviet/Egyptian relationship. Throughout the period, Iraqi public rhetoric was almost entirely anti-American (anti-imperialist), anti-Zionist and full of praise for 'our Soviet and socialist friends.' Of course, the Soviet Union was obliged to swallow some fairly bitter pills along the way, including the massacre of much of the Communist left in1963, the Ba'th's crude national socialist demagoguery, and the abandonment of any pretence that it was following a 'non-capitalist road' after the late 1970s. There were some little triumphs, perhaps most notably the nationalisation of Iraqi oil in 1972, which had been undertaken with generous (and widely acknowledged) technical assistance from the Soviet Union. Although oil nationalisation was wildly popular in Iraq, and added greatly to the cachet of the Ba'th government, the lack of accountability meant that much of the proceeds of the nationalised oil went into the pockets of Saddam Hussein and his cronies, and was a major factor in enabling them to stay in power for so long.

For the United States, obsessed by its crusade against Communism, the overthrow of Qasim in February 1963 and the massacre of the left which followed were regarded as positive developments, akin to the overthrow of Musaddiq ten years earlier, and the overthrow of Allende ten years later. While the Shah was alive, it was reckoned that he could contain the Iraqi regime, and act as the US policeman in the Gulf. Until the 1970s, Iraq could be written off as hopelessly 'socialist' and 'pro-Soviet', and was an object of fashionable concern and approval in some more short-sighted and more forgetful European leftist circles (Farouk-Sluglett 1982). After the oil price rise which followed the Arab–Israeli war of 1973, Iraq's income from oil tripled within two years, and went up almost tenfold between 1973 and 1982. With the disappearance of Iran from the scene in 1979–80, Iraq became the second largest market in the Middle East after Saudi Arabia for European, American and Japanese goods.

Finally, with the fall of the Shah and the rise of the Islamic Republic, the United States became very anxious to find another policeman to take the Shah's place. Thus implicitly, perhaps explicitly, it encouraged the invasion of Iran in 1980, probably thinking, along with Saddam Hussein, that the chaos within Iran would mean that the new regime would fall with comparative ease. When it became clear that this was not going to happen, the United States supplied Iraq—either directly or through third countries—with the latest military technology and advanced weaponry, and either gave Iraq, or otherwise allowed it to receive, the means to manufacture chemical (and most probably biological) weapons (Farouk-Sluglett and Sluglett 2001: 266–8), often in contravention of its own laws. Soviet–Iraqi relations had been under intense strain since 1978, when the Ba'th had turned against the communists again, and Iraq was moving steadily closer to the United States. However, after Khomeini banned the Tudeh party and cancelled a number of agreements with the Soviet Union, and especially after Iran began to gain footholds within Iraq in 1982–83, the Soviet Union shifted its support back to Iraq, although only for the duration of the war (Golan 1992: 47–53). Thus, the Cold War came to an end with the Soviet Union having spent its final few years on the same side as the United States in the war between Iran and Iraq.

The Effects of the Cold War

I would like to go back to something I mentioned at the beginning, to discuss briefly some of the distortions which the Cold War created in the internal politics of the states of the Middle East. To my rather pleasant surprise, counterfactual history, thought to be a rather risqué activity for historians, seems to have its adherents in international relations and political science, or at least this is what I take Joseph Nye to be saying (Nye 1997: 42–5). Thus, apparently, it is perfectly 'all right' (within reason, that is, provided the speculation remains within the parameters of common sense) to speculate on how Middle Eastern history and politics *might* have developed if such and such had or had not happened, or if such and such an action had or had not been taken. This speculation, however, will form the subtext, rather than the text, of what follows.

It is often alleged that democracy has no 'natural' roots in the Middle East, or more generally in the Islamic world, and hence that the growth of democratic institutions in such stony soil cannot and should not be expected. It is worth pointing out to such doubting Thomases that Western/Westminster democracy has no roots in Japan, and that what roots of it there may have been in Weimar Germany or Italy were extirpated almost entirely by the excesses of the 1930s and 1940s. However shakily, all three countries (as well as Turkey and India in their own ways, while they are not exactly the obvious heirs of it), have maintained a fair semblance of democracy for some six decades. Whether this is natural or unnatural is rather beside the point.

In the geographical space between Western Morocco and Eastern Iran, only two countries have more or less recognisable parliamentary democracies, Turkey and Israel, in which the opposition can and has become the government on several occasions. Even here the record is less than spotless, given the number of military interventions in Turkish politics, and the fact that about one third of those whom Israel rules has no say whatever in most of the basic aspects of its governance. Besides Israel and Turkey, Morocco has a lively if controlled party life, Egypt, Iran, Jordan and Yemen, and to some extent Bahrain and Kuwait, have some sort of controlled democracy, and Algeria, Iraq, Libya, Saudi Arabia, Syria and Tunisia, have none at all.

It was not always so. In the inter-war and immediately post-war period, there were lively and contested parliamentary elections in Iran, Iraq and Syria, perhaps also in Egypt. Part of, probably most of, what killed this off in the 1950s was the pressure of the Cold War. Mostly founded in the 1930s, the Middle Eastern communist parties had fairly limited connections with Moscow, which, as we have seen, did not have particularly strong ties with the region. Unfortunately the nature of the East/West conflict meant that, for example, when the monarchy was restored in Iran after the overthrow of Musaddiq, or the United Arab Republic of Egypt and Syria set up, or Qasim's regime overthrown in Iraq, such events were followed by the round-up and imprisonment, torture and, especially in Iraq in 1963, the execution, of thousands of local communists and leftists and their suspected sympathisers.

If one looks at what the communists were actually advocating, or what they did achieve in the limited arenas in which they were able to take some brief charge, it was quite modest and restrained—the creation of trade unions, the fundamentals of compensated land reform, the nationalisation of leading industries, free health and welfare programmes, and so on. In fact, with the exception of land reform, which was not on the agenda in Western Europe, these goals were prominent on the platforms of almost all Western European social democratic parties. In Britain, for instance, mostly during the post-war Labour government between 1945 and 1951, the railways and the mines were nationalised, a national health service was put in place, there was a free educational system from elementary school to university, and so on.

In the Middle East, the communists and the left were increasingly persecuted and driven underground in the 1950s and 1960s. This group included, it is reasonably safe to say, most of the leading intellectuals of their day, those who could not be bought and/or co-opted by the regimes which came to power. Their influence on the cultural life of the region was paramount and lasting. For the most part, potentially leftist or left-leaning regimes were replaced by more or less vicious forms of national socialist dictatorship, or, in the case of Iran under the Shah, by an autocracy that became increasingly less benevolent as the years passed. The CIA and British intelligence were behind the coup that overthrew Mussadiq and restored the Shah in 1953; perhaps less well known is that the CIA was involved in the coup which overthrew Qasim in Iraq in February 1963, and that it had also been in touch with members of the Ba'th party, most probably including Saddam Hussein, since the late 1950s, on the grounds that the party was both the 'force of the future' and virulently anti-communist.[10] Obviously, being a leftist in Egypt was somewhat less dangerous than being a leftist in Syria or Iran, and being a leftist in Syria or Iran was still less dangerous than being leftist in Iraq. In any case, survival, or at least not being persecuted, was largely a matter of chance and connections.

Perhaps the most unfortunate general consequence of this pathological fear, or hatred, of local communists and leftists, which the Cold War encouraged if it did not actually engender, was that *secular* opposition was driven underground almost everywhere in the Middle East. In such circumstances, 'politics' either became extraordinarily dangerous, or degenerated into sycophancy. Opposition to, or criticism of, the regime, or of the leader's policies, became tantamount to treason,[11] and could be punished as such. In consequence, what opposition there was drifted into the hands of religious organisations of various kinds, since, in Islamic countries, governments cannot, ultimately, close down the mosques.

This, then, seems to have been one of the major tragic consequences of the Cold War. The obsession with persecuting and reducing the influence of the left had two results, first, the maintenance in power of a series of unattractive, unrepresentative and generally dictatorial regimes of whatever political hue, and second, the rise of the religious right. In the latter, we are now faced with uncontrollable forces which believe, or purport to believe, in place of more rational political programmes, that 'Islam is the only solution'. The Soviet Union has collapsed, the Cold War has come to end—but the scars that this conflict has left on the Middle East will not go quickly away.

In Southey's *Battle of Blenheim*, young Peterkin asks his grandfather Kaspar:

'Now tell us all about the war
And what they fought each other for.'

'It was the English' Kaspar cried
'Who put the French to rout.
But what they fought each other for
I could not well make out;
But everybody said' quoth he
'That 'twas a famous victory'.

. . .

'And everybody praised the Duke
Who this great fight did win.'
'But what good came of it at last?'
Quoth little Peterkin.
'Why, that I cannot tell,' said he
'But 'twas a famous victory.'

Further Reading

ABRAHAMIAN, E., *Iran between Two Revolutions* (Princeton, NJ: Princeton University Press, 1982). In-depth study of the formation and activities of the Tudeh Party of Iran.

BATATU, H., *The Old Social Classes and the Revolutionary Movements of Iraq: a Study of Iraq's Old Landed and Commercial Classes and of its Communists, Ba'thists and Free Officers* (Princeton, NJ: Princeton University Press, 1978). Study of the Iraqi Communist Party, that charts the chequered and tragic progression of this organisation for much of the Cold War.

CARRÈRE d'ENCAUSSE, H., *La Politique Soviètique au Moyen Orient, 1955–1975* (Paris: Presses de la Fondation Nationale des Sciences Politiques, 1975). The clearest account of the beginnings of Soviet involvement in the Middle East after the death of Stalin.

FAROUK-SLUGLETT, M. and SLUGLETT, P., 'Labor and National Liberation: the Trade Union Movement in Iraq, 1920–1958', *Arab Studies Quarterly*, 5, 1983, 139–54. This article traces the linkages between the struggle for national independence and the activities of the Iraqi Communist Party.

FAWCETT, L., *Iran and the Cold War: the Azerbaijan Crisis of 1946* (Cambridge: Cambridge University Press, 1992). A comprehensive account of attempts to form an independent Azeri government in northern Iran with a measure of Soviet assistance.

KUNIHOLM, B., *The Origins of the Cold War in the Near East: Great Power Conflict and Diplomacy in Iran, Turkey and Greece* (Princeton, NJ: Princeton University Press, 1980). See in particular the sections on Greece and Turkey which have probably not been superseded.

LOUIS, W.R. and OWEN, R. (eds.), *A Revolutionary Year: the Middle East in 1958* (London and Washington D.C.: I. B. Tauris and Woodrow Wilson Center Press, 2002). The volume contains a number of useful essays on the various crises of 1958.

LOUIS, W.R., *The British Empire in the Middle East 1945–1951: Arab Nationalism, The United States and Postwar Imperialism* (Oxford: Oxford University Press, 1984). The most authoritative account of the gradual replacement of Britain by the United States as the dominant power in the Middle East.

NYE, J., *Understanding International Conflicts* (New York: Longman, 1997). An immensely helpful work in trying to understanding the wider ramifications of the Cold War.

SAYIGH, Y. and SHLAIM, A. (eds.), *The Cold War and the Middle East* (Oxford: Clarendon Press, 1997). The most comprehensive work on this period.

Notes

1. 'Only when we begin to allocate full agency to Arab governments can we allocate full agency to the populations; a deterministic worldview of a hegemonic United States or West has a disempowering effect, since it locates the source of all ills exclusively in the West.' Farouk-Sluglett (1994: 105). On 'victimhood', see Makiya (1993: 253–60).

2. The full text of Truman's speech of 12 March 1947 enunciating 'the doctrine' is in Kuniholm (1980: 434–49). See also McGhee (1990). Between 1947 and 1953, McGhee was successively 'Co-ordinator of Aid to Greece and Turkey, Assistant Secretary of State for Near East, South Asian and African affairs and US ambassador to Turkey' *ibid.*, p. xvi.

3. It probably also reflected local disappointment at the fact that much of the promise of the Constitutional Revolution had not been fulfilled. Fawcett (1992: 12). See also Sluglett (2002).

4. 'It has been taken for granted . . . that American interests must have actual physical control of, or at least assured access to, adequate and properly located sources of [sc. oil] supply.' Herbert Feis (wartime economic advisor to the State Department) quoted in Stork (1975: 29).

5. In 1970, 6.8% of OPEC crude oil went to North America, 55.8% to Western Europe and 21.3% to the Far East. In 1990, 22.7% went to North America, 34.9% to Western Europe, and 30.7% to the Far East. Relatively small amounts of OPEC crude, mostly from Iran and Iraq, went to the USSR and Eastern Europe: 0.2% in 1970 and 2.3% in 1990. Although Soviet oil production doubled between 1970 and 1990, it represented only about 0.6% of world production in 1970 and 1.3% in 1990. OPEC (1991: Tables 25, 26). [This source does not separate the Middle Eastern/North African members of OPEC from the non-Middle Eastern/North African members (Ecuador, Gabon, Indonesia, Nigeria and Venezuela). In 1970 and 1990, oil exports from these countries accounted for 20.8%

and 23.3% of the OPEC total respectively. *Ibid.*, Table 23].

6. The incident caused a major, if temporary, rift in Anglo-American relations, since the United States had already accepted the principle of fifty-fifty profit-sharing between Aramco and the government of Saudi Arabia, and could not understand why Britain did not see that it would eventually have to bow to the inevitable and follow suit. See Louis (1988). In *The British Empire in the Middle East 1945–1951*, Louis quotes George McGhee, the Assistant Secretary of State for the region, himself an independently wealthy oil man, as having 'left the British in no doubt whatever that he believed "Anglo-Persian" to be niggardly and short-sighted' (Louis 1984: 655).

7. Admittedly this lament was uttered in the context of very considerable European hostility to US policy in Vietnam. Echoing the Blair government's support of the United States in 2002-03, the British government was one of the US' few unwavering supporters in the late 1960s. Louis (2002: 1–25).

8. In the sense of this comment by the associate dean of the Faculty of International Affairs at Columbia University at a conference in December 1968: '[The West] accepts the idea of full national self-determination in the Middle East, as elsewhere. The last doubt on that score was dissipated by the clear United States stand in the Suez crisis of 1956'. Mosely (1969: 227).

9. Thus Iraq spent $12 billion on military *matériel* between 1985 and 1989, of which $7 billion worth was purchased from the Soviet Union. Iraq's second largest supplier was France, which received $2 billion.

10. See Farouk-Sluglett and Sluglett, (2001: 327 note 3), quoting Batutu (1978: 985–6) and Mufti (1996: 144–6).

11. The atmosphere which this created is wonderfully evoked in Makiya (1998).

3

The Middle East since the Cold War: Torn between Geopolitics and Geoeconomics

Bahgat Korany

OVERVIEW

Rather than a chronology, this analytical chapter emphasises some milestones in the region's evolution in the last fifteen years. Influential conceptual lenses such as 'the End of History', and 'The Clash of Civilisations' could not explain the region's international relations. With the US as a real rather than a virtual Middle East power after its invasion of Iraq, and its roadmap as the way out of the Palestinian–Israeli impasse, the region best substantiates global unipolarity. The chapter analyses three factors synonomous in the public mind with this region: oil; conventional and newer conflicts; and religio-politics. Data-based, the chapter attempts also to compensate for gaps in the established literature, such as some negative effects of the oil boom, and the attempts at regional cooperation to provide 'peace dividends'. It also draws attention to the diversity and wider conception of threats to national security.

Introduction: Sorting Out Post-Cold War Conceptual Lenses

Both during and after the Cold War, the Middle East and North Africa (MENA) occupied centre stage. However, many countries in the region feared initially that the end of the Cold War would devalue the region's worth and deprive its members of their capacity to manœuvre at the global level of unipolarity. For instance, Palestinians and Syrians lost not only a staunch ally but also a cheap source of conventional arms with the disappearance of the Soviet Union in 1991. Fear of the region's strategic devaluation was best exemplified by concerns in Turkey, a member of NATO, a listening post on the Soviet Union and guardian of the Dardanelles Straits.

But the end of the Cold War coincided with the Gulf War, 1990–91. The building up of an American-led international coalition to expel Iraqi invading forces from Kuwait dissipated doubts that the region might become marginalised. The attacks of 11 September 2001 against New York and Washington; al-Qaida's jihadism; President Bush's crusade against 'the axis of evil'; and the 2003 Anglo-American invasion of Iraq confirmed the region's centrality and its dubious distinction as an epitome of conflicts, old and new. As a result, factors shaping Middle East politics and society and their interaction with the global system have not changed—at least on the surface. But their variations and varied combinations give the region a different texture and chemistry. For despite differences between opponents of globalisation (a majority in the region) and its proponents (a minority), all agree that this reality liberates us from a blinkered state-centred approach and shows internal/external connectedness in social dynamics. Indeed, MENA after the Cold War might help popularise a new term in social analysis: INTERMESTICS, that is, not the conventional separation, but rather the growing organic connectedness between international relations and domestic politics. Whereas the all familiar state-centreed geopolitics are still predominant, the new geoeconomics of globalisation with its market vagaries and involved social forces are increasingly present.

The end of the Cold War naturally triggered visions, theories or conceptual lenses about the future system (see Figure 3.1 below). To identify the post-Cold War world, policy-makers and analysts talked about a new world order, but soon this overall picture became that of 'globalisation', the buzzword of the 1990's. The earliest and most influential conceptual lens was that of Fukuyama's *End of History* (1992).

According to this optimistic vision, the end of the Cold War decided the outcome of ongoing world conflict in favour of Western Liberalism, thus the 'end of history',

Oil
Conflict
Globalisation
Religio-Politics

Fig. 3.1 Post Cold-War conceptual lenses

the history of ideological indecision. We can thus look forward to a period of ideological assuredness, mental comfort and social harmony.

In MENA, socialist rhetoric and pseudo-socialist regimes have been in decline in the face of political Islam and petro-dollars for decades, and yet there was no social harmony or inter-state peace. On the contrary, with the proliferation of conflicts and the intensification of outside hegemony, one could talk not about the end of history, but rather about its return and continuation.

At the other end, was Huntington's pessimistic *Clash of Civilizations* (1996), whose subtitle is *the Remaking of World Order*. According to Huntington, Fukuyama's illusion of harmony is merely a reflection of a moment of euphoria, for 'the one harmonious world paradigm is clearly far too divorced from reality to be a useful guide to the post-cold war'. Instead, this world is one of multiplicity of conflicts, ethnic cleansing and the breakdown of law and order. The reason, according to Huntington, is what we can call cultural zero-sum power politics, where warring states and blocks have been replaced by equally warring civilizations (Huntington 1996: 21).

To explain the place of MENA in the world, Huntington's culture-centred determinism seemed plausible, in fact too plausible. After September 11 and the primacy of the New Conservative ideology in the US, described in Chapter 13, the West seems to be against the rest and is in fact the best placed to face of the 'axis of evil'. Huntington's is thus much more a self-fulfilling prophecy than a scientific theory. The evidence does not support it, and in fact goes against it. The longest war since the Second World War was the 1980–88 Iran–Iraq war between two Muslim countries. The present world crisis around the Gulf stems initially from one Arab Muslim country, Iraq, invading another, Kuwait. Al-Qaida and other pseudo-Islamic movements are up in arms more against their own Islamic regimes than against the 'unbelievers'. And we do not need to mention Islam's doctrinal internicine sects and feuds throughout history. Briefly the warring demarcation line Islam/non-Islam does not hold to explain the region's post Cold War international relations, neither conceptually nor factually. Intra-Islamic conflicts are as numerous, if not more so, than those between Muslims and non-Muslims.

A third, less-known conceptual lens was much more specifically about the *structure* of the post-Cold War world. After East-West bipolarity, would the system be uni-polar or multi-polar? The debate raged on the pages of such periodicals as *Foreign Affairs* and *International Security*, but without really being decided. Finally a compromise was achieved with the idea that the world system was going through a transition period, and its final structure was still in the making. At present, with the US occupying Iraq, and becoming THE Middle East power, native MENA literature repeats ad nauseam 'I told you so', and equates post-cold war globalisation with US unipolarity. An American-Arab sociologist and novelist of Georgetown University, Halim Barakat, expressed this dominant view:

The information revolution has not brought about harmony, cooperation, and mutual support among states and peoples for the common good of humanity, but rather provided a new and effective tool for entrenching the hegemony of those who control the means by which that revolution is taking place. What we are seeing is a shift to what is erroneously termed the 'global village' or 'family', but amounts to nothing more than sweeping American hegemony. (*Al Hayat*, 25 July 1997)

Consequently this chapter emphasises—in the established political economy tradition—globalisation's characteristic inter-connectedness betwen internal and external dynamics. It finds the region highly prone to conflict because of an increasing resource-gap. A resource-gap should be understood here not only in the limited material sense, but in the wider one of deficits. Deficits could be in capital, both financial and social, in management capacity, both of human resouces and of conflicts, and in the availability of goods necessary for nourishing body and mind. As a result, among the myriad factors helping to decode MENA's present international relations, three are particularly emphasised: oil; the primacy of conflict; and religio-politics. In analysing these three factors, this chapter attracts attention to some aspects that have been overlooked in the recent literature. For instance, whereas so much has been written about the Arab–Israeli conflict with its payoffs and pitfalls, very little has analysed the different international conferences that tried to put MENA on the road to economic integration and political rapprochement.

This chapter's four sections deal with what are considered in the public mind three synonyms of the region. Section one deals with oil, its assets and its disadvantages. Section two deals with conventional geopolitical conflict: the eternal Arab–Israeli conflict, as well as Arab–Arab conflicts and their global repercussions (e.g. Gulf Wars). Section three continues the analysis of conflict by focusing on newer socio-economic deficits and the highly conflictual domestic environment. Section four follows logically and deals with religio-politics with its mobilisational effect and international spill-over. Though attention is drawn to the importance of religion in the region generally (e.g. Israel's birth and present politics), the emphasis is on Islamic protest. To show the characteristics of this protest in different regimes, this section cites two illustrations: an erstwhile Third-World leader, Algeria; and an orthodox Islamic country, Saudi Arabia.

Oil: A Mixed Blessing?

Though Chapter 4 is devoted to the subject of oil, some aspects have to be remembered here. Oil is still a highly strategic energy supply, and MENA occupies a central position in providing it. The region still controls 68 per cent of all world reserves. It exports about 35 per cent of the world total and by 2020 it is estimated to export just over 75 per cent (Cordesman 2001). The 1973 oil embargo lasted only five months but it brought panic in Western streets and recession in the world economy for years afterwards. The US has learnt to reduce its own dependency on MENA oil. While it still imports 48 per cent of its oil needs, its major providers are now Venezuela, Canada, then Saudi Arabia and Mexico; MENA represents no more than 20 per cent of these imports. Moreover, the US has built a Strategic Petroleum Reserve in case of emergency.

But as the current imperial power of the post-Cold War system, the US has a special responsibility in guaranteeing the smooth functioning of the world economy and polity, including its oil provisions. Since, contrary to previous optimistic estimates, Caspian Sea oil reserves are equivalent only to those of the North Sea, MENA keeps its prime place as THE oil-provider. Indeed, Western Europe continues to be quasi-totally dependent on it for its oil supplies. Moreover, growing energy needs in Eastern Europe and Asia increase pressure on Middle Eastern oil.

For the peoples of the region, oil has been at best a mixed blessing. Oil has intensified world covetousness and implication in their fate since the 1930s and the industry reveals at present the dangers of counting on an extremely extraverted and one-product economy. On average, Gulf economies count on oil for 75 per cent of their national income. This leaves them victims to the vagaries of globalisation and forces beyond their control. Between 1981 and 1986 Algeria's oil revenues dropped from $26.3 billion to $6.2 billion, and Libya's from $46 billion to $7.1 billion. This story is representative of all oil-producing countries. Thus Saudi Arabia's revenues soared from less than $3 billion in 1972 to $113 billion in 1981 before plummetting to less than $23 billion in 1987. Indeed, most oil states' budgets have serious structural deficits and open or concealed internal debt. The result is that population growth could offset any increase in oil revenues. Saudi Arabia, for the period 1980–2000, saw its population grow from 9.9 million to 22 million, a rise of over 120 per cent. But its per capita income went down from $21,425 to $3,000, or a seventh of what it had been two decades earlier (Richards & Waterbury 1998: 59). Moreover, the budget deficit for the period 1996–2000 is on average 10 per cent. Yet accustomed to the easy money of the rentier state that derives substantial revenue from foreign sources, in the form of rent rather than really sweating for it, the population does not easily accept hardships (Beblawi and Luciani 1987: 1–21). It is not only the state and its economy that are rentier, but it is as if the contagion trickles down into the society's structure and organisation and even to individual mindsets. In such a socioeconomic context, reward does not depend on work or productive efficiency but on the outside—a huge recipe for laziness and effortless spending. The serious problem starts when this easy money suddenly declines. We will consider some of the domestic consequences in the sections on the yawning resource gap and religio-politics.

Hardship or not, the fluctuation of financial flows are not allowed—by conviction or by persuasion—to affect 'national security'. Consequently, many of these countries 'recycle' a substantial sum of their petro-dollars in arms purchases from Western countries, especially the US. Though the two Gulf Wars proved that none of the six members of the Gulf Cooperation Council could defend itself—individually or collectively—against either Iran or Iraq, they have nevertheless 'invested' since the late 1980s $75 billion of their oil wealth in the purchase of weapons systems. Since Iraq's invasion of Kuwait in 1990 and until 2000, the Saudi government has signed contracts for US weapons systems worth $36 billion, or 32 per cent of US global arms exports.

The Primacy of Conflicts: Conventional Geopolitical Ones

The eternal *Arab–Israeli conflict* naturally tops the list. It is a protracted social conflict, i.e. a multidimensional one where religious, political, cultural, economic and psychological elements pile up and feed on each other to create a seemingly indissoluble impasse. Consequently, it is so central to MENA' regional dynamics that they are mostly analysed through its prism. Six regional wars as well as two *Intifadas* have shaped both inter-state and inter-society phenomena: state-formation, regime patterns, regional alignments and realignments, collective psychology as well as the region's overall process of negotiations and governance. Historically, this conflict even shaped the balance between the two super powers in the Cold War. In the 1950s, it brought in the USSR to foil Western arms monopoly, and ended by promoting non-alignment. In the 1970s, its peace process marginalised Soviet regional impact. The Arab–Israeli conflict is even supposed—through lobby politics—to influence elections to top political positions in the unique super-power: the United States.

At the regional level, the Arab–Israeli conflict is at the basis of the region's militarisation and the rise of the so-called national security state. For instance, three coups d'état took place in Syria in the first year following the Arab defeat in the 1948 Arab–Israeli war, and the Nasserist coup was primarily motivated by the debacle in Palestine. Military spending as percentage of government expenditure for some individual states is simply staggering: 21.17 per cent for Israel; 35.17 per cent for Jordan; more than 40 per cent for Syria, Oman and Saudi Arabia; more than 50 per cent for the United Arab Emirates; and almost 60 per cent for Iraq (Richards and Waterbury 1998: 336–7). Figures (Henry and Springborg 2001: 104–5) for the 1993–97 period show decline for some countries: Syria 40 per cent to 28 per cent; UAE 50 per cent to 48 per cent and Saudi Arabia 41 per cent to 37 per cent. They are still far above world average. Even if not all of this military expenditure is directly motivated by the Arab–Israeli conflict, it has been presented as such. Did not Saddam Hussein's Iraqi regime invade Kuwait in 1990 to liberate Jerusalem?

But the end of the Cold War presaged an initiative towards a collective peace process with the convening of the Madrid Conference in October 1991. Typically this conference got bogged down in procedural polemics and ended without even fixing another meeting. Because of this failure, negotiations moved to the bilateral level as Israel always preferred: e.g. Syrian–Israeli negotiations in Washington. But it was second track or informal diplomacy that proved the most capable of making things move. The secret Israeli–Palestinian negotiations in Oslo in 1993 were the result. Oslo was indeed a qualitative shift for at least three reasons: (a) the two main protagonists announced mutual formal recognition; (b) there was agreement on a specific program of action and timetable for Israeli withdrawal from Gaza and most of the West Bank, and the emergence of a formal Palestinian authority recognised internationally (e.g. internationally-supervised Palestinian elections took place in January 1996); and (c) it allowed other protagonists to join—officially—the peace process (e.g. the signing of the Jordanian-Israeli peace treaty in 1994). Optimism was so widespread that talk of the New Middle East joined the rhetoric of the new world order. The idea was best expressed by Shimon Peres, Israel's former head of the Labour Party and Prime Minister, in 1993:

Peace between Israel and its Arab neighbours will create the environment for a basic reorganization of Middle Eastern institutions ... It will change the face of the region and its ideological climate. (For) the problems of this region of the world cannot be solved by individual nations, or even on a bilateral or multilateral plane ... Our ultimate goal is the creation of a regional community of nations, with a common market and elected centralized bodies, modeled on the European Community. (Peres 1993: 62)

Consequently, four economic conferences were convened: Casablanca 1994, Amman 1995, Cairo 1996 and Doha 1997. But these conferences were controversial and some on the Arab side mistrusted their raison d'être. They were skeptical about an Israeli warfare state becoming overnight a welfare state and thought of these economic integration conferences not in terms of balance of benefits to replace balance of power, but rather as Israeli hegemony by other means. (I have detailed the debates in Korany 1996.) Though usually overlooked, the story of these conferences needs telling because the issue of potential 'peace dividends' probably provides a glimmer of hope for escape from the Arab-Israeli impasse.

From Casablanca to Doha 1994–97: Why Peace Dividends did not Materialise

Though it fixed no place or date for another meeting, Madrid initiated multilateral negotiations and the exploring of economic cooperation. This multilateral economic emphasis was a reminder that the region badly lagged behind other world regions. For instance, while in 1990 trade among members of the European Union was 60.4 per cent of their international trade, inter-Arab trade was only just over 8 per cent. Establishing any form of regional economic integration would thus bring the Middle East into line. The four economic conferences 1994–97 do show, however, that Arab–Israeli *political* problems had first to be contained for any economic integration to take place.

The aim of these conferences was foremost to integrate Israel in the region by building economic cooperation and attracting international investment. This was the peace dividend to bolster the nascent political settlement. This emphasis on regional economic cooperation was a reflection of 'functionalist' thinking, of 'peace through trade', the origin of present European integration. Consequently, to import this Jean Monet approach, Morocco's King Hassan II—who had championed the social integration of his substantial Jewish minority and maintained close relations with Israel—initiated the first conference: Casablanca, in Fall 1994. Three thousand participants representing sixty-one countries, including heads of state or their representatives as well as public personalities and businessmen, came. This was the 'privatisation' of the peace process, since the official convenors were two non-governmental organisations, principally the World Economic Forum of Davos. Casablanca established a 'permanent' institution for regional economic integration, The Middle East Economic and Strategic Group, to integrate Israel in the region. But a prerequisite for this integration was an end to the Arab economic boycott of Israel. Since this was the last Arab card to pressure Israel for political settlement, many—notably the Syrians and their Lebanese allies who boycotted the meeting—hesitated to use up this card so early in the game.

But Casablanca came at a time of optimism, even euphoria. It followed Oslo and Israeli-Palestinian mutual recognition, the 1994 Jordanian–Israeli Peace Treaty and the initiation of formal Syrian–Israeli contacts. All hopes were thus permitted. Israel, which had long planned its integration in MENA, came with 150 investment projects, including many for the development of regional tourism. Although Egypt came with forty and Jordan with ten, there were no equivalent collective Arab projects.

Casablanca's final communique was a reflection of Israel's preparedness. It insisted on the elimination of all trade barriers (i.e. ending the Arab economic boycott), and set up three specialised mechanisms for regional integration: a Development Bank, a Regional Council of Tourism and a Regional Office for Trade and Business. An executive secretariat was also set up with headquarters in Casablanca. Moreover, to show the institutionalisation of the process, the conference fixed the date for the next meeting in Amman.

Whereas Casablanca was intended to prepare for the peace dividends, thought to be assuredly in the works, Amman, on the contrary, faced some dark clouds of doubt. For instance, in the year separating the two conferences, Israel continued its assassination policy by killing Fathi El-Shakaki, Secretary General of Palestine's Islamic Jihad. Moreover, Israel's Labour Prime Minister, Rabin, insisted that Jerusalem was the eternal capital of Israel. The US Congress followed suit by asking the Administration to transfer the US embassy from Tel Aviv to Jerusalem by the end of 1999. This decision contravened all UN resolutions on this matter and embarrassed the US's Arab allies who usually insisted on the primacy of Washington as a credible go-between. Still 2,000 participants came to Amman primarily to activate Casablanca's three mechanisms for integration. This brought Israel's regional integration closer and—given this country's technological and managerial advance—bestowed on it the lion's share of the advantages of the new Middle East. In addition, bilateral agreements were signed: e.g. transfer of Qatar's natural gas to Israel.

But the doubts that loomed over the Amman conference became opposition, both regional and international, to the convening of the next conference; Cairo 1996. For despite some earlier misgivings about Rabin's declarations, both he and Peres were of the Labour Party, which championed comprehensive peace and Middle East integration. However, 1996 brought to power the Likud and its right-wing coalition who considered the Palestinians more as 'terrorists' than equal peace partners. Likud also mistrusted regional integration and thought of the conferences as a restriction on Israel's manoeuvrability. Instead, they preferred to impose the political settlement reflecting Israel's military hegemony. Things came to a head when Prime Minister Netanyahu all but formally cancelled the Oslo Declaration of Principles.

To avoid political escalation, and as an alternative to cancelling the Cairo conference, the compromise was to change its raison d'être and formula in three respects. First, the conference became much more a businessmen's conference with only a few foreign ministers attending. The bulk of the 1,400 participants were 500 Egyptian businessmen who would probably not have attended had the conference been held elsewhere. Second, the focus of the conference was redirected more toward international than regional concerns, involving Arab-Arab and Arab–international cooperation. The avowed objective was to devalue Israel's presence and to treat it as one among many other international participants, without any preferential treatment. Consequently regional blueprints were put on the back burner. Third, the conference documents show that workshops and panels focused on topics of a general nature such as 'Europe and Middle East Partnership', 'Privatization; Obstacles and Consequences', 'Energy' and 'IT and Communications'. Though Israel still came with 162 projects totaling $27 billion, it faced a much more effective and spontaneous Arab boycotting stance. Even when Israeli businessmen invited their Egyptian counterparts to meet and indicated beforehand their criticisms of their Prime Minister, Egyptian businessmen were pressured by public opinion not to initiate 'normalisation' before steps for political settlement advanced (El-Saadani 1997: 246–54). Some individual gains notwithstanding, the whole atmosphere was morose, and collective mechanisms were in limbo. But the worst was still to come with the next meeting in Doha, Qatar.

Opposition to the Cairo conference became rejection and boycott in Doha. The rejectionists insisted that since Likud declarations and intransigent behaviour reneged on both Madrid and Oslo, no economic cooperation could be initiated. Hence Doha would be a waste of time. But both Israel, and especially the US, insisted on holding the conference as originally planned. The US pressured many countries to attend. Thus, on the eve of the conference, Yemen saw its debt reduced by the Paris Club from $7 billion to $400 million. Similarly, Kuwait had declared its non-participation but, following the visit of Secretary of State, Madeleine Albright, made a volte face and attended. Despite the formal representation of sixty-five countries and the participation of about 850 businessmen, the Doha conference, given the raison d'être of the whole process, appeared to be the last nail in the coffin of regional projects of economic integration.

First, though Albright herself headed the US delegation, only nine out of twenty-two Arab countries attended. They did not include the main protagonists: Syria, Lebanon, the Palestinian Authority, or such US allies and pivotal states as Morocco, Egypt and Saudi Arabia. Second, many of those finally attending chose to be modestly represented: Mauritania's delegation was headed by its Assistant Foreign Minister, and Kuwait's by the Undersecretary of its Ministry of Commerce.

Third, though some previously-negotiated bilateral agreements were signed (e.g. a Jordanian–Israeli industrial zone; renewal of the natural gas agreement between Qatar and Israel), mega-projects that characterised the previous three conferences were noticeable by their absence (El-Saadani 1998: 299–302).

Despite earlier efforts to separate economic projects from the vagaries of the Arab-Israeli conflict, the Doha communique was, against Israeli objections, highly politicised and critical of Likud policy. It emphasised the deteriorating economic situation in Palestine and the increasing suffering of the Palestinians. Given the failure of the original objective of regional cooperation, it was only natural that none of the Arab countries was ready, then, to continue the process of a new Middle East. How can you get peace dividends from non-existent peace, was the question posed by most of the Arabs and their allies. Israel's proposal to hold a sequel conference in Bethlehem was rejected, as was Canada's to host it outside the region.

So the Exclusivists on both sides ended by having their way, at least for the moment. Arab Exclusivists pointed to the meagre political and economic results of the four conferences despite the international and regional energy invested. They aimed to prove Israeli incapacity to shift from a warfare to a welfare state, and its primary interest in hegemony rather than comprehensive peace and cooperation. They even quoted Peres to support their idea of Israeli hegemony by other means.

In any case the polemics lost their importance as the Arab–Israeli peace process stagnated and a second Intifada began in 2000. More than ten years after Oslo we are back to suicide attacks, dynamiting houses and even a new wall to concretise the barriers between the Israelis and the Palestinians. The result is that the idea of a real Israeli–Palestinian peace has regressed in the hearts and minds of the whole region, the US roadmap continually restarts and the arms race continues unabated.

Border Disputes can also Trigger International Wars

Related to the Arab–Israeli conflict and old conflict types are the myriad border disputes. Almost every MENA country has a border-demarcation problem with its neighbour(s).

An Arab–Arab conflict, the one between Algeria and Morocco in 1963—one year after Algeria's independence—was about the tracing of their borders. This conflict continued to poison their relations as we see in the contemporary conflict over the Western Sahara. The largest and costly war in the post-Cold War era—the eight-year one between Iran and Iraq—was ostensibly about the tracing of borders on the Shatt al-Arab waterway. Rough estimates suggest that there were more than one and a half million war and war-related casualties and millions were made refugees. Iran acknowledged that nearly 300,000 people died in the war. Iraq suffered an estimated 375,000 casualties, the equivalent of 5.6 million for a population the size of the United States. The final cost is estimated at a minimum of $200 billion (http://globalsecurity.org/military/world/war/iran-iraq.htm, http://us-israel.org/jsource/iraniraq.html).

The invasion of Kuwait and Gulf War of 1990–91 were also about (colonial) border-demarcation. But globalisation and technological advance have left their impact. Though much shorter, the war's cost was staggering. According to US estimates more than 100,000 Iraqi soldiers died and 300,000 were wounded. Many human rights groups claimed a much higher number of Iraqi casualties. In purely monetary terms, estimates of this war's cost range from $61 to $71 billion (http://www.cnn.com/specials/2001/gulf.war/facts/gulf-war/index.html). The Iraq War or *second* Gulf War (2003–)—a direct continuation of the first—is still on-going. The total number of casualties are still unknown but we have an idea already of the enormous economic costs: according to American sources until April 2003, the US cost is over $20 billion in direct military expenditure. The reconstruction of Iraq will need at least $20 billion a year. The indirect impact of the war cannot be neglected. In Europe, though the Euro appreciated against the US dollar during the war, the European Commission has lowered its forecast for economic growth, from 1.8 per cent to 1 per cent. The aviation and tourism industries have been two of the worst hit sectors: $10 billion and three million jobs lost. Most countries cancelled their air flights to the region, and the sector lost more than $30 billion in economic value. The military attack in Iraq also brings unpredicted risks to the shipping industry. Insurance companies increased the so-called special war premium for shipping stationed around the Gulf to as high as one per cent per week. The fee is much higher if the ship is owned by the United States, as it is more likely to be a target for attack by terrorists (http://www.cctv.com/lm/942/19/14.html).

A twenty-year low on Tokyo's benchmark stock index, a volatile world oil market and a huge drop in airline passenger volume and cut in numbers of airline employees—nothing can impact international economic relations as much as war.

The result of this primacy of conflicts is that MENA has become a highly-militarised region, compared even to other turbulent Third World zones. Compared to nuclear South Asia for the 1997–99 period, the ratio of Middle East military expenditure to GNP is almost four times as much, military expenditure per capita is on average three times as much, the ratio of armed forces per 1,000 is more than ten times as much, and arms deliveries twelve times as much. Globalisation's technological advance has made weapons' destructive power more lethal and more widespread. On the surface, the Gulf Wars have brought to the fore the looming danger of weapons of mass destruction from chemical and biological weapons to nuclear proliferation. Among the countries of the region, pressure is building to carry out the economists' 'demonstration effect', the 'keeping up with the Jones', or what I can call a 'contagion effect', i.e. to accelerate proliferation both of nuclear and chemical-biological weapons. If there is a 'coming crisis' of this type at the global level, it will manifest itself very vividly and dangerously in MENA. For instance, Israel is perceived by its Arab neighbours as being increasingly nuclearised, with '...no less than 264 nuclear bombs...in addition to tactical neutron bombs...all supported by a sophisticated delivery system (*El-Mustaqbal Al Arabi*, Jan. 2000: 175–82). As a result, there is a huge pressure from vocal sectors of Arab civil society on their governments to go nuclear to attain the level of nuclear deterrence of their adversary. A conference at the Center for the Study of the Future (Assiut University, Egypt, Nov. 1999) suggested that Arab governments abstain—in the case of the failure to establish MENA as a nuclear-free zone—from signing the NPT and to work seriously to establish an active nuclear programme—individually or collectively.

To the conventional inter-state conflicts, nuclear or not, are added new ones. They are no longer 'domestic' since globalisation is increasingly blurring the internal/external demarcation line (Korany et al. 1998).

Globalisation, Yawning Resource Gaps and Newer Threats/Conflicts

On average all comparative socio-economic indicators for the twenty-year period 1980–2000 are negative and show this gap as the new threat in MENA. GNP growth rates are not more than half that achieved in South Asia, and the comparison with rates for East Asia-Pacific makes the MENA situation look really bad (World Bank 2000: 23).

The gap in *real terms* is much worse when demographics are included. With globalisation and increased health standards and health education, MENA countries have increased their population on average more than three times in the last fifty years, Algeria four times and Saudi Arabia seven times. All analysts agree that true development rate normally requires 2 per cent *more* annual growth rate than population growth. If MENA population growth hovers around 2.5–3 per cent on average, a minimum of 5 per cent economic growth rate is needed to avoid negative growth. For the period 1991–95 the comparative figures of real per capita GDP growth were also unfavorable to MENA—0.2 vs 2.2 per cent for South Asia and 8 per cent for East Asia (Cordesman 2001: 48).

A timebomb is thus ticking in terms of potential social upheavals and their possible spill-over in interstate conflicts. Indeed, the relationship between demographics, social upheaval and interstate conflicts is no longer guess-work. Based on the analysis of forty-five conflicts in developing countries in the period 1945–71, one of the findings is that the higher the rate of population growth, the more salient a factor population increase appears to be in the development of conflict and violence (Choukri and North 1975).

The resource gap has another impact that is hidden no longer, and that is the age of the population: or MENA's increased youth of the population dilemma where 40 per cent or more are fourteen years or younger. This age bracket taxes the system in terms of education needs and job opportunities. Unemployed, these young people are easily recruited by protest ideologies and militant pseudo-religious organisations. Yet in MENA resources are at present unavailable to drastically increase employment opportunities. For the period 1990–2000, budget deficit hovered on average around 2.5 per cent. Moreover, jobs in the private sector tend to emphasise imports and related service sectors rather than real economic development.

The region failed to compensate for its resource gap by attracting foreign rsources: e.g. trade, FDI (foreign direct investment). For the period 1980 to 2000, the gap between MENA and the rest of the world is big. Whereas MENA's exports have risen by 5 per cent the rate for Latin America-Carribean was about 350 per cent, for South Asia-Pacific more than 400 per cent and for East Asia 550 per cent. Even for Sub-Saharan Africa, the growth rate was almost five times that of MENA, i.e. 24 per cent (Cordesman 2001).

In MENA, FDI—one of the salient characteristics of the 'global metropolis'—is very low as a percentage of GDP. As globalisation predicts, world private capital does exist and is increasing, but because of MENA's negative risk-assessment this capital has gone to other regions. Thus whereas in 1998 FDI flows as a percentage of GDP were 3.9 per cent for East Asia and 3.5 percent for Latin America, it was only 0.7 per cent for MENA—i.e. almost half of the flow for Sub-Saharan Africa. Moreover, for 1960–90 the FDI global rate of increase was 800 per cent but was not even 300 per cent for MENA. As a result, infrastructural needs are not met and societal daily management in many MENA countries is in danger of being stalled.

MENA's external debt burden, a hemorrage on its already declining resources, has risen as a percentage of GNP from 22.1 per cent to 31.2 per cent, as percentage of exports from 40.4 per cent to 93.8 per cent. Egypt has seen its debt rise by 60 per cent, Jordan by 400 per cent and Syria by 700 per cent.

Moreover, the region failed to make up for this decline by raising its productivity. In fact, whereas MENA productivity dropped by about 6 per cent in the period 1960–90, East Asian-Pacific productivity rose by 54 per cent (Cordesman 2001: 79).

Even oil-producing countries are no longer immune to the negative societal effects of this deteriorating resource gap. For instance, most oil states' budgets have serious structural deficits and open or concealed internal debt. As a group, oil economies have actually underperformed the rest of MENA. The result is that population growth will more than offset probable increase in oil revenues. For instance, Saudi Arabia for the period 1980–2000 saw its population rise from 9.9 million to 22 million—a rise of over 120 per cent. Yet its per capita oil income went down from $21,425 to $3,000 or a seventh of what it was two decades earlier. Moreover, the budget deficit for the period 1996–2000 is on average around 10 per cent. The Saudi case is indeed representative of other oil producing countries in the Gulf.

This worsening economic situation—in all its facets—increases societal stress and leads to a situation of overall insecurity—of both society and state. This overall insecurity, together with the state's legitimacy deficit, feeds discontent and protest which often take a religious form in a highly religious region.

Religio-Politics: From Mobilisation to International Spill-over

As is well known, the region witnessed the birth of three main world religions: Judaism, Christianity and Islam. Though dominant Western media tend to talk mainly about Islamic fundamentalism and radical Islam, the whole Middle East is characterised by the politicisation of religion. Lebanon suffered from two long civil wars in the 1950s, 1960s and 1970s because of the distribution of political posts between different Muslim and Christian communities and their sects. Israel's identity and very birth are based on its Jewishness. In the Spring 2003 US-Israeli-Jordanian-Palestinian summit in Aqaba, Jordan, President Bush had to accept that Israel's national security rests on it keeping its Jewish character. Many present Israeli laws, from the law of return to the recent ban on marriage between Israeli Arabs and Palestinians, cannot be understood without remembering this linkage between Israel's Jewishness and its national security. But because more than 95 per cent of the population of the Middle East are Muslims, the phenomenon of islamisation of politics and protest should be emphasised in the space available here.

In Algeria, Egypt or even the Islamic Republic of Iran, Islamic movements try to topple the regime. In Egypt since 1990 about 1,200 have been killed following terrorist action or police repression. By 2003 more than 100,000 had lost their lives in Algeria's civil war. Despite the purely domestic character of these movements, there seems to be a contagion or—in today's terms—a globalising effect.

Since its birth in the seventh century among the tribes of Arabia, Islam has been a globalising phenomenon, and at present it constitutes the second religion in France. Nowadays, its original pioneers, the Arabs and Arabised populations in the Middle East, constitute only 20 per cent of the 1.2 billion world Muslims. Given the importance of that religion, the West exploited it during the Cold War to defeat Marxism and the Soviet presence worldwide. In 1982 between 20,000 and 30,000 Muslims from all over the globe joined the war in Soviet-occupied Afghanistan, and indeed managed to make Soviet troops bleed and finally withdraw. This is in reality the international origin of the al-Qaida organisation which immensely benefited from Saudi-Gulf funding and US training. But al-Qaida is not the only transnational group, for the Encyclopedia of World Terrorism lists no less than sixteen Islamic organisations and groups that have international objectives.

Before the events of September 11, scholars usually focused on the domestic dimension of Islamic protest. Karawan is a good case in point:

Despite the transnational language and ideology that Islamists adopt, their actions are primarily driven by national issues and concerns. These actions often reflect particular tendencies and sub-national, ethnic concerns. The 'Islamic solidarity' fashioned over the years is often empty rhetoric. There is no good reason to expect relations between Egyptian Islamists, should they ever come to power, and Islamists in Sudan to be fundamentally better than those between Iran and Saudi Arabia, or between Syrian and Iraqi Baathists. (1997: 67–6)

But it is also true that islamised opposition movements can prosper in countries that are extremely different in per capita income, domestic political organisation and international orientation: in Algeria, a paradigm of an erstwhile Third World revolutionism; and in Saudi Arabia, an Islamic othodox state. Socioeconomic ills are cerainly an important factor but so are the threats to identity in the context of globalisation and uncontrolled forces of external penetration. Hence the contradictory phenomenon of an Islamic opposition in an Islamic orthodox state:

Central to the Saudi opposition's vision is the idea that 'Islam' and its values are under attack both globally and locally and that the Saudi government has failed to protect Islam and Muslims. The opposition is involved in globalization through both the means and the issues. According to Al-Shamrani, the group used to meet and discuss whether the Saudi state conformed with Islamic teachings, how the state followed secular law and supported the United Nations, and how the Ulama such as Bin Baz and Bin Otheimein were conspiring with the state to undermine Islam. (Fandy 1999: 3)

But such underlying societal insecurity cannot be camouflaged for ever and has to come out in the political arena. In this situation, political conflict comes to the forefront and legitimacy deficit increases. Hence, we face the rise of the seemingly contradictory phenomena of an Islamic opposition in an orthodox Islamic country. Moreover, this opposition can spill beyond state borders. This is the case with the Afghan Arabs and Osama bin Laden (deprived of his Saudi citizenship in 1994) who constitute an extreme and bloody example of uncivil society contesting global governance.

Consequently at present many more scholars are in search of systematic evidence to emphasise the transnational dimension of Islamic cells as network actors. Network actors refer to non-formal illegal and clandestine groups not necessarily tied to a state, and usually supported by a sophisticated financial network—Hawalah (i.e. informed financial transfers). Whether terrorist or not, they are increasingly part of the global civil society and their funding and logistical networks cross borders and are thus less dependent on formal state interaction or disrupted by economic sanctions. They have capitalised on available technologies to communicate quickly and securely. The root problem of the mushrooming of political Islam as a mobilisation force lies in the legitimacy deficit of many regimes in this area and the increasing threats to identity from uncontrolled globalisation forces.

So-called domestic religio-politics, then, has international spill-over: fifteen of the nineteen September 11 hijackers were Saudi citizens. Attacks on tourists (e.g. Luxor, Egypt, 1997) are meant to embarras governing regimes, threaten their economic base and guarantee international visibility. The US and its citizens are usually the prime target, as in the attack on the World Trade Center, and the 1995 truck-bombing of the National Guard headquarters in Riyadh which killed at least five US servicemen. The 1996 bombing of the Khobar Towers killed nineteen US servicemen. The 1998 attacks on the US embassies in Kenya and Tanzania left 257 dead and almost 6,000 injured. The 3,000-member Afghan–Arab movement under the financial leadership of bin Laden takes the US as a major target because it incarnates the largest power in the region, because it has close ties with Israel, because attacks on the US produce the most worldwide publicity and act as a proxy for less popular attacks on Middle Eastern regimes.

Both to defend its threatened national security, and as the hegemon that must maintain global governance, the US restructured its strategic doctrine and made it pre-emptive. With its 139,000 troops in Iraq close to the borders of Syria, Iran and Saudi Arabia, and spending close to one billion dollars a week to maintain these troops, the US is becoming a real and not only a virtual Middle East power.

Conclusion: Which Direction MENA?

Neither the 'End of History' nor the 'Clash of Civilizations' has characterised the Middle East since the end of the Cold War. Conflicts have been primary, but these are political and social rather than purely religious and directly involve the present world hegemon. These conflicts will continue, given the increasing self-assertiveness of minorities such as the Kurds in Turkey, Syria, Iraq and Iran, or the Berbers in North Africa. Through the literature, I have identified twenty-six factors of instability ranging from the proliferation of weapons of mass destruction, to over-urbanisation and desertification. These conflicts will intensify given the yawning resource gap. The accumulation of deficits—economic, political and social—will make the distinction between internal and external conflicts even harder to discern. The example of the water resource gap in a barren region and potential water wars are a case in point. Decline of water per capita in MENA is far greater than the world average. Whereas between 1960 and 1990 world decline was 43 per cent and by 2025 the decline is estimated to be 64 per cent, the respective figures for MENA are more serious. They are for Jordan 58 per cent and 83 per cent; for Yemen 54 per cent and 75 per cent; for Iran 63 per cent and 82 per cent; for Iraq 64 per cent and 86 per cent; for Oman 67 per cent and 90 per cent; for Libya 71 per cent and 90 per cent; for Saudi Arabia 71 per cent and 91 per cent; and for the UAE 94 per cent and 96 per cent. Ominous as they are, these figures may be rather conservative since real population increase could be more than that factored in. As examples, population increase for the period 1993–2025 is estimated at 52 per cent in Israel; 73 per cent in Lebanon; 86 per cent in the West Bank; 117 per cent in Jordan; 171 per cent in Gaza; and 172 per cent in Syria (Shapland 1997: 2).

Moreover, a major part of MENA, like the above-mentioned case of Saudi Arabia, lives divided in time due essentially to the invasion of IT, satellite TV and especially the Internet. Internet users in the Arab world have increased from 2 million in 2000 to 3.5 million in 2001, an increase of 75 per cent. By 2003 they reached over 10 million. With the increasing efforts to introduce computers in school, these figures are too modest. These problems, whether water or IT, cannot be settled by routine conflict-management. They raise the issue of socioeconomic change given the region's double problem of aging leadership but increased youth of the population. In 2004, King Fahd and Egypt's President Mubarak have been in power for twenty-three years, and the revolutionary Qadhafi for thirty-five years. Syria, Morocco and Jordan had their succession in place when their leaders died: Assad senior after thirty-one years, Hassan II after forty years and King Hussein after forty-seven years. It was a process of pure political inheritance with sons replacing their fathers. But no major socio-political change has taken place in these systems up till now. Though confirmed democratically in 1996, Arafat has also been in power for over forty years. But at present he is facing increasing marginalisation under the pressure of the Israelis and the Americans. It is too early to affirm whether or not this externally-engineered change is the wave of the future. This is why what is taking place following the invasion of Iraq has a significance that goes beyond this country. It seems safe to predict that in the era of globalisation—through international aid, NGOs or the mere travelling of ideas—external factors are bound to impact on the interplay between the region's domestic and international relations.

Religion will also impact on the type and direction of change. The present debate is about which pattern of religio-politics will shape the future direction of the region and its place in the world. Will it be the orthodox Saudi-type increasingly under fire both internally and externally? Will it be the Iranian revolutionary type, increasingly factionalised between Reformers and Radicals, a factionalisation that proved for some the failure of political Islam? Will it be the Israeli-Turkish type, attempting to combine religion and Western democracy? Or will it be the myriad of restrictive pluralist regimes in Jordan, Egypt, Tunisia and Kuwait, to name just a few, which continue eternally to experiment with finding the appropriate formula to satisfy internal pressures and external aid donors? In the globlisation era, MENA's international relations cannot any longer be separated from type of regime and society's good governance.

Further Reading

Note on non-English language publications

One of the notable characteristics of recent MENA literature is the consolidation of contributions by scholars publishing in their own 'native' languages. For those reading Arabic, the *Arab Strategic Yearbook*, (Cairo: Al-Ahram Centre of Political and Strategic Studies) is both solid and balanced in its analyses. From Tel-Aviv, *Middle East Survey*, though more chronological, is equally good. Apparently it will cease publication shortly, but earlier yearly issues are available. Among periodicals, *El-Siasa El-Dawliyya* (Cairo: International Politics Quarterly), and *El-Mustaqbal El-Arabi* (Beirut: Arab Future, monthly) provide a wealth of information. Among newspapers, *Al-Hayat* (daily, London) and *Al-Ahram Weekly* offer good coverage and reliable analysis.

BROWN, L. C., *International Politics and the Middle East* (Princeton, NJ: Princeton University Press, 1984). This classic attempts to develop a theory about Middle Eastern international behaviour and uses historical data to substantiate the theory.

DEKMEJIAN, R., *Islam in Revolution.* (Syracuse: Syracuse University Press, 1985). One of the early surveys of this phenomenon that goes beyond pure description to provide conceptualisation and explanation.

GUAZZONE, L. (ed.), *The Middle East in Global Change* (London: Macmillan and New York: St. Martin's, 1996). Focused on change, the twelve authors analyse aspects of interdependence and fragmentation.

HEYDEMANN, S. (ed.), *War, Institutions and Social Change in the Middle East* (Berkeley & London: University of California Press, 2000). One of the few works on the region that goes beyond analysing war as an inter-state phenomenon and integrates wider national and regional dynamics.

HUDSON, M. (ed.), *Middle East Dilemmas* (New York: Columbia University Press, 1999). An up-to-date analysis of challenges facing the region, both in conflict and cooperation.

KEPEL, G., *La revanche de Dieu* (Paris: Seuil, 1991). An established French scholar provides a comparative field-based analysis of current religious revival in Christianity, Islam and Judaism.

KERR, M. and YASSIN, S. (eds.), *Rich and Poor States in the Middle East* (Boulder, Colo.: Westview Press, 1992). A pioneering analysis of emerging political economy trends in the region following the oil era.

KORANY, B., NOBLE, P. and BRYNON R. (eds.), *The Many Faces of National Security in the Arab World* (London: Macmillan, 1993). Middle Eastern and Western scholars collaborate to criticise the narrow approaches to security and to show the presence of wider threats.

REICH, B. (ed.), *Handbook of Political Science Research on the Middle East and North Africa.* (Westport, Conn.: Greenwood Press, 1998). A good inventory of approaches to the region's various political facets with an excellent overview of the literature.

ROY, O., *L'echec de l'Islam politique.* (Paris: Seuil, 1992). The untraditional thesis about political Islam's weakness and even failure, based on the author's fieldwork.

SIFRY, M. and CERF, C. (eds.), *The Iraq War Reader* (New York and London: Simon and Schuster, 2003). An excellent collection of historical documents and political analyses. Some very good appendices.

TESSLER, M., NACHTWAY, J., and BANDA, A. (eds.), *Area Studies and Social Science: Strategies for Understanding Middle East Politics* (Bloomington and Indianapolis: Indiana UP, 1999). A credible effort to combine general concepts and specific cases in decoding the region's different facets.

PART 2

THEMES IN INTERNATIONAL RELATIONS AND INTERNATIONAL POLITICAL ECONOMY

4

Oil and Political Economy in the International Relations of the Middle East

Giacomo Luciani

OVERVIEW

Oil and oil-related interests have had, and continue to have a profound influence on the political economy of the Middle East—domestically as well as from the point of view of international relations. Indeed, it is difficult to resist the temptation to conclude that practically everything is related, conditioned and justified by oil: which is the widespread, yet simplistic and essentially erroneous 'conspiracy theory', according to which the 'black gold' is the only value that matters. The ambition of this chapter is to offer a synthesised yet balanced view of the impact of oil: presenting the multiple ways in which oil has shaped the recent history of the Middle East, but also making it clear that oil is not the only relevant explanatory variable.

Introduction

Oil is commonly considered a political commodity. Because of its pivotal importance as primary source of energy, governments are concerned for its continued availability, and seek to minimise import dependence.

In fact, that oil deserves to be considered a political commodity is debatable. For the past century or longer, oil has been in abundant supply, and the leading industrial players—the major international oil companies in the past, the OPEC producers today—have been primarily concerned with avoiding that excess supply should bring about a collapse in prices.

For about three decades—from about 1930 to about 1960—control of large oil reserves, notably in the Middle East, allowed a small group of international oil companies to reap extraordinary profits. Governments at the time may have been justified in making sure that such profits were preserved or by-passed, depending whether the international oil companies were national or foreign. Since 1973, it is the governments of the OPEC countries—and of non-OPEC producers that benefit from the fact that OPEC keeps prices high—that have reaped extraordinary rents.

Apart from these rents, control of oil reserves or logistics has not entailed special political or military benefits, and conversely the lack of such control has not exposed individual countries to special costs. Oil is essentially allocated through the market, not through power and appropriation.

The Middle East plays a special role in the international oil industry (Table 4.1). Five Gulf producers possess 65 per cent of the world's proven oil reserves. Their oil is by far the cheapest to produce and, if oil were a competitive industry, they would probably be the almost exclusive source of world oil. However, because oil is not a competitive industry, the Middle East producers' share of global production has been kept low, well below their share in global reserves. Over the years, this has been especially true of Iraq—this being both cause and consequence of Iraq's difficult relations with the rest of the world.

Figure 4.1 shows the evolution of production from the major Gulf countries. Iran was the first country in the Gulf to become an oil exporter, and kept the pride of first place until 1950. In that year, the controversy between the company controlling all Iranian production—Anglo-Iranian—and the nationalist government of Mussadiq erupted. Following the nationalisation of Anglo-Iranian, all international oil companies boycotted Iranian oil; production collapsed to almost nothing in 1952 and 1953, and recovered only after the coup which overturned Mussadiq and the formation of the Iranian Consortium, in which Anglo-Iranian's role was reduced to 40 per cent.

Production in Iraq started in 1928 but remained at a low level due to the con-tinuing controversy between the Iraq Petroleum Company (IPC) and the Iraqi government. Saudi Arabia began producing in 1938, but production was constrained during the war, and took off only after 1945. Kuwaiti production began only in 1946 but grew very rapidly, and in 1953 had already overtaken Saudi production. The

Table 4.1 Proven oil reserves, Middle East and North Africa at end 2002

	Thousand million barrels	Share of world total
Iran	89.7	8.6%
Iraq	112.5	10.7%
Kuwait	96.5	9.2%
Oman	5.5	0.5%
Qatar	15.2	1.5%
Saudi Arabia	261.8	25.0%
Syria	2.5	0.2%
United Arab Emirates	97.8	9.3%
Yemen	4.0	0.4%
Other Middle East	0.1	◆
Total Middle East	685.6	65.4%
Algeria	9.2	0.9%
Egypt	3.7	0.4%
Libya	29.5	2.8%
Total North Africa	42.4	4.1%

Source: BP Statistical Review of Word Energy.

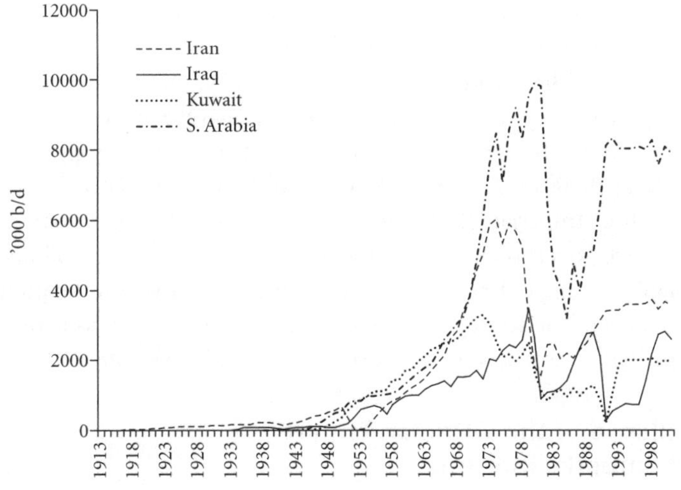

Fig. 4.1 Historical production of 4 main Gulf producers

Source of data: OPEC.

production of all three countries—Iraq, Saudi Arabia and Kuwait, increased rapidly to compensate for the collapse of Iranian production in 1951–54; but Saudi and Kuwaiti production remained high, while Iraq's was reduced. Kuwaiti production reached a maximum of 3 million barrels per day in 1973, and has since declined. It was reduced to close to nothing by the Iraqi invasion in 1991, and has since recovered. Iranian production reached a peak in 1974, and declined precipitously after the revolution in 1979 and the onset of the Iran–Iraq war. It recovered after the end of that war. Iraqi production peaked in 1979, before the war with Iran. It recovered in the final stages of the war, but collapsed again when Kuwait was invaded. It recovered under the UN oil-for-food programme but collapsed again in 2003, when the Coalition invaded and occupied the country. Saudi Arabia's production peaked in 1980, when it had to compensate for the loss of Iranian and Iraqi oil. It has since been constrained primarily by OPEC quotas.

In discussing the Middle East, oil is inescapable: it has influenced the region's relations with the rest of the world, notably the major powers; it has influenced relations within the region, because it is not uniformly distributed, on the contrary it is highly concentrated, creating a very distinctive polarisation between oil-haves and oil-have-nots; it has influenced the domestic politics of the Arab countries, allowing the consolidation of regimes which, in the absence of the oil rent, would probably not have survived to the twenty-first century.

Oil and the Consolidation of the Middle East State System

The presence of oil in the Middle East has had a crucial influence in the consolidation of the regional state system. Interest for Middle Eastern Oil focused initially on Kirkuk—then part of the Ottoman vilayet of Mosul—and Southern Persia, and was already active at the turn of the twentieth century. Oil was discovered in Persia by William Knox D'Arcy in 1908 (Yergin 1991: 135–49; Stocking 1970: 8–14), and the involvement of the Imperial UK government was immediately clear (Yergin 1991: 150–64; Stocking 1970: 14–22). Winston Churchill, then First Lord of the Admiralty, decided that the Imperial fleet should be converted from coal to oil, and argued for direct government involvement by acquiring a controlling interest in Anglo–Persian—as Anglo–Iranian was then named—as a way to guarantee cheaper supplies to the fleet. The strategic interest in oil, at a time when none of today's Gulf States, except Persia, could be said to exist, was already very obvious.

Oil, the collapse of the Ottoman Empire and British imperial interests

Oil interests fundamentally shaped British policy in the Gulf, first emphasising freedom of navigation, later guaranteeing the independent existence of the

Trucial States, as they were called at the time, against the momentum of Saudi expansionism.

Oil was also a major factor in the shaping of states, which emerged from the collapse of the Ottoman Empire. However, interest in the political control of oil reserves was not uniformly shared: it continued as a quintessentially British objective, which other Powers did not attribute the same importance to. After the First World War, the San Remo conference attributed to the UK the mandate on a newly formed country called Iraq, composed of the three Ottoman vilayets of Mosul, Baghdad and Basrah. Previously, the Sykes–Picot agreement had attributed Mosul to France, but the latter surrendered that choice morsel and was content with a minority participation in the Iraq Petroleum Company (IPC), the producing consortium that acquired a concession to Kirkuk oil.

The political rationale behind the composition of the IPC shareholding group is manifest, especially when we take into account the evolution from its early version— the Turkish Petroleum Company, which Caliste Gulbenkian sponsored before the war, including German and Italian interests—to its final shape (47.5 per cent to British companies, another 47.5 per cent equally divided between American and French companies, the remaining 5 per cent to Gulbenkian) (Stocking 1970: 41–6; Yergin 1991: 184–206).

Not all UK policies in the Middle East can be said to be functional to its oil interests, though. The Balfour declaration, which was due to have such a momentous impact on the future of the region, certainly was not conceived of in connection with oil interests. Neither was support to the Hashemite revolt, later contradicted by Sikes–Picot; nor, especially, the acquiescence to the expansionary policies of Abdul Aziz ibn Saud which led to the disappearance of the Hijaz and the formation of contemporary Saudi Arabia. The British oil interests simply completely overlooked the possibility that Saudi Arabia might have significant oil deposits, and were not interested in seeking a concession there, thus opening the door to a total parvenu on the scene—such as Standard Oil of California, later to be called Chevron, was at the time. The US quickly filled in any space that the UK would leave unoccupied, and contributed to the consolidation of some of the region's states, Saudi Arabia first and foremost (Stocking 1970: 66–107; Yergin 1991: 280–92).

Oil production in the Gulf before 1972 was controlled by producing companies or consortia in which the major international oil companies cooperated in a web of interlocking interests (Table 4.2). Producing consortia held huge concessions and frequently were the only producers in the company, thus commanding enormous bargaining power vis-à-vis the national government. The company having the largest reserves in the Gulf was by far Anglo-Iranian. It changed its name into British Petroleum following Mussadiq's nationalisation, and is today's BP.

The cornerstone of the system was IPC. Five of the eight major international companies were present in IPC, whose equity was carefully divided: 50 per cent to British interests, represented equally by Anglo-Iranian and Royal Dutch-Shell;

Table 4.2 Composition of major producing consortia in the Middle East before 1972

	Kuwait Oil Company (KOC)	Iraq Oil Company (IPC)	Arabian American Oil Company (ARAMCO)	Abu Dhabi Marine Areas (ADMA)	Iranian Consortium
British Petroleum	50	23.75		66.6	40
Royal Dutch Shell		23.75			14
Standard Oil New Jersey		11.875	30		7
Standard Oil California			30		7
Texaco			30		7
Mobil		11.875	10		7
Gulf	50				7
CFP		23.75		33.3	6
Others		5			5

25 per cent to American interests, represented equally by Standard Oil New Jersey (one of the companies issued from the break-up of John D. Rockefeller's Standard Oil in 1911; later known as Esso Oil Company, today ExxonMobil, after its merger with the latter) and Mobil (previously known as Standard Oil Company of New York or SOCONY, another of the offspring of Standard Oil); and 25 per cent to French interests, represented by the Compagnie Française des Petroles (today's Total). The internal rules of IPC were designed to discourage competition between the IPC partners in the downstream markets as well as upstream elsewhere in the region. The partners were bound by the Red Line agreement not to enter in any other producing venture in the former Ottoman Empire except in the same combination as in IPC. Hence many other producing consortia, notably Abu Dhabi onshore, exactly mimic the composition of IPC. Kuwait, however, was not considered to have been part of the Ottoman Empire, which allowed Anglo-Iranian to take 50 per cent of the concession, sharing it with Gulf Oil (an American company that has since disappeared, taken over by Chevron). Saudi Arabia, on the other hand, was part of the Ottoman Empire, and the IPC partners showed no interest in acquiring a concession there; this went to Standard Oil of California (or SoCal, another Standard Oil offshoot; today called Chevron) that discovered oil alone, but was taken aback by the magnitude of its discovery and started looking for partners, with the active participation of the State Department (which at some point even considered taking a direct interest, much as the British government had a direct interest in Anglo-Iranian). SoCal brought in first Texaco, which was its partner in the East in a joint venture called Caltex (today Chevron

and Texaco are merged in a single company); later also Standard Oil New Jersey and Mobil.

The Iranian Consortium was formed after the coup, which overthrew the Mussadiq government and paved the way to the return of the Shah. Anglo-Iranian, the original sole concession holder, maintained a 40 per cent interest, but had to surrender the rest to Royal Dutch Shell (14 per cent, so that British interests still controlled a majority) and various American companies (the CIA had been instrumental in orchestrating the coup).

The system collapsed after 1972, when most producing companies were nationalised.

Oil and the Middle East boundaries

As we look at today's political map of the region, we find that oil has had little influence in determining boundaries and state structures within the former French mandate (i.e. Syria and Lebanon) as well as in the Mediterranean portion of the British mandate (i.e. Jordan and the Palestinian/Israeli conundrum). It has, on the other hand, had fundamental influence in shaping the boundaries and independent existence of all other states in the Middle East.

The British action which stopped Saudi expansionism to the North (towards Iraq) and to the East (towards the Trucial States) was clearly dictated by the wish to see the region subdivided in several, competing states, avoiding excessive concentration of powers and resources in the hands of a single state (the old Roman strategy: divide and rule). This can only be understood in the light of oil interests, and the need to maintain control on oil resources through diversity and competition. We can speculate what the political map of the Gulf might have looked like in the absence of oil, but most historians would, I believe, agree that the UAE, Qatar, Bahrain and possibly even Kuwait would not have survived as independent entities without their oil.

Indeed nor, possibly would Saudi Arabia have survived. The third Saudi state, established by Abdalaziz, would have had a hard time consolidating itself purely on the basis of revenue from the pilgrimage and domestic taxation of an extremely poor population. It is oil that has allowed the consolidation of the Saudi state, bringing sufficient financial resources to pay for a modern state bureaucracy, and eliminating the urge to conquer just to replenish empty coffers. Similarly, it is oil money which has allowed the Gulf emirates to develop modern state structures, which otherwise they could not possibly dream of, and establish themselves on the map. Outside the Gulf, the same is certainly true also for Libya.

In short, oil in the region has led to the consolidation and in some cases the emergence of independent states—which otherwise might easily have disappeared—alongside the states with deeper roots in history, such as Egypt—first and foremost—and the states in the French sphere of influence: Morocco, Algeria, Tunisia, to a lesser extent Lebanon and Syria.[1] This dichotomy between the older and the newer states, which largely coincides with the oil-haves and the oil-have-nots, has come to be one of the fundamental dimensions of regional and international relations of the Middle East.

Oil was instrumental in the consolidation of Middle East states also in the sense that it predominantly favoured aggregation rather than disaggregation, centripetal rather than centrifugal forces. The same has not been the case elsewhere in the world—witness the case of Biafra.[2] But in the Middle East, although oil is, in some cases, the prerogative of one region only—in countries where national allegiance is weak and regional allegiance is strong—no visible separatist temptations have emerged. The clearest case is Saudi Arabia: oil is entirely in the Eastern region, which is far from the traditional cultural and political centre—in the Hijaz—as well as from the new political and administrative centre in Ar Riyadh; but the Hassa oasis lacked a tradition of autonomy, and supported the return of the al Sa'ud from early on. The UAE is another example, in as much as oil resources are almost exclusively concentrated in Abu Dhabi: there, however, the oil centre and the political centre coincided, and the oil-rich region had no temptation to secede, because it dominated. The non-participation of Bahrain and Qatar in the UAE project might be explained with their relatively more abundant resources, which allowed them to refuse the hegemony of Abu Dhabi—in this sense a case of secession. In Libya, oil sits primarily in the Syrte desert, in the middle of the three historical regions of Cyrenaica, Tripolitania and Fezzan, thus discouraging any secessionist project. In Iraq, the Kurdish question has been intertwined with oil interests, but the Kurdish claim on control of Kirkuk oil is too feeble to allow Kurdish separatism to plan confidently to walk away with the fields: also, oil is available elsewhere in Iraq—in fact primarily in the North and South, but the centre of the country also has some reserves—thereby diluting the possible feeling that 'our oil is paying for all'.

Finally, oil has been instrumental in encouraging the definition of boundaries, and accepting international arbitration in contested cases. The definition of boundaries has frequently been a successive stage to mutual acceptance and recognition. The potential for finding oil has been an incentive to adopt a tougher negotiating stance, but at the same time also to seek a speedy resolution. Thus it has been the case in the Gulf (between Bahrain and Qatar; Qatar, the UAE and Saudi Arabia; Saudi Arabia and Yemen, etc.) as well as elsewhere (e.g. between Libya and Tunisia). The problem of oil fields straddling across boundaries (for example between Qatar and Iran, Iraq and Kuwait, and Libya and Algeria) was not eliminated, and in most cases such transboundary fields continue to be independently exploited on the two sides of the frontier, as the solution based on unitisation and condominiums has not taken roots. The original 'neutral zones' between Kuwait and Saudi Arabia and Iraq and Saudi Arabia have been divided up, further demonstrating a preference for clear division over joint exploitation. Although Iraq mentioned Kuwaiti pumping of oil, which Iraqis claimed to be theirs, as one reason for invading Kuwait, it would be difficult to argue that this was an important, even less a determinant reason. So far, potential conflict over the sharing of common resources has not erupted, leading at most to competition to develop each country's side of the field more rapidly. In contrast, several non-oil-related boundary conflicts have not been resolved, one suspects, primarily because neither side has a strong interest in resolving them. In this sense, and possibly counter-intuitively, oil has contributed to the peaceful solution of boundary conflicts, rather than to their exacerbation.

Oil and the International Relations of the Middle East

Oil is a very important factor in the international relations of the Middle East states, both with respect to regional, i.e. inter-Arab relations, and with respect to inter-national relations at large, i.e. relations with industrial and other developing countries.

The West and Arab oil

It is quite evident, and amply documented in the historical literature, that preoccupation with oil has been paramount in shaping the attitude of the UK, and later the US towards the region. We have noted this already with respect to the formation of the state system in the region, but almost all policies of the key outside players towards the region were evaluated mainly with respect to their implications for oil. Consider, for example, the key episode of Iraq's independence, whose final granting was subordinated to the interests of the Iraq Petroleum Company; or the overthrow of the Mussadiq government in Iran, which was tied primarily, though not exclusively, to the nationalisation of Anglo-Iranian Oil Company. Similarly, the United States entered in very close alliances with Saudi Arabia—which was, and continues to be problematic on most accounts, yet remains inescapable because of oil—and Iran. The latter developed following the inclusion of American companies in the Iranian consortium, which became possible after Mussadiq's demise and the return of Mohammed Reza Shah, and ended the monopoly of Anglo-Iranian on Iranian oil, forcing it to share its control with several other, primarily American, companies. (Anglo-Iranian also changed its name into British Petroleum.)

The diplomacy of other countries was also shaped by oil, albeit at a lower level of intensity, simply because they had far fewer assets, and were rather interested in a reshuffle of the cards, than in continuation of the existing order. Thus France attempted to hold on to Algeria, and did what was necessary to protect the interests of CFP (today's Total) in the UAE, but otherwise tried to distinguish itself from 'the Anglo-Saxons' by taking a line emphasising 'cooperation' with the oil producing countries (e.g. France's immediate acceptance of the Iraqi nationalisation in 1972; refusal to become member of the IEA when it was established, in Paris, in 1974;

promotion of diplomatic initiatives for a 'new international economic order' and later for the International Energy Forum; finally, the active undermining of US sanctions against Iran, and the flirting with the Saddam Hussein regime for oil concessions after the lifting of the UN oil embargo—a love story which was never consummated).

Italy too supported the creation of a national oil company, ENI, which became the prime mover of Italian diplomacy towards the Arab countries, leading to active support to the Algerian war of liberation (raising the suspicion that the bomb which downed Enrico Mattei's plane in 1962 may have been planted by the French secret service) as well as support for Mohammed Reza Shah when he fled Iran in conflict with Mussadiq, and the close relationship with Libya.[3] More recently, ENI has disregarded the US embargo against Iran, and has, imitating the French, flirted with Saddam Hussein's Iraq—without getting much in return. In actual fact, however, none of these attempts ever was terribly successful: ENI got its best results out of purchasing oil from the Soviet Union (a move which made the US furious), and finding oil in the Sinai, in Egypt.

Oil has influenced diplomacy towards the region, but in most cases diplomacy has failed to yield the results that were expected of it, at least as far as oil is concerned. In more recent years, oil has more frequently been used as a tool, rather than as objective: witness the American embargo against Iran, then Libya, and the UN-imposed embargo against Iraq. In all cases, the major industrial powers have made their own access to oil more difficult, in order to pursue a political priority. Or is it the case that oil needs not only to be abundant and cheap, but also politically correct, in the sense of coming from a country whose government is friendly to us? Many seem to believe that this is indeed a priority or requirement, and rank suppliers in accordance to political proximity, although there is no empirical support to the belief that oil produced from a friend is either more reliable or cheaper.

Middle East oil exporters and their international relations

The oil producing countries have naturally taken notice of the importance attributed to oil by the major powers, and attempted to take advantage of it, acquiring guarantees for their security against external and internal challenges, as well as access to sophisticated weapons systems. (The guarantee against internal challenges was 'lifted' from Iran by President Carter, who wanted to uphold basic human rights and democracy, and thus allowed the Imperial regime to collapse—with consequences that most observers would consider quite disastrous, to this date.)

The less obvious point is that in fact oil does not appear to be a prominent preoccupation in shaping the foreign policy of the oil producing countries. International oil policy is entrusted to a Minister of Petroleum or Energy, who is generally regarded as a technician; and is discussed in OPEC or other similar fora, which have a narrow, technical mandate. The only case in which there was an attempt to use oil as a weapon—in 1973—was a short-lived affair and oil never truly became physically scarce (see Figure 4.2).

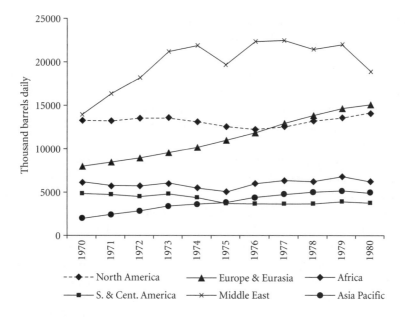

Fig. 4.2 World oil production by region

Source: BP Statistical Review of Word Energy.

At the outbreak of war between Israel and its Arab neighbours in October 1973, OAPEC (the Organisation of Arab Oil Exporting Countries) declared an embargo against the United States and the Netherlands (Yergin 1991: 588–612). Prices increased rapidly on oil markets, precipitating the first 'energy crisis'. The chart above shows that the embargo was fictional: Middle East oil production increased steadily and rapidly until 1974. It declined the following year because of the recession and decrease in oil demand triggered by the increase in prices. In fact, oil was never used as a weapon. Nevertheless, commentators still refer to OAPEC's decision as to a dangerous precedent and proof of the unreliability of Gulf oil supplies.

That episode was a success from the point of view of provoking an increase in prices, but politically a disastrous failure, which the Gulf oil producers still regret today. In fact, the perception that Gulf oil supplies are insecure and unreliable is still based essentially on just that one decision, and persists notwithstanding the fact that since that time Gulf producers have demonstrated more than once that they are able to deliver all the oil that is required even in the presence of conflict in the region.

Mostly, the diplomacy of the oil producing countries has been busy pursuing objectives that are either irrelevant or dysfunctional to their position as major exporters of oil: be it the promotion of Islam or the fight against Israel, pan Arabism or some milder form of pan-Africanism, or sheer military expansionism. Indeed, most oil producing countries should blame their ill-advised foreign policy initiatives for most of the problems they find themselves mired in. Even the Gulf countries, which have a record of less pernicious adventurism than Iraq, Libya (culminating in the Lockerbie bombing) or even Algeria (still mired in conflict with Morocco on Southern Sahara, a late heritage of its Third-Worldism), still bear the consequences of their support for Arafat, the Afghan mujahideen and Islamist tendencies everywhere. The advantage of Norway, one is tempted to say, is that it has no Great Cause that it should sponsor—although the cases of Nigeria, Venezuela and others are there to demonstrate that it is possible to create a disaster out of oil even in the absence of a Great Cause.

It is remarkable how little attention the oil exporting countries have otherwise devoted to oil in International Relations. OPEC members meet to discuss production and prices, but otherwise no resources have been devoted to shaping a full-fledged, well-structured oil diplomacy. For example, one would expect major oil producers to engage in dialogue with their most important clients to reassure them about the reliability of supplies: we would expect countries like Saudi Arabia, Kuwait or Iran to have intense diplomatic exchanges and dialogue with Japan, China, India and other key destination countries—but this is not the case at all. Oil producers have not promoted an international oil and gas regime, and remain at the margin or outside the Energy Charter Treaty.[4] They have welcomed the initiative of establishing the International Energy Forum as a way to overcome the contraposition between OPEC and the IEA, but the Forum remains very much of a loose meeting ground, notwithstanding the recent creation of a permanent secretariat in Riyadh.[5]

Oil and Domestic Politics: The Rentier State Paradigm

The availability of oil resources profoundly affects the domestic political order and contributes to explaining the Middle East difference. Several authors have dealt with the oil/domestic politics interplay, and a lively discussion has developed in the literature. Without attempting a complete survey, I will introduce the rentier state paradigm, which was proposed originally by Hossein Mahdavy (1970), and systematised by Beblawi (1987) and Luciani (1987); it has become a common tool in the interpretation of the political dynamics of oil producing countries.

The rentier state paradigm

The essence of the rentier state concept is that while in 'normal' countries the state is supported by society, and must, in order to pay for itself, establish a system to extract from society part of the surplus the latter generates; in oil exporting countries the state is paid by the oil rent, which accrues to it directly from the rest of the world, and supports society through the distribution or allocation of this rent, through various mechanisms of rent circulation.

Hence the distinction between production states, in which society is the source of value added and the state pays for itself by imposing taxes; and allocation or distributive (or rentier) states, in which the state is independent of society, and directly or indirectly supports a large part of the latter through the process of spending domestically the rent which it receives from the rest of the world.

The emphasis in this approach is on the fiscal function of the state. The (production) state is viewed essentially as a tool to subtract resources from the actors originally possessing them and reallocating them in a way different from that which the original owners would have chosen. Politics in (production) states consists in justifying the predatory function and influencing the destination of the 'booty' in the name of an asserted common interest. In order to justify this process, states need the acquiescence or acceptance of their people, and seek legitimacy, including through democratic institutions.

In contrast, rentier states do not need to tax, or may tax more lightly, and their primary function is the distribution of resources accruing from abroad. These resources enter the domestic circulation and have an impact on the domestic economy only to the extent that they are domestically spent by the state. Spending is therefore the essential function of the rentier state, and generosity (as opposed to accountability) the essential virtue of its ruler.

Not all Arab states are rentier. The details of the definition of rentier state are essential, and generalisations that blur our understanding of reality rather than improving it should be resisted. In particular:

1. It is essential that the source of the rent be the rest of the world. States that use the control of a specific domestic source of rent to extract surplus from society are not rentier states, because they are supported by society rather than vice versa.

2. It is also essential that the rent should accrue *directly* to the state. Some authors consider the inflow of remittances from workers having migrated to the oil exporting countries (believed to incorporate a share of the oil rent) as a potential base for a rentier state in the receiving country. There is a double fallacy here, because expatriate earnings, if they contained an element of rent in the past, certainly don't do so any longer, beyond the normal differences in remuneration levels in different labour markets; and secondly because in any case remittances are private income flows, and the state must resort to taxation in order to appropriate them.

The rentier nature of the state is empirically connected primarily to the case of oil exporters, but there may be other sources of rent that have essentially the same impact. These may be tied to control of strategic assets, generating payments from other governments; of important logistical assets, such as the Suez Canal; of other minerals, such as diamonds in Africa; or of drugs production or trade, such as in Afghanistan, among others. However, *these activities are not always controlled by the state,* and then the political impact is quite different: for example, the production of qat is not controlled by the Yemeni state, and the drugs cartel in Colombia is in conflict with the state; diamonds for many years allowed Unita to continue in the civil war against the Angolan government.

In historical experience the oil rent suddenly increased for approximately a decade, from 1973 to 1983, and 'flooded' the entire region, engulfing everybody in the process of rent circulation. But this was a limited experience: oil-exporting states have been rentier, in the sense of being essentially independent of domestic taxation, before 1973 and continue to be so in the twenty-first century. To the rest of the region, the encounter with large-scale oil rent was short lived.

The rentier state, taxation and democracy

The most important feature of the rentier state is that, being financially independent of society and indeed having in a sense society on its payroll, it is autonomous (in the sense of not being accountable) and does not need to seek legitimacy through democratic representation. It is an historical fact that demands for democratic representation and government accountability rose out of the attempt of the ruler to impose new taxes. The rentier state paradigm has become most popular through the reversal of the well known saying 'no taxation without representation' into its mirror image: 'no representation without taxation'. In fact, neither of the two is strictly speaking correct, yet both capture a simple casual link, which remains fundamentally true.

Rentier states inherit a political order from history; they do not create their own political order. A few were democracies when they acquired access to external rent, and remained democracies, although maybe with a slightly different modus operandi. A majority were authoritarian, and the advent of the rent allowed them to reinforce and consolidate authoritarian rule. Patrimonial states ruling segmented (tribal) societies are a specific subset among the authoritarian rentier states: it has been argued that this specific form of government is especially adapted to the rentier state, because the state is viewed as the property of the ruler, and the distributive function, which is played in order to maintain a desired balance in the segmented society, is understood as the essential function of government.

It is to be expected that rentier states will not be subjected to important pressure from below to allow for democratic participation. Everybody understands that a democratically elected ruler will be seriously tempted to turn authoritarian, as soon as he acquires control of the oil rent and the great power this gives to him over society. The possibility of alternation is essential to democracy: no opposition will remain loyal to democratic institutions, if it does not stand a chance to ever win elections; and no political force will accept a transition to democracy, if the first elections are also likely to be the last.

The difficulty of establishing representative democracy in a rentier state is an objective fact—the very recent literature about how to democratise Iraq is full of references to the fact that the central government should not have full control of the oil rent. (This poses a very difficult dilemma: some have suggested that the rent be distributed directly to the people, others that it should be locked in a fund not accessible to the government—but then, to whom?—others again have suggested various forms of federal government; but what is to prevent an independent, and democratically elected, Iraqi government from asserting its control over the rent?)

Conversely, it may be expected that non-rentier states, because they need to rely on taxation, will experience pressure from below to allow for democratic representation. However, when faced with pressure to democratise, non-rentier states can, first and foremost, resort to repression, a task facilitated by constant refinement of control methods and technology; second, they can make the most of whatever small sources of outside rent are available to them; and, finally, they can develop forms of taxation that are less politically demanding—from taxes on international trade to money creation and inflation. The region offers examples of various combinations of all of the above, but there is yet no convincing case of transition to democracy.

The ability of authoritarian governments to resist economic, fiscal and political reform is indeed very considerable: the common assumption, whereby economic stagnation will breed dissatisfaction and fuel demand for participation, has frequently been disproved in reality: having a hard time simply to survive leads to passivity and fatalism, rather than to the revolt of those 'having nothing else to lose than their chains'. Furthermore, in Middle East non-rentier states the option of exit (i.e. migration) is normally always available: it contributes to letting the steam off, and concentrates the minds of the left behind into getting out, rather than getting better. The youth, especially, concentrates on the option of leaving—to Europe, the US or at least one of the oil producing countries. The fact that few succeed is not very important—it is the constant delusion of capitalism that everybody can become rich, but very few actually do so.

In the early years of the twenty-first century, conventional expectations—persistent authoritarianism for the rentier state and pressure towards democracy for the non-rentier states—have tended to be contradicted by actual developments, as several rentier states have seemingly engaged in the road towards wider political participation, while the non-rentier states have further barricaded themselves behind their security apparatuses. How is this paradox to be explained?

Possibly, the explanation can be found in the different strength of the private sector in the rentier and non-rentier states: the private sector has become remarkably strong in the Arab Gulf rentier states, while it has remained weak in the non-rentier states as well as in those rentier states, such as Iraq or Libya or Algeria. In fact, the rentier state remains very strong because of its financial independence from society, but the national private sector is also very strong, thanks to the accumulation of assets internationally, combined with the continuing attachment to its country of origin. The private sector in the Arabian Gulf countries commands financial resources far in excess of those of the state, and is keen to invest at home. The rentier state must then redefine its role relative to the private sector, reducing its commitments in certain areas and opening new opportunities to private investment. A new public/private relationship is required in order to accelerate growth, exiting the doldrums of stagnant or declining GDP per capita, and entering a new phase of rapid development, also in order to stem the growth of unemployment. Thus the state remains rentier; nevertheless, while in the earlier phase of the rising rent tide, the private sector was allowed to make very good profits, but lost the levers of economic power, the ebbing of this tide is manifesting increasing investment opportunities which complement the ambitions of the state.

The politics of economic reform

The issue of democracy is indeed closely connected to the question of economic reform. The Middle East countries must—as all countries—reform their economies in order to keep pace with the globalisation process, and have notoriously resisted doing so. What is possibly even more important, the two or three cases (Jordan, Morocco, Tunisia) of countries having accepted the need to reform, and followed the precepts of the Washington consensus over the past twenty years, have failed to reap major benefits. The region has no success story, no Middle Eastern 'cub tiger' that it can show to galvanise support towards reform and participation in the globalisation mainstream.

With the exception of the Gulf Arab oil producers, the turn towards an open and competitive market economy is hindered throughout the region by the weakness of the private sector. This weakness is in most cases due to the fact that the praetorian regimes, which prevailed in some Arab states (Egypt, Syria, Iraq, Algeria, Libya), have moved against their historical bourgeoisies and caused their ruin (Henry and Springborg 2001). The new private sector, which emerged in praetorian regimes thanks to closeness and access to political power—cronyism— remains extremely weak when assessed in terms of financial or managerial capabilities. But even in states such as Jordan or Morocco, that did not go through the experience of praetorian rule and 'socialist revolution', we find a not altogether different situation: their private sectors are also weak by international standards, and not truly able to compete. The Gulf Arab oil producers are different because over the decades they have nurtured a private sector that is well integrated in the globalisation process.

The distinction between praetorian republics and globalising monarchies proposed by Henry and Springborg only captures one aspect of the story: while it is certainly the case that the praetorian republics, having destroyed their bourgeoisies, have a hard time reintegrating into a global economy inspired by the Washington consensus, it is misleading to bundle two oil-poor countries such as Morocco and Jordan with the oil-rich countries of the GCC: the private sector in the former commands a fraction of the financial resources of the private sector in the latter. If we could draw a map of the region based on the capabilities of each country's private sector as measured by their net worth, Saudi Arabia would probably account for close to half of the entire region, and the rest of the GCC for more than a further third. The remainder of the region is in the hands of business characters of no weight in the global context, and can only integrate by 'surrendering' to foreign capital—a prospect in stark contrast with its persistent nationalist rhetoric (e.g. net assets accumulated internationally by GCC investors are estimated at around $1.3 trillion. Saudi holdings are probably in the region of $750 to 850 billion, the rest belonging to other GCC nationals. All holdings of all other Arab countries are certainly less than $200 billion, probably less than half this sum.).

The implication of the weak private sector is that economic reform (privatisation, liberalisation of international trade, and liberalisation of capital movements) is bound to result in the domination of all major productive assets on the part of foreign interests—mostly multinational corporations. However, the prospect of selling all major economic assets to foreign owners runs against the residual nationalist feelings, which the authoritarian incumbent exploits to justify maintaining control over some levers that are essential to his survival.

Successful economic reform and integration in the globalisation mainstream requires the presence of a strong national private sector, which has the means to take over from the state all those tasks that the state should relinquish, and is able to compete internationally. This of course does not mean excluding international investment, but being able to establish balanced and mutually rewarding alliances, rather than simple sell-outs.

It is only the rentier states of the Gulf that have a private sector with the required combination of financial and managerial capabilities, and commitment to their country of origin. (Interestingly, a section—albeit not a very large one—of this private sector is constituted of entrepreneurs from other Arab countries that have prospered in the Gulf and might some day return to their places of origin—but precious few have done so until now.) The rentier states face fewer obstacles in pursuing economic reform, as they have much better tools and opportunities available to them than the non-rentier states. They have been slow to reform because of weak leadership and complacency: but these weaknesses can be overcome if the required feeling of urgency prevails.

The connection between the rentier nature of the state, economic reform and the path to democracy is therefore more complex than initially expected.

The non-rentier states are loath to embrace economic reform because doing so might weaken their grip on power, in the absence of democratic legitimation. At the same time, conditions do not exist for reform to be a great success—as the experience of the few neighbours that did reform appears to prove. A vicious circle is therefore created between the absence of democracy and the absence of economic reform, and political stability increasingly rests on repression and authoritarianism.

In contrast, the rentier states are waking up to the need to reform, enjoy very favourable conditions to turn reform into a success, and are considering opening the political space to greater participation in order to facilitate the shaping of the relevant consensus around reform. Such opening of the political space, however, is not necessarily a precursor of democracy: the state remains rentier, and all that it truly needs is just the consensus of the private entrepreneurial class in order to establish a new public/private relationship. This consensus is not automatic and entails some political cost in terms of enlarged political participation; yet the relevant entrepreneurs remain very largely loyal to the incumbent regimes.

Oil and Inter-Arab Relations

Oil has had a fundamental influence on inter-Arab relations, primarily because of the dialectic between oil-poor and oil-rich states. Interestingly, the oil-rich states, as stressed earlier, also are relatively 'new' in history, while the oil-poor states have deeper historical roots. Finally, the oil-rich states are rentier, while the oil-poor states only became rentier for a short season, as recipients of unilateral transfers from the oil-rich states.

The dichotomy between oil-rich and oil-poor states is certainly not the only factor in the extraordinary divisiveness of Arab regional relations, but it has been significant.

The call of Pan-Arabism

Pan-Arabism has been the dominant discourse on regional relations in the Middle East. Pan-Arabism is not, in itself, directly related to oil—although it is a reaction to the Balkanisation of the Arab region which, in turn, is certainly due also to oil—but quickly became entangled with it, hardening the conflict between the historically longer-established, progressive, more developed, but oil-poor Arab States; and the newly formed, traditional, conservative and oil-rich states in the Gulf and North Africa.

Nasser's ideology was not primarily conceived of as a tool to destroy the oil monarchies and assert control over their oil riches, but it quickly was perceived as aiming at exactly this outcome. Nasser was defeated by the inability to deliver progress with respect to Palestine, but possibly even more so by his inability to come to terms with the oil monarchies, or, to be precise, with all oil exporting countries in the region, even when they shed their monarchies and followed the 'revolutionary' path. He lost his battle when he could not prevail in the civil war in Yemen, nor was able to overcome the rivalry with Iraq, even before 1967. The advent of a regime with strong Nasserite and pan-Arab temptations in Libya received little more than an opportunistic and profiteering response from Egypt. Simply put, the 'historical' Arab states cannot accept that the basis of power in the contemporary world has changed: not only are oil barrels more important than guns, but also money is more important than population.

The constant temptation of Arab oil exporters to become embroiled in issues that transcend their national boundaries and are not functional to their national interest is indeed a feature of rentier states. The authoritarian rentier state does not need to refer to a national myth, because it is supported by a rent accruing from the rest of the world and does not need to impose taxes on the domestic economy. A national myth is necessary to justify the redistributive function of the state, which requires a concept of collective good and legitimacy to be justified. Rentier states simply distribute without the need for taxes, and tend to deny that 'the people' should have a say in the way the rent is distributed, presenting themselves as invested of some superior or wider mission. The authoritarian rentier state thus tends rather to assert its legitimacy by reference to a constituency that is larger than its own population—Islamic in Saudi Arabia or the Islamic Republic of Iran; Arab in Iraq or Libya; technocratic in Dubai. Inevitably, these assertions of legitimacy tend to compete and conflict with each other, creating a difficult regional climate. (The Shah's insistence on a purely Persian national myth—the continuous reference to the imperial and pre-Islamic past, as symbolised by the coronation in Persepolis—did not help in creating a feeling of belonging or consensus.)

In contrast, the oil-poor states have articulated a claim to a share of the oil rent, which the oil-rich states never truly accepted as legitimate. The primary recipients initially accepted mechanisms to circulate the rent regionally—direct budget subsidies to their neighbours, as well as labour migration and remittances—but expected a political return, which was denied to them. This has little to do with the nature of the regime, as it has been true of the Gulf monarchies as well as of Libya and Iraq. The claim to sharing in the rent combined with a statist (étatist) ideology, which attributed the primary role in promoting economic development to the State, leading to a vision of regional integration based on politicised government-to-government relations. This approach proved totally sterile.

It is interesting to note how both oil-poor and oil-rich states sometimes embraced the same ideological discourse, but with entirely opposite intentions. Hence pan-Arabism in Egypt and Ba'thism in Syria were meant to lay a claim to a share of the oil rent of neighbouring countries, while the same pan-Arabism in Libya or Ba'thism in Iraq were used to justify the rentier state's bid for hegemony.

Egypt turned its back to pan-Arabism and Nasser's legacy when it signed its separate peace with Israel. It also turned its back to the oil money of its neighbours, embracing, in theory, the credo of openness to international trade and market-based development. But implementation of the new strategy was—and continues to be—painfully slow. The Gulf oil producers have always combined a leading role of the state in promoting development—an essential facet of circulating the oil rent—with openness to international trade. In so doing, they have nurtured a domestic private sector that has grown more competitive and well integrated in the global economy. In contrast, none of the non-oil Arab states has succeeded in establishing a truly competitive economy, which is capable of following the example of the Asian emerging economies. Their attractiveness for private investment from the Gulf is limited, contributing to estrangement and resentment.

The ascendance of the Gulf rentier states

In the 1970s, the increase of the oil rent was so sudden, and its concentration so extreme, that the rentier states felt it was prudent to be generous outside as well as inside their boundaries. They therefore created institutions to redistribute a share of the rent internationally, and engaged in granting direct subsidies to neighbouring governments. Jordan, Syria, the PLO and, until it made peace with Israel, Egypt were major beneficiaries of these direct grants. Later, Iraq became a recipient during its protracted war with Iran.

However, the effectiveness of such generosity in purchasing lasting goodwill was dubious, to say the least. Iraq's decision to invade Kuwait, and the attitude that Jordan or the Palestinians took on that occasion, was abundant proof that generosity sometimes breeds resentment. More recently, the fact that al-Qaida has turned against the Saudi regime is again a demonstration of a client turning against its patron.

So, after a short period of time in which the tide of the rent rose so high that it covered the entire region, and almost every government became rentier—in the sense of being primarily occupied with capturing oil or strategic rents under the form of direct grants—we have returned to a condition that was common before 1973; that is of a region which is dominated by the dynamics between rentier and non-rentier, or oil-rich and oil-poor states, and the impossible integration between them.

In the meantime, as noted above, the private sector in the rentier states has become much stronger, and the rent has declined: rentier states can therefore propose a much more conventional model of regional cooperation, based on free trade and private investment, be it direct or financial. They can rely on international organisations such as the IMF, the World Bank or the WTO to promote this model, playing down the Arab nationalist discourse and dimension. However, the latter refuses to die, and the non-rentier states are not keen on a model of regional integration that may substantially downsize their political influence.

Slowly but surely, the balance of power (opportunities and capabilities) has shifted in the region, away from the older established but oil-poor states and in favour of the newly consolidated oil-rich ones. Furthermore, within the latter group some have wasted their opportunity, engaging in regional adventurism and ill-advised state-led investment policies. The GCC states, certainly the most fragile at the beginning of the process, have bred a wealthy, sophisticated private sector, which is reasonably well integrated in the currents of globalisation; they therefore have a much better chance of success than the rest of the region.

The regional balance in the Arab region has been moving relentlessly away from the historically better established states towards the oil-rich 'parvenus'. As military power loses importance—in a world in which only one superpower counts—and traditional industry and agriculture is less important than services and the e-economy, the traditional centres of Arab politics are in decline while the oil exporters enjoy all opportunities. Regional politics has not yet come to terms with the new reality, but unless it does so, it will remain sterile. The very evident problems of the Arab League and most other regional institutions are linked to the incongruence of ambitions and assets: some countries have ambitions and no assets, other have all the assets and very few ambitions—hence the very typical combination of the empty rhetoric of some, and the paralysis and lack of direction of others.

The international and regional environments and the emerging political order in the Middle East

Notwithstanding the prediction that the world will grow increasingly dependent on Middle East oil, after September 11 a new political agenda has emerged with greater vigour in the US and Europe: priority is now very clearly laid on fostering or even forcing political and economic reform in the Middle East, leading to the establishment of democratic governments in all key countries in the region and their integration in the globalisation process. This agenda is, in fact, not entirely new: the European Union's Barcelona Process explicitly targeted democracy, good governance and the respect of human rights in parallel with the establishment of a regional free trade zone: but it did not involve the largest oil producers, and was pursued with little vigour. Only too often, the US and Europe have preached democracy but then bowed to the persistent or worsening authoritarianism of regimes they deemed as friendly.

The international environment is moving against the incumbent regimes in the Middle East and North Africa. They can survive by tightening up repression with modest or even poor economic results, but the main industrial countries find this scenario unacceptable. It is also that, again because of the circulation of oil money, extremist opposition finds better opportunities to raise finance, and has therefore become more dangerous. Finally, the dependence of local regimes on outside support for their survival is so obvious that the foreign patron is a target just as the domestic client.

The war in Iraq and the demise of the Saddam Hussein regime may or may not succeed in establishing a democratic government there. The outcome is certainly very important, because Iraq is a major oil producing country, potentially second only to Saudi Arabia. In any case, it is very unlikely that Iraq may become the model for the rest of the region, at least for quite a long time. The destruction of civil society and the private sector has been such that the recreation of an Iraqi entrepreneurial class will take decades. The country will, for quite some time, be primarily concerned with reconstruction: if it is forcibly opened to international trade, investment and competition it may simply turn into a hunting ground for international investors, including Arab, and never see the birth of a strong national private sector.

The Middle East and North Africa will be forced to open up to international trade, and at least partially to democratise. The US and the EU are both pursuing schemes towards the establishment of free trade areas that will eventually also liberalise trade within the region. In this way, the objective of Arab free trade that has always eluded the countries of the region will eventually come about because of international pressure and initiative. The enforcement of free trade will erode the authoritarian governments of the non-rentier countries, limiting their control on the economy and power of patronage, and restricting their ability to tax trade. Their legitimacy will be further restricted, and a period of instability will ensue. Even if there is rapid progress towards democratisation, it is highly unlikely that, after such a long period of constrained political life, a stable political system will emerge. In short, the times ahead will not be easy for the oil-poor states.

The oil-rich rentier states of the Gulf also face a difficult adjustment, but they are in a much more favourable position. Their economies are much more open, they will enjoy continued access to the oil rent, and their private sector is strong and loyal to their country. They need to adapt their political system, but the required change is in the direction of greater efficiency and wider participation, not true democratisation: the system will essentially remain authoritarian, although it must avoid paralysis.

The Gulf countries suffer a very difficult problem with their aging and sclerotic leadership, but are showing signs of reacting to the new challenges. Although it may require difficult institutional innovations to separate the responsibility of government from that of the ruling family, in order to isolate the government from the inevitable aging of the rulers, the external and domestic pressure for reform may well succeed in precipitating the required changes—which however fall very much short of democracy or government accountability to popularly elected representatives.

The Gulf-based entrepreneurs are best positioned to take advantage of the new opportunities that will be created by the imposition of a new order, whether from the US or the EU or both, beginning from the reconstruction of Iraq. International investment will be attracted to the region but will remain wary of political instability (newly established democratic governments will be viewed as fragile) and difficult local conditions, and will seek risk mitigation. The Gulf entrepreneurs are ideally placed to offer risk mitigation, because they are 'indigenous' and at the same time have large financial tools and are ready to invest. They will remain mostly keen to invest in their own countries, where most 'control functions' will concentrate, but will be ready to irradiate from there.

Will this outcome be acceptable to the oil-poor states? Will they view Arab investment from the Gulf countries any more favourably than investment from multinational corporations? Will the traditional tension between oil-rich and oil-poor states gradually dissolve? It will not be an easy process. The other Arab states may attempt to resist the hegemony of the Gulf-based private sector, by favouring investment from the rest of the world, but this would result in even less control over their own fate. A national alternative is essentially ruled out.

A possible scenario, in a context of greater regional integration, is that the Gulf-based private sector might gradually become more regionalised and less closely tied to the Gulf. The Gulf-based entrepreneurs that originate from other countries (for example Syria, Lebanon, Jordan, Palestine, Iraq, Egypt) may progressively return to their countries of origin, although this will be a slow process. And the Gulf entrepreneurs may progressively move the centre of their activities and interests to other Arab capitals. In this way, a progressive adjustment of the existing disequilibrium might take place—but again, it will take time.

Conclusion

This chapter has attempted to map the multiple ways in which oil has influenced international relations and domestic politics in the Middle East. We argued that historically interest for oil, especially in the UK and the US, strongly influenced the attitude of these two countries towards the Middle East and the formation of the state system in the region, following the collapse of the Ottoman Empire. However, we also highlighted that not everything can be explained by oil.

We stressed the historical dynamic between states that have deeper roots in history but generally little oil, and states which were formed only much more recently and consolidated primarily thanks to their oil resources and the rent that these generated.

The polarisation in the region between oil-rich and oil-poor states is an essential tool of analysis. The parallel distinction between rentier and non-rentier states was introduced to explain how oil affects the domestic political development of the oil-rich states, and influences their regional relations.

We explained how rentier states feel little pressure to become democratic, while this pressure may be expected to exist in the non-rentier states. However, we also stressed that, faced with the need to engage in economic reform, non-rentier states are in a much more difficult position, because of the weakness of their private sectors, than rentier states—notably the Arab Gulf states, whose governments always supported private business. This explains why in fact we see little progress towards democracy and economic reform in the non-rentier state; quite the contrary, the state is progressively barricading behind an increasingly intrusive repressive apparatus. In contrast, rentier states in the Gulf are moving towards economic reform as well as wider political participation; the latter however is likely to fall short of democracy as we normally recognise it.

Such domestic dynamics are important because they underlie regional relations. The progressive ascendance of the oil-rich, rentier states continues, supported by their much greater adaptability to the dictates of globalisation. The oil-poor states are bound to continue in their relative decline, but have not yet come to terms with it; they are not willing to subscribe to a model of regional relations based on the liberal recipe of the Washington consensus, which would inevitably consolidate the hegemony of the private sector of the Arab Gulf countries. The process will be influenced by external intervention as well as the circumstances of the international oil market.

International organisations, the United States and the European Union are all pursuing, albeit at times in competition with each other, an agenda aiming at economic and political reform in the region. Incumbent authoritarian regimes have been very successful in resisting such pressure until recently, but September 11 and subsequent events may signal a radical change in the rules of the game.

Oil is important because it affects the power balance within the region as well as outside attitudes. If the price of oil were to significantly increase due to scarcity of global supplies, the incentive to reform in the rentier states might quickly evaporate. Rent circulation would again become the most important determinant of regional relations, as it was in the 70s and early 80s, although a return to the past is probably not to be expected. If, at the opposite extreme, oil prices became very soft, the rentier states might experience serious short-term budget difficulties, sending shock waves throughout the region. Instability might then become acute, which is unlikely to be the most favourable condition for economic and political reform. Finally, if—as it is officially sought by the US, the EU, Russia and many more—prices remain stable at a moderate level, conditions may indeed become favourable for promoting economic and political reform in the Arab Gulf states; in turn, this development might improve regional opportunities and encourage economic reform in the non-rentier states, facilitating their progressive democratisation.

Further Reading

GAUSE, F. G. III, *Oil Monarchies: Domestic and Security Challenges in the Arab Gulf States* (Washington D.C.: Council on Foreign Relations, March 1994). A good introductory reference to the politics of the Arab Gulf countries.

HENRY, C. M. and SPRINGBORG, R., *Globalization and the Politics of Development in the Middle East,* (Cambridge: Cambridge University Press, 2001). The most recent effort at offering a political economy interpretation of Middle East politics.

KERR, M. H. and YASSIN, EL SAYED (eds.), *Rich and Poor Nations in the Middle East* (Boulder, Colo.: Westview, 1982). A classic for understanding the regional dynamics between oil-rich and oil-poor countries in the Middle East.

LUCIANI, G. (ed.), *The Arab State* (Berkeley: University of California Press, 1990). Contains the essential reference essays on the rentier state paradigm.

PENROSE, E. T., *The Large International Firm in Developing Countries—The International Petroleum Industry* (Boston: MIT Press, 1967). A true classic and still a must read for understanding the international oil industry; the analysis of the workings of IPC and the control of international majors on world oil production remains important to the understanding of contemporary realities although the situation has by now changed completely.

STOCKING, G. W., *Middle East Oil* (Knoxville; Tenn.: Vanderbilt University Press, 1970).

An account of the history of development of Middle East oil that contains
all the important details presented very
effectively.

SALAME, G. (ed.), *Democracy without*
Democrats: the Renewal of Politics in the
Muslim World (London: I. B. Tauris,
1994). The best reference on the question
of democracy in the Middle East.

WATERBURY, J., *The Egypt of Nasser and*
Sadat: the Political Economy of Two
Regimes (Princeton, NJ: Princeton
University Press, 1983). Essential to

understanding the promise and pitfalls
of Nasserism, and the problems of the
non-rentier Arab states.

YERGIN, D. *The Prize: The Epic Quest for*
Oil, Money and Power (New York: Simon
and Schuster, 1991). A history of the oil
industry that is the best introductory
reading to get the basic facts and references. It differs from Stocking (1970)
inasmuch as it covers more than just the
Middle East and has a lot of entertaining
details, which however are not always
truly important.

Web Links

http://www.eia.doe.gov/—The web site of
the Energy Information Agency of the US
Department of Energy is the largest freely
available source of information on energy
affairs on the web.

http://www.grc.to/—The web site of the Gulf
Research Center, a privately sponsored

research and documentation centre on
the Arab Gulf.

http://gulf2000.columbia.edu/—The web site
of the Gulf 2000 project established at
Columbia University. Very extensive
documentation on the Gulf.

Notes

1. Ilya Harik (1987) has argued that,
contrary to the frequently held view according
to which all contemporary Arab States are a
creation of the colonial powers, most of them
have substantial roots in history. This is
certainly the case not just for Egypt, but also
for the Maghreb—although in the case of
Libya the three constituting provinces of
Tripolitania, Cyrenaica and Fezzan have
greater historical legitimacy than the unitary
state which has emerged. The situation is
different in the Mashreq, where the division
between Syria, Iraq and Jordan (the latter
a state invented totally *ex novo*) was shaped
by the colonial powers; Mount Lebanon had
a clearly recognisable separate identity in

history, but today's Lebanon was deliberately
defined by the French with considerably wider
borders than the historical precedent. About
Israel/Palestine, the impact of the British
mandate is only too obvious. In the peninsula,
a Saudi state has existed in the Nejd (central
Arabia) almost without interruption since the
eighteenth century, but today's Kingdom
includes the historical Hijaz and the emirate of
Hail, which have disappeared. Kuwait has
roots in history but all other Gulf emirates
were such small and unimportant places that
to discuss of their 'independent' existence in
history is moot.

2. Biafra is the province in Nigeria where oil
is concentrated. Biafra tried to secede from the

Nigerian federation but lost the ensuing bloody civil war (1966–70).

3. Enrico Mattei was the charismatic founder of the Italian state oil company ENI, which brought together two pre-existing companies, Agip and Snam. He died in the crash of the company's plane in very bad weather while returning to Milan from Sicily; the causes of the crash were never satisfactorily clarified (Yergin 1991: 530–1). Mattei battled the major international oil companies (he coined the term 'the Seven Sisters') and sought to find independent reserves for his company in Iran and Libya, but was especially successful in Egypt.

4. The Energy Charter Treaty was born as a European initiative to establish co-operative energy relations with the Former Soviet Union and the countries of the former Soviet block, following the collapse of the Iron Curtain. Negotiations were extended to Japan and Austrialia, which became members, as well as Canada and United States, which in the end refused to sign. The Middle East producers were invited only after the Treaty was signed, and most of them currently have the status of observers. Details in the Annual Report of the Energy Charter Secretariat, various years.

5. The International Energy Forum is a conference of the major industrial, developing and oil producing countries which was convened the first time in 1991. The 8th and latest International Energy Forum was convened in Osaka in September 2002. There the decision to establish a permenent Secretariat based in Riyadh was made, and a Secretary General was appointed in June 2003.

5

The Clash of Globalisations in the Middle East[1]

Clement M. Henry

OVERVIEW

Globalisation connotes the removal of barriers between states to the movement of capital, goods and labour. While the lowering of barriers to the movement of factors of production has resulted in transnational networks of production and elements of an international civil society, it has also facilitated international terrorist networks, drug cartels and the like. In the Middle East, for strategic reasons discussed in this paper, the spectrum of barriers to be removed includes not just protectionist trade or monetary policies but the regimes as well. 'Regime change' can be brutal or gradual, imposed or developed from within. This chapter examines the sorts of political change envisioned by the authors of the *Arab Human Development Report 2002* to overcome the region's 'freedom deficit' as well as the darker, by now all too familiar scenarios associating this dimension of globalisation—regime change—with American (multilateral or unilateral) military operations. The Middle East is home to most of the oil that fueled the world's first truly global industry, but the region may also become the epicentre of forces that reverse the globalising tendencies of states.

Introduction

It is not so much Seattle or New York as the Middle East that is becoming the principal battleground for contending visions of the new global order. The clash of globalisations[2] is most acutely perceived in this vulnerable, strategic region. The Middle East is caught between the imperialistic impulses of the neo-conservative Bush Administration and other, apparently more benign, multilateral proponents of globalisation such as the World Bank, the International Monetary Fund and the United Nations family of organisations. Pitted against these forces are the states of the region and some of their more radical internal oppositions.

Globalisation connotes the removal of barriers between states to the movement of capital, goods and labour. New information technologies may encourage states to remove barriers, but globalisation is not a sociological abstraction like modernisation. Some of the older technologies, such as printed media, telephones and transistor radios, used to be principal indicators of the abstract but conceptually inevitable modernisation of traditional societies (Lerner 1958). Globalisation, however, is far from inevitable, for it depends largely on the political acts of states, notably those of the great powers. As John Gray (1998) and other have noted, the world economy is less globalised on some dimensions, such as capital flows, than in 1913. One recent commentator goes so far as to write that '... globalization is a myth: it never really occurred ...' because most manufacturing is organised regionally, not globally (Rugman 2000: 1). Few industries, indeed, are truly global, but globalisation in the sense of the removal of barriers to various sorts of transnational exchanges has increased dramatically since the Second World War. The victorious allies founded a new world order in 1945 that encouraged these trends.

Certainly, transnational corporations (TNCs) have pioneered productive trade and networking across borders even if few industries are truly global. The top five hundred TNCs account for 90 per cent of foreign direct investment and over half of world trade (Rugman 2000: 3). New technologies have facilitated not only corporate networking but also new non-corporate forms of transnational association. With the help of the Internet, NGOs are straddling across continents and articulating a new public sphere, international civil society, working sometimes in broad consultation with the United Nations. Some have opposed further global initiatives that might favour transnational corporate activities. Before the riots in Seattle, for instance, a powerful transnational coalition sidelined the Multilateral Agreement on Investments (MAI), a treaty that was to have improved the environment for foreign direct investment (Kobrin 1998).

Technology facilitates new forms of association, but globalisation also has a darker side. Other transnational associations overlooked by liberal theorists include international drug cartels and terrorist networks, often serviced by cross-border money transfers (Hoffmann 1995). The decisions of states to open up to international traffic and capital flows are reversible, as the First World War and the Great Depression illustrated. Globalisation is not inevitable like the 'Passing of Traditional Society'. One dilemma of the United States since 11 September 2001, was to tighten controls on international money laundering while continuing to support the free flow of capital.

Globalisation, understood as the removal of various barriers that states erected over the past two or three centuries, is now rooted in a liberal world order that the United States and its allies constructed in the final days of the Second World War. The end of the Cold War, symbolised by the tearing down of the Berlin Wall in 1989, opened up new possibilities for globalisation but it also introduced new threats. The breakup of the Soviet Union hollowed out the core of power relationships that had deterred the US superpower from acting unilaterally. Multilateral commitments to collective security underlay the liberal order, and the first Bush Administration (1988–92) respected them by staying within the rules of the UN Security Council (and even sacrificed domestic political capital by omitting to veto a Security Council resolution critical of Israel, in order to maintain the coalition to liberate Kuwait). But the new Bush Administration habitually circumvented treaties and multilateral undertakings, whether the ABM Treaty with Russia, the Kyoto Protocol, the International Court of Criminal Justice, or WMD inspections in Iraq. By going to war against a member of the United Nations without a second resolution of the Security Council, the United States and the United Kingdom have created an alternative recipe for globalisation in the Middle East, whether or not, as many observers claim, they actually violated the United Nations Charter. 'Regime change' extends the spectrum of possible barriers to be removed by 'globalisation' to include the regimes themselves. Images of an Anglo-American occupation of Iraq also confirm perceptions of globalisation that were already widely shared in the region—the idea that globalisation is a new form of imperialism.

The purpose of this chapter is to examine these perceptions and to analyse the various responses of Arab regimes and their oppositions to the new challenges that they face. First we discuss the special characteristics of the region and why the tensions associated with globalisation are most acute in this part of the world. Then we examine the challenges to governments in the region associated with liberalising trade and attracting foreign direct investment. Major political as well as policy changes are clearly needed. We focus upon the analyses and prescriptions of leading Arab social scientists expressed in the *Arab Human Development Report 2002* because they represent the most candid positive regional response to the economic and political challenges of globalisation. As the authors are clearly aware, however, the upgrading of governance needed to implement effective economic reforms is likely to endanger incumbent regimes and further exacerbate their respective oppositions. They in a sense also favour regime change, just like the neo-conservatives in the Bush Administration. But to the extent that the United States pre-empts the gentle persuasion of multilateral institutions with direct military intervention, the potential targets are likely to harden their opposition to globalisation. The United States currently seems to be reinforcing the perception in the region that globalisation is just a cover for a new version of nineteenth century imperialism.

The Middle East as 'Shatterbelt'

The Middle East is predominantly Muslim and, with the big exceptions of Iran and Turkey and the more recent one of Israel, predominantly Arab, but its most distinctive characteristic is neither religion, language nor culture but rather its peculiar colonial legacy. Leon Carl Brown has succinctly captured this legacy:

For roughly the last two centuries the Middle East has been more consistently and more thoroughly ensnarled in great power politics than any other part of the non-Western world. This distinctive political experience continuing from generation to generation has left its mark on Middle Eastern political attitudes and actions. Other parts of the world have been at one time or another more severely buffeted by an imperial power, but no area has remained so unremittingly caught up in multilateral great power politics. (Brown, L.C. 1984: 3)

Political geographers tell us why. Evidently the Middle East is closer to the traditional Great Powers of the eighteenth and nineteen centuries, including Russia, than is Sub-Saharan Africa, South or Southeastern Asia, or Latin America. Sir Halford J. Mackinder offered an overarching geopolitical interpretation of the Middle East's strategic significance in 1904, when the imperial powers (including the United States after 1899) took geopolitics seriously. It lies at the centre of the Rimland surrounding Russia, the inherently expansionist 'pivot state' of the Eurasian continent. And 'if the pivot state should ever gain control of the marginal lands, thus gaining access to the sea, "the empire of the world would then be in sight" ' (Drysdale and Blake 1985: 23, citing Mackinder 1904). These ideas would resurface during the Cold War, when the region was viewed as a 'Shatterbelt', as depicted in the map below.

This region also roughly coincides with the 'Arc of Crisis' depicted by Zbigniew Brzezinski, President Jimmy Carter's National Security Advisor; it acquired added strategic significance with the Soviet Union's invasion of Afghanistan in 1979 (Brzezinski 1998: 7, 53).[3] Mackinder's geopolitics may be outdated but the region's strategic significance had already dramatically increased shortly after he wrote, when oil was first discovered in Iran and subsequently in Iraq, Kuwait, Saudi Arabia and the United Arab Emirates. Adding Algeria, Libya and other minor Arab producers, the region contained 69 per cent of the world's proven oil reserves at the end of 2001 (BP 2002). Indeed oil, the world's first truly global industry, seems to have reinvigorated Mackinder's geopolitical legacy. Not only was the international hydrocarbon economy the driving force behind Bush Senior's drive to liberate Kuwait—remember, as Secretary of State James Baker admitted, it was American jobs that were at stake. More seriously for understanding the current clash of globalisations, the younger

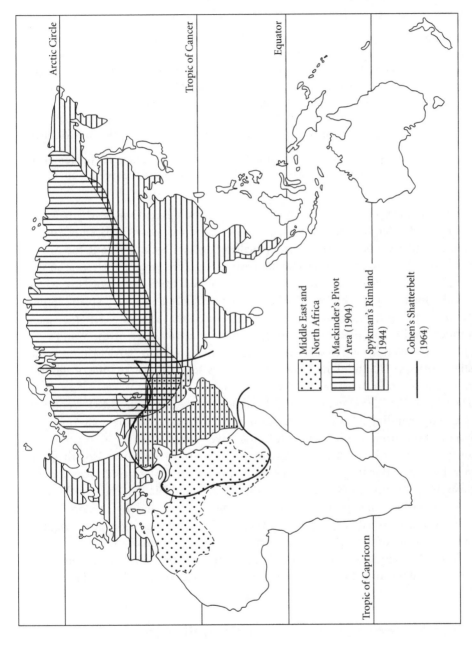

Fig. 5.1 Geopolitical views of the world: Mackinder, Spykman, and Cohen

Source: Figure 2.5a: Geopolitical views of the world from THE MIDDLE EAST AND NORTH AFRICA by Alasdair Drysdale and Gerald H. Blake. Copyright 1985 by Oxford University Press, Inc. Used by permission of Oxford University Press, Inc.

Bush's principal strategic planner, Paul Wolfowitz, was apparently already thinking along Mackinder's lines while serving Bush Senior's Administration in 1992. Here are the relevant excerpts of his draft memo, 'Defense Planning Guidance for the 1994–99,' first leaked to *The New York Times* on 8 March 1992.

We continue to recognize that collectively the conventional forces of the states formerly comprising the Soviet Union retain the most military potential in all of Eurasia; and we do not dismiss the risks to stability in Europe from a nationalist backlash in Russia or efforts to reincorporate into Russia the newly independent republics of Ukraine, Belarus, and possibly others ... We must, however, be mindful that democratic change in Russia is not irreversible, and that despite its current travails, Russia will remain the strongest military power in Eurasia and the only power in the world with the capability of destroying the United States.

In the Middle East and Southwest Asia, our overall objective is to remain the predominant outside power in the region and preserve U.S. and Western access to the region's oil. (Tyler 1992: 14)

The available excerpts did not mention any other region except the nearby Balkans. Turning Mackinder on his head, preserving world domination apparently entails preventing any rival outside power from challenging US hegemony along the Arc of Crisis.[4] No other external power may be permitted to challenge the US role in the region, and regional powers, too, must be prevented from exercising any wider regional influence (Lustick 1997). As Telhami and Hill (2002: 170–1) explain, 'From 1949 to the present, American planners have worried that a hostile state may gain too much wealth and power by controlling the dominant share of the world's oil supply ... Today, Iraq and, to some extent, Iran have replaced the Soviet Union as the hostile powers in U.S. thinking.' The United States still targets Iran, one of the two surviving states in President Bush's 'Axis of Evil'.

The 'Shatterbelt' depicted in Figure 5.1 can be perceived as the world's geopolitical cockpit, commanding oil as well as maritime communications. Virtually all American administrations from Truman to Bush Junior have viewed it as central to US global security. The Truman Doctrine the Eisenhower Doctrine, the Nixon Doctrine, the Carter Doctrine, the Reagan Doctrine and now the Bush Doctrine focus almost exclusively upon this critical region. It is thus understandable that the globalisation that is primarily being propagated by the United States and by predominantly American transnational corporations is viewed with some suspicion in the region, with its memories of the experiences of various European imperialisms to which Leon Carl Brown has alluded. Although the United States may be exercising 'hegemony of a new type' (Brzezinski 1998), it seems to many like old-fashioned imperialism.[5]

Middle Eastern Perceptions of Globalisation

Globalisation has been internalised in Arabic as 'awlaama', a newly coined word, but it is still more widely perceived as an external threat than as an opportunity to join the world economy. Addressing the United Nations in 1998, Abdul-Qader Ba-Jammal, who was Yemen's deputy prime minister and foreign minister, expressed these sentiments:

Many of us understand that globalization is the theoretical economic option of free trade and liberalism following the collapse of the socialist economies and the end of the cold war in the twilight of this century. Some of us understand that globalization is a new tool to control the division of labor in the world and to maintain the status quo of the poor and consumers without ideological or political slogans . . . We, the group of least developed countries, view globalization with terror, because isolation and marginalization will threaten our countries if we do not help one another . . . Globalization does not present any tangible picture of equality. What is even more dangerous is that we are talking about globalization as if it were a future, providential destiny and a single option. Such logic . . . makes it appear as if we were engaging in contracts of submission. (UN—ESCWA 2001: 52)

The IMF discipline exercised over various indebted MENA economies in the 1980s did not seem too different from other 'contracts of submission' enforced by the Great Powers with gunboats a century earlier (Henry 1996: 32, 135–40, 161–6, 212–16). Although this multilateral sort of intervention has not led to military occupation and protectorates or international mandates, it chastens and chastises regimes and induces responses that echo those of early generations to colonial rule. The Anglo-American occupation of Iraq may indeed make its neighbours 'view globalization with terror.'

A colonial dialectic of sorts is being reenacted, despite the nominal sovereignty of most of the principal actors on the receiving end of globalisation. The stimulus, like the colonial penetrations of nineteenth and early twentieth centuries, elicits a range of responses from the positive acceptance of putative globalisers to utter rejection on the part of some Islamists as well as Arab and local nationalists nostalgic for the 1960s and 1970s. These 'negations' recall those of the traditionalists reacting against nineteenth and early twentieth colonial European occupations of Arab lands. Wistful of an imagined golden age, many reject the western influences, symbolised today by MacDonald's and high-rise hotel chains, which are supposedly corrupting their societies. In some colonial situations the traditionalists, too, were swept away as new generations, more impregnated with western as well as 'traditional' world views, synthesised them in ways that could liberate their societies by playing on the con-tradictions of colonial occupation with western liberal values. It became possible to be both nationalist and pro-western, for adopting modern political styles and values rendered nationalism more effective, in turn offering better protection of the authentic aspects of tradition that were worth preserving. From Ataturk's Turkey to Bourguiba's Tunisia, nationalism went hand in hand with a cosmopolitan acceptance of the modern (European) world.

In much of the Arab world, however, independence came before the nationalists had time to reach any broad social consensus, and power fell into the hands of traditional notables, only to be seized after independence by military rulers who incorporated newly participant strata. And even where, as in Tunisia and Turkey, a colonial dialectic ran its course, subsequent generations questioned the synthesis. Over the past decade, with the end of the Cold War and the opportunities now lost of playing one side against the other, the MENA is again confronting the old problem of a potentially invasive western presence. Yet the targeted countries lack the domestic political space in which to negotiate compromises between the putative globalisers and the recalcitrant moralisers, whether Islamist or nationalist, within their respective communities. The minority of Islamists who would favour positive responses to the challenges of international markets tend to be excluded from politics because they threaten incumbent regimes. The principal resistance to reform comes from vested interests within these regimes. Diminishing oil revenues or strategic rents (Egypt, Israel, Morocco, Turkey) tend to concentrate teams of economic reformers on the need for change, but rising oil revenues or other rents then have the effect of relaxing their efforts. The result, to date, is that the MENA's economic performance, especially that of the Arab world and Iran, has been weaker, compared to most other regions of the world, on a wide range of indicators. The countries of the region still tend, with the exception of some of the wealthy petrostates, to hide behind high (but diminishing) tariff barriers and capital controls, and the foreign direct investment that they attract outside the petroleum sector is virtually nil compared to other regions.

Trade Policies

The record of the MENA countries is mixed with respect to their trade policies. Admission to the World Trade Organization usually requires a variety of internal reforms to insure a level playing field between trading partners. Joining the Mediterranean Partnership proposed in 1995 by the European Union requires a progressive lowering of tariffs on nonagricultural products until the year 2010, when virtually all protection is to be eliminated. Meanwhile, the dismantling by the Uruguay Round of the Multifiber Agreement's quotas threatens a number of local textile industries, and the EU has been helping to finance its southern partners' programmes to bring these and other local industries up to standard ('mise à niveau').

Most of the countries bordering on the southern Mediterranean tried to join the WTO and to benefit from the EU's Partnership Programme. Egypt, Israel, Morocco, Tunisia and the city states of Bahrain and Kuwait were among the first to become full members of the World Trade Organization, in 1995, and Tunisia and Morocco were also first to sign up for full partnerships with the European Union. Jordan, Oman, Qatar and the United Arab Emirates subsequently acceded to the WTO, and Jordan also entered into an association agreement with the European Union, as did Israel. Egypt, Lebanon and Algeria eventually signed agreements with the EU in 2001 and 2002, while the latter two were also in the final stages of negotiating membership with the World Trade Organization. All of these countries were trying with various reservations to liberalise their trade policies to take advantage of the new division of labour connoted by 'globalisation'.

Almost as many countries of the important countries in the region, however, were delaying the internal changes that new agreements might impose. Saudi Arabia's negotiations with the WTO, for instance, stalled when rising petroleum prices in 2000–03 relaxed any internal pressures for reform. Iraq and Syria were two Arab nationalist holdouts against the WTO, and Syria's negotiations with the EU were long and inconclusive. Libya had observer status at some meetings of the EU and Mediterranean Partners.

Most of Arab countries were pushing for a General Arab Free Trade Area (GAFTA) as a halfway house, to be implemented by 2008. Arguably countries could benefit from complementarities in certain industrial sectors and enhance their ability to trade outside the region, although intra-Arab trade constituted only 7.5 per cent of these countries' total trade in 2001. Meanwhile the Gulf Cooperation Council, established in 1981, took major strides to coordinate trade policies among its six members, Bahrain, Kuwait, Oman, Qatar, Saudi Arabia and the United Arab Emirates, and they were committed to a common currency by 2010.

Eliminating protective tariffs not only carried serious consequences for local industries. For some countries it had major fiscal repercussions because tariffs constituted an important proportion of the total tax revenues. The region was more dependent on tariff revenues than East Asia or Latin America or, for that matter, any comparable middle and lower middle-income countries. A well administered country like Tunisia could gradually adapt to the new state of affairs by introducing a value-added tax and applying it effectively. Lebanon, however, was less fortunate. Although Prime Minister Hariri reduced tariffs (slightly) in January 2001 to stimulate the economy, his hands were tied by the country's crushing debt, and the tariffs were a major source of revenue for servicing it. Virtually all of the major countries in the region except Turkey were depending on tariffs for over 10 per cent of their current revenues.

The Problem of Attracting Private Capital

In the 1960s and 1970s the international climate had been relatively favourable to developing countries. They were encouraged to industrialise and to expand their administrative infrastructures, even to emulate the welfare states of the advanced industrial countries. Official development assistance was relatively generous, even if the industrial countries outside Scandinavia never quite reached the 1 or 2 per cent of GDP advocated by the international development community. But then the international climate changed with the emergence of OPEC, the tightening of international oil markets, and the explosion of oil prices triggered by the October

(Ramadan, Yom Kippur) War of 1973. While the industrial countries continued to provide some development assistance, developing countries had to rely more on loans from international banks. These banks, flush with oil revenues that most major oil exporters could not invest at home, encouraged the other developing countries (and some major oil producers such as Algeria and Mexico) to borrow as much as they could possibly absorb. The banks profited enormously until 1982, when Mexico's problems initiated an international debt crisis, structural adjustment programmes, and much suffering in the third world. Meanwhile, Maggie Thatcher and Ronald Reagan led an international offensive against wasteful public sector spending. In the 1980s and 1990s foreign direct investment replaced official development assistance as the principal source of capital for financing third world development. The end of the Cold War in 1989 further encouraged the reliance on private capital.

The Middle East and North Africa, however, is one of the regions, along with South Asia and Sub-Saharan Africa, which has experienced the greatest difficulties in adapting to these new tendencies. A recent study of the United Nations' Economic and Social Commission for Western Asia (ESCWA) analysed the share of the Arab World in the world economy. While it includes 4.7 per cent of the world's population, it accounted for only 2 per cent of the world's GDP in 2001 and attracted a bare 0.8 per cent of the world's foreign direct investment (UNESCWA 2002: 1).

Figure 5.2 highlights the significance of foreign direct investment (FDI) as a source of capital for developing countries by comparing it with the various other types of capital flows since 1970. Despite the Asian financial crisis, FDI to developing countries has consistently exceeded $150 billion since the mid-1990s. Official development assistance, by contrast, reached a plateau of $59 billion in 1991 and has steadily diminished, even in current dollars without controlling for inflation. The MENA has not adapted effectively to global financial markets. While the region has received more than its per capita share of official development assistance and bank loans, it has not attracted private investment in quantities that are commensurate with its population.

Figure 5.3 displays MENA's share of these three principal sources of international finance, bank and trade financing, foreign direct investment and official development assistance, over the years 1970–2001. The percentages refer to MENA's share of the totals received by the developing countries of East Asia Europe and Central Asia, Latin America, the MENA, South Asia and Sub-Saharan Africa. These populations totaled just over 5 billion in 1999, so that MENA, including the Arab world and Iran, constituted about 5.7 per cent of it. Since 1970 this region has accumulated on average about 10.8 per cent of the banking and trade financing resources and 18.2 per cent of the official development assistance—substantially more than its aggregate population would predict. Figure 5.3 shows, however, that MENA's share of the declining pie of official development assistance has been diminishing. Its average share of FDI turns out to be negative because of large disinvestments, understated in Figure 5.2, in 1974 and 1980.

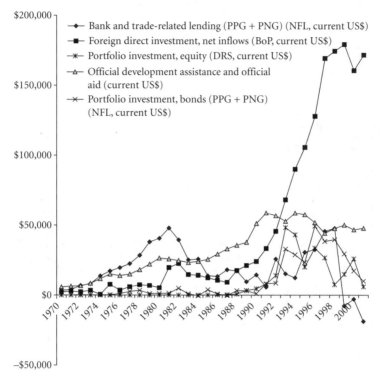

Fig. 5.2 Types of capital flows to LDCs 1970–2001 ($000)
Source: World Bank, World Development Indicators 2003.

At the turn of the century the region was still receiving more than its 'fair' (in terms of population) share of bank and trade credits and official assistance, but it was clearly failing to attract much foreign direct investment or portfolio investment. The one apparently 'bright spot', 43 per cent of the international bond market in 2001, amounted to little in absolute terms (because of the declining bond market charted in Figure 5.2) but did have interesting implications. Some of the MENA countries were able to raise funds on the international bond market, a cheaper source of funds than commercial banks. In 2001 the aggregate funds raised by the MENA region reached 5.7 per cent of the total pie available to developing countries, so that performance was commensurate with population. But the principal performers in the region were Israel, Morocco and Lebanon. Israel attracted tremendous amounts of foreign direct investment—and official development assistance as well, mainly in the form of US economic aid—and Morocco did almost as well in absolute but hardly in per capita terms. As for Lebanon, there was little foreign direct investment: the country was converting part of its unmanageable internal public debt into external, less expensive bonds. Egypt and Tunisia were also becoming active in the international bond market, thereby explaining the MENA's one apparent 'bright spot' in 2001.

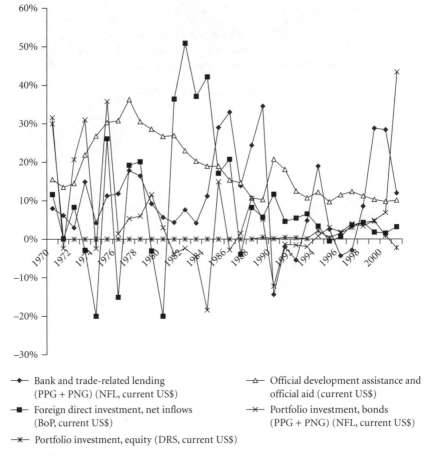

Fig. 5.3 MENA's share of captial flows to LDCs 1970–2001

Source: World Development Indicators 2003.

Part of the MENA's difficulties in attracting private capital may relate to purely economic considerations, such as the costs of skilled labour and the sizes of national markets. But the political regimes are also an obstacle. A major problem is flow of information that investors need. In the antiseptic language of economists, there are information 'asymmetries' between private and public actors: the latter may have better information than private sector owners or managers, although even this distinction between the 'public' and 'private' sectors is problematic, however, since public officials may be less informed than ostensibly private actors enjoying close personal relations with rulers.[6] Most economic as well as political information is kept out of any public domain, even of government officials. Under such conditions it may be difficult to attract private investment, whether national or foreign. With respect to foreign capital, the information needs vary, depending on the type of financial flow, whether 1) foreign direct investment, 2) bond issues, 3) portfolio investment in local stock markets, or 4) international bank and trade-related lending. FDI (outside the energy sector) and portfolio investment will be particularly demanding, as will many local private investors.

Hypotheses about Investors' Information Needs

Most investors care little about political structure, whether or not, for instance, a polity has competitive elections or a strong human rights record. Assuming, however, that laws are in place encouraging foreign investment and permitting the repatriation of profits, prospective investors—indigenous as well as foreign—will still need certain kinds of information.

Of the four sources discussed above, international bank and trade-related lending is least in need of public information. The international bankers have their own confidential sources, such as their borrowers, other banks, local government officials, in-house country risk analysts, teams of external consultants and expensive country risk publications. Commercial banks used to be the principal source of private capital flows to developing countries, and they carried the fewest potential ripple effects on the political structures of borrowing countries. Although they supported IMF and World Bank policies of economic adjustment crafted in the interests of the creditors in the 1980s, their direct impact upon host political structures was minimal. International bankers continue prudently to avoid any appearance of involvement in host country politics, and governments can rely on their discretion. But unfortunately for information-shy regimes, traditional commercial bank lending has given away to more open capital markets which require greater transparency if they are to function properly.

As Figure 5.2 indicated, commercial bank lending peaked in 1982, and since the eruption of the Mexican crisis the banks have been more concerned about being repaid than about injecting new cash into overly indebted economies. The MENA drastically reduced its overall indebtedness; in fact today only Lebanon, followed by Syria and Jordan, displays debt-to-GDP ratios comparable to those of the heavily indebted Latin Americans. And few of the important MENA countries rely on commercial bank credits any longer. Algeria leads the way in repaying its international debt. The debt servicing wipes out any new lending, so that since 1995, the cash flows to the region as a whole were negative every year except 1997, reflecting the general tendency of countries in the region. Like official development assistance, commercial bank lending has become a diminishing source of funds for most LDCs, whereas foreign direct investment, bond issues and cross-border portfolio equity became major sources in the 1990s.

Portfolio investments in stocks and bonds peaked respectively in 1993 and 1996 at about $50 million each for the entire group of less developed countries; in 1996, in fact, these portfolio investments accounted for almost one-third of the private sector capital that was replacing official development assistance and bank and trade financing. It is perhaps no accident that countries in the MENA region developed their national stock markets at this time—even the Palestinians developed their bourse with online trading capabilities in the occupied territories. The investment behaviours of private investors residing in industrialised countries were perhaps changing. In the United States individuals have moved their funds from banks to mutual funds, and managers of mutual and pension funds have sought to diversify their investments into emerging markets.

All three of these expanding streams of private capital—foreign direct investment and the two types of portfolio investment—require more publicly available information than the commercial banks or foreign aid donors. Portfolio investors and managers have become particularly demanding in the wake of the collapse of 'emerging markets' in Southeast Asia in 1997 and the broader collapse since 2000. Demands for public information and signals are potentially more troubling and politically destabilising for information-shy regimes than are the discrete private queries of international bankers or public donors.

While bondholders will be less demanding than shareholders or certain kinds of direct investors, their requirements may still significantly constrain a country's economic policies. Investors in bonds are principally concerned with the macro-economic stability of the country issuing or guaranteeing the bond. One sign of future long-term stability may be the independence of the country's central bank. Sylvia Maxfield argues, in fact, that one reason for the recent increase in the number of independent central banks is that politicians desire to signal investors that orthodox macro-economic policies will be sustained (1997: 35–7). Just how much central bank independence can be tolerated, however, is a question that deserves to be addressed in the MENA. Any real independence—and greater transparency of the country's commercial banking system—may expose sensitive political patronage networks, yet international managers of bond portfolios may insist on greater openness, especially in light of recent experiences with the Thai, Indonesian and other Asian banking systems.

Information-shy regimes will presumably face even greater challenges in attracting portfolio investment in local stock markets and certain kinds of foreign direct investment. In addition to macroeconomic stability, required as a protection against foreign exchange risk, portfolio investors in equities seek active, relatively liquid local stock markets, displaying a wide variety of traded companies. During the decade 1992–2001, stock markets were indeed being introduced—or reopened in countries such as Egypt—and were representing substantial amounts of capital as a percentage of GDP. Only East Asian markets seemed better endowed. In the MENA, however, the local stock markets seemed less active than those of any other region. As regards the turnover, or value of shares traded, as a percentage of the average market capitalisation, this was thin in the MENA except in Israel and, surprisingly, Saudi Arabia. And of the 2,020 companies listed on MENA exchanges in 2001, 1,109 were Egyptian, 647 were Israeli, 316 were Iranian, and 161 were Jordanian. Saudi Arabia and Morocco followed with 76 and 55 companies, respectively.

Only with difficulty can family firms in the MENA be persuaded to go public, much less to submit to the fuller disclosures required by international investors. Listings of public sector companies and banks pose other problems as well. Token privatisation may not be palatable to international investors, yet real privatisation transferring a public sector company to a private core management group may conflict with political patronage imperatives. Without foreign investors, moreover, local investors may also be wary. Under the new conditions of globalisation local investors have been observed to follow the lead of foreign portfolio managers (Maxfield 1997: 45).

The very distinction, indeed, between local and foreign investors may be more problematic in the MENA than in other regions of the developing world. In most of the region foreign direct investment outside the energy sector is inseparable from local private investment. Many of the 'foreign' investors are other Arabs who are in close touch culturally and politically with the recipient country. Other 'foreign' direct investment seems to come from local investors redeploying their foreign assets. Local rulers and their close associates, operating through dummy foreign companies, may also account for some of the private foreign direct investment. They of course take advantage of inside information about publicly financed projects, but other Arab investors have preferred to place their funds abroad in the absence of adequate information. Their information needs easily spillover from economic to political matters and hence may be more threatening to incumbent regimes than those of the foreign multinationals focused on the energy sector.

The local investors, in turn, tend to be wary of their respective regimes. A survey of local entrepreneurs sponsored by the World Bank in sixty-nine countries in 1997 included entrepreneurs from Morocco, Jordan and the West Bank and Gaza. A full half of them registered dissatisfaction with unpredictable changes in government policies, and 70 per cent were dissatisfied with the judiciary (World Bank 1997). Their major concerns were with possible effects to their businesses of political instability and an unreliable judiciary. Surprisingly, they were less concerned than entrepreneurs from other regions with unpredictable changes in laws and policies, insecurity of property, and corruption and they even rated their respective governments slightly more favorably on a 'credibility index' than the samples from Central and Eastern Europe, Latin America and the Caribbean, Sub-Saharan Africa and the Commonwealth of Independent States. Nevertheless, the survey's findings were universal: there is a major credibility gap between the entrepreneurs and regimes of developing countries. This finding may carry more negative implications for direct foreign investment in the MENA, however, than in parts of the world where foreign investors are less identified with indigenous entrepreneurs. Outside their relatively insulated energy sectors, the MENA countries may have greater difficulty attracting foreign direct investment because its investors are more discriminating and demanding of information than the foreigners who invest in other regions. As discussed elsewhere, even Egyptian investors close to the Sadat regime (and therefore privy to much inside information) invested relatively little of their fortunes in *infitah* companies and projects (Henry 1996: 232–4). The climate was so restrictive that outsiders had little

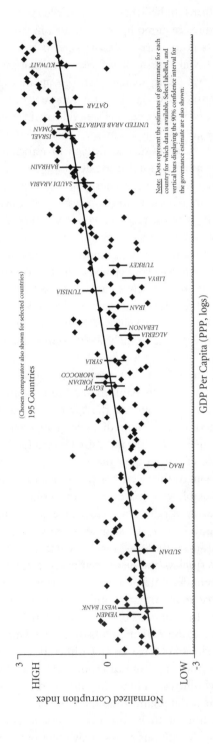

Fig. 5.4 Control of corruption—2002

Source: "Governance Matters III: Governance Indicators for 1996–2002" by Daniel Kaufmann, Aart Kraay and Massimo Mastruzzi, 2003.

http://www.worldbank.org/wbi/governance/pdf/2002kkzcharts_ppp.xls

incentive to invest whereas insiders had little need to, since political connections enabled them to use public capital instead of risking their personal fortunes on new projects. Much of the 'foreign' direct investment that flowed into the country was Egyptian capital seeking the protection accorded to foreign investors.

Apart from the energy sector, TNCs have tended to minimise their involvement in the region, yet they bring the bulk of FDI to the developing areas and promote much of its international trade. Foreign or local, investors need reliable information and they also require institutional credibility that has been spelled out into a battery of indicators by the World Bank. Readily available online, these data summarise impressions derived from polling local and international businesspeople. They may render foreign direct investment more problematic by drawing comparisons between potential investment opportunities inside and outside the region. The potential investor may readily compare countries with respect to government effectiveness, regulatory quality, rule of law, corruption, political stability and, possibly of less concern to the businessperson, voice and accountability.[7] Figure 5.4 offers one illustration, the Control of Corruption, comparing the different MENA countries and controlling for their level of economic development (per capita income). The reader (or potential investor) may easily generate others.

Most prospective investors, foreign or domestic, of course also need to borrow funds if they are not wealthy TNCs and cannot raise local equity. Consequently, domestic credit allocation will have to be efficient if investment and economic growth are to be sustained. Since the local stock markets remain weak, the primary source of finance capital will be the commercial banking system, yet maximising its efficiency may be incompatible with sustaining vital political patronage networks. Banks may have to be kept in politically safe hands to insure that lending follows political as well as economic criteria.

To summarise, the MENA risks falling behind other regions of the developing world in the race to attract foreign private capital. While part of the problem may be that its earlier advantages of greater oil rents, workers' remittances and foreign aid protected it too long from adjusting to the new era of globalisation, it is also a latecomer to the global information revolution. Part of the problem is hypothesised to be political: its information-shy regimes seem to find it more difficult than the Asians or Latin Americans to disclose the information or attain the credibility needed to attract private foreign investment or to promote local stock markets. Their likeliest 'foreign' investors are their own citizens with foreign assets or citizens of neighbouring countries whose information needs may be more demanding than those of corporate outsiders. Increasing the capital flows needed for sustained economic development may require painful political reform to break down barriers to the flow of information. Financial reform, in particular, touches on sensitive nerves because the state-owned banks prevailing in much of the region (Algeria, Egypt, Iran, Libya, Syria and Tunisia) protect patronage networks that prop up their respective regimes, and private sector oligopolies in most of the monarchies perform similar functions.

Increasing Transparency and Accountability

The most candid exposition of the Arab world's problems in adapting to the new world order of globalisation is the United Nations Development Programme's *Arab Human Development Report 2002*, drafted by Arab intellectuals. Trained in economics and other social science disciplines, they are part of the international establishment of Western educated consultants and technocrats that wants the region to jump on the bandwagon of reform. Yet of course they are only technocrats, without the political authority needed to cope with those who reject the reforms associated with globalisation.

The Report recognises that the Arab world is falling behind the rest of the world. Per capita GDP grew annually on average by only 0.5 per cent between 1975 and 1998—'in effect a situation of quasi-stagnation' (2002: 88). Until 1981 the region's per capita income appeared to be catching up with the world average, but it declined by 1998 to the equivalent, in real purchasing power parity, of only one-seventh that of the average inhabitant of OECD countries. 'Among Arab countries, only Egypt and to a lesser degree Jordan and Tunisia had a tendency toward convergence with OECD. All other countries, without exception, moved in the opposite direction' (2002: 89). The small indigenous populations of Kuwait, Qatar and the United Arab Emirates already enjoyed OECD per capita income levels but had not reached the OECD along other critical dimensions of human development. Average Arab growth rates look only a little better by slightly modifying the time span so as to limit the distorting effects of high or low oil prices.[8]

The Report singles out three 'deficits' in the Arab world that conventional economic growth indices overlook and that the UNDP's classic Human Development Index (HDI) also ignores. These are 1) the freedom deficit, 2) the women's empowerment deficit and 3) the deficit, at least relative to wealth, of human knowledge capabilities. Three of the Report's eight chapters focus on this third deficit and try to tackle the problem of harnessing the region's human potential to the tasks of economic growth and development. The Arab (mostly male) intellectuals writing this report pay less attention to gender problems, but they are not shy about discussing the 'freedom deficit' because they view civic and political freedom as intrinsic to human development.[9] There is no attempt to hide the essentially political obstructions to human development in the region. Instead of camouflaging 'governance' in Arabic translation as some antiseptic sort of management problem, the authors come out up front:

...Efforts to avoid the political aspects of governance when discussing the question sometimes reflect fear of expected or imagined consequences of dealing directly with the subject. However, restricting discussion of governance in this way does not serve the long-term interests of developing countries, many of which still face tremendous challenges in building good governance or in achieving the levels of human development that only good governance, including its political aspects, can ensure. (UNDP 2002: 106)

'Governance' or *al-hokm* is modeled on universal democratic principles. The Report calls for participation, the rule of law, transparency, responsiveness to the various interests of civil society, equity, accountability and wise leadership or 'strategic vision' (2002: 106). Most authoritarian rulers, as well as their Islamist oppositions, pay lip services to these principles, but the Report advocates policies that would, if actually implemented, amount to gradual regime change in many Arab countries. Many of the policies suggested to stimulate economic and educational development are explicitly conditioned on better governance. Constitutional democracy is viewed not only as an intrinsic good by the putative globalisers who drafted this Report; it is also an instrumental necessity if the region is to stop stagnating and begin to catch up with the rest of the world.

The observed deficit of 'human knowledge capabilities' further highlights the importance of good governance. The Arab world has consistently trailed the rest of the developing world in gross primary education enrollment ratios, despite out-spending it until 1985. Arab spending went more to secondary and university edu-cation, where it outperformed the average of developing countries (although not Asia or Latin America). Obviously, urban middle-class rulers and administrators were looking after their own interests, not those of poor country folk, especially not their daughters. Illiteracy rates very slightly improved between 1980 and 1995 but remained wretched compared to the average of developing countries. Over half the women living in the region remained illiterate in 1995 (2002: 52–3). As the Report discusses elsewhere concerning alleviating poverty, the best way to correct such major bias is to deepen democratic participation.

An urban class policy bias also helps to explain the 'mismatch' deplored in the Report between educational curricula and labour markets (p. 60). Parental and teacher pressures usually propel vocational schools into a dysfunctional academic status (Moore 1980: 62–83). The combination of inadequate vocational training and the declining quality of primary schools helps to explain why Arab unemployment is more severe than in other parts of the world. Too many aspiring but poorly trained youth, male and female, are graduating from secondary schools and universities to be constructively absorbed by the local economies, and labour productivity has actually declined (p. 87). Workers tend to produce less for equivalent wages than in most other regions of the developing world.

The Report's proposals to revitalise economic growth sound like the familiar list of reforms proposed by the World Bank in structural adjustment programmes. In order to create 'an enabling environment for the private sector', states must insure the rule of law, an efficient judiciary, etc., just as the World Bank (1997) has been insisting since 1997. Whether for encouraging more private sector activity or generating and using knowledge effectively, strong institutions are needed (2002: 96). Possibly more controversial is the proposal to build 'growth triangles' between countries endowed with abundant labour and those endowed with capital; from the given examples (p. 97) it is not clear whether the third technology leg of the triangle is to come from inside (as in Jordanian-Israeli industrial zones) or outside the region. Partnerships between local universities and research establishments and the private sector are encouraged but the Report also highlights the need for more foreign direct investment, virtually absent outside the petroleum sector, as a 'critical force for transfer and development of new technologies' (p. 95). To this end the Report stresses the importance of good governance alongside the basic basket of economic reforms advocated by the World Bank's structural adjustment programmes.

Thus, for the sake of programmes for poverty reduction and job creation, 'civil society institutions need to develop into a broad-based, inclusive, efficient and sustainable grass-roots vehicle for efficient sustainable collective social action that effectively combats the powerlessness that lies at the heart of poverty' (p. 102). Nothing less than a social revolution may be needed: 'The crux of the process of poor-enabling development is major institutional reform that radically raises the share of the poor in the power structure of society ... it is institutional reform rather than economic growth per se that constitutes the heart of poor-enabling development.' In practice, however, such reform might have profoundly destabilising effects. In Morocco, for instance, King Hassan once exclaimed that the poor couldn't eat pencils; his strategy was to preserve the clienteles of notables in the countryside designed to keep them under control (Hammoudi 1997: 25–43).

Using Freedom House data collected over the years by a conservative American foundation, the Report documents the region's freedom 'deficit': the fact that on their indicators most Arab countries are not free (although some of the monarchies attain 'partly free' status) and that the region's mean score is far lower than those of other regions, including Sub-Saharan Africa. Indeed, the freedom deficit has apparently widened rather than narrowed in recent years as the cases of Algeria, Egypt, Morocco and Tunisia show; only Kuwait registered significant progress.

On the indicators of voice and accountability, political instability, government effectiveness, regulatory burden and extent of graft and quality of institutions, the averages of Arab countries tended to be lower than the mean for the sample of 147 countries.[10]

The Issue of Regime Change

If, as the Report argues, the Arab world is to catch up with the rest of the developing world, it needs above all else to tackle the issues of governance that the region's freedom deficit reveals. In the Report, as in the UNDP's Programme on Governance in the Arab Region, the dimensions of good governance are laid out as objectively as possible as a reform agenda calling for: fair and free elections with 'a solid electoral system that permits the peaceful rotation of power' (p. 115), an elected, representative legislature that can exercise some real control over the executive power, a constitution that effectively defines the rules of the game separating executive, legislative and judicial powers, the rule of law and autonomy of judicial institutions, local self-government and reforms to invigorate civil society and guarantee a free press. The Report is not country specific but does urge some reforms that are widely applicable, such as the need to scrap systems that authorise associations in favour of just permitting them to declare themselves.[11]

Evidently, the Report is articulating a new requirement for the Arab world. Not only, as during the debt crisis of the 1980s, is the region being summoned to remove its trade barriers, to plug up its fiscal and current account deficits, to stabilise its macro-economic indicators and structurally to reform various sectors of the economy and privatise public enterprises. Now it is being called to move from economic policies that few people understand (apart from job losses in the public sector) to straightforward efforts of political reform. Backed by citations from the Prophet's son-in-law (appealing to both Sunnis and Shi'ites) the Report calls in essence for the transformation of Arab regimes into constitutional democracies like those of most OECD countries.

The UNDP is continuing its benevolent political intervention through its Programmme on Governance in the Arab Region (POGAR). Its web site (www. undp-pogar.org) fleshes out the detail of country practices that the *Arab Report on Human Development* could not cover. Mirroring the Report, UNDP-POGAR focuses on eight broad themes or substantive dimensions of governance that embody the normative principles of participation, the rule of law and transparency and account-ability. Although these standards all apply as yardsticks for evaluating political insti-tutions and practices, their relevance varies with the nature of the concrete theme. Thus, extending participation is the primary concern behind the themes of civil society, decentralisation, elections and the role of women in public life. Corresponding to the rule of law are the themes of the judiciary and constitutions, while legislatures and financial institutions are primary agencies of transparency and accountability.

As explained on its web site:

Democratic participation hinges on the free exchange of ideas and information. In this arena, the UNDP promotes freer expression through the creation of new laws and regu-lations, by strengthening media, and by developing knowledge through national Human Development Reports. In line with these priorities, POGAR aims to increase access to information about governance in the Arab world by encouraging public institutions to make information more widely available to the general public. POGAR contributes to this process through information on its website; by commissioning original research from think tanks, research centres and individuals; and by organizing conferences and workshops in which information is widely shared. (http://www.undp-pogar.org/activities/index.html)

POGAR's primary audiences are the government officials directly involved in the various UNDP programmes, but they may also include new generations of citizens with access to the Internet—these are growing despite the substantial digital divide between the Arab world and other regions documented by the Arab Human Development Report.

The governance practices of twenty Arab countries are documented online. Description is neutral, intended to be credible without raising unnecessary controversy because POGAR's partners include the governments in question. Behind the reform agenda lies the hope of liberal globalisers that publicity will gradually induce changes in the regimes by changing mentalities and concrete behaviours and practices. The strength of this approach is that it enjoys legitimacy in the eyes of the concerned parties. POGAR is quietly expanding the scope of globalisation, defined, it will be recalled, as the elimination of various state barriers, to include barriers of domestic government practices. In the spirit of the Enlightenment good ideas and practices are expected to drive out bad ones, and significant changes, such as Bahrain's or Qatar's new constitutions, are visible to all to be criticised or emulated by the neighbouring monarchies.

POGAR is one of a growing number of regional and international intermediaries conveying experiences and lessons in economic and political liberalisation from international institutions and from a variety of bilateral development programmes in the OECD countries as well as multilateral agencies. The distinctive contributions of POGAR are to synthesise these experiences for the Arab world and to offer channels for exchanges among Arab countries of their own reform efforts. Since it is a distinctively Arab regional agency, it also helps to legitimate international perspectives on governance and to mitigate what might otherwise be perceived as outside meddling by various donors, notably the European Union. The EU's partnership agreements with a number of Southern Mediterranean Arab states call on the partners to engage in political (governance) as well as economic reform. POGAR encourages reformers within the region to compare notes and generate their own demonstration effects.

Conclusion

The Anglo-American invasion and occupation of Iraq have further compromised the chances for gradual, incremental change in the region. The backsliding over the previous decade of the larger Arab countries already reflected a growing polarisation between the regimes and their political oppositions following the original American-led war against Iraq to liberate Kuwait. That war polarised regimes and Islamist oppositions not only in Saudi Arabia but also in Algeria, Egypt and Tunisia, the countries whose freedom scores diminished the most in ensuing years. The American 'War Against Terrorism' following the attacks of 11 September 2001, will inevitably lead to further polarisation. Incumbent regimes use the US example to legitimate their crackdowns on 'terrorists,' and the occupation of Iraq invites recruitment of more terrorists.

A clash of globalisations may intensify in ways that further diminish democratic prospects. Multilateral international and regional efforts to promote good governance gradually through exchanges of information have already in Iraq given way to more rapid regime change by Anglo-American military intervention and may result in increases in domestic violence against regimes viewed as their 'collaborators'. Globalisation is now associated with regime change in the region, whether gradually through multilateral efforts or by more extreme methods. Underlying the clash between these alternatives is the conflict between the unilateralist tendencies of the Bush Administration and the proponents, in the United States as well as in the international community, of the gentler liberal conception of globalisation. One may expect more or less transparency and accountability in the region, depending upon how this conflict over the nature of world order plays out.

Either way, the experience of globalisation in the Middle East has introduced a new dimension of regime change. Globalisation now entails democratisation as well as economic liberalisation. When the democracy does not happen with apparent spontaneity, pushed by internal forces and regional 'snowball effects' as in Latin America and Eastern Europe, it gets imposed in other ways, by the bayonet if necessary. Sovereignty is eliminated. The logic of eliminating national barriers to commerce threatens to eliminate the nations themselves. Globalisation in this sense, however, pushes against very stubborn forces of nationalism, and notably the Arab and local nationalisms of the MENA, including an Iraqi one, awakened over the past century. New colonial incursions cannot but build up new national resistances, notably in this strategically located region.

The Middle East, home to most of the oil that fueled the world's first truly global industry, may yet prove to be the battlefield that reverses the tendencies of most states to open themselves up to the benefits of commerce and investment associated with globalisation. The Anglo-American occupation of Iraq has weakened virtually all of the regimes in the region, except Israel's. Those resisting the coalition are isolated and economically weakened, saved only for the moment by higher oil prices. Potential allies are also ever more fragile, embarrassed by their ties with the United States and fearful of being perceived as imperialist lackeys. Minorities of liberal globalisers are necessarily weakened. A prolonged occupation of Iraq also risks further weakening of the United Nations family of multilateral institutions, including the UNDP, while increasing the likelihood of more transnational terrorist attacks. The logical responses of victim states may be to build defenses that impair the global coordination and diminish the transnational flows of factors of production. Globalisation, which is the effect of numerous sets of reforms expressing the political wills of states, might then again be called into question, as in 1914, but this time by a never-ending 'War on Terror'.

Further Reading

Brown, L. C., *International Politics and the Middle East: Old Rules, Dangerous Game* (Princeton, NJ: Princeton University Press, 1984). An excellent analysis of the complex colonial situations undergone by various Arab societies and the dilemmas of external powers intervening into the internal affairs of these countries.

CARNEGIE Endowment for International Peace, *Arab Reform Bulletin* (June, 2003–) *http://www.ceip.org/files/Publications/arb-archive.asp* (4 Feb. 2004). A monthly online publication with substantive timely articles about reforms in various Arab countries.

HENRY, C. M. and SPRINGBORG, R., *Globalization and the Politics of Development in the Middle East* (Cambridge: Cambridge University Press, 2001). Offers an analysis of the progress and impediments to reform in the Middle East and North Africa.

KHALIDI, R. *Resurrecting Empire*, (Boston: Beacon Press, 2004). Explicitly compares the American intervention in Iraq to European practices of imperialism in the region over the previous century.

LEENDERS, R. and SFAKIANAKIS, J., *Middle East and North Africa, Global Corruption Report 2003*, (Transparency International, London: Profile Books, 2003) , 203–14. An excellent snapshot of issues of transparency and corruption in the Arab region.

RICHARDS, A. and WATERBURY, J., *Political Economy of the Middle East*, 2nd edn. (Boulder, Colo.: Westview, 1996). Required background reading for any student of Middle Eastern economies, economic policies and political structures.

United Nations Development Programme and Arab Fund for Economic and Social Development, *Arab Human Development Report 2002*: Creating Opportunities for Future Generations, (New York: United Nations Publications, 2002): *http://www.undp.org/rbas/ahdr/english.html* (5 Oct. 2002). Path-breaking analysis of Arab intellectuals of the 'freedom deficit' and other hindrances to sustainable development in the region.

——. *Arab Human Development Report 2003*: Building a Knowledge Society, (New York: United Nations Publications, 2003). Following up on the earlier report, with a focus on the constraints, including political ones, on developing and disseminating applied knowledge and research.

World Economic Forum, *Arab Competitiveness Report 2002–2003* (New York: Oxford University Press, 2002). Presents a careful analysis of problems faced by the various Arab countries in competing for private investment and offers an assessment of the conditions, structures and policies that are integral to the region's competitiveness in the global economy. *http://www.weforum.org/site/homepublic.nsf/Content/Global + Competitiveness + Programme%5CRegional + Competitiveness + Reports%5CArab + World + Competitiveness + Report + 2002–2003* (4 Feb. 2004)

Notes

1. This chapter develops an earlier draft published in *Review of Middle East Economics and Finance* (Routledge Taylor and Francis Group), 1:1 (2003), 3–15.

2. I take the title from Hoffman (2002) but he has informed me that he most certainly did not select it for his *Foreign Affairs* article but 'wanted to emphasize, first, the difference and the overlap between interstate politics and the politics of the kind of world society globalization fosters and, secondly, the different directions in which economic, cultural and political globalizations are going' (Letter of 20 November 2002).

3. In his recent book Brzezinski (1998: 53) extends the Arc of Crisis into Central Asia and labels the entire region 'The Global Zone of Percolating Violence'. Oddly, the book deals at length with the new 'Eurasian Balkans' but has little to say about the Middle East, perhaps because Brzezinski considered it already to be under US hegemony.

4. In the end, once his first draft was leaked, Wolfowitz was obliged to water it down, because there were widespread criticisms that it had violated the principle of collective security in favour of unilateral action to preserve American hegemony. In the current Bush Administration, however, he and Vice President Cheney (who was Secretary of Defense in 1992) enjoy greater influence.

5. For a recent discussion of America's efforts to transcend geography, see Neil Smith, *American Empire: Roosevelt's Geographer and the Prelude to Globalization* (Berkeley: The University of California Press, 2003).

6. Leenders and Sfakianakis (2003: 203) observe, 'it is... often difficult to separate private sector venality from that in the public domain, given the intimate links between the family networks that hold power and the principal business interests in the region.'

7. The data are available at the World Bank online: *http://info.worldbank.org/governance/ kkz2002/mc_indicator.asp* For other political indicators see the Polity IV database online: *http://www.cidcm.umd.edu/inscr/polity/report. htm.* Concerning corruption, Transparency International also presents a somewhat different scale based on similarly derived polling data, the Perceptions of Corruption Index: *http://www.transparency.org/pressreleases_archive/ 2002/2002.08.28.cpi.en.html.*

8. Consider, for instance, average growth rates from 1972, before the first major oil price hikes, and 1998, a year when oil prices were bottoming out. Calculating the per capita growth rates from the World Bank's World Development Indicators 2001, Algeria doubles its average annual rate from 0.2 to 0.4 per cent if the base year is 1972 rather than 1975.

Egypt's is slightly reduced, to 4.9 per cent from 5.3 per cent. Morocco's and Tunisia's remain the same, respectively 2.0 and 2.9 per cent. Syria's is substantially increased, from 1.4 to 2.3 per cent, while Saudi Arabia's losses are reduced from an annual average negative growth rate of 1.3 per cent to 0.9 per cent. These data include all the major Arab countries with populations of 9 million or more; data was unavailable for Iraq.

9. Team leader, Nader Fergany, devised a special Alternative Index of Human Development (AIHD) that includes the HDI dimensions of life expectancy and educational attainment but replaces per capita wealth with 1) Freedom House averages of civic and political freedom, 2) a gender empowerment measure devised by the UNDP, 3) Internet hosts per capita and, 4) negatively scored, carbon dioxide emissions per capita. Ranked along the AIHD, the Arab countries all fall into medium and low categories.

10. The average of seventeen Arab countries was lower by about three-quarters of a standard deviation on voice and accountability, and only with respect to the rule of law was their average (barely) above the mean. AHDR, pp. 111–13, cites Kaufmann et al. (1999a and 1999b). Renamed and updated data produced by the World Bank is on at: *http://www. worldbank.org/wbi/governance/govdata2002/.*

11. Morocco and Bahrain receive special attention for exemplary political reforms (p. 108). Morocco brought opposition parties into a government of 'Consensual Alternation' in 1998 (albeit without releasing control over the strategic 'sovereignty' ministries of the interior, defense, foreign or religious affairs), and Bahrain's National Action Charter reiterated various individual liberties promised under its original Constitution, suspended in 1975. A new element in the revised Constitution of 2001, however, is an appointed upper house equal in number and thus able decisively to influence the elected lower house, much as Jordan's did with only half as many appointed notables until King Abdullah II dissolved parliament in 2001.

6

The Puzzle of Political Reform in the Middle East

Augustus Richard Norton

OVERVIEW

Authoritarian governments prevail in the Middle East and experiments in political reform have enjoyed only limited success. The persistence of autocratic rule in the region stems from several factors, including the dominant role of the state in the economy, a 'ruling bargain' whereby citizens are promised prosperity in return for restrictions on freedom, and the preference of external great powers for stability over democracy. In recent years, disillusionment has spread, often to the benefit of Islamist groups that promise an attractive moral alternative. In response, governments stifle peaceful dissent, lending further momentum to culturally entrenched Islamists. Since 11 September 2001, the United States and several European powers have declared their intention to foster reform and spread democracy in the Middle East. The reform project provokes deep suspicion among many people in the region, who see the United States, especially, as self-serving and biased in favour of Israel. Even so, dissatisfaction with government remains pervasive and, suspicions notwithstanding, debates about political reform and democracy are gathering momentum in the region.

Introduction

Most Middle Eastern states won their independence from European domination only in the latter half of the twentieth century. The new governments that emerged faced formidable challenges, particularly promoting prosperity and sustaining growth in late developing economies that were ill-equipped to compete in the world economic system. The chosen path centered on a large statist economy that, in term, swelled government employment and disadvantaged private enterprise.

Another challenge was to foster a collective sense of identity, the essence of citizenship. In general, personal freedom was sacrificed in the interest of state security, often with reference to the Arab–Israeli conflict, which has continued since 1948. If political space was dominated by the state and controlled by ubiquitous police apparatuses, this reflected a tacit compact between government and citizen. In short, in return for loyalty to the state the citizen would be offered a healthier, more prosperous life.

Clientelism and often its handmaiden, corruption, defined the relationship between ruled and ruler. Democracy was not much discussed. Democracy refers most basically to the ability of citizens to hold their governments accountable, and to change their political leaders at regular intervals. Instead, accountability to the public is generally weak in the region, and rulers are more likely to change as a result of actuarial realities than a withdrawal of public confidence. The unavoidable fact is that most of the region's governments are not simply undemocratic but anti-democratic.

The exceptions to the rule, namely Israel, Turkey and, less compellingly, Kuwait and Lebanon are reminders that democracy is not a condition, such as being left-handed, but an experiental process. With more than half a century of democratic experience, democracy is still strikingly incomplete in Israel and Turkey, where ethnic minorities (some non-European Jews and especially Arab citizens in Israel, and Kurds in Turkey) often find their freedoms curtailed and quite incomplete. In culturally diverse Lebanon one finds all the formal trappings of democracy but only a shallow respect for democratic principles among sectarian politicians or in nearby Syria, which often has the last word in Lebanese politics.

In the quarter century since a revolution toppled the monarchy and established the Islamic Republic in Iran, some institutions of democracy, such as competitive elections for parliament have gained legitimacy, but the levers of power remain in the hands of conservative clerics who evince little enthusiasm for loosening their grip on power. The Iranian case illustrates that even in the face of broad disenchantment a failed regime retains an impressive capacity to forestall change through coercion and repression.

In the remaining score of Middle East countries democracy has enjoyed only spotty success. Fledgling reform experiments in Kuwait, Bahrain, Qatar, Jordan and even Saudi Arabia are reminders that the process of becoming democratic—democratisation—is not irrelevant in the region but that process is not only gradual but also reversible.

While literacy rates in the Middle East may be unimpressive by western standards, the simple fact is that access to education has proliferated, including at the university level so that many peoples' expectations have become more complex. In an era of straitened resources, government's capacity to sustain the loyalty of citizens through patronage and subsidies is strained, if not overwhelmed. Yet, this does not necessarily create conducive conditions for democracy to emerge and may actually buttress the power of hardliners who see political liberalisation and democracy as a formula for their losing power.

Given that the exceptional cases of Israel and Turkey entail predominantly non-Arab societies, it is clear that the democracy deficit applies significantly to the Arab world. An appropriate first task is to weigh what is known about the correlates of democracy and to determine what patterns emerge in Arab states. In a pathbreaking study published by a United Nations agency, a group of respected Arab scholars examined political, social and economic conditions in the Arab world (UNDP 2002). This incisive and rich report attracted wide attention in government circles and in the press.

The authors identified thirty-one indicators to reflect the level of democracy and freedom. These indicators are summarised in three major clusters: government process, government capacity to implement and shape sound policy and the level of respect displayed by both citizen and state for social and economic institutions. When these clusters of indicators are co-related to measures of human development and then compared to the rest of the world, the findings show clearly that even wealthy Arab states provide fewer outlets for political expression, fair government and responsive government than states with comparable incomes and quality of life outside the region. Using a carefully designed composite measure, fewer than nine per cent of Arab citizens rank in the middle level of material well-being and freedom, and none are found in the highest level.

It has often been argued that as income and other measures of well-being increase, the chances for democracy grow. Across the region utter poverty (living on less than one US dollar per day) is relatively uncommon and afflicts less than five per cent of all Arabs. In the aggregate, per capita income in the Middle East is considerably higher than either East Asia, or Africa, yet both regions have shown much more democratisation than the Middle East. The Arab middle class varies widely in size but in many countries, such as Egypt, Saudi Arabia and Algeria, it is quite large. The presence of a large middle class is often instrumental for democracy because the middle class has the means and the incentives to protect its interests against government encroachment, as well as the ability to articulate political demands. However, since the government sector is often massive and employs a large percentage of the middle class, government employees are reluctant to slap the hand that feeds them. For instance, despite programmes to privatise state firms in Egypt, more than half of the non-agricultural labour force is still employed by government.

The corollary is that the large state sector stifles the development of market economies that might produce more challenges to the autocratic state, or even lend momentum to democratic demands.

Explaining the Democracy Deficit

The weak progress of democracy in the Middle East has fascinated many scholars. Some have a one-size-fits-all answer to explain the absence of democracy. So the late Elie Kedourie asserted that 'the idea of democracy is quite alien to the mind-set of Islam' (Kedourie 1992). This implies that only by changing the mind-set of the adherents of Islam is democracy likely to be embraced, and Kedourie held that to be improbable. Yet, it is apparent that Muslims do practice democracy in a variety of settings, including India, Indonesia, Holland, Lebanon, the United Kingdom and the United States. To discover whether Muslims embrace democracy one may learn less by examining non-democratic settings than by democratic contexts. The idea of democracy did not originate in the Islamic world, yet the notion that Muslims are unwilling to embrace democracy for deeply seated cultural reasons simply does not stand up, whether the focus is on Muslims in general, or Arab Muslims in particular. Given the opportunity to play by democratic rules, Muslims have been quite adept at forming political parties, interest groups and building effective coalitions. There is no question that some Muslims are hostile to democracy in principle because they argue that law is not made by man and woman but by God. Nonetheless, many pious Muslims do embrace democracy as wholly consistent with their religion. We need to look at factors other than religion to grapple with the weakness of democracy in the Middle East.

Public opinion

Viewed from the West, political attitudes in the Middle East are often hidden from western view not just by barriers of language and distance but by metaphors that betray stereotypes rather than reveal reality. An example is the use of 'the street' to refer to opinion in Muslim countries, especially in Arab countries. The term is used by Arab journalists and others, often in a sense that corresponds with a Lebanese proverb, 'ra'i al-baqir ahsan min siyasa al-bashar [the opinion of a cow is better than the politics of the people].' Certainly in western usage the term 'the street' implies a formless mass of people swayed by the sentiments of the moment and manipulated by autocrats, a modern parallel to 'the mob' in revolutionary France. The street implies that there are few nuances of opinion, no need to stratify points of view to discern class, gender, age, regional or occupational distinctions. 'The street thinks...' intone sage-sounding commentators, as though talking about tidal movements (Norton 2002).

While public opinion polling is a relatively new phenomenon in most Middle Eastern settings, a number of leading polling firms (e.g., Gallup and Zogby Associates) have turned their attention to the region and the broader Muslim world.[1] In addition, a cadre of regionally-based public opinion specialists has produced high quality scientific surveys of opinion (e.g., Khalil Shikaki, the Palestinian scholar).

The picture that emerges from these opinion studies are highly differentiated views. For instance, when questioned about US policy in Iraq, or in the Arab-Israeli conflict in 2002 and 2003, views are overwhelmingly negative with approval ratings of less than five per cent. In contrast, US democracy and institutions evoke robust approval ratings. Of course, the opinions vary by age and education with younger people (18–35 years) more likely than older respondents to offer a favourable view (Zogby 2002).

While there is no unified view about remedies, there is widespread unhappiness with government in the Middle East. What conclusion are we to draw from the fact that the ruling party in Turkey, then led by Prime Minister Bulent Ecevit, garnered less than two per cent of the popular vote in the 2002 parliamentary election? Complaints of corruption, incompetence and general unresponsiveness dot common discourse, not to mention humour. None of this is direct evidence that the people of the region wish to be democrats or imagine transforming their own political systems into democracies. The evidence does suggest that many people wish they were governed better than they are in fact.

> Egyptians are famous for their political humor, and this joke offers a sample: President Husni Mubarak's son 'Alaa is widely reputed to be quite corrupt and he often enriches himself by becoming a 'partner' of legitimate businessmen. One day he decides to stop in a Mercedes automobile showroom in Muhandiseen, a middle class section of Cairo. As soon as the owner sees him entering the showroom, he despairs that his profits will disappear if 'Alaa becomes a business partner. The dealer effusively greets the powerful young man who is eyeing a shiny new Mercedes coupe. The nervous businessman decides on a strategy: he will give the man a shiny new Mercedes and send him on his way. He walks up to 'Alaa, hands him the keys and says 'Your Excellency, it is yours'. 'Alaa says, 'no, my father taught me to pay for things, not to take them.' The dealer replies, 'in that case, pay me ten pounds, and it is yours.' At which point 'Alaa peels off a twenty pound note (worth about four US dollars at the time). 'I will get you change.' 'No need,' the president's son answers, 'I will take two.'

The role of outside powers

While western diplomats and political leaders paid lip service during the 1990s to encouraging democracy in the Middle East, there was little real pressure on the region's governments to permit people an expanded voice in politics. Major powers, not least the United States, preferred stability over the uncertainty of democratisation. Those who wielded power in Cairo, Tunis and Riyadh and other Arab capitals grew accustomed to empty western rhetoric about democratisation. In the United States, President Bill Clinton spoke melodiously in the 1990s about the promotion of democracy around the globe, while his administration's leading Middle East diplomat, Martin Indyk, simultaneously disparaged the notion of democracy for Arab states as destabilising and threatening to the 'peace process' and to Israel. Indyk's perspective underlined the cold fact that he and many of his colleagues in government were perfectly happy to cling to autocratic rulers, rather than gamble on the uncertainties of more open political systems (Indyk 2002). Put another way, Arab governments held more accountable to their citizens would be compelled by public opinion to insist that the US couple its concern for Israel's security with a more serious commitment to meeting the aspirations of Palestinian Arabs living under occupation.

Officials were able to fragment or suppress those groups that were calling most strenuously for reform with few criticisms from western capitals. The Islamist political movements of various stripes, the best organised opposition forces, posed a direct challenge to the monopoly on power held by the ruling élites. Where parliamentary elections were held, the Islamists' participation was carefully circumscribed (as in Egypt) if not outlawed completely (as in Tunisia). When Islamists were allowed to fully participate in elections in Algeria they proved to be a popular alternative to the discredited secular ruling party.

Thus, the contemplation of democracy in the Arab world prompted major outside powers and local dictators to see eye-to-eye in terms of the virtue of continuing the status quo and sustaining stability, which has been the obsessive focus of western and, in particular, US officials.

Western, and particularly US perspectives on political reform were changed dramatically by the attacks of 11 September 2001. The carnage inspired a rethinking of assumptions. While stability was long the 'drug of choice' in Middle East policy-making, officials now argued that stagnant political systems and stifled hopes were a formula for further disasters. Former US Secretary of State, Madeleine K. Albright revealed in 2003 that she regretted not pushing harder for reform and she admitted that Middle East democracy was not a priority during the eight years of the Clinton presidency. 'We did nudge at times, supporting Kuwaiti leaders in their initiative to give women the vote and encouraging the creation of representative bodies in Bahrain and Jordan. But we did not make it a priority. Arab public opinion, after all, can be rather scary' (Albright 2003).

At the dawn of the twenty-first century, powerful external powers, especially the United States, embraced secular democracy as a panacea for the region's ills. Top officials referred frequently to the 'freedom deficit' in the Middle East, and concluded that economic failure and political oppression fed despair and conditioned people to succumb to ideologies of hatred and violence. President George W. Bush declared in February 2003 that 'The world has a clear interest in the spread of democratic values, because stable and free nations do not breed ideologies of murder.'

There is considerable evidence to support the proposition that mature democracies do not invade other mature democracies or promote murderous chaos. This is somewhat irrelevant to the Middle East, where democracy is often inchoate at best. In fact, democratising states are not necessarily stable and are actually more prone to instability than authoritarian systems. Thus, while there are other good reasons to wish for more freedom for Middle Easterners, the project of democratisation may not produce the democratic peace presumed by Bush and other US officials, at least not in the foreseeable future.

Iraq as a model?

When the United States and Britain invaded Iraq in 2003, it was widely asserted by officials and proponents of toppling Saddam Hussein from power that Iraq would be transformed from a republic of fear into a republic of freedom. Iraq would lead the way as a beacon of democracy for the region. Speaking before the US Congress in July 2003, Prime Minister Tony Blair declared: 'We promised Iraq democratic government. We will deliver it.'

In November 2003, President Bush declared a sea change in policy that would see America exchange its obsession with stability for the promotion of democracy and argued: 'Sixty years of Western nations excusing and accommodating the lack of freedom in the Middle East did nothing to make us safe—because in the long run, stability cannot be purchased at the expense of liberty. As long as the Middle East remains a place where freedom does not flourish, it will remain a place of stagnation, resentment, and violence ready for export.' Given the broad disdain for US policies in the Middle East, especially Bush's enthusiastic support for Israel, even when it acts in morally obnoxious ways against Palestinian civilians under occupation, such pronouncements often evoke incredulity.

Like Blair, Bush promoted Iraq as a poster child for democracy, especially after the predicted massive stockpiles of weapons of mass destruction that were supposed to be uncovered by the March 2003 invasion proved evanescent. Ironically, one of the most influential Iraqi advocates of this transformation from fear to freedom was the dissident Iraqi intellectual Kanaan Makiya who argued persuasively in 1989 that the regime of Saddam Hussein had obliterated civil society, the middle space between citizen and state, leaving Iraqis exposed to the naked power of the state and able to find security only in the basic institutions of family and tribe and sometimes not even there (Makiya [writing as Samir al-Khalil] 1989). If a democracy is to be durable, then an essential ingredient is a vibrant civil society, which certainly requires much more time than the few months anticipated initially by the US architects of the invasion.

America and Britain's perking interest in democracy may prompt ruling autocrats to clean up their acts a bit but only provided that Iraq does not go badly awry. Neither the US nor Britain anticipated the difficulties that they would face in consolidating their occupation of Iraq following the toppling of Saddam Hussein's regime. Some ill-considered decisions, such as the much-regretted edict to dismantle the Iraqi army shortly following the capture of Baghdad, only exacerbated the problems. The deadly resistance to the allied occupation, the anger of many Iraqis at America's often club-footed response to violence, and a series of bombings and assassinations against international and Iraqi institutions, mock the project of democratising Iraq.

The political economy of the state[2]

In Iraq, as elsewhere in the Middle East, the public sector is massive and any thoughtful effort to promote political reform must address the state's overarching economic role. The Middle Eastern state extends well beyond the seraglios of the rulers. Outside of agriculture, the state is the leading employer. Thus, many citizens have a stake in the state, and their interests do not lie in destroying it but improving its performance. Government dominates the formal economy, in some instances through a phalanx of public sector companies, in others through the flow of oil earnings and other 'rents' directly into the state coffers. As a result, government expenditures in the Middle East often make up a larger share of the GNP than in other countries of comparable income level outside of the region. In some cases, the government spending amounts to nearly half of the GNP (e.g., Egypt), compared to less than 25 per cent in middle-income countries generally (al-Sayyid 1991).

While the state's grip on the economy is important, considerable economic activity and resources lie outside of the state's control. A significant amount of largely undocumented economic activity occurs in the realm of the informal sector, which encompasses an array of craftspeople, doctors, lawyers, petty traders in licit and illicit goods, altier operators, piece workers and many others whose income is undocumented by the state. In post-revolutionary Iran, the informal economy has mushroomed dramatically and is pointedly visible in the urban areas in a variety of crucial money lending institutions. In Egypt, the informal economy is commonly estimated to be comparable in size to the formal economy. In effect, the steady growth of the informal sector has been a natural byproduct of failures in the government-dominated formal sector. The informal economy is an important site for undermining and quietly contesting the state's authority (Singerman 1995).

Rentierism

Yet, the prevalence of rentier states in the Middle East means that governments are highly resistant to change. Unlike states that depend on taxation extracted directly from citizens, rentier states distribute rents rather than extract taxes. Rents are direct payments to government that may derive from natural resources, especially oil, as well as other significant transfers such as foreign aid. (For instance, Egypt receives $2 billion in annual assistance from the United States that reduces the state's dependence on conventional taxation.) Some of the smaller states in the region, such as Qatar or the United Arab Emirates receive almost all of their income from oil or natural gas sales, rendering the government much more removed from public pressure than governments that depend upon taxation.

The emergence of the rentier state in the Middle East has had a detrimental effect on both economic development and political liberalisation. This has in turn discouraged the emergence of an independent bourgeoisie that can engage the state in economic give and take or contest the state in delineation of rights, responsibilities and obligations. The state has in effect attempted to satisfy the population at large through provision of a host of services and economic activities paid through rent income. As long as rents from the outside world are available, the state will respond only to those concerns of the population that it finds necessary for maintaining its power and position. Moreover, the rentier state's often extensive economic programmes tend to co-opt the bourgeoisie and reward it economically in projects conceived and funded by the state. Hence, the bourgeoisie's fortunes come to centre on the state and its defined economic goals.

The rentier state tends to become increasingly autonomous from society. The state can use the income from rent to enlist compliance and to pursue goals not necessarily in the best interests of society. Since most of the state's revenues are not extracted from the population, the corollary sense of obligation and responsiveness to society does not necessarily develop. So long as the rent continues to flow, rentier states have no incentive to liberalise their political systems. As Luciani indicates in his chapter and elsewhere, the oil rent becomes 'a factor perpetuating authoritarian government' (Luciani 1994).

A state facing fiscal crisis and forced to resort to increased taxation will generate demands from within the society for accountability and democratic institutions. Programmes of political reform in Jordan and Morocco bear out this argument, in that each state sought through political reform to salve the pains of extensive economic belt-tightening and tax increases.

Does economic reform induce political reform?

Major international financial institutions, such as the World Bank and the International Monetary fund have promoted the dogma that the path to democracy begins with economic liberalisation. This may be true over the long term, but the short term consequences of economic liberalisation are often reduced freedom. The case of Syria illustrates that economic crisis followed by a relatively steady economic liberalisation does not lead to political reform. Similar to some other authoritarian states, Syria has controlled the bargaining process in its economic liberalisation programme by confining it to a privileged few (Heydemann 1993).

Following the death in 2000 of Hafiz al-Asad, who ruled Syria for twenty-seven years, there was much hope that his son and successor Dr. Bashar al-Asad would shepherd Syria toward more freedom. Whatever Bashar's intentions, he promptly revealed his dependence on the authoritarian structure of power that his wiley father had mastered. Although there was a flush of excitement in 2000, opposition voices were soon stifled by the state. It is now widely presumed in Syria that even the gingerly pace of reform (including the release of a fraction of the 3,000 political prisoners) would be in jeopardy were it not for the carrot of a trade pact with the European Union. The pact may come into force in 2004.

Divergent paths in rentier states: Iran and Turkey

The examples of Iran and Turkey also shed some light on how rentierism influences the prospects for political reform. In Iran, rentierism came to define the state in the 1970s. Its systematic growth was conclusively evident after the oil boom that followed the 1973 Arab–Israeli war. Supremely confident of its economic and political positions in domestic, regional and international arenas, the state's economic policies resulted in two simultaneous developments. It created a heavily dependent commercial and industrial modern bourgeoisie that benefited enormously from the state policies but remained subservient to it. The private sector's influence 'was limited to implementation. Being totally dependent on the state, Iran's rentiér bourgeoisie had neither the incentive nor the means to "capture the state"' (Shambayati 1994).

Growth of rentierism also made the state essentially oblivious to the concerns and priorities of civil society. The pre-revolutionary Iranian state decided what was good for society and acted accordingly. When the state was eventually challenged during the revolutionary years, it was the traditional bourgeoisie from the bazaar, which had preserved some of its autonomy from the state that took the lead and in reality bankrolled the revolution. Using the well-established bazaar–mosque alliance networks, the opposition legitimised its attack on the Pahlavi state utilising powerful Islamic ideology. The sharp lines of cleavage were defined in cultural and moral terms, much more so than economic ones, in order to mobilise support and attack the state where it was most obviously vulnerable (Shambayati 1994; Ashraf 1988; Ashraf 1990). The bazaar provided the funds to the clerics' organisational structure and networks of mobilisation. The expression of opposition was an example of pragmatic use of Islam to gain advantages in the political arena. The Iranian rentier state was confronted with a major political challenge that was expressed in moral and cultural terms that enjoyed deep resonance in the society at large. The state, which was alienated from significant segments of civil society, was incapable of sustaining itself. Political liberalisation, granted under intense revolutionary pressures, came too late in the game to help preserve the state.

The Turkish case offers a sharply different model. Although certain features of rentierism, remittances from workers abroad, are also present in Turkey, the state's income is based primarily on domestic sources, not external rent. Hence rentierism has not dominated the Turkish economy. To increase revenues in the 1970s, the state had to increase taxation and domestic production. A number of policies, including import substitution industrialisation, were adopted to increase domestic production and reduce external dependence. Although these attempts did not help Turkey's negative trade balance and foreign exchange crisis, they did prompt the state to engage in serious bargaining with the business community through chambers of commerce and industry. The ensuing cleavages within the private sector led to the creation of several organisations devoted to management of commerce and industry. It is instructive that an Islamist group, the National Salvation Party, was established to protect the interests of petite bourgeoisie against some of the more prominent organisations that were tied to the interests of larger industrial and commercial capitalists. Economic issues rather than religious ones defined much of the political agenda of this Islamist party as well as the industrialists in their interactions with the Turkish state. Organised in a set of autonomous organisations, the private sector was a serious force in the society at large and in its relationship with the state. The private sector's concerns and demands could not be ignored by the state (Shambayati 1994).

The end result of the private sector's interactions with the state through a set of autonomous and semi-autonomous economic and political organisations was the growing pressure for political liberalisation. In short, in the absence of fully developed rentierism, increasing domestic taxation and extraction, foreign exchange crisis and the willingness to engage opposition from within the society in an inclusionary way combined to increase prospects for democracy in Turkey. This pattern stands in sharp contrast to the Iranian case in the pre-revolutionary decade where rentiérism and exclusionary politics were dominant.

The pressure mounts

Especially in the 1980s and 1990s, as the manifest failures of state dominated models of economic development left other governments unable to meet the burgeoning demands of fast growing populations, space for political contestation opened a bit. In effect, repression lightened as a means of accommodating dissent and reducing government's culpability for failure. The population pressures are immense, as reflected in the aggregate figures on youths fourteen years or younger who account for nearly 40 per cent of the Middle Eastern population according to 2002 data, and well over 50 per cent in some cases, such as Syria and Palestine. It is easy to visualise the serious challenges the youth bulge poses for government, not least in terms of schooling and job creation. While per capita measures of gross domestic product increased per annum by over three per cent over the past quarter century, population growth rates of approximately three per cent wiped out any prospect of benefit from the growth.

In the swelling working class neighbourhoods of the region's largest cities, rural to urban migration fueled massive urban sprawl. To begin to grasp the sheer magnitude of the phenomenon one needs only to consider that some cities, such as Riyadh in Saudi Arabia, were growing so fast that populations doubled in as little as seven years, while already massive cities, such as venerable Cairo were adding millions of new residents each decade.

Where political space opened, individuals began to organise giving new life to long-suppressed associational life. The result was a rapid expansion of civil society, the mélange of associations, clubs, syndicates, guilds and other groups that enjoy a measure of autonomy from the state's control and ideally serve as a buffer between the citizen and the raw power of the state (Norton 1995). By the late 1980s, more than

70,000 such groups were counted in the Arab world (Ibrahim 1995). While the components of civil society that attracted the most international attention were oriented to the protection of rights, such as the Egyptian Organisation of Human Rights, or the Palestinian al-Haqq, the vast majority was not overtly political and focused on aiding the indigent and the ill, or providing religious or educational resources. In cities like Cairo, Istanbul and Algiers, intricate networks defined by kinship, locality and reciprocity intersect with elements in civil society, the informal economy, opposition political movements and government functionaries to define a complex setting for politics (White 2002; Singerman 1995).

Equally, if not more important, large informal and undocumented sectors of the economy grew as previously noted. Across the region vast numbers of labour migrants were attracted to the employment opportunities in the oil economies of the Gulf. These workers, as they returned home to Syria, Egypt, Lebanon, Jordan and Yemen, among other countries, bringing hoards of hard currency that would be used not only to improve their families' standard of living and to start businesses, but to also fund opposition groups, especially Islamist movements.

Muslims and the Question of Political Reform

There are 1.2 billion Muslims in the world, including 350 million in the Middle East, and more than 200 million in the Arab world alone. While it would be convenient if a preponderance of Muslims embraced western secular ideals, not to mention western-style democracy, the dominant oppositional forces in the broader Muslim world—not least in the Arab world—emphatically reject secularism as contradictory to Islam and are deeply skeptical of democracy on normative grounds. If political reform is to take root in the region, it will necessitate more than a relative handful of pro-western liberals to cultivate the ideas. In a region in which religion is an important source of personal identity, any opening of a political system brings with it a debate about the proper role of religion in society and the relationship of religion to the state.

There are many variants of democracy, but a core component is the conduct of reasonably fair competitive elections. In many of the countries of the region open elections would either bring Islamist parties to power or, at a minimum, provide them a substantial voice in politics. This prospect leads to unease in western circles, and usually evinces a go-slow approach even when coupled with a commitment to accept the prospect of Islamists politicians playing a prominent role in democratising regimes. Richard Haass, formerly a prominent Bush official and now the President of the Council on Foreign Relations, notes that 'In promoting democracy, the United States is well aware that a sudden move toward open elections in Muslim-majority countries could bring parties with an Islamic character greater power' (Haass 2003).

The sections that follow offer several case studies of Islamist parties seeking, with varying success, a place in the political system.

Algeria

In the face of horrible unemployment, discontent and economic failure, Algeria attempted democratisation in the late 1980s and early 1990s. The ruling National Liberation Front (FLN) had monopolised power for three decades, ever since Algeria won its hard fought independence from France in 1962. The FLN was soundly trounced by the Islamic Salvation Front (FIS) in Algeria's first free elections, including municipal and then parliamentary elections. The Algerian army intervened in January 1992 to prevent the FIS from realising its victory and civil war ensued. It is impossible to know whether the FIS might have ruled competently or incompetently and whether it would have been able to impose its religious values on a divided society split between secularism and religious conservatism.

More than 100,000 people have died and Algeria has become a cautionary tale invoked routinely by Middle East dictators, secularly inclined intellectuals and western officials alike. The failure of the Algerian reform experiment certainly illustrated the likely fate of ruling parties when exposed to reasonably free elections.

Algerian secularists who enthusiastically supported the coup in 1992 now often concede that it would have been far better to permit the FIS experiment to go forward, especially since the option of intervention on the Turkish model would have continued to be an option for the Algerian generals.

Less noticed is that the debacle in Algeria also prompted a lot of soul-searching amongst Islamist thinkers concerning whether and how they should accommodate themselves to the prevailing autocratic regimes (as in Egyptian example that follows). Some leading thinkers, such as the late Lebanese cleric, Muhammad Mahdi Shams al-Din argued that FIS erred in seeking power and did not take into account the strong secular impulse in Algerian society. Others urged a path of peaceful political accommodation and playing within the rules of the existing game.

Egypt: Hizb al-Wasat

What happens when Islamists go against the grain, and declare their commitment to democracy and their toleration, if not endorsement for the separation of religion and politics? One such case is the Party of the Center (or Hizb al-Wasat), a remarkable attempt by a group of moderately-oriented Islamists, to play by democratic rules in Egypt in the 1990s. The case of Hizb al-Wasat illuminates the impediments that are routinely placed in the path of non-violent political forces intent on playing by the rules-of-the-game in Egypt, and elsewhere. The initiative was the product not of western designed projects of reform; to the contrary, it grew from debates among younger members of the Ikhwan, many of whom were actively involved in public and professional life, especially in the syndicates of doctors, engineers and other professions (Baker 2004).

The case of the Hizb al-Wasat is interesting for a number of reasons, including the fact that the thwarted organisation embraces precisely political participation and toleration while it rejects a privileged interpretation of religion. The attempt by the

Hizb al-Wasat to gain legal status as a political party was not only opposed staunchly by the Egyptian government, but the official suppression of the fledgling party was emphatically endorsed by Egypt's venerable Islamist organisation, the *Ikhwan al-Muslimun* (the Muslim Brethren). The Ikhwan's own efforts to lawfully participate in politics have been frequently sabotaged over the past two decades by the government. Hizb al-Wasat is a case of a new political generation attempting to play by new rules. The motives of the Ikhwan in joining in the suppression of the party reveal the spectacle of a new generation being held at bay by an old guard that only retires in the grave.

For its part, the government believed that the party initiative was a scheme by the Ikhwan to find a side door into legitimate party status. Three founding members along with nine others were then arrested for attempting to reorganise the Ikhwan and for plotting against the government (they were released three months later without being charged).

Among leading independent thinkers, the Ikhwan's riposte to al-Wasat was described as heavy-handed and unfortunate. For instance, Shaikh Yusif al-Qaradawi, a widely viewed Egyptian cleric often featured on al-Jazeerah and other satellite stations, argued that al-Wasat was a way to break the isolation that the government imposes on the Islamic movement. 'I fear that the Islamic movement constrains the liberal thinkers among its children and closes windows of renewal (*tajdid*), interpretation (*ijtihad*), and stands on one side of ideas and thought while not accepting the other point of view or those holding different opinions about objectives or the means to accomplish them.'

Following its first failure, the aspiring party was reorganised but it failed to win registration and it lost again on appeal in June 1999. Two years earlier, the party filed an application with the Ministry of Culture to start a newspaper, *al-Mustaqbal* (the Future), but the application simply disappeared into the bowels of the ministry. In 2000, seemingly as a consolation prize, the organisers of the failed party were permitted to constitute an NGO for the discussion of contemporary issues. Thus, the government succeeded in thwarting the organisation of a credible opposition party that embraced precisely the 'rules of the game' that the regime claims to stand for but actually observes only in the breech. One is left to wonder whether a well placed nudge in 1996 might have eased the path for al-Wasat, but the focus in western capitals at that time, and certainly in Washington, embraced static stability not reform. Were a new Hizb al-Wasat to emerge would the United States deploy her diplomats to seek is legalisation or would the US be dissuaded by the fact that the party would be have an 'Islamic character'?

One wonders whether the embrace of democracy extends to self-consciously Islamic groups such as al-Wasat. The emergence of al-Wasat does not mark a new azimuth as much as a new context and a new era in Islamist politics. In this sense, it is an instructive sample of modern political parties that may appear with increasing regularity throughout the Muslim world. Important policy statements by Bush and others seem to envisage a secular model of political parties that might not only exclude the Ikhwan, but even parties like al-Wasat emphasising the *shari'ah* a lection of principles. The al-Wasat example illustrates that 'parties with an Islamic character' may well invoke creative political ideas and pragmatic principles.

Lebanon: Hizballah

The Lebanese political system is especially intricate because it is designed to accommodate nineteen recognised confessional or sectarian groups, and especially to distribute political office between the leading sects, the Maronite Catholics, the Greek Orthodox, the Sunni Muslims and Shi'i Muslims and the Druze Muslims. In this sense the system includes clear structural constraints that prevent any single sect from seizing control of the system, even if a sect could speak with a single voice, which is impossible in practice. Beginning with independence in 1943, the power office of president was allocated to the Maronites, prime minister to the Sunnis and speaker of the parliament to the Shi'i Muslims.

The civil war that engulfed Lebanon from 1975 to 1989 stemmed in considerable measure from Lebanon becoming a regional battleground, not simply between Israelis and Palestinians, but between rival ideological forces in the Middle East. Equally important, the collapse into civil war reflected the lack of capacity for new political voices, not least the Shi'i Muslim community, which was feeling the impact of modernisation on many levels. Indeed, many newly politicised young Shi'i Muslims joined Palestinian guerrilla groups, sometimes motivated by ideological affinities but often simply by the prospect of a job. Even before the civil war, protest movements and opposition parties such as the Communists attracted significant numbers of Shi'i Muslims. (Although no single sect may claim to be a majority of the population, by far the Shi'is comprise the plurality, presently with about 40 per cent of the population.)

The Israeli invasion of Lebanon in 1982 lent momentum to groups inspired by the exemplar of the 1979 fall of the Shah in Iran. One of these Shi'i groups was Hizballah, initially established as little more than a cat's paw of Iran, which was involved in a number of horrendous incidents, including the suicide bombing of US and French forces in 1983, and dozens of kidnappings of foreigners, including journalists, priests, spies, diplomats and hapless foreign residents of Beirut. In its own programme, published in 1985, Hizballah declared its aversion to ever participating in the corrupt political system of Lebanon. Instead, the group committed itself to establishing a system of Islamic rule in Lebanon while fighting to expel foreign influence from Lebanon, especially the influence of the 'Great Satan', the United States.

With the civil war behind it, Lebanon held the first parliamentary elections in twenty years in 1992. By this point Hizballah had released its foreign hostages, and it was in the process of converting itself into a political party with a broad base of support among the Shi'i community. This process was helped by the group's reputation for integrity in contrast to less violent rival groups. Thus, after a stormy internal debate during which a minority declared that participating in Lebanese politics would lead to the party's co-optation into a corrupt political system, the majority (with Iranian encouragement) opted to play the game of politics. Starting in 1992 Hizballah has participated successfully in parliamentary consistently winning about twelve seats in the 128 seat body.

Until Israel's unilateral withdrawal from Lebanon in 2000, Hizballah was also the dominant element in the resistance front that eventually persuaded Israel that the costs were too high to continue its occupation of southern Lebanon. Hizballah skillfully used its place in the resistance to elicit political support. One of its 1996 campaign posters declared 'they resist with their blood; resist with your vote [vote for Hizballah]'.

Is this a success story? While Hizballah is frequently referred to in western commentary as a terrorist group, the fact is that its campaign against the Israeli occupation targeted occupying forces not civilians. Since the Israeli withdrawal, the border between the two countries has been reasonably calm, far more so than in the preceding two decades of Israel's occupation. Meantime, the party is now a central player in Lebanese politics. Its migration into politics was marked by a significant broadening of its membership base. Over two decades it has increasingly institutionalised itself as a political party with a stake in the political system. This has lent Hizballah political credibility it lacked previously, but it also imbues the party with restraints so long as it wishes to sustain its broad popular base of support. The verdict on Hizballah's transformation is arguably mixed, but it is clearly inadequate to simply denote it as a terrorist group.

Conclusion

The Hizballah example raises a key question: How should we understand the political efforts and potential of the Islamists? Are they behaving instrumentally in order simply to seize power or are they actually habituating to democracy? In his seminal article, Dankwart Rustow conceptualised the process of democratisation as a process of habituation whereby the players learn and grow used to democratic rules of the game (Rustow 1970). This is an important insight because it is unrealistic to presume that democratic systems begin with all parties fully imbued with democratic principles. Indeed, even mature democracies are still evolving, still democratising, as witness the case of the United States where full political rights were only extended formally to women less than a century ago, and where many groups are still marginalised in the political system.

Are the Islamists somehow different and exempt from the habituation process? This is a key debate and it is sparked by the fact that Islamist groups have been particularly successful in building a broad array of associational groups intended to fill the vacuum of services that are not fulfilled by government or the private sector. Some scholars, often evoking the rise of Nazism in Germany, argue that the vibrant associational life created by Islamists constitutes a step toward illiberal radicalism rather than fostering a vibrant civil society (Berman 1997; Berman 2003).

The failure of state institutions has given rise to the associational life associated with the Islamists. In Egypt, for instance, the state has tried to meet the challenge of Islamism by burnishing its own Islamic credentials in the media and in its public actions, further legitimating the Islamists as a political force.

In the absence of independent political parties that permit people to freely participate in politics, there is no doubt that segments of civil society, such as professional syndicates and labour unions often play a decidedly political role. In any case, the presence of strong parties would be no guarantee of a freer or more liberal political system and unfettered political parties would have a propensity to become engines of patronage and corruption. While the Nazi case is a warning of one disastrous path of development, the simple assertion that Islamists are simply Muslim replicas of European fascists misunderstands the vast array of attitudes and ideological perspectives that define Islamist groups in the contemporary Middle East.

It is also an overstatement to presume that Islamists have become the sole focus of quotidian life in much of the Middle East. Skeptics like Berman underestimate the persistence of Islam as a value system in Middle Eastern societies and the long-standing role of Muslim beneficence in helping the needy. The Islamist groups that often enjoy high visibility in western assessments are only one component in the complex webs and networks that intersect urban life in the Middle East (Singerman 1995). It is certainly unreasonable to expect that its associational life will reveal predominantly secular impulses, especially since secular values are often perceived as hostile to Islam at the popular level.

No doubt, the region has been strikingly resistant to democracy. As we have seen, the factors include the political economy of the states as well as the reluctance to permit to Islamists a hand in the game of politics. Indigenous and exogamous factors point to a process of liberalisation and democratisation that will play out over decades. The defects and failures of existing governments are easy enough to catalogue, and the ruling élites cling fiercely to power. Missing until now are élites committed to serious rather than cosmetic reform. In an important article, Eva Bellin puts this succinctly: 'regime elites possess both the will and the capacity to suppress democratic imitative' (Bellin 2004).

External players, such as the United States, remain too apprehensive about Islamist parties to push the process very hard. The longstanding comfort of western policy-makers with stability has been shaken by the terrorism of September 2001, but stability is still the default setting for policymakers. While models for Islamist participation in politics according to the 'rules of the game', as with Hizballah, do exist, the special constraints found in Lebanon are not easily reproduced elsewhere. Nonetheless, the important albeit failed model of Hizb al-Wasat shows how Islamist thinking is evolving in important ways.

What is not in doubt is that, given the opportunity, the quest of Middle Easterners for a better life, and for politics free of corruption and coercion will continue.

Unfortunately, abiding suspicions of the motives of the United States often contaminate the project of democracy and the hypocrisy of outside players is much discussed in the region. In any case, as the British diplomat Chris Patten emphasises: 'if we in the West think that democracy as a political form holds universal appeal, we should not force-feed it to subservient states as a Western geostrategic option' (Patten 2003: 43). Thus, the coming years will be as much a test of the power of external encouragement (not imposition) as of the ability of the regional political players to embark on incremental processes of reform.

Further Reading

BAKER, R. W., *Islam without Fear: The New Islamists* (Cambridge, Mass: Harvard University Press, 2004). A rich and informed account of renewal trends in Islamic political thought, especially in Egypt.

BELLIN, E. *Stalled Democracy: Capital, Labor, and the Paradox of State-Sponsored Development* (Ithaca, NY: Cornell University Press, 2002). A revealing case study of Tunisia that shows how the state-dominated economy breeds contingent democrats whose weak commitment to political reform stems from material interests in the economy.

BRYNEN, R., KORANY, B. and NOBLE, P. (eds.), *Political Liberalization & Democratization in the Arab World: Theoretical Perspectives* (Boulder, Colo.: Lynne Rienner Publishers, 1995). In addition to the authors' superb introduction and overview of the issues, this volume contains several important contributions by leading scholars.

EICKELMAN, D. F. and ANDERSON, J. W. (eds.), *New Media in the Muslim World: The Emerging Public Sphere* (2nd Bloomington: Indiana University Press, 2003) An invaluable collection of studies that show how Muslims are not only exploiting new media, such as the Internet, but also participation in a broadened public sphere.

FELDMAN, N., *After Jihad: America and the Struggle for Islamic Democracy* (New York: Farrah, Straus and Giroux, 2003). A readable account of the debates among Muslims on the prospects for reform and democracy.

HEFNER, R. H. (ed.) *Muslim Democrats: Prospects and Policies for a Modern Islamist Politics* (Princeton, NJ: Princeton University Press, 2004). Leading scholars come together to analyse the reflexivity of Muslim thinkers, reformist movements and institutions.

NORTON, A. R. (ed.), *Civil Society in the Middle East* (Leiden: E. J. Brill, 1995, 1996). The most comprehensive collection of studies on state-society relations in the Middle East covering virtually every country in the region.

SALAMÉ, G. (ed.), *Democracy without Democrats: Renewal of Politics in the Muslim World* (New York: St. Martin's, 1994). A pathbreaking volume that explores the prospects for democracy in a region where leading opposition forces initially may spurn the concept.

UNDP, *Arab Human Development Report* (Geneva: United Nations Development Program, 2002). A fact-filled and wide-ranging analysis the Arab world that emphasises three key deficits: freedom, education and women's rights.

WHITE, J. B., *Islamist Mobilization in Turkey: A Study of Verncacular Politics* (Seattle: University of Washington Press, 2002). The author's extensive fieldwork in Istanbul is the basis for a compelling and nuanced account of the social and cultural roots of the Islamic parties in Turkey.

Notes

1. The Pew Charitable Trust also offers extensive polling reports. See the widely discussed *Views of a Changing World 2003*, *http://people-press.org/reports/display. php3?ReportID = 185*.

2. This section draws upon work done jointly with Professor Farhad Kazemi.

7

The Politics of Identity in Middle East International Relations

Raymond Hinnebusch

OVERVIEW

The powerful challenge to state identities offered by both sub and supra-state identities makes the Middle East unique. Section one examines the struggle over identity within states. Section two looks at the impact of identities on the conduct of foreign policy in Middle East states examining, specifically the effect of Pan-Arabism and Pan-Islam on both the regional and international politics of the area. The chapter locates the identity issue within the wider debates in International Relations theory, particularly between constructivism and neo-utilitarianism.

Introduction

Identity and International Relations Theory

Middle East area specialists have always acknowledged the importance of identities for an understanding of the region (Barnett 1998: 5). However, it took a sea-change for this to be acknowledged in the International Relations literature long dominated by materialist/structuralist approaches such as neo-realism. Debates over nationalism

Box 7.1 Debates on nationalism

The problem of the origin of identity in the region is framed by the debates over nationalism. 'Primordialists' stress nationalism's roots in unchanging historically inherited ethnicity; 'modernists', such as Ernest Gellner, see it as chiefly a product of modernization, notably the spread of the market, while 'instrumentalists' see identity as 'constructed' by élites and counter-élites in their struggles for power.

None of these positions is wholly credible. To be sure, contra the primordialists, there is no self-evident single historic identity uniformly embraced in any of the Middle Eastern states; rather rival identities are tested through discourse, debates in a 'public sphere' (Lynch 1999: 46–9) among élites, intellectuals and publics. Moreover, the existence and actions of the state may be decisive for the construction of political identity. Nevertheless, the likelihood that the construction of a particular identity will succeed depends on objective factors such as shared historic memories, a dominant religion and the social communication facilitated by a common language (Deutsch 1953). Thus, the domination of a particular identity is the product of a complex interaction of ideational and 'objective' factors.

have, for some time, underlined how far the congruence of nation and state, merely assumed by neo-realism, is a contingent outcome of complex historical factors, although disagreement persists over the relative malleability of national identities (see Box 7.1). The more recent rise of constructivism's challenge to the 'neo-utilitarian' schools has now secured a place for identity as a factor in shaping international politics. But still at issue is *how much* identity matters as opposed to material structures and how far the study of discourse as opposed to that of material factors allows a better understanding of International Relations in the Middle East and elsewhere.

Arguably, the Middle East is a very good test case of these theoretical issues. There is an ongoing struggle in the region between multiple competing identities that can throw light on the process of identity formation. Sub-state groups contest loyalty to the state and its boundaries, spreading irredentism. Pervasive trans-state identity movements, Pan-Arabism and Pan-Islam, have mobilised popular loyalties more effectively than most states. In the 50s and 60s, Egypt's Nasser used Pan-Arabism to put normative constraints on the ability of Arab states to conduct sovereign foreign policies. Since the 70s, political Islam has sought to Islamise states from below, aggregate them for Islamic causes, and mobilise Muslims against Western threats. Precisely because the Middle East is the world region where such popular identities are ostensibly most at odds with externally imposed structures of material power, particularly the states system, it is a valuable test case of the relative power of ideational and material factors.

Identity and the Middle East State

The identity/sovereignty problematique in the Middle East

The relative incongruity between state and identity is perhaps the most distinctive feature of the Middle East states system. In the Westphalian model that European expansion ostensibly globalised, it is the congruity between identity and sovereignty, nation and state, that endows states and the states system with legitimacy. In an age of nationalism, there is, in fact, a powerful drive by identity communities to attain a state and by state leaders to forge a shared national identity among their populations. Where the drive to bring state, territory and nation into correspondence is obstructed, states' legitimacy is weaker while *irredentism* (the desire to overcome the identity-territory incongruence) fosters intra- and inter-state conflict. The Middle East stands out because of its unique combination of *both* strong *sub-state* identities and powerful *supra-state* identities that, together, dilute and limit the mass loyalty to the state typical where it corresponds to a sense of nation distinctive from the 'other' (neighbouring states) (Ayoob 1995: 47–70; Hudson 1977: 33–55).

One reason for this divergence from the Westphalian model is that in most of the Middle East, an arid region of trading cities and nomadic tribes, identification with the territorial state was historically weak and tended to focus instead on the sub-state unit—the city, the tribe, the religious sect—or on the larger Islamic community or *umma*. As Weulersse (1946: 79–83), pointed out, states, typically the products of outside conquerors or of desert-based religio-tribal movements, tended to disintegrate after a few generations and when a new wave of state-building came along the states' boundaries were often quite different. To be sure, Harik (1987: 19–46) has argued that a potential basis for contemporary nation-states exists in a multitude of geographical entities within the Arab world that had distinct historical experiences: where minority sects established autonomous regimes (Yemen, Oman, Lebanon); where tribal or tribal-religious movements founded regimes (Saudi Arabia); or where Mamluk élites achieved autonomy as Ottoman power declined (Tunisia, Algeria). It is indisputable that the boundaries of these entities have been frozen in contemporary times, but far less clear that distinct national identities differentiate them from their neighbours. It is only in those societies with substantial peasantries, hence attachment to the land—Turkey, Iran and Egypt—that contemporary states have inherited clear features of the nation-state model.

Aggravating the identity deficit of contemporary regional states was the way the states system was imposed by the Western imperial powers. Instead of the natural processes of sorting out boundaries through war and dynastic marriage which took place in the northern world, the imposed boundaries of the modern Middle East state system fragmented the region arbitrarily into a multitude of competing, often artificial, state units on the basis of great power interests, not indigenous wishes (Ayoob 1995: 33). This sacrificed the nation-building potential of the pre-existing cultural unity deriving from a long history of extensive empires ruling in the name of the Islamic *umma*. It also disrupted a multiplicity of regional ties while reorienting many economic and communications links to the Western 'core'.

One consequence of the creation of new artificial states was that loyalties often remained attached to pre-existing *sub-state* identities which often spilled across the haphazardly imposed state boundaries—becoming 'trans-state' and giving rise to irredentism. This, in turn, has generated inter-state conflicts as states contest each other's borders or 'interfere' in each others 'domestic' affairs by supporting irredentist groups, a practice which can escalate into actual military confrontation between states. The best example of this is the case of the Kurds who have been regularly used by their host states in their rivalries with each other and who have attempted to exploit these state rivalries in their struggle for national rights; this has regularly led to inter-state conflict, notably between Syria and Turkey and between Iran and Iraq (Gause 1992: 444–67; Ayoob 1995: 7, 47–70). (See Box 7.2.)

The second consequence of the arbitrary imposition (and freezing) of the states system is the enduring power of *supra-state* identities, expressive of the lost cultural unity. The collapse of the Ottoman empire created an identity vacuum and the region-wide struggle against Western imperialism allowed Arab nationalism, beginning after the First World War, to fill this gap among the educated Arabic speaking classes; secular in character, Arab nationalism had the advantage of including in the putative Arab nation the significant Christian and Islamic heterodox sub-state minorities. Beginning in the 1930s, Pan-Islam arose among the traditional lower middle classes and after the loss of the 1967 war by Arab nationalist states captured the loyalties of big parts of the middle classes as well. Both ideologies challenged the legitimacy of the individual states and spawned movements promoting their unity as a cure for the fragmentation of the felt community.

Box 7.2 The Middle East 'Mosaic'

There are ethnic minorities in all Middle East countries, notably the Kurds, spread between Iraq, Iran, Turkey and Syria, and the Berbers, who spill across North African boundaries. Iran is the premier multi-ethnic society, its Persian core flanked by Azerbaijanis, Kurds, Turkomans, Arabs and Baluchis. Religious pluralism is even more striking: Sunni Muslims are the majority community in the Arab world, but not in particular states (Lebanon, Iraq) while Shi'a Muslims, the majority in Iran, spill across the Arab region where they are pivotal minorities or deprived pluralities in Bahrain, Kuwait, Iraq, and Lebanon. Several Shi'a offshoots, notably the Druze, Ismailis and Alawis, are historically important in Syria and Lebanon, while the Zaydis dominate Yemen. Offshoots of the purist Kharijites (Ibadies) dominate Oman. A multitude of Christian minorities, divided by the languages of their liturgies or allegiances to Eastern Orthodoxy vs. Rome, are scattered across the region.

The rapid rise of Pan-Arab identity in the 1950s corresponded to the advance of education and literacy and was often spread by the Egyptian teachers employed throughout the Arab world who helped socialise the emerging middle classes. But the shared cultural basis was already there: similar food, marriage and child-rearing practices, music and art and, most important, the common Arabic language—the critical ingredient of nationhood. The spread of a standard newspaper and radio Arabic made the language more homogeneous, stunting the evolution of national dialects into the linguistic basis of separate nations. The recent advent of Arab satellite TV has sharply reinforced cross-border participation in a common discourse. All this has made the Arab world, in Noble's words (1991: 56), a 'vast sound chamber' in which ideas and information circulate widely. Extended family ties frequently crossed borders and cross-border immigration has been constant: in the 1950s there were major flows of Palestinian refugees; since the 70s labour migration to the Gulf oil producing states has been substantial. Niblock (1990) argues that the interests of the separate states are too intertwined—by labour supply, investment funds, security, water, communications routes, and the Palestine issue—for them to develop self-sufficient coherence. Long after the creation of the Arab states system, Noble (1991: 57) could argue credibly that the Arab world was less well represented by realism's impenetrable 'billiard balls' in which governments insulated domestic society from foreign influence than by a set of interconnected organisms separated only by porous membranes.

As a result, there has been a widespread feeling of belonging to a distinct Arab World (al-'alam al-arabi); indeed, survey majorities in the Arab states through the 80s have agreed that the Arabs constituted a *nation* and that the state boundaries dividing them were artificial (Korany 1987: 54–5; Reiser 1984). Thirteen of fifteen Arab state constitutions define the nation as the *Arab nation* (Ayubi 1995: 146). Uniquely in the Arab world, not this or that border, but state boundaries in general have been seen by many Arabs to be arbitrarily imposed as a divide and rule strategy by imperialism and hence to lack the legitimacy and sanctity they enjoy elsewhere. Historical memories of greatness under unity and experience that the Arabs are successful when they act together and are readily dominated when divided, keep Pan-Arabism alive. The loss of Palestine, the 1967 defeat by Israel, the sanctions against Iraq and its 2003 conquest, are all seen as shared Arab humiliations while the 1973 war and oil embargo and Israel's evacuation of southern Lebanon under Hizballah pressure in June 2000 have been experienced as shared victories. At the level of formal ideology, this sentiment was manifest in the doctrines of Pan-Arab nationalism which viewed all Arabic speakers as forming a nation, the states of which ought to act in concert (a norm established by Nasser of Egypt) or be confederated, or, in its most ambitious form (as in Ba'thism), be merged in a single state embracing this nation.

More even than Arabism, Islamic identity is deeply embedded in the beliefs and daily practices of Middle Eastern societies. Nevertheless, the rise of Islamic political movements was the outcome of a specific interaction between objective factors and 'political entrepreneurship'. The traumatic shock of the 1967 Arab defeat and the Israeli conquest of the holy city of Jerusalem, blamed by many on secular nationalism, generated an identity crisis and stimulated the belief that only a return to God's path could reverse the disaster. This belief seemed partially vindicated by Islamic Saudi Arabia's use of the 'oil weapon' during the more successful 1973 Arab–Israeli war, by the subsequent oil boom which enriched conservative Islamic states and by the success of Islamic revolution in Iran. At the same time, however, political Islam was also a reaction against the corruption, inequality and 'Westoxification' unleashed by oil-fuelled modernisation. The accompanying threat to small traders and artisans by 'infitahs' (economic openings) to foreign competition, and the oil price booms and busts which first raised, then frustrated the aspirations of partly-educated rural migrants to the city who found themselves under-employed and excluded from established networks of patronage, created large marginalised classes that found refuge in Islamic identity. With the decline of the secular ideologies that had once expressed the discontent of subordinate classes, and given the absence of effective channels of legitimate political activity, the *dawa* (call) of a new generation of politicised preachers and activists, often funded by Saudi Arabia or inspired by revolutionary Iran, found fertile ground in the suqs, campuses and, above all, the mosques, the main surviving political shelter from the authoritarian state. Islamist activists tried to transmute the powerful 'everyday' allegiance that Islam already commanded among the masses into a political counter-ideology able to mobilise them against ruling regimes. Indicative of the subsequent growing societal influence of political Islam is its ideological capture of big parts of the formerly secular middle classes, its emergence as the main opposition to the state everywhere, its filling of the welfare gap left by the 'infitah state's' reneging on the populist social contract, and its assumption of leadership in the region's continuing nationalist struggles. It is symptomatic of the region that the identity gap left by the relative decline of Arabism in the 70s was filled less by state identities than by another supra-state identity, political Islam. Parenthetically, this does not mean that Islamic identity has wholly eclipsed Arabism. Indeed, they often reinforce rather than compete with each other.[1]

The effect of political Islam on the states system is, however, not straightforward. Except in Iran, it has failed to seize state power and institutionalise an enduring Islamic order. Moreover, it is doubtful that the rising identification with political Islam poses a threat to the individual states comparable to that of 1950s Pan-Arabism. Some do argue (Vatikiotis 1987: 42–4) that Islam withholds legitimacy from nationally separate states in the name of a Pan-Islamic *umma* and this is certainly true of radical Islamists such as Sayyid Qutb; also in this tradition are the radical Islamic networks, above all al-Qaida, operating on a trans-state scale in opposition to states perceived as Western clients. Others, however, argue that Islam has always been comfortable with a plurality of states within the *umma* and that Islam currently takes distinctive 'national' forms compatible with individual statehood (Piscatori 1986; Shaikh 2003) Certainly, Middle Eastern rulers have routinely used Islam to legitimise their separate states; indeed, Saudi Arabia deployed Islam as a defence against Pan-Arabism. Islamic movements constitute the main political opposition in most Middle East states but typically they seek to Islamise the state, not to abolish it. To the extent that regimes permit Islamists to join the political process and to work toward the Islamisation of public life (education, law and media), Muslim discontent with the secular state is assuaged and state identity brought into greater congruence with Islamic societies; alternatively Islamist energies have been diverted into attempts to build a Islamic counter-society—schools, health clinics, welfare institutions—at the grass roots level (rather than contesting the legitimacy of the state). In cases such as Syria, Egypt and Algeria, regimes, battle-hardened by facing down Islamic revolution, now present more obdurate obstacles to Islamic movements than Pan-Arabists ever faced.

Thus, against the pervasive incongruity of boundaries and identity must be set the durability of the regional states system. Once ruling élites and state apparatuses were created in the individual states, they acquired vested interests in the new post-Ottoman fragmentation. In nearly a century of ongoing state formation, state builders have struggled to contain the penetration of their territory by trans-state forces and tenaciously defended their sovereignty against a redrawing of boundaries. Indeed, the individual Arab states outlasted the Pan-Arab movements that in the 50s and 60s sought a solution to the 'one nation-many states' dilemma by merging them in Arab unionist projects such as the abortive UAR between Egypt and Syria. The international system, in guaranteeing state borders, obstructed Bismarkian attempts at forceful absorption of neighbouring states, such as Saddam Hussein's attempt to annex Kuwait. Thus, the borders imposed at the birth of the state system remain largely intact.

The durability of the states system does not, of course, necessarily imply the legitimacy of the individual states; on the contrary, they have suffered from chronic legitimacy deficits ultimately rooted in the shallowness of the popular identifications they command. In principle, the territorial state based on habitation of a common territory (especially where boundaries correspond to some historical memory) and guaranteeing equal citizenship rights under a common government could constitute an identity alternative to supra-state Arabism or Islam. Commanding the instruments of socialisation—mass media, mass education—as well as job opportunities in state-dominated economies, state élites enjoy some advantages in promoting identification with the state among the rising generation. The very durability of boundaries means that, inevitably, new generations would, in the usual course of things, tend increasingly to view the existing states as the normal framework of political life.

Yet, this potential has been retarded by a vicious circle in which Arab state builders are caught. Their inability to take their citizens' political identities for granted and the ability of counter-élites to deploy sub- and supra-state identities to mobilise opposition has pushed state-builders into authoritarian strategies in which tightly knit ruling cores are constituted through extensive use of *sub-state* loyalties (kin, tribe, sect) while *supra-state* identities—Arabism and Islam—are deployed as official legitimating ideologies. Such tactics keep non-state identities alive while states' access to external rent—oil revenues and foreign aid—allows them to avoid trading political rights for taxes and support. The resulting top-down state building has limited the mass mobilisation and democratic inclusion that was a crucial ingredient in the West's prototype nation-building.

The complex interaction of multiple identities ensures that, in reality, there is considerable *variation* in the level of incongruence between identity and state boundaries in the region. Significantly, nation-building has proceeded with most success in non-Arab Turkey, Israel and Iran where indigenous state builders were relatively better able to determine borders and ensure a rough correspondence between them and the dominant ethnic-linguistic identity or where a history of separate statehood survived into the modern era. Turkey and Iran have long histories as imperial centres and have constructed modern nations around their dominant ethnic-linguistic cores with considerable success. Israel is a unique case, a state founded by a trans-state movement, Zionism, that, believing the Jews (whatever their diverse ethnic origins) to constitute a nation entitled to a state on the territory of Biblical Israel, successfully claimed most of the land of that ancient state—at the expense of the indigenous Palestinian population—for its modern reincarnation. In a virtuous circle, the greater congruity of state and identity in the non-Arab states made democratisation less risky and this, in turn, consolidated identification with the state. Nevertheless even these states each face an unfinished task of integrating minorities: indeed, Turkey and Israel have been at war with sub-state identity groups—Kurds, Palestinians—which they cannot assimilate and will neither grant full rights nor allow to separate. Moreover, the perceived lack of full correspondence between Biblical Israel and the contemporary state keeps irredentism alive in Israeli politics.

In the Arab states, multiple, often equally potent, levels of identity co-exist in quite varying ways, from cases where identification with the separate states overshadows without wholly displacing Arabism to those where state identities remain subordinate to the sense of being an Arab or a Muslim. At the first end of the continuum is an oil city-state such as Kuwait where Farah's study (1980: 141–2) found state identification came first (24.3 per cent), then religious affiliation (14.4 per cent) and Arabism last. The geographically separate Maghreb has always identified less with Arab nationalism than local statehood, although neither Arab or Islamic identities have been effaced as the strong reaction in the Maghreb to the 1991 Western attack on Iraq showed.

In Egypt, a strong sense of territorial identity is based on the Nile valley and a history of statehood predating the Arabs. Yet, Egyptian identity is Arab-Islamic in content, and attempts to construct alternative definitions of Egyptianness—'Pharaonic' or 'Mediterranean'—have failed. Thus, even in the late 70s when Sadat was withdrawing from Pan-Arab commitments and engaged in bitter disputes with other Arab states, a survey of high status Egyptians (normally less receptive to Arabism) indicated that, although 71.3 per cent identified with Egypt first, 71.1 per cent said Egypt was a part of the Arab nation, indeed the natural leader of the Arabs (Hinnebusch 1982: 535–61). This strong sense of kinship with the Arab world meant that decisions taken purely on grounds of state interest—Egypt's separate peace with Israel, membership in the anti-Iraq Gulf war coalition—which would be perfectly natural were Egypt a consolidated nation-state—were extremely controversial and damaging to regime legitimacy. Similarly, Yemenis see their identity as distinct, by virtue of Yemen's special pre-Islamic existence as a state, but nevertheless see Yemen as part of the wider Arab community (Halliday 2001).

In many Mashreq cases, where externally-imposed borders corresponded to no history of independent statehood, much less nationhood, Arabism was long the dominant identity. It is no accident that the main Pan-Arab nationalist movement, Ba'thism, was born in Syria, and was most successful there and in Iraq and Jordan. If the natural geo-historical unit, *bilad ash-sham* (historic and geographical Syria), might have supported a viable nationhood, its fragmentation into four mini-states (Syria, Jordan, Lebanon, and Palestine/Israel) prevented the truncated Damascus-centred rump from becoming a strong uncontested focus of identity. The attempt to generate a non-Arab Syrian national identity by the Syrian Social Nationalist Party came to nothing, although when a Pan-Syrian identity is defined as Arab in content, it carries resonance. In Iraq, the opposite case of an artificial state constructed by throwing rival communal groups together, Arabism was embraced by some as the only satisfying solution, but rejected by others.

The case of a stateless people, the Palestinians, well illustrates the evolution of multiple identities. As they had no historical memories of a Palestinian entity, a distinct Palestinian identity was a function of the enforced separation of Palestine from Syria and the struggle with Zionism. Yet, needing the protection of membership in a larger whole, Palestinians also identified with Arabism until its 1967 failure. After that, a more specific Palestinian nationalism arose, although it was retarded by the lack of a state and was contested by an Islamic identity. None of these identities were, however, mutually exclusive; thus, Palestinian Islamicists assimilated nationalism and nationalist resistance to Britain and Israel used Islamic discourse (Khalidi 1997; Buderi 1997).

In summary, while state identities have everywhere developed as supplementary or, in a few cases, primary bases of legitimacy in the region, given the continuing popular credibility of Arab and Islamic identities, rulers vacillate between legitimising themselves as Arab or Islamic leaders and relying on state identities; they cannot fully rely on the former since their borders are not congruent with the Arab or Islamic communities and because adherence to their norms might sacrifice state interests; yet they cannot fully rely on state identities as long as these lack sufficient credibility to marginalise their supra-state rivals (Anderson 1991: 72). They may try to overcome this dilemma by 'statising' a supra-state identity as the official state ideology, as when Ba'thist Syria claims to be the special champion of Arabism or Saudi Arabia of Islam.

The Impact of Identity on the International Relations of the Middle East

Inter-Arab politics amidst supra-state identity

The importance of identity for the international relations of the Middle East system is championed by constructivism in opposition to the 'materialist' so-called 'neo-utilitarian' theories that dominate the international relations field (see Box 7.3).

Box 7.3 IR approaches and the impact of identity

For the neo-utilitarians (including Marxist structuralists and neo-realists), the system-level is constituted of material structures, specifically the balance of power (for neo-realism) and assymetric core-periphery relations (in structuralism) which, outside of the control of most states, are the main factors shaping and constraining their behaviour. By contrast, for constructivism, the system-level is primarily constituted by normative inter-subjective understandings which state élites construct through their discourse and interactions with each other and their publics and through which their identities are constituted (Pan-Arabism being a pivotal example in the Arab world).

In utilitarianism, states are assumed to seek material interests (wealth and power) and their strategies toward this end are shaped by their *position* in systemic structures (for the mostly-weak Arab states, normally one allowing limited autonomy from the core powers and entailing threats from more powerful non-Arab neighbours); identities and norms are merely *used* by state élites either as instruments of power (using foreign threats to stir up supportive nationalism) or to legitimise their material interests.

For constructivism, however, states' identities shape their conceptions of their interests (thus, the high value put by Arab and Islamic identities on autonomy from Western domination infuses conceptions of Arab state interests with a natural anti-imperialism, even if this has material costs). A more qualified version of constructivism acknowledges that the pursuit of material interests may motivate state élites but the necessity to legitimise this in terms of the norms and identity (Arabism, Islam) shared with their populations constrains their policy options. Analysts of the Middle East tend to lean to one or the other of these rival poles.

Constructivism would seem to be particularly relevant to the Middle East, given the exceptional power of supra-state identities (Arabism and Islam) over state conduct and the near-absence of the national-states assumed by realism. This arguably makes for a different, even unique, kind of regional system in the Arab core of the Middle East. Rather than an international system of self-contained national communities whose borders distinguish between 'us' and 'them', the Arab world, according to Kienle, might better be seen as an 'overarching Arab polity' within which the individual states constitute a set of semi-permeable autonomous units (Kienle 1990: 9, 27; Sela 1998: 9–10). Yet, just because the Arab world has made up a single political arena, inter-state competition has been endemic and precisely because boundaries lack the impenetrability of the Westphalian model, with ideological influences readily crossing state lines, each state has been highly sensitive to the actions of others and vulnerable to trans-state movements. In this context, moreover, aspirations for Pan-Arab leadership were seen as realistic and rival leaders had an incentive to manipulate trans-state ideological appeals against each other in ways that would be either ineffective or viewed as a violation of sovereignty in a conventional states system. Despite this, the states are formally sovereign, the norm of sovereignty is acknowledged by state leaders and the putative (Arab or Islamic) supra-state community, lacking a common centralised authority or even an effective inter-state 'regime', appears highly anarchic, hence given to state self-help, as in the realist model. Indeed, Stephen Walt, in his classic realist study, *The Origin of Alliances* (1987), disputes the uniqueness of inter-Arab politics, insisting that Pan-Arabism was merely an instrument of state power used, much like an army, by stronger states pursuing their 'national interests' against weaker ones. As such, how far the conduct of *inter-Arab* politics is qualitatively different from *international* politics remains a matter of controversy.

The rise and decline of Arabism: constructivist vs. utilitarian explanations

The rise and fall of Arabism allows an assessment of the relative power of constructivism and its rivals for understanding the region's international relations. According to Michael Barnett's classic constructivist account, *Arab Dialogues*, norms had a decisive impact on state behaviour but not in any pre-determined way. Rather, owing to the rivalry built into the Arab system between the norms of sovereignty and of Pan-Arabism and because Pan-Arab norms had themselves to be interpreted in changing contexts, the actual impact of norms on foreign policies was inevitably a product of on-going contestation among the Arab states, what he calls inter-Arab 'dialogues' (1998: 6, 28, 40). He argues that in this dialogue the balance between Pan-Arabism and sovereignty was altered, swinging first against sovereignty and then back in its favour.

While the ingredients of Arab identity long existed, it was, ironically, inter-Arab leadership rivalry that played a central role in the overt 'construction' of Pan-Arab identity and the semi-institutionalisation of its norms. This game was played by ideological competition in which leaders ambitious for Pan-Arab leadership, trumpeting their own Arab credentials and impugning those of rivals, sought to sway public opinion and to mobilise the Arab 'street' to pressure (even overthrow) rival governments from below. The first episode in this struggle was the early 1950s debate over whether to join the Baghdad Pact, a Western-sponsored security alliance against the Soviet Union. While pro-Western Iraq wanted to join, Egypt's Nasser, seeing it as a form of neo-imperialism, mobilised Arab public opinion on behalf of an alternative Arab collective security pact. Nasser's victory in this debate established a powerful Pan-Arab norm against foreign treaties or bases. His emergence from the 1956 Suez war as a popular Arab hero and the 1958 overthrow of the pro-Western Iraqi regime put all those who contested his view of Pan-Arabism on the defensive. Egyptian hegemony was thereafter exercised on behalf of an informal 'Pan-Arab regime' that constrained the foreign policy options of individual Arab states within bounds determined by Cairo's view of the overarching Arab national interest. The core issues that defined Arabism were rejection of Western domination, defence of the Palestine cause, the desirability of Arab unity, and the expectation that the Arab states should act in concert in world politics in defence of all-Arab interests. Once Nasser's Pan-Arab discourse galvanised trans-state Arab nationalist movements across the region, even pro-Western élites were forced to protect themselves from subversion by defending their own Arab nationalist credentials and being seen to adhere to Arabist norms.

As Barnett argues convincingly, this inter-Arab competition, though intense, was quite different from a conventional 'realist' power struggle. It was not chiefly over territory or other tangibles but over the desired normative order of the Arab system. Crucially, the typical currency in this struggle—in stark contrast to that between the Arab and non-Arab Middle East—was not military power but ideological appeal: it was legitimacy, derived from being perceived to observe the norms and play roles grounded in Arabism, which gave the power to affect outcomes (Noble 1991: 61; Barnett 1998: 2, 6, 16). Nasser's blessing was sought and his censure feared not because of his army but because he was seen as the guardian of Arab nationalist norms and could bolster or subvert the domestic legitimacy of other leaders. Before Nasser, Egypt had enjoyed no such advantage over its Arab rivals and after he died, Egypt's trans-state power dissipated overnight; for while its material power had barely changed, his successor had none of the moral authority that had enabled him to make Egypt a pole of attraction for the populations of other states (Hudson 1999: 86).

With Pan-Arabism on the ascendancy as the dominant discourse, a process of 'outbidding' began in which rival state leaders sought to mobilise mass support by escalating its standards. This led to demands first for more militancy toward imperialist footholds in the region (as in the Gulf States), for greater integral unity between Arab states (as embodied in the UAR and subsequent unity projects) and later for greater militancy on behalf of the Palestine cause. Even if Arabism was manipulated to serve the interests of states in their competition more than to advance all-Arab interests, this competition tended, Barnett argues, to establish norms of behaviour that constrained all states. Even Nasser, the main architect of the Pan-Arab order, found that he, too, was bound by them, so long as he wished to retain his Pan-Arab leadership (even as the material costs of his Arab commitments, such as his support for the Yemen revolution, rose). Indeed, trans-state Pan-Arab movements were autonomous of Cairo; they used Nasser as much as he used them and they constantly pressured him into increasing his commitment to the common cause against his own better judgment.

At a certain point, however, Pan-Arabism began an apparent decline or at least underwent a reinterpretation to the advantage of sovereignty, a 'deconstruction' driven, in Barnett's view, by the zero-sum interactions of Arab leaders. First, the very trans-state vulnerability of most Arab states gave them an incentive to defend the rival norm of sovereignty (implying non-interference in the domestic affairs of other states). As Walt rightly pointed out, even at the height of Pan-Arabism, balancing against Egypt's use of Pan-Arabism to impose hegemony was pervasive within the Arab world, at the expense of co-operation for common interests. This was practised not just by the conservative monarchies but even by ostensibly Pan-Arab regimes in Syria and Iraq when Nasser posed a threat to them. However, the power of Pan-Arab norms could still be seen in the fact that 'balancing' against Nasser took the form of propaganda wars over who was truest to Pan-Arabism and in the eschewing of alliances with non-Arab partners which might have made sense in classic forms of balancing, notably ones between the weaker Arab monarchies and Israel against stronger radical republics.

Second, over time, inter-Arab rivalry, forcing competitors to act on their Pan-Arab rhetoric, 'entrapped' Arab leaders in unrealistic or risky commitments that were potentially damaging to the interests of the individual states. This tendency climaxed in the provocative rhetoric by which Syria, Jordan and Egypt blundered into the 1967 war with Israel. As Sela shows, once the costs of outbidding had become prohibitive for many individual states and once it became manifest that the actions of one Arab state affected them all, the individual states agreed to institutionalise the Arab summits system in which all could participate in a mutual deflation of the standards of Arabism. The most portentous outcome of this was the collective legitimisation of a political settlement with Israel in return for its evacuation of the territories occupied in 1967. The growing acceptance of the view that Pan-Arab norms had to be defined by an inter-élite consensus in which the interests of the individual states would inevitably be prioritised shifted the normative balance toward sovereignty (Barnett 1999: 40–52; Sela 1998: 3–8). Sadat's separate peace with Israel was a watershed event in prioritising sovereignty (the right to recover lost Egyptian territory) over Pan-Arab norms; Saddam Hussein's invasion of Kuwait shattered what remained of a Pan-Arab normative order. In Barnett's view, the zero-sum interactions of Arab leaders led to a norm dissensus that broke the moral power of Pan-Arabism over their conduct. Gradually, the disillusionment of the public with Arabism's failures and costs also enervated popular constraints on their pursuit of state-centric policies. In essence, just as the Arab leaders constructed Pan-Arabism through their rivalries and rhetoric, so they also deconstructed it.

While constructivist accounts give valuable insights into the micro-processes at the level of actor 'agency' whereby interactions and discourse shape normative change, they typically make only passing reference to constraints deriving from underlying macro-level structures. A full appreciation of why Arabism, an identity so thoroughly grounded in the stuff of nationhood (language, history), should have failed to sustain enduring normative power over Arab states is impossible without careful analysis of the material context within which Barnett's 'Arab dialogues' took place. This context was, for the most part, hostile to the institutionalisation of a Pan-Arab normative regime.

First, neglect of structural constraints leads constructivists to exaggerate the agency possessed by 'periphery' powers such as the Arab states to construct their own regional order. While Nasser did mobilise popular identity to successfully defy the West in constructing a Pan-Arab order, this was only possible temporarily because of the unique bi-polar structure of world power in the period after the Second World

War. It was the existence of countervailing Soviet power that to some extent temporarily sheltered the Arab world from direct Western intervention against nationalist projects; the truth of this is dramatically revealed by the resumption of such intervention in the post bi-polar era.

Second, identity and norms, to endure, must be congruent with economic structures. Amin (1978) has shown how the regionwide trade interdependence fostered under the Middle East's extensive empires was associated with universalistic Arab-Islamic identities. However, with the West's fragmentation of the regional market into state-bounded economies dependent on the export of primary products to the 'core', the economic interests of dominant classes (exporting landlords, petro-shaikhs) were pulled out of correspondence with Arabism even as it was itself emerging as a dominant identity. Ironically, the efforts of Arab nationalist states to break their economic dependence only issued in protected inward-looking economies and demolished the potential Pan-Arab industrial bourgeoisie which might have had a stake in regional markets. Only about 9 per cent of Arab foreign trade is with other Arab states and over 90 per cent of Arab foreign investment takes place outside the Arab world. Thus, Pan-Arab norms corresponded to no Pan-Arab economy, no material infrastructure that could sustain them in the face of adversity.

Third, the West's creation of protected client states in the region constituted profound structural obstacles to Pan-Arabism. This is nowhere better illustrated than in the case of Jordan where the Hashemite regime was created and sustained by the West as a *buffer state* charged with containing popular mobilisation on the basis of Arab/Palestinian identity (Salibi 1998). Identity certainly mattered since, had popular identity shaped that of the state, Jordan's foreign policy would have been very different. Indeed the association of breaks in Jordan's traditional pro-Western policy with brief episodes of internal democratisation is striking. It was evident in the 1950s under the elected Nabulsi government and again when King Hussein's stand with Iraq in the 1991 Gulf war gave him the legitimacy to engineer another brief democratic opening. In spite of such episodes, however, Jordan was repeatedly restored to the buffer state role with which it was endowed at its creation by some combination of the Western economic dependence of the regime and actual or threatened intervention by Israel or the West against threats to the monarchy—that is, by the structure of *material power*. Indeed, precisely because permanent democratisation would have transformed Jordan's identity and its conception of its interests, it could not be allowed; thus, once the Gulf war crisis had passed and the palace again prioritised structural constraints over popular identity by its peace treaty with Israel and re-alignment with the West, Jordan's democratisation had to be reversed. Hence, the role of the regime remained one *of containing, not expressing* mass identity, a scenario most exaggerated in Jordan but typical of many other Arab states.

Fourth, the contest between Arabism and sovereignty was not played out exclusively at the level of inter-state discourse (as in Barnett's account) and a state's adoption of Pan-Arabism (or not) was in good part a result of internal (partly class) struggles over state power. Radical versions of Arabism were the ideological weapon of rising social forces with an interest in change, specifically the new middle class challenging the oligarchy in the 50s. Middle-class élites newly arrived in power, especially in states insecure in their separate identity or with the potential for Pan-Arab leadership, used Pan-Arabism to legitimise their often-precarious rule at home. Sovereignty, on the other hand, was the ideology of satisfied social forces, normally traditional élites on the defensive and without the potential for Pan-Arab leadership; moreover, once middle-class élites evolved into new state bourgeoisies, they also began to embrace sovereignty. Identities were, as Marxist materialism holds, intimately connected with the *social structural position of the social forces* that advocated them.

Fifth, a dynamic beginning in the late 70s whereby the anarchic structure of the regional states system shaped state-centric conceptions of state interests at the expense of Pan-Arabism is indisputable. The much increased insecurity issuing from Israel's overwhelming post-1967 military superiority and the growing militarisation of the Arab–Israeli conflict increasingly encouraged, as realism predicts, a resort by each Arab state to 'self-help,' both in defending itself and seeking exit from war at the expense of shared Arab norms. Specifically, Egypt's pursuit of a separate peace with Israel upset the Arab–Israeli power balance, heightening the insecurity of other Arab states, notably Syria, and encouraging them to similarly look to self-help through militarisation and separate diplomacy. The Iran–Iraq war had a similar effect in the Gulf. In this new environment where survival depended more on raw military power than success in ideological competition, the world of constructivism was giving way to that of realism.

Sixth, neo-utilitarian approaches agree that a stable transnational 'regime', far from being self-enforcing (as constructivism implies), requires a 'hegemon' which, the chief beneficiary of this order, is prepared to use its ideological hegemony and its material power to enforce regime norms. Arguably Egypt performed this role (although not very effectively) for the Pan-Arab order under Nasser but abandoned it under Sadat. Egypt has historically wavered between more Arab and Egypt-centric identities and, as constructivism would predict, these have indeed been associated with quite different conceptions of Egypt's interests and different foreign policies. However, it was only as long as Pan-Arabism corresponded to élite views of Egypt's interests that Pan-Arab identity dominated and Egypt played the Pan-Arab hegemon; once Sadat found it would serve his material interests in winning American aid and diplomatic help, he defected from the Arab consensus and fostered a rival Egypt-centric identity. To be sure, this was a contested, not a mechanical process and Coldwell's (2003) constructivist account shows that much of Egypt's attentive public continued to hold Arab or Islamic identities, and hence perceived Egypt's interest as inseparable from that of the Arab world. Nevertheless, for Egypt's ruling élites, identity seemed to shift according to immediate material costs and benefits which, in turn, were a function of objective systemic constraints, much as realism would predict (Karawan 2002). And Egypt's foreign policy transformation had far reaching consequences: Pan-Arabism lost its hegemon and the same Egypt that had once enforced Pan-Arab standards pioneered their sacrifice to individual state interests under the banner of sovereignty.

Finally, the material consequences of the 1970s oil boom had an ambivalent but mostly deleterious effect on Arabism. Oil differentiated the interests of the Arabs into rich and poor. As the oil producers invested their petrodollars in Western banks and real estate, their interests were increasingly detached from the Arab world and attached to the core. Oil also financed a decade of state building which made states' populations less susceptible to trans-state ideological mobilisation and consolidated the individual states as the sources of wealth and welfare on which citizens now depended, allowing parts of the formerly Pan-Arab middle classes to be co-opted by the individual states. As the Pan-Arab mobilisation of the public declined, élites were freer to put state interests over Pan-Arab interests in their foreign policies.

Thus, if sovereignty later displaced Pan-Arabism as the dominant official norm governing foreign policy, this was not simply because it won a contest of discourses among publics, which did not decisively attach their loyalties to the individual states. Rather it was because it better corresponded to the short run material (security, wealth) interests of local élites who normally (not always) prioritised these over the identity they shared with each other and their publics, realities congruent with Marxist structuralism and realism. Compared to the pull of these interests, Arabism remained unanchored in a material substructure.

Yet, the persistence of Arab identity remained, as constructivism would expect, a durable obstacle to the legitimisation of élite interests. The embedding of the Arab states system in a supra-state community built an enduring tension into it, trapping foreign policy-makers between the logic of sovereignty, in which each regime, insecure both at home and amidst the anarchy of the states system, pursues its own interests and security, often against its Arab neighbours, and the counter norm held by their publics which conditioned the legitimacy of the individual states on their acting together in defence of the shared identity (Barnett 1998: 10–11, 25–7).

Pan-Islam in the international relations of the Middle East

It is a matter of debate whether political Islam, in the form of Pan-Islam at the inter-state level, constitutes a functional substitute for Pan-Arabism as a supra-state ideology able to constrain the state's pursuit of pure raison d'etat and generate Muslim power in world politics. One might expect this to be so partly because the two identities overlap in the Arab world and their foreign policy preferences largely reinforce each other (although they differ over models of domestic order). Islam and Arabism both prioritise Arab or Islamic unity over individual reason of state; both insist on economic and cultural autonomy of the Western-dominated world system and both reject the legitimacy of Israel. Radical Islamic movements such as Hamas and Hizballah are as much manifestations of Arab national resistance to Israel as they are of Islamic resurgence (Munson 2003). It is apparent, too, that Islam has succeeded, where secular nationalism failed, in seriously challenging the enemies of Arab-Islamic causes: it was Islamic activists that overthrew the formidable Pahlavi state, forced the withdrawal of the powerful Israeli military from southern Lebanon and inflicted human costs on Israel for its colonisation of the West Bank/Gaza. Given this, the existence of trans-state Islamic movements shaping the identity of publics across the region appears to give political Islam some potential to shape (and concert) the foreign policies of ostensibly Muslim states against common enemies.

Moreover, the revival of Islam has potentially enormous significance for the global position of the Muslim Middle East. Over one billion Muslims worldwide constitute majorities in over forty states while the Muslim diaspora in the West numbers in the millions (Murden 2002: 185). Political Islam is the main ideological competitor of globally triumphant Western liberalism. In Murden's view (2002: 204): 'In a world rapidly being swallowed by an all-pervasive global system, Islam [is] a diffuse grassroots counter-hegemony'. But this does not necessarily mean that a growing clash of civilisations between Islam and the West is becoming the major axis of post-Cold War international relations or even that Islam is becoming a power in world politics.

As regards the clash of civilisations, it is not so much Western civilisation that Muslims contest (or 'envy' in Washington's discourse): ordinary Muslims avidly consume Western products and Muslim militants seek to selectively incorporate Western technology and practices, including democracy and capitalism, into an Islamic version of modernity. The battle is more within the Muslim world between state and society and over social practices within homes and schools than between Islam and the West (Halliday 1999: 130–1). Far from there being a monolithic Islamic animosity to the West, Iranian President Khatemi's call for a dialogue of civilisations was widely endorsed in the Islamic world

Rather, what generates conflict (and spawns anti-Western terrorism) is the West's penetration of and subordination of the region: the themes that Osama bin Laden believed to have the greatest resonance for his potential constituency were, like the grievances of Arab nationalism, explicitly rejections of the US *impact on the region*: its perceived support for Israeli denial of national rights to the Palestinians, its post-1991 vendetta against a defeated Iraq, its imposition of neo-liberal economics, its military bases in the Gulf, and its control, via client regimes, over the disposition of the region's main resource, oil. It is less a clash of civilisational values than of material interests, hence one resolvable through compromise (Fuller and Lesser 1995: 9), although it is certainly possible that the systematic targeting of Muslim states and movements by the Bush regime could elevate a conflict of interests to the higher civilisational plane (Munson 2003).

So far, however, Islam has had no impact, comparable to Arabism at its height, in generating shared foreign policy norms which could effectively organise Islamic states against common enemies (George 1996: 79–80). To be sure, given the continued legitimacy deficits of the individual states, state élites still need to be seen to defend

Arab-Islamic norms in the face of a public periodically aroused by Islamic (in place of Pan-Arab) movements. Even if regimes can now more easily weather dissent in the streets than hitherto, there is still a legitimacy cost to be paid for openly violating such norms and in certain circumstances Islamic activists have been able to call leaders to account for that; arguably the assassination of Sadat was in part for his separate peace with Israel while the 1982 Islamic rebellion against Asad's Syria was in part a result of the legitimacy loss suffered by the regime for its intervention in Lebanon against the PLO, keeper of the Palestine cause (Noble 1991: 53–4). Particularly in time of crisis with Israel or the West, the older generation of Arab nationalists and younger Islamic militants have come together to pressure regimes from below and it is chiefly the fear of de-legitimisation at home which forces states to justify, disguise or refrain from policies that affront the Arab-Islamic identity of their populations. But under pressure from without—increased exponentially from the US hegemon in and after the second Iraq war—many have been forced to pay such domestic costs. While there may be a growing clash of civilisations at the popular level—where opinion polls in the Muslim world since September 11 have shown overwhelming negative views of the US—this has not seeped up to the level of state policy.

Indeed, even where Islamists themselves have managed to gain access to the levers of power (as in Turkey in 1997 and 2002) or amassed influence in the legislature (as in Jordan, Kuwait, Morocco and Yemen), they have not been able to force a significant Islamisation of states' foreign policies. To be sure, in Iran where Islamic revolution wholly overturned the previous power structure and its pro-Western foreign policy, the Islamic regime explicitly sought to export a Pan-Islamic revolution aimed at creating similar Islamic states that would have acted against 'world arrogance'—the United States and its regional client regimes—in the name of the oppressed (*mustaza'fin*) of the Muslim and Third worlds (George 1996: 82). Iran's example and encouragement did much to spread Islamic movements across the region, but the export of Islamic revolution was ultimately contained within Iran, not least by the alignment of the mildly Islamic Gulf states with secular Iraq in the Iran-Iraq war. No secular regime was overthrown; rather, it was Iran's Islamic ideologues that were displaced from power in Tehran by pragmatists bending before global pressures and seeking to put Islam in the service of the Iranian state rather than the reverse. Moreover, although there are now more overtly Islamic states than hitherto, these regimes—in Afghanistan, Iran, Pakistan, Saudi Arabia and Sudan profess different versions of Islamic ideology, are more often than not in open conflict with each other, and in several cases are actually aligned with the US, the perceived enemy of most Islamists.

At the supra-state level, the Pan-Islamic institution, the Organisation of the Islamic Conference (OIC), is based on mutual acknowledgement of state sovereignty, has no power to co-ordinate common action, has no record in settling inter-Muslim disputes and is less an actor than an arena in which Muslim states seek legitimacy or allies on behalf of state interests. The rivalry between its three pivotal members, Saudi Arabia, Iran and Pakistan, and their different relations to the US hegemon have paralysed collective action. For the Saudis, who initiated the OIC as a legitimising tool against Pan-Arabism, an effective Muslim foreign policy would bring conflict with their US patron; thus, in deference to Washington, they blocked OIC initiatives to resolve the Iraqi occupation of Kuwait and to arm Bosnian Muslims. Fear of offending Washington prevented an OIC stand against US sanctions on Iran and on Pakistan for its development of the sole nuclear capability in the Muslim world. The OIC was silent on the genocidal UN sanctions against Iraq until quite late in the day and on the US bombing and invasion of Muslim Afghanistan. Most Muslim states, themselves multi-national, had an interest in the principle of states' territorial integrity that prevented OIC stands in defence of Muslim self-determination in Kosovo and Chechnya (Sheikh 2003). The OIC was, ironically, a vigorous defender of state sovereignty which it saw as a defence against Western hegemony. Yet the very existence of the OIC as a regularly convened Pan-Islamic conference made it a focal point which accentuated consciousness of all-Muslim issues and, more rarely, articulated a consensus on them. Thus, after the 11 September events, the OIC condemned terrorism but rejected 'any linkage between terrorism and rights of Islamic and Arab peoples, including the Palestinian and Lebanese...to self-determination... [and] resistance to foreign occupation [which are] legitimate rights enshrined in the United Nations charter' (OIC Qatar communiqué, 10 October 2001 in Murden 2002: 204). But the OIC could hardly be said to aggregate Muslim power in world politics.

In summary, while decision-makers cannot wholly ignore political Islam in foreign policymaking, no Islamisation of foreign policy has resulted and no Muslim bloc has emerged to redress the global power imbalance against the Islamic world. As with Arabism, state structures, the anarchy of the states system, the absence of economic interdependence among Muslim states and their dependence on the core, all deprive Pan-Islam of a material substructure that could make identity the basis of effective common action.

Conclusion

Identity matters and constructivism has done Middle East studies a service in providing a theoretical approach for understanding it in the region. But constructivist accounts that neglect the material context of identity are as misguided as materialist attempts to reduce it to an epiphenomenon. Material and normative variables are autonomous, but a stable social order depends on a relative congruence between them. When norms do not correspond to material structures, the former lack the material anchor to endure and the latter the legitimacy to survive without the continual application of coercive power. Arguably, the main source of the enduring instability of the Middle East is the continuing contradiction between externally imposed structures (the fragmenting states system, the region's international dependency) and the region's Arab and Islamic identities. The regional states system seems here to stay but, equally, Arabism and Islam are too deep rooted in historic memory and social communication to be readily superseded by newly-constructed state identities as 'instrumentalists' might imagine. But the incongruence between state and mass identities does generate continuous attempts by both states and opposition trans-state movements to bridge the gap.

Understanding this dynamic requires a theoretical approach that charts the *interaction* of material structure and norms, of interests and identity, and this requires bridging the constructivist–utilitarian gap. One commonly proposed compromise is to use constructivist methods in a first step to trace how domestic identity shapes states' conceptions of their interests; thus rather than *a priori* defining interests as wealth and power, Arab nationalism and Islam could be shown to shape a notion of interest putting a high value on regional autonomy. In a second step, utilitarian analysis would then show how states pursue these interests through rational strategies in a world of constraints—which, for small Middle Eastern powers, would likely require that they be considerably compromised. This at least acknowledges the equal importance of identities and structural constraints in explaining state behaviour; but in artificially separating the international and domestic levels it obscures the vital significance of their interactions (Seidman 2002).

Thus, Pan-Arab identity and norms were constructed, not just in a domestic struggle within states but also through state interactions amidst the discourses of trans-state movements and against a backdrop of shared language and culture. Secondly, states cannot simply be assumed to represent popular identity in their foreign policies; on the contrary, in the Middle East external (Western) constraints increasingly force states to *contain* it. In doing so, state élites attempt to reconstruct popular identity by pointing to the 'realities' of external constraints—Israel's power, economic dependence on the West—as requiring a deflation in the normative expectations of Arabism and Islam.

As a recent text on the issue shows (Telhami and Barnett 2002), because identities are multiple, fluid and open to various interpretations, state élites have been able, at least within sprawling state establishments, to construct alternative state-centric identities that better suit their immediate material interests (whether security or wealth). Contested at every step by counter-élites seeking to mobilise popular support on the basis of Arabism and Islam, they have failed to marginalise these supra-state identities. Nevertheless, the material structures of repression, socialisa- tion, and co-optation at their disposal, reinforced from without, give them some advantage in this contest. In such circumstances, supra-state identities only set the broadest boundaries beyond which certain foreign policies are, for a period, excluded and within which several, chiefly expressive of élite material interests, are normally possible. As such, the partial key to understanding the international politics of the Middle East provided by constructivism must be deepened by attention to identity's interrelations with the materialist structures analysed by neo- utilitarian approaches.

Further Reading

BARNETT, M. N., *Dialogues in Arab Politics: Negotiations in Regional Order*, (New York: Columbia University Press, 1998). The classic constructivist account of Pan-Arabism.

JANKOWSKI, J. and GERSHONI, I. (eds.) *Rethinking Nationalism in the Arab Middle East* (New York: Columbia University Press, 1997). State of the art on the construction of national identities in the Arab world.

MURDEN, S., *Islam, the Middle East, and the New Global Hegemony*, (Boulder, Colo.: Lynne Rienner Publishers, 2002). Masterful interpretation of the clash of civilisations as a reaction against Western hegemony and penetration of the Muslim world.

TELHAMI, S. and BARNETT, M., *Identity and Foreign Policy in the Middle East* (Ithaca, NY and London: Cornell University Press, 2002). Applies the constructivist-realist debate to country case studies.

Note

1. That Arab identity remained important was indicated by the fact that, in one of the few episodes where people were forced to choose between it and Islam, in the Iran–Iraq war, Iraqi Shi'a put their Arab identity over their religious ties to Iranian Shiism.

8

Alliances, Cooperation and Regionalism in the Middle East

Louise Fawcett

Overview

International Relations approaches to the study of cooperation in the Middle East have been heavily influenced by traditional power politics or realist approaches. At first sight this is convincing. Cooperation between states of the region has often been frail and transient, alliance making reflective of internal and external power balances, and regionalism, as the building of international regimes or institutions, perfunctory. This chapter reviews the experience of the Middle East in the light of the International Relations literature and suggests that it is more complex and diverse than commonly assumed. There are deep forces for cooperation, particularly in the Arab world—deeper than many other regions—and the potential for cooperation in both broader and narrower regional contexts, but suspicion and rivalry, together with regime insecurity and external intervention, overlie attempts to create any regional community. Global trends push the Middle East into new arenas of cooperation, but there is a need to map these on to local realities.

Introduction

How and why states cooperate, and the related questions of when they build alliances and with what effect, and the ways in which regionalism, regional institutions and regimes contribute to regional and global order are all issues which exercise scholars of International Relations. Theories have been designed and refined to help answer these questions, and have been applied to different regions. This intellectual effort is clearly important in terms of explaining and predicting state behaviour, but also in highlighting ways in which states can cooperate for pacific and productive purposes, and thereby promote regional, and international community. Building regional peace and security is an important stepping stone to the construction of a more secure global order. Indeed it has been singled out as a priority by different UN Secretary-Generals since the end of the Cold War, notably by Boutros Boutros-Ghali in his *Agenda for Peace* (1992). Middle Eastern scholars are also concerned with these themes, but their focus is different. Their domain is the local rather than the global. Alliances, cooperation and regional order and important because they help guide and frame the debates over domestic politics and society, about peoples and governments. In this way, the state, society and the region are intertwined.

The introduction to this volume noted some of the challenges involved in bringing together the strands of Middle Eastern and International Relations scholarship. Some of the possibilities, alongside the difficulties involved, are discussed in the different chapters of the book. This chapter addresses the problem in terms of the politics of alliance, bloc or region building. It looks first at some problems of relevant theory and its application to the Middle East case; second at the definitional questions that arise when speaking of regions, regionalism and the dynamics of cooperation; third at the record of different forms of alliance making and cooperation across the region; and finally, offers a contemporary balance sheet. It argues that such issues are central to the study of the international politics of the Middle East because of the special nature of its security dilemma. Insecurity operates at three interrelated levels: the domestic, regional and international. And, in contrast to many parts of the world, it is only poorly mitigated by the effects of cooperation between states, institutions, and other actors.

International Relations Theory and the case of the Middle East

Mainstream International Relations theories see alliance or bloc building as principally self-interested behaviour by states to maximise security and relative position. When states cooperate it is not because they seek to promote any greater regional or global good, but because their interests are served or preserved by so doing. Regional groups, agencies and regimes, have been cast in similar light, as power and security maximisers. Strong states are often identified as key agents in this process, though small states also initiate cooperation to consolidate strength or balance opposing power. States that lack security and power on the international stage, might be expected to construct alliances or regimes to bolster their power, or to look to strong states for help in their construction and maintenance.

The most important of these theories, realism and neorealism, ascribe to states certain unitary properties, but while the former acknowledges certain national attributes and 'social texture' (Ruggie 1998: 7), the latter focuses on the structure of the international system (Waltz 1979). In giving prominence to security and anarchy in international relations, such theories have functioned well as all purpose explanations of many patterns of state behaviour: inter-European relations until the period of the two world wars for example. In the Middle East, where cooperation between peoples across borders was far denser, and until the Second World War was still a state system in the making, they seem less appropriate. Nonetheless, realists would argue that such cooperation as exists is merely contingent upon the restless drive of empires and states for security. In the short life of the modern Middle East, they would point to the different arrangements and groupings of both Arab and non-Arab states: whether in the Arab League, Baghdad Pact, or the Gulf Cooperation Council, as well as the different bilateral alliances including those of the United States with Israel and Iran (before 1979); or the USSR with Egypt and Syria as evidence of this. In this account states are mainly involved in securing or consolidating their position and power, or balancing against the power and threats of others (Walt 1987). Indeed, every major regional alignment, from the positions adopted in the Cold War and the Arab–Israeli conflict, right through to the Gulf War coalition of 1991 have been thus explained.

Dominant states are facilitators and perpetrators of such projects, for they possess the requisite power to influence outcomes in the international system. Yet again, while the history of Europe, the Americas and East Asia, offers many examples of the exercise of hegemonic power, and the ability of strong states to exercise and extend their influence in the regional and international system, the Middle East has a poor record (Lustick 1997). Different states have had such aspirations: Egypt has often been regarded as the 'natural' leader of the Arab world, and at times displayed the characteristics of a hegemon, particularly under the charismatic presidency of Nasser, but its economic, cultural and military power were not robust enough, or robust enough for a sustained period to warrant that title. Saudi Arabia has displayed similar qualities in terms of claims to religious legitimacy or the power conferred by oil wealth on a large, though thinly populated state; both Iraq and Syria have made different bids for regional dominance, using military and nationalist tools; so, in different ways, has pre- and post-revolutionary Iran. If power is about the ability to influence outcomes, it is clear that most Middle Eastern states have failed to acquire it (Nye 2003: 67). The exception is Israel, the obvious regional great power, yet one which has failed, so far, to help construct a viable order, for reasons that relate to its regional isolation, external dependence and domestic structure alike.

Looking to regional great powers and power balancing techniques to explain and predict the behaviour of Middle Eastern states in war and peace thus only provides a partial picture. Middle Eastern states have been bad balancers and weak hegemons. First, because of the absence of obvious hierarchies between states; second, because of their feeble balancing behaviour; and third, because of presence of powerful identities that overlap and even conflict with the existing state system. We could extend the range of our discussion to external powers, and demonstrate how they have frequently called the tune in the Middle East, citing France and Britain before the Second World War, the US and USSR during the Cold War, and the United States since, but again our explanation would be incomplete. The Middle East system may be deeply 'penetrated' but it is also highly resistant to external pressure for change (Brown, L.C. 1984: 3). System-level analysis is inadequate therefore, because the behaviour of the Middle East also demonstrates the power of ideas—of both shared and conflicting identities—and their constant interaction with regimes and peoples. In short the International Relations of the Middle East is shaped, and constantly reshaped, by local, regional, international and transnational pressures.

The obvious difficulties with realist accounts in analysing the behaviour of regional states are only partly resolved by a consideration of competing approaches. Admittedly these are diverse, and cannot be done full justice here. Structuralist arguments which employ a core-periphery perspective in describing imperial-type orders, have their uses in explaining the postion of not only the Middle East (Hinnebusch 2003: 14–53) but a range of developing countries in the international system. Inasmuch as they focus on the unequal distribution of power—economic, political and social— they suffer also from the weaknesses of realist approaches in their failure to examine the diverse capacities of states, and the shifting fabric of Middle Eastern peoples and societies. Other theories that similarly critique traditional understandings of the international system have value in forcing us to rethink the appropriateness of existing paradigms, but cannot be taken too far, as Sami Zubaida demonstrates for the case of Islam in the Middle East. Rejecting 'essentialist' or 'orientalist' theses which demand a different starting point for a study of Middle East politics, he shows how Islam in its modern form has grown and developed alongside the modern state system (Zubaida 1989). Constructivist theories, which also prioritise shared experi- ence, norms and values, as against crude measurement of state power, would appear to have considerable purchase in a region where ideas and identity retain strong explanatory value (Barnett 1996). Yet, as John Esposito has pointed out, diversity and differential experience across states is a feature of both Arabist and Islamist movements in the region (Esposito 1992: 202).

For many international relations theorists, rejecting realist descriptions of state behaviour does not mean engagement with the type of critical approaches described above. Rather, it means an adaptation of realism, to acknowledge the significance of actors and forces other than states, and to incorporate types of cooperative behaviour. This adjustment to pluralism may be small, but significant. Newer liberal theories, while rejecting idealist claims about the declining salience of states, or the future emergence of world government, focus instead on the possibilities of cooperation amid anarchy, through the positive and norm-enforcing role of regimes and insti- tutions (Keohane 1984). They capture aspects of broader theories of interdependence which similarly see states moving towards common goals and policies, shaped by shared interests: economic, political, strategic and social.

Applying the latter types of theory to the Middle East appears no less problematic than either realist, or more radical approaches. International regimes—as agreements over common rules and procedures—and institutions in the Middle East have been notoriously flimsy: states may agree on certain principles and norms that should govern behaviour but cannot trust others to keep or enforce them; hence the rate of defection is high and the (relative) security of bilateralism often preferred. The weakness of institutions is closely related to the relatively weak interdependencies between states, at least of the economic and political kind which would make states prone to cooperate. Functional cooperation, of the sort identified at the core of cooperation in Europe, has taken place but remains limited in comparison with other regions. The nature of the oil economy, despite evidence of common strategy and design within the Arab states of OPEC, helps to explain the limits of economic cooperation, while diversity of regime type and interest, together with external influence have in turn constrained political cooperation. Taken together liberal theories of interdependence, or institutionalism, cannot be said to have real impact. At the risk of generalisation this might once have held also for regions outside Europe or the North Atlantic area, but recently Latin America, Southeast Asia, and Africa have all enjoyed some success in embracing a wider economic and security agenda.

Of the approaches outlined above, those that appear useful are aspects of realism and structuralism, combined with elements of constructivism, and domestic level explanations, which question the state system as the primary determinant of regional behaviour. The region has a history of external dependence and interference, which explains the attractiveness of both realist and structuralist theory, but the short life and artifical nature of many states together with the common bonds of language and religion—among the Arab states at least—highlight aspects of constructivism. In addition, the interests of individual states—reflecting regime type, and a range of domestic considerations, as well as regional and broader systemic constraints—are also crucial to understanding how they will position themselves in the international arena.

Considering the behaviour of Middle Eastern states in the international system demands a flexible and inclusive theoretical framework that incorporates the politics of power and influence, but includes the role of diverging ideas and interests. No single theory, or level of analysis offers a way of exploring satisfactorily the shifting and complex dynamic of interregional politics, or the international politics of the region, or explaining why high levels of cooperation and intercourse, coexist alongside equally high levels of competition and conflict. One reason for this would appear to lie in the fragile relationship between state and identity in the Middle East, which helps to explain the relative weakness of states. This in turn accounts for the disjuncture between ideas and institutions, and the low levels of institutional cooperation generally.

The above reiterates the difficulties that the Middle East presents for International Relations scholars. The region, like many other parts of the non-western world, defies attempts at generalisation, and resists standard explanations. There is some validity in the complaint that theories of international relations have failed to take the Third World seriously and therefore cannot be relied upon to provide a guide to understanding its past or present (Ayoob 1995; Korany 1999). Still, even within this broad critique, the Middle East does appear to have been particularly unreceptive to these exercises.

Against this background, the chapter moves forward to look at the types of cooperation and alliance behaviour that have occurred in the Middle East. What have been the opportunities and constraints for the states of the region? Which arrangements and institutions have evolved? Apart from the different approaches outlined above, there is also considerable comparative material to draw on. These comparisons are useful in terms of revealing how the experience of the contemporary Middle East can effectively be mapped on to that of other regions. The study of regionalism in the Middle East has often been condemned as a sterile exercise, theoretically limited and empirically uninteresting. Such critiques reflect a narrow view: regionalism is not merely about identifiying bands of economic, political or security cooperation or integration; it should be seen as a flexible and evolving concept encompassing a wide range of actors and actions. It is about discovering and making effective an identity and purpose that relate to the needs of the region, and informs its interactions with the outside world. Successful states in International Relations belong to successful regions. Such regions are the major stakeholders in any given international order. The failure of regionalism reflects the failure of the region itself.

Regions, Regionalism and Understanding the Dynamics of Cooperation

Speaking of types of cooperation at the regional level as a prerequisite for successful participation in the international system invites a discussion of which regional unit or level of cooperation is best. We use the word 'region' freely. In the introduction we noted the formal definition of the region now known as the Middle East. But in talking about cooperation and regionalism, more precision is needed. If we are trying to understand how the countries of the Middle East interact with themselves and with the broader international system, do we understand the Middle East as a single coherent entity or as a set of distinct, if related parts? Is it indeed meaningful to speak of processes like alliance-making, cooperation and regionalism in the Middle East as a whole, or is it sensible to subdivide the area in terms of explaining patterns of identity and behaviour? Which regional type is most useful? These are key questions, not just for the Middle East, but for regions generally, as the process and practice of regionalism takes on ever greater significance in the international system.

The term region has been analysed and explained in many different ways. It may be no more than a geographical reality, from a continent to a mere cluster of states or territories sharing a common space on the globe. Or it may be likened to a nation in the sense of an imagined community: a region held together by common experience, custom and practice. A mid point might be to see a region as a group of states linked together both by a geographical relationship and a degree of mutual interdependence. (Nye 1968: vii) Alternative approaches focus on regional patterns of security and conflict (Buzan and Waever 2003).

If we understand the Middle East as a region, we can see how elements of such definitions are useful: geography, history and a range of common concerns do indeed 'unite' the region, at least in one sense. Certainly, any durable peace settlement will require broad regional engagement. But security and other interdependences do not imply cooperation. There are deep divisions reflected in the absence of 'pan-regional' (as opposed to pan-Arab or pan-Islamic) institutions, despite recent efforts both by Europe and the United States, to promote them. Cooperation, when it occurs, is often fragmentary and transient. Alliances shape and reshape rapidly across a conflictual terrain where deep or institutionalised cooperation—regionalism—of which I will say more in a moment is limited in scope and purpose.

At one level, the idea of the broader Middle East as a region or as a system is a useful analytical tool (Hinnebusch 2002; Gause 1999) but it is also too limited and undemanding for our present purposes. Further division is required to highlight patterns of affinity, activity and cooperation. The Arab states, for example, form an obvious system (Sela 1998): a tightly knit community revealing dense patterns of both conflict and cooperation. For Paul Noble 'the Arab world is arguably the only meaningful international political system among the various continental or macro-regional grouping of states in the Third World' (Noble 1991: 72–3). This claim makes even more puzzling its relative lack of durable institutional cohesion (the Arab League notwithstanding). Other patterns and insights emerge when we consider sub-regional domains, where groups of states—Arab and non-Arab—come together for different purposes in a variety of settings. Some of these smaller settings—the Gulf, Northern Tier and the Mahgreb (North African) regions are examples—provide useful points of departure in a studies of cooperation.

Defining regions, their size and membership, is obviously important when we turn to a disussion of regionalism. Different regional configurations have yielded very different regionalisms. There is no ideal model. Europe is often cited as one, though in reality there are many different European experiences. In discussing regionalism, and the related process of regionalisation, I am not merely interested in a framework which looks for European-type institutions and structures, which might conform to some of the theoretical approaches described above, but use regionalism as a way of exploring the wider patterns of cooperation and conflict in the region.

Regionalism, as the process where states (and other actors) coordinate strategy and policy in any given region, is central to the debate about cooperation in the Middle East. The aim of regionalism is to pursue common goals in one or more issue areas. At its softer end, it may be little more than the promotion of regional awareness or belonging—a move towards the creation of a regional society. At its harder end it is represented by formal arrangements, treaties and organisation. It includes links between states, but also groups and individuals that operate both above and below the level of the state—a range of non-governmental, private sector, or civil society actors now operate at the regional level and can play important roles in promoting dialogue and cooperation. Negatively, it can also be taken to include regional terrorist and criminal networks, the object of much study both before and after September 11. In most formal arrangements—certainly in the case of the Middle East—the state continues to play the predominant role, and the bulk of the literature on regionalism focuses on the more measurable institutional forms of interstate cooperation.

Regionalisation is a related term, used in describing aspects of international order. It refers to a process (as opposed to a policy) that encompasses an increase in region-based interaction and activity: of doing things at the regional as opposed to some other level. Like globalisation, it may take place as the result of spontaneous forces. It has frequently been used to describe concentrations of economic activity, often as a precursor to the emergence of formal organisation or agreement. In recent usage it refers also to activity at the regional level that contributes to the promotion of international peace and security. This might involve the interaction of regional with global actors, like the UN. Post-Cold War international crises—including examples from Africa, Southeast Asia, Europe and the former USSR—have seen different experiments in regionalising peace and security. Indeed the success or failure of regionalism at the security level has increasingly been measured in terms of the ability of regional actors to act as providers of security within within different regions, to contribute to an 'evolving architecture of regionalization' (Fawcett 2003).

This discussion is relevant not because the Middle East is replete with examples of successful regional action, but precisely to highlight the low levels of regionalisation (Aarts 1999). While certain features are present—in migratory and labour movements, private sector networks, the disbursement of aid and development funds—its relative absence in other key spheres is notable. In particular regionalisation has been slow to generate common strategies or agreements. The regionalisation of conflict is real enough, but it too has failed to produce unified responses. In a recent study of non-UN peace support operations, Middle Eastern actors do not feature (Pugh 2002; UNDPKO 2004).[1] In a world where regional agencies have increasingly come to play a role in determining the parameters of peacekeeping and other activity within their respective areas, or where there are real signs of regionalisation—as cases in Europe, the Americas, Southeast Asia and Africa demonstrate—giving rise to elements of economic and security community, the Middle East remains on the periphery. In short neither regionalism, nor regionalisation have made a significant impact.

Cooperation and Regionalism: A Review

The next part of the chapter focuses on the history and experience of Middle East cooperation and regionalism from a comparative perspective, looking at the Cold War and post-Cold War periods respectively. This temporal division may prove to be something of an artificial one from the Middle Eastern viewpoint. There, unlike some other regions, the end of the Cold War had ultimately limited effects in terms of region building and conflict management, but from an International Relations perspective, the Cold War and post-Cold War provide rather different frameworks to analyse the experience of alliances and cooperation (Laidi 1994).

A long view

Viewed from an historical and comparative perspective, Middle East regionalism has a respectable pedigree, both from an institutional and non-institutional perspective. During the Ottoman period, a regional order, an informal regime by all accounts was clearly recognisable. The sense of community and belonging, born of Islamic authority and custom was strong. There was also a degree of pluralism in the sense of religious and minority toleration. The collapse of the Empire, abolition of the Caliphate, and the parallel emergence of a new state system had deleterious effects, but the notion of Islamic community persisted alongside the more recently dis-covered notion of Arab community.

In the period between the two world wars, as the new states moved towards independence, the absence of the formal institutions of cooperation was unre-markable. First, Middle Eastern states were concerned with the building of domestic structures. Second, no other regions in the world outside the Americas (with the Inter-American system) had any such institutions. Still, Middle Eastern states became acclimatised to the new culture of international organisation through membership of the League of Nations: Persia (later Iran), though not an original member, was invited to accede to the League Covenant in 1919; by 1935 Iraq and Turkey (and Afghanistan) were members, and by 1938 Egypt (Zimmern 1945: 526–7).

Regionalism, in theory and practice, met with mixed responses from the founding fathers of the League of Nations or the United Nations, for whom universalism lay at the foundations of a successful international order. In the case of the United Nations, however, it was the demands of American, Arab and Commonwealth states that influenced the final wording of the Charter, highlighting—in Chapter VIII—the role and responsibility of regional agency (Claude 1968: 5–6). And membership of the United Nations and its related institutions—most Middle Eastern states, with the exception of the Gulf and North Africa joined in 1945 (Roberts and Kingsbury 1993: 530–6)—became an important vehicle for representation and legitimacy.

As regards the Arab League, founded in 1945 (see Box 8.1), if Arab 'unity' was the theme which underpinned discussions over its shape and form, the organisation that emerged was built on the lowest common denominator principle, making it heavily state centric, with the preamble to the Charter emphasising the need to respect the independence and sovereignty of states. State sovereignty and Arab unity were awkward partners, but for Arabs, fear of domination by a single state and the multiple agendas of regimes, prevented a common stance. As Gomaa argues in his study of the League, this was a starting point: 'the loose form of association provided for in the Pact represented the most that Arabs could agree on in the circumstances' (Gomaa 1977: 26).

Box 8.1 Regional groups and unity schemes in the Middle East

The Arab League   1945–
Algeria, Bahrain, Comoros, Djibouti, Egypt, Iraq, Jordan, Kuwait, Lebanon, Libya, Mauritania, Morocco, Oman, Palestine, Qatar, Saudi Arabia, Somalia, Sudan, Syria, Tunisia, United Arab Emirates, Yemen

Baghdad Pact/CENTO   1955–79
(Great Britain) Iran, Iraq (left in 1959), Pakistan, Turkey

United Arab Republic   1958–61
Egypt and Syria

United Arab Emirates   1971–
Abu Dhabi, Dubai, Sharjah Ras Al-Khaimah, Umm Aal Qaiwain, Ajman, Fujairah

Federation of Arab Republics   1971–73
Egypt, Syria, Libya

Islamic Conference Organization   1971–
Middle Eastern members: Arab League States (see above) Iran, Turkey

Gulf Cooperation Council   1981–
Bahrain, Kuwait, Oman, Qatar, United Arab Emirates, Saudi Arabia

Economic Conference Organization   1985–
Afghanistan, Iran, Turkey, Pakistan, (Central Asian Republics)

Arab Mahgreb Union   1989–
Algeria, Libya, Mauritania, Morocco, Tunisia

Arab Cooperation Council   1989–90
Egypt, Iraq, Jordan, North Yemen

Unification of Yemen   1990
Creation of Republic of Yemen (ROY) uniting the former Peoples Democratic Republic of Yemen (PDRY) and the Yemen Arab Republic (YAR)

Euro-Mediterranean Partnership Programme   1995–
EU member states, Algeria, Cyprus, Egypt, Israel, Jordan, Lebanon, Malta, Morocco, Palestinian Authority, Syria, Tunisia, Turkey

The Arabs were not alone in achieving only a limited a modest form of interstate cooperation. Unity and solidarity were also on the agenda of the Organization for African Unity (OAU), but the scope of its activities was likewise modest. Sovereignty was a prize to be nurtured, not one to be sacrificed on the altar of a pan-movement, or one that extolled the virtues of integration. Other agencies and alliances emerging in this period had a heavily statist and often specifically Cold War agenda. Selective security pacts like the North Atlantic Treaty Organization (NATO), the Warsaw and Rio and Baghdad Pacts, the South East Asian Treaty Organization (SEATO) developed as products of the East–West divide, designed in part to serve the interests of the superpowers. Outside NATO and the Warsaw Pact (until the end of the Cold War), superpower dominance and the absence of a regional rationale limited their acceptability and influence. The Baghdad Pact, later the Central Treaty Organization (CENTO), was conceived by the Western powers as an instrument of Cold War containment, to supersede failed attempts to build a Middle East Defence Organization. Sponsored by Britain, but counting also on US support, the Pact was widely identified as an instrument of the colonial powers and their successor. It excited the hostility of non-members, while failing to command the support of its own (see Box 8.1). The regional justification for its existence dissipated after Iraq's exit in 1959. Subsequent US initiatives—like the Eisenhower Doctrine—to construct an effective regional alliance system met with equally mixed results.

The Arab League and Cold War alliances were not the only options. The West European experience of integration seemed to offer a different model and became a source of emulation throughout the developing world. It is true that the early European institutions had a strong realist rationale—that of securing Europe in an anti-Soviet alliance, but they went much further. The early successes of the original six European Community members presented a new regional challenge, which though rooted in the particular experience of Europe, was seen as a starting point for other such experiments. Attempts to create common markets and free trade associations in Asia, Africa, the Pacific and the Americas proliferated.

In the Middle East, Arab attempts between 1957 and 1967 to create a Common Market were characteristically ambitious, but ultimately failed. The European example and the consequences of the Suez crisis of 1956, assisted the drive towards economic cooperation and common resource management leading to the signature in 1964 (under the aegis of the League's Economic Council), of a treaty agreeing to the establishment of an Arab Common Market, scheduled to come into being in 1974. But lack of consensus over the type of agreement sought, over common tariffs and trade policies meant that the scheme soon failed, a failure shared by similar projects elsewhere (Kanovsky 1968; Owen 1999). The relevance of the European experience to what were, in the main, poor and insecure states with only the rudiments of a regional market, along with the assumption that such states would benefit from a customs union or similar, was brought into question. By the end of the 1960s the different experiments in regional integration had faltered; even in Europe, its proponents would question the continuing relevance of regional integration theory.

External penetration, inter-Arab tensions, domestic politics and the nature of the regional economy all help explain the fitful progress of cooperative efforts at the regional level. Despite the potential benefits of functional cooperation, particularly in areas like resource management, few durable achievements resulted. Typically, regimes found that their economic and military interests were better supplied either in ad hoc or bilateral alignments: through oil sales to the developed world, or through the receipt of military assistance and material from one of the superpowers. This did not mean that Arab identity or unity were irrelevant, simply that they could not supply the framework to overcome the security dilemma that different regimes faced.

The failure of an institution like the Arab League was by no means absolute. The League has always had its share of critics, but also supporters (Salame 1988). If the idea of the League as a vehicle for collective security went unrealised, a study of three cases of conflict between members, in which the League council was involved, the Lebanon-UAR conflict of 1958, the Kuwait–Iraq conflict of 1961 and the Yemen Civil War, 1962–7, shows that in the first two at least, the League had played a significant negotiating role[2] (Nye 1971: 161–5). Further, the League did achieve a certain unity of purpose and action in its stance against Israel and boycott of Israeli goods. Like the League of Nations, however, the Arab League has been criticised for its failure to achieve universality (in excluding key regional players) and judged more for its 'high politics' record in conflict prevention than for its achievements in other areas, of which development support through the Arab Fund is one example (Waterbury 1996: 368).

Other attempts at union and cooperation, with mixed results, deserve brief mention: the United Arab Republic (UAR), the Federation of Arab Republics, the Gulf Cooperation Council (GCC) and Economic Conference Organization (ECO). In a different category—and not strictly a Middle Eastern organisation—was the Islamic Conference Organization (ICO) (see Box 8.1 for details). While the first two briefly raised the tantalising vista of greater Arab unity, the middle two were of a more functional quality—perhaps that is why they lasted. The UAR revealed the many tensions inherent in any pan-Arab project (Kerr 1970). Behind the rhetoric of unity and cooperation lay the reality of state and regime interest. While those of Syria and Egypt briefly coincided the UAR survived. When seen as a vehicle for Egyptian hegemony, it collapsed.

The UAE and GCC provide two examples of how common regime type and security concerns can help sustain groupings whose members believe their interests and freedom of action are sustained by so doing (Tripp 1995). Britain's withdrawal from the Gulf in 1971 helped bring the Emirates together as a federation, an arrangement reflecting 'political necessity' as well as 'economic and social convenience' (Heard-Bey 1999: 136). As regards the GCC, it was the continuing insecurity of the region in the face of the Soviet invasion of Afghanistan and the Iranian Revolution (1978–79) that drove Gulf States into a new security alliance. Security certainly appeared as the major motivation behind the GCC—its lofty talk of economic integration notwithstanding—and remained a central preoccupation during its first ten years of existence which saw first the Iran–Iraq war (1980–88), then the

Gulf War of 1990–91. External dependence and continuing rivalries among its members have prevented the emergence of what Karl Deutsch has called a 'security community' (Deutsch 1957): indeed in this regard the GCC has done rather less well than a number of parallel sub-regional security organisations like ASEAN, or ECOWAS, though probably better than SAARC in South Asia (Barnett and Gause 1998). Despite its limitations, however, and the powerful presence of the Saudis, the GCC has come to be regarded as one of the region's more successful organisations, though the Gulf War and subsequent developments were to test its unity and independence of action, while also exposing its limited capacity to act against powerful external threats.

There were windows of opportunity for Arab states in this period as in the period which followed the Cold War. A high point of Arab solidarity can be identified between 1967 and 1974, followed by fragmentation and breakdown from the mid-1970s till the outbreak of the Gulf War in 1990 (Sayigh 1991). In those years a consensus emerged over the desired regional order—as evidenced in Arab summit meetings,[3] the October 1973 War and the oil embargo—which, however briefly, saw a coordinated set of Arab responses to the US–Israel position. It did not last. The consequences of the war, the Camp David accords (1979), the lost economic opportunities and the threatening regional environment, caused introspection—a decline in support for core issues and a shift away from Arabism to state nationalism. The structures of cooperation were too fragile to endure: regional states proved as willing to break the consensus as they were to lead it.

Outside the region itself, there were other opportunities for Middle Eastern states to participate in diverse multilateral fora, where regionalism based on a 'southern' identity engaged different groups of developing countries. The Non-Aligned Movement (NAM) provided an important venue for Arab countries, while other developing states in turn enjoyed the fruits of the short-lived Arab successes of the 1970s. Collective action among Arab states in OPEC was inspirational in terms of the broader Third World movement, particularly in articulating demands by the Group of 77 (developing) Countries for a New International Economic Order. These achievements, like those of the Arabs themselves were ultimately ephemeral, but deserve mention in the context of broader regionalisms seen as expressions of resistance to the existing international order.

By the end of the Cold War, the individual and collective achievements of Middle East states—whether at the regional or southern level—were few. The system was in deep crisis, reverberating from the consequences of the Iranian Revolution, the Iran–Iraq War which followed (1980–88), and the Camp David Accords (1979) which had exacerbated Arab divisions, and resulted in Egypt's temporary expulsion from the Arab League. Certainly, inter-Arab cooperation and bloc creation appears insignificant against the record of US and even Soviet alliance-building in the region. Not that either of the two superpowers were ever fully satisfied with their efforts, particularly the USSR, but also the US, despite a series of intiatives designed to put in place a viable containment strategy. Taken overall however, the different relationships forged between the United States and key Arab states, to say nothing of Israel, Iran (until 1979) and Turkey (a member of NATO since 1952); and the USSR with—albeit temporarily—Egypt, Iraq and Syria, are a more robust memory of the international politics of the region than the fitful efforts of the Arab League or the GCC. Inter-Arab alignments whether bilateral or multilateral had all too often proved transitory and fragile.

Beyond the Cold War

So what changed with the end of the Cold War? From an International Relations perspective, this was a period of major global change, with the perceived delivery of a substantial peace dividend and the expansion of the related processes of regionalism and globalisation. Globalisation, because of the continuing opening of markets and demolition of alternative economic strategies, and the revolution in communications and technology which assisted in the flow and fusion of ideas, politics and societies. Regionalism because of the once more powerful example of Europe, taking off again around the mid-1980s, but also the removal of superpower overlay, contributing to greater regional purpose and empowerment. Obviously, these processes, like the end of the Cold War itself, affected different parts of the world in different ways, both positively and negatively. For some states, the old world of International Relations—of interstate war, alliances, balances of power and threat—now seemed strangely irrelevant; for others the change was outwardly dramatic but ultimately less profound.

In the Middle East, the response to the Cold War's end was particularly mixed, for the new era was characterised by both continuity and change (Sayigh 2000; Miller, 2003). The region's most important rivalries and tensions were not of the Cold War type: the Arab–Israel conflict, the Iranian revolution and the Iran–Iraq War all were profoundly affected by the both the Cold War and its ending, but their causes lay elsewhere. More generally, there was necessarily a rethinking of external alliances and commitments, particularly where the USSR and Eastern Bloc were concerned, and, to some extent the United States also, though for the latter, Cold War or no Cold War, regional security and oil remained top priorities and continued to condition regional alignment. Still, the fear of marginalisation, common to many developing countries, was also felt by different states of the region, prompting new cooperative ventures. Early responses to the so-called 'new regionalism' (Fawcett and Hurrell 1995) came in the form of the two new schemes: the Arab Mahgreb Union (AMU) and the Arab Cooperation Council (ACC) both formed in 1989 (see Box 8.1). The revival of the Yemeni unification movement that year was also related to the changed post-Cold War environment and the drying up of Soviet support for the South Yemen regime (Halliday 2002: 272). In 1992, following an Iranian initiative to bolster indigenous security initiatives, the ECO was expanded to include the six Muslim Central Asian states and Afghanistan. These developments were more than matched by a proliferation of new groups in other areas including MERCOSUR in South America, and the Asia Pacific Economic Conference.

As far as the specifics of the Middle Eastern case are concerned a few points should be noted. The AMU was no new idea and flowed logically from the renewal of diplomatic relations between Algeria and Morocco in 1988; it was also a response to and borrowed heavily from the European experience. In its early commitment to the creation of a common market—commitments repeated in new regional experiments in South America and Southeast Asia—the impact of Europe is apparent. In contrast however, inter-regional trade was slow to take off and political quarrels have often kept AMU leaders away from the summit table. In contrast, relations between individual Maghrebi states and the European Union have been consolidated as part of the Euro-Mediterranean Partnership Programme (see Chapter 14).

In relation to the short lived experiment that was the ACC, it appears that the European challenge was also a factor. So too was the chronic state of regional instability in the wake of the Iran–Iraq war and the eruption of the Palestinian *intifada*. Many speculated that the ACC aimed at Iraqi containment—as such it was a failure. Iraq's invasion of Kuwait in 1990 demonstrated the fragility of previous attempts to build a regional order, and revealed that the end of the Cold War, for the Middle East at least, had not diminished its security dilemma, or even the spectre of interstate war.

The emergence of these new regional alignments within the space of a few years highlighted the impact of regional and global change. At the regional level, if bloc building had been profoundly influenced by the Arab–Israeli conflict, the Iranian revolution and the Iran–Iraq war, it continued to be shaped by the rapid pace of events. Two related developments—both to some extent products of the new era—were of prime importance and interacted with the ongoing debate about post-Cold War regional cooperation: the Gulf War and the start of the Arab–Israeli peace process in 1991. The former had enormous knock on consequences for the institutions and axes of cooperation, killing off the ACC, dividing the Arab League and loosening Arab alignments. The Gulf War was a salutary reminder of the limits of regionalism and of the greatly preferred, but hitherto unimplemented Arab option. But Arab states lacked the power and the will to match Iraqi might and this task fell to a US-led coalition, a tactical alliance par excellence.

Preferring an Arab solution was a way of demonstrating the continuing power of identity politics, of doing things the 'Middle Eastern way', but the failure to achieve it merely reinforced the futility of such ideas unless accompanied by the appropriate level of cooperative commitment, whether of the military or diplomatic kind. Again, this was supplied by outside actors. In other parts of the world, in contrast, regional actors, inside or outside institutions, started to take on larger roles in the management of regional security—whether in South East Asia where ASEAN became involved in regional consensus building; in Africa where regional actors have taken on security and development tasks previously within the UN's remit; or in Latin America where the Central American peace processes and democracy building have been in part fashioned by regional actors.

The Gulf War itself could have ignited a positive regional response. Its consequences were profound, and continue to reverberate throughout the region.

The League's Secretary General resigned as the organisation divided over the invasion: this was probably the most serious crisis it faced. Its survival however, demonstrated the resilience of institutions to overcome serious internal strife. So did the GCC, though the Damascus Declaration, with its talk of a '6 + 2' arrangement which would have brought Egypt and Syria into the regional security frame, did not materialise. The GCC has continued to expand its functional cooperation and attempts to coordinate trade, with a commitment to a common currency by 2010. On the critical question of security, the organisation's profound weakness in respect of its powerful neighbours remains an insurmountable obstacle to strategic independence, and its members have not so far moved in the admittedly difficult and dangerous direction of including rather than excluding Iran or Iraq.

In regard to the Arab-Israeli peace process initiated in Madrid in 1991, the consequences of the Gulf War and the end of the Cold War were important facilitators, prompting external and internal actors to frame new responses to the conflict. While these efforts are dealt with in some detail in other chapters, a few observations are in order here. In the early post-Oslo days there was widespread talk of a new regional order. This was incorporated both in the rhetoric of a 'New World Order', articulated by President George Bush, and in the concept of a 'New Middle East' by former Israeli Prime Minister Shimon Peres (Peres 1993).

The new order under discussion was inclusive and ambitious. Underpinning it was the belief that a peace settlement, and reduction of military expenditure, would free up resources for economic and social development and promote wider economic integration on the European model. Reality tested such assumptions, and by the turn of the century the hoped-for dividends of the Oslo Accords, and the multilateral economic conferences that followed, failed to materialise. Resource and security interdependence, once more produced not cooperation, but conflict. Still, many would agree that the events and discussions of the decade, including the Euro-Mediterranean Partnership initiatives discussed in Chapter 14, remain an important point of reference, and could yet provide the cornerstone for further developments. Like the broader process of détente between the superpowers in the 1970s, which helped to put in place some early foundations for the end of the Cold War, this period in the history of Middle East regionalism may one day also be seen as having contributed towards a more viable order.

The prospects in 2004 are not encouraging. When one surveys the strategic impasse reached in the Palestine-Israel conflict, a situation to which both regional and external powers have contributed, the limitations of regional institutions and actors are striking. Neither the intermediary efforts of foreign powers, nor those individual Arab states—like Saudi Arabia in 2002, have succeeded in brokering a durable settlement.

These difficulties have been compounded by the unilateral turn in US foreign policy since 2001, epitomised by interventions in Afghanistan and Iraq, which have added further to regional confusion and fragmentation, yet also ignited further discussions about possible regional orders. Some considerable sympathy for United

States has become more muted since the events of September 11, with the elaboration of an 'axis of evil' and its remedy in a war on terror and weapons of mass destruction—both with particular focus on the Middle East. Ambivalence over the Afghan intervention turned to outright hostility over the Iraq War. Most Arab states publicly pronounced against US intervention—signalling that acquiescence or cooperation, of the sort some offered in the previous Gulf War or Afghan invasion, would not be forthcoming—but the war and occupation have failed hitherto to generate a common response.

Whether or not any new Iraqi regime will be conducive to regional stability and cooperation remains an open question. Certainly the United States and Europe—though not always in concert—have been party to considerable discussion about the best modalities for promoting regional cooperation in the Middle East in the longer term. One proposal has been for a security condominium, like the Conference for Security and Cooperation in Europe (now OSCE), which the Barcelona Process could also help to reinforce; another has been the creation of a Middle Eastern NATO, or a fomal defence pact between US and the Gulf states (Pollack 2003). The latter two would surely be unwelcome in the current climate where overt US involvement is resisted by many states. The former, with the European precedent in mind, may offer more promise as a broad forum in which confidence building and other cooperative measures can be aired. Other projects, including the 'Road Map', a peace proposal envisaging the creation of a Palestinian state by 2005, devised by the so-called Quartet (US, Russia, EU, United Nations), as well as the 'Greater Middle Eastern Initiative', on the agenda of the G-8 Summit in 2004, suffer from their over-reliance on external agency and their neglect or ignorance of regional priorities and actors.

Future problems and prospects

Far from opening up new vistas of unity and cooperation, the post-Cold War Middle East revealed serious forces of fragmentation and division—even before the destructive events of 2001—which key actors seem powerless to check. Identity politics, or the politics of Arab consensus, which in the past seemed to offer a way forward, have been seriously buffeted by the blows of recurrent wars and ongoing crises. They are not dead—the Arab world is quick to forgive its own—but a successful means of marrying identity and interests has not been found. The multiple allegiances that have long characterised the region have taken on new colours with Islamic groups competing with Arabism and states for popular loyalty and support. Collective Islamic voices in an organisation like the Islamic Conference Organization, have a role to play, and may lay some groundwork for cooperative strategies, but so far have a limited and often symbolic impact (Esposito 1992: 202).

Most worrying are the continuing calls to violence among radical Islamic groups and actors, which have not so far met with any concerted regional response. Again, in contrast to some other regions where September 11 and subsequent events have reinforced the desire to cooperate and yielded concrete measures, Arab states have so far failed to coordinate any common strategy, or even to reach consensus on the admittedly difficult task of defining terrorism (Laqueur 2003).

The oldest regional organisation, the Arab League, appears strangely irrelevant to the region's pressing most concerns, its difficulties epitomised by the absence or exit of key members from the Arab Summit in Tunis in May 2004, making meaningful resolution hard to achieve. Here, a useful contrast can be made with the African Union's ongoing projects, of which the New Economic Partnership for African Development is an example. Efforts to move other regional agendas forward continue, like the proposal for a Greater Arab Free Trade Area, with a projected completion date of 2008, or the GCC's commitment to a common currency, though both at the time of writing offer only limited prospects.

Recent developments in the region seem superficially to support a victory for the realist paradigm, which posits the USA, the external hegemon, holding, albeit with increasing difficulty, a regional balance of power between Israel and diverse Arab interests. Lesser players have minor roles: Russia (and the Central Asian states) also condition the regional balance of power on a somewhat different axis, through relations with states like Iran and Turkey. While Turkey's stance is both to the East and West, with EU membership a priority, Iran is currently developing a range of strategies to the make more of its immediate environment (Herzig 2004). Europe's potential to mediate—and to offer new roads to regionalism by policy and example—remains real but still underutilised. The region seems rudderless, without a core. Institutional progress is retarded by nature of US power and influence, and the contested shape of regional order. There are obvious Cold War parallels here, and many continuities. For alongside external powers and the enduring role of ideas, it is regime security, and this is critically linked to regime type that determines the positioning of Arab states and paralyses cooperative initiatives. In this regard the Middle East has fallen behind the rest of the world.

In addressing the question why the regional system still behaves in such anarchic fashion, we need to focus on the state. The state remains the essential ingredient in determining what makes for successful regionalism and cooperation in the long term. What initiates regional activity—for example external pressures—may not sustain it, so the role of states is central. Here capacity and regime type are crucial: where regionalism and cooperation are successful, states and regimes have a major role to play in promoting, generating and maintaining the processes that drive it. And when we look at state capacity, not only in the Middle East, but in a range of developing countries, the state is chronically weak, except for some, in a coercive sense. The state lacks legitimacy, being unaccountable to its own peoples, to say nothing of peoples and states belonging to a broader regional entity. Middle Eastern states have typically lacked the capacity, but also the will to make cooperation and regional institutions work, except in a narrow and self-regarding sense. Hence, the need to turn outside to resolve their security dilemmas. In this formulation regionalism and anything more than functional cooperation is merely a symbol, a valuable but disposable source of legitimacy for regimes whose own legitimacy quotient is low (Hudson 1977).

Democracy may be a sufficient, if not a necessary ingredient in this process—some successful cooperation at the regional level has occurred in the soft authoritarian states of South-East Asia—but it helps. It may be no coincidence that in regions like South America, and parts of the wider Europe also, the return or consolidation of democracy has helped to provide cement to the processes and institutions of coop-eration. For the case of the Middle East, we may be better off thinking of political *transformation* rather than 'transition to democracy', but the prospects for realistic regional engagement and cooperation do seem to lie beyond this transformationist phase.

It is perhaps unsurprising in this regard that the Arab Human Development Reports (2002, 2003, 2004)—important documents much cited in this volume—highlight governance, modelled on universal democratic principles as the key to change. While the reports are concerned with economic or what is called 'human development' they stress the necessity for fundamental political reform if the Middle East is to catch up with the rest of the world. And this relates as much to its inter-national relations as to its economic and social development. The message here may be that only regime change can finally give real purchase to the marriage of identity and interest, to viable forces and institutions of cooperation.

Conclusion

The three terms introduced in the title of this chapter, cooperation, alliances and regionalism might have been fairly peremptorily despatched with a discussion of their past and present limitations. That is the types of cooperation and alliance-making that have occurred have been limited, transitory, self regarding acts accomodated well within the realist state-centred analysis that forms the cornerstone of International Relations theory. There is no Middle East region that corresponds to any existing institution, no successful free trade area, no security community; no longer perhaps a core community of shared ideals. Despite some hopeful advances in the 1990s, the different regional groups and initiatives remain of relatively limited interest given their weak economic, political and security cooperation.

From the perspective of the early twenty-first century it is tempting to see the Middle East through the lens of US policy, as representing the backwater of regionalism, understood as both meaningful collaboration and engagement at the regional level and the possibility of translating that engagement onto the interna-tional stage. But this is a simple stereotype. It is true that the progress of the region has been enormously encumbered by external agency, the product of its strategic vulnerability and resouce capacity. External powers have undoubtedly contributed to the democracy deficit in some ways, not least in keeping the rentier state alive. But external agency will also be a crucial part in enabling the region to move forward. Alone, of course, it will not suffice, for the progress of the region depends critically on the successful and meaningful engagement of its own members. And here we need to look much harder at the fabric Middle Eastern states and societies to understand its current position. There are many opportunities for regional level action—engaging not only states but a range of non-state or civil society actors—for enabling the region to connect with the broader processes of regionalisation and globalisation. Staying on the outside, on the periphery of global trends, is not an option.

Nothing that has been said undermines the basic thesis that multiple identities and linkages bind together the Middle East, and that these will invariably affect regional outcomes and choices. In some ways the Middle East is privileged in this regard. In Europe identity is still in the process of construction and has flowed from other types of cooperation. But until identity and material interests coincide we cannot expect any liberal interpretation to prevail in explaining the International Relations of the region. If states feel threatened by Israel or Iraq, or even by a drop in oil prices, the politics of identity will not save them. There must be other compelling reasons to act. The success of the European project depended in the first instance on US power, and shared security and economic concerns. Similar factors explain the relative success of some regional arrangements in the Americas—a recent example is MERCOSUR. So together, but in different combinations, the quest for power and security, the actions of strong states, levels of interdependence, institutional frameworks and shared identities and values, can all play a role in promoting community and cooperation at the regional level, though ultimately we must move down to the domestic level of analysis to explain what makes such arrangements work. And in the Middle East, domestic arrangements inhibit rather than promote meaningful collective action.

The limitations and dangers of realism when applied to the Middle East, and the need for a multilevel approach to understanding the International Relations of the region, has been a constant theme of this and other chapters and is well brought out by Bahgat Korany: 'Foreign policies are shaped by national situations, values and perceptions of policy makers and global and regional environments. Systemic conditions provide opportunities or constraints to action and generate pressure that push or pull states in different directions' (Korany 1991: 49). The history of alliances, cooperation and regionalism in the Middle East amply bear this out.

Further Reading

BARNETT, M. N., *Dialogues in Arab Politics: Negotiations in Regional Order* (New York: Colombia University Press, 1998). A constructivist approach to understanding Arab order which challenges realism.

HINNEBUSCH, R. and ANOUSHIRAVAN, E., *The Foreign Policies of Middle Eastern States* (London: Lynne Reinner, 2002).

A fine work combining the skills of a number of authors and offering an up-to-date analysis of the foreign policy of Middle Eastern states, with useful insights on both their regional and international relations.

HUDSON, M., *Middle East Dilemmas. The Politics and Economics of Arab Itegration,*

(London: IB Tauris, 1999), A comprehensive volume which describes the different experiments in regional integration and cooperation across the region.

GUAZZONE, L. (ed.), *The Middle East in Global Change* (London: Macmillan, 1996). A useful work which examines different processes of interdependence and framentation in the region.

LUCIANI, G. and SALAME, G. (eds). *The Politics of Arab Integration* (New York:

Croom Helm, 1998). An earlier, though still very helpful volume, to be read in conjunction with Hudson (1999) above.

SELA, A., *The Decline of the Arab-Israel Conflict* (New York: State University of New York Press, 1998) Though superseded by events of recent years, this volume is a sustained attempt to apply an Arab system approach to understanding the dynamics of this conflict.

Notes

1. The possible use of Arab troops as peacekeepers in Iraq, after US withdrawal has been mooted.

2. In the case of the Kuwait–Iraq dispute, Arab League forces were deployed to thwart possible Iraqi aggression.

3. The Arab Summit process was initiated by Nasser in 1964. Summits have since been held at regular, often yearly intervals.

9

War and Security in the Middle East

Janice Gross Stein

OVERVIEW

The history of the modern Middle East shows that the prevention and management of conflict remains a major political as well as military challenge. While other states have moved beyond traditional security concerns to embrace a wider agenda to include human development and security, the Middle East still faces this fundamental dilemma. Using the Arab–Israeli wars as a case study, this chapter examines how theories of international relations can help understand the persistence of war, violence and intervention in the region. It tests and challenges traditional realist notions, arguing that the balance of military power can only partially explain patterns of war and conflict in the region. Finally, it suggests that fundamental political accommodation is required for the states of the Middle East to move beyond the current spiral of violence and retaliation.

Introduction

The modern Middle East has proven to be the graveyard of many contemporary theories of international relations. Theories of the origins of war, deterrence, compellence and negotiation have all come to grief when tested against the evidence of the last half-century in the Middle East. Tragically, the Middle East, along with Africa, has been and remains one of the most war-prone regions globally.

While other regions of the world have expanded their security agendas to include the safeguarding of the environment and water, the protection of people and the promotion of rights-based security, the Middle East has been largely resistant to the strategies of war prevention and conflict management that have had some degree of success in other parts of the world. The litany of war, violence and foreign intervention is long and continuing.

The Arab–Israeli conflict punctuated the modern history of the Middle East with full-scale war in 1948, 1956, 1967, 1969–70, 1973 and 1982. The most deadly war since the Second World War began in 1980 between Iraq and Iran and lasted for eight years. It was followed by Iraq's invasion of Kuwait in 1990 and the war to force Iraq's military forces from Kuwait in 1991. In the interim, the first *intifada* by Palestinians against Israel exploded in 1987 and continued for five years.

The last decade of the twentieth century sowed the seeds of hope that the trajectory of violence could be changed. In the wake of the Gulf War in 1991, intrusive UN inspections began in Iraq to disarm its nuclear and chemical weapons programmes. Intensive bilateral and multilateral processes of negotiation between Israel, Palestine and Arab states culminated in the creation of the Palestine Authority, and, with a few important exceptions, region-wide discussions of arms control, water, the environment, refugees and development. It seemed, for a few short years, that the wealth of the Middle East—its people and its resources—could be put to productive use in giving broader and deeper meaning to security.

That promise was dissipated, as expectations were frustrated through painfully slow processes of negotiation between Israel and the Palestine Authority that bitterly disappointed both. A second, more violent and more lethal *intifada* erupted in September 2000 that has killed over 500 Israelis and disabled thousands. Israel's retaliation and reoccupation have killed more than 2,500 Palestinians, wounded thousands more, and wrecked havoc with Palestinian institutions and society. Both communities are angry, embittered, despairing of progress and deeply distrustful of one another.

One year later came the al-Qaida attacks against Washington and New York, and the Middle East became the overwhelming preoccupation of the United States. Violence in the region was no longer a local concern, or related only to the security and stability of oil. The 'grand bargain' between the United States and the oil-producing states in the Gulf, where the United States imported oil and turned a blind eye to governance in the region, has come unstuck. In two successive wars, the United States removed the Taliban from Afghanistan and Saddam Hussein's government from Iraq.

The United States is merely the latest of the foreign powers—Britain, France and Soviet Union—to intervene with force in the modern Middle East. We begin the twenty-first century with an American occupation force entrenched in Iraq, in the heartland of the Arab world, and the Middle East wracked by ongoing violence.

In this context of seemingly unending rounds of violence, the security agenda in the Middle East is sharply focused. Safeguarding the environment and the promotion of human rights seem to many of the peoples of the region a fantasy, connected to a world that they have never experienced and cannot imagine. Attention is concentrated overwhelmingly on an end to violence and war, the creation of security from violent death, the development of accountable governments and governance and the creation of a viable and legitimate Palestinian state that can craft a solution for Palestinian refugees. In the Middle East, peace is intimately interconnected to legitimacy and rights. Peace without legitimacy and rights, and legitimacy and rights without peace are each unachievable.

How can theories of international relations help us to understand the persistence of war and violence and the repeated intervention of the great imperial powers? The dominant theory—realism—has traditionally brought a narrow focus to the understanding of war: the single variable of military capabilities. It explains the occurrence of war largely as a function of an imbalance in military capabilities and changes in that balance. Theories of deterrence, or the prevention of war, have focused on the denial of opportunity to attack through the accumulation of a preponderance of military capabilities which is so obvious that no would-be attacker would go to war, and demonstration of firm resolve to use force so that intentions can never be in doubt. There are several variants of realist theories, but, at their core, they all reduce the outbreak of war to fatal uncertainty about military capability and resolve.

This reading of the history of war in the modern Middle East is deeply flawed. An examination of the large-scale wars in the Arab–Israeli conflict and in the Gulf demonstrates that superior military capabilities and a demonstrated willingness to use force have rarely prevented an attack in the face of deep-rooted grievance or fear. Domestic pressures have interlaced with often fragile and authoritarian government structures to shape grievance or a perception of threat. It shows as well, contrary to realist expectations, that the 'learning from defeat', which is central to some realist theories, has been slow, uneven, and non-linear. Saddam Hussein in Iraq learned little from the costs of stalemate at the end of the eight-year war with Iran. Moreover, learning about the costs of violence has frequently been overwhelmed when grievance mounts. Angered by Kuwait's demands for repayment of loans at the end of the war with Iran, and convinced that the United States would exploit its status as the sole superpower to dominate the Gulf, Saddam made the catastrophic decision to attack Kuwait in 1990.

It is not enough to learn from defeat about the high absolute and relative costs of the use of force. Over time, leaders have had to learn about the costs of 'victory' as well as the costs of 'defeat' to break a cycle of violence and move to accommodation. As long as learning is constrained—by 'winners' and 'losers' alike—security will remain elusive in the Gulf and in the Arab–Israel conflict.

Analysis of the origins of war and of periods of accommodation also points to domestic economic and political factors as important proximate causes. We need to understand the Middle East from the 'inside out', paying close attention to the political struggles within as well as to the more traditional military balance. Finally, the struggle for legitimacy and rights are the overarching motifs that animate most of the war and violence within the region. At best, military balances are enablers rather than precipitants of war. If we focus our attention exclusively on military factors, we miss the most important part of the story.

The story the modern Middle East tells is that the prevention of war and violence is a political as well as military challenge. We first examine the limited currency of realist explanations of war by testing them in a detailed analysis of the long cycle of Egyptian-Israeli rivalry, punctuated repeatedly by war. We use this rivalry as a critical case, both to test theory and to extend the analysis of its successful termination to the ongoing Israel–Palestine conflict and other enduring rivalries. In the course of the analysis, we examine deterrence and compellence as theories and as strategies of conflict management that failed and explore how leaders have 'designed around' superior military capabilities and crafted strategies that compensate for military inferiority. Finally, we assess the likelihood that strategies of negotiation can accomplish more than simply introduce pauses in an unending spiral of violence and retaliation. Until and unless states within the Middle East reach fundamental political accommodation with one another, the region will continue to be hostage to basic security. Resources will continue to flow to military expenditures and away from the human development and human security that will define the future of the region.

War and the Failure of Deterrence: The Inadequacy of Balance of Power Explanations

Contemporary realists explain the origins of war through the breakdown of the balance of power and the failure of deterrence. These structural explanations look at the 'objective' capabilities of states and posit a set of conditions when states are likely to attack. They may attack when they identify an 'opportunity' for gain created by a favourable military balance, or they may attack when their power declines relative to others and they anticipate a less favourable future in which they can defend their interests. The first environment creates the conditions for an 'offensive' war and the second enables a 'defensive' war by a declining hegemon (Waltz 1979; Gilpin 1989). In both cases, it is the balance of military capabilities, a balance that can be measured objectively, that creates an environment conducive to war.

1948–49: The first war

Realist arguments have their greatest currency in the first war of the modern Middle East, the war by Arab states against the newly created state of Israel in 1948–49.

The balance of military power between Arab states and Israel was uncertain; it had never been tested. It was extraordinarily difficult for Arab leaders to estimate the forces that the new state would be able to field. Determined to prevent the partition of Palestine and the creation of the state of Israel, and uncertain of the balance of power, the Arab attack is consistent with realist theories.

The defeat did have a significant impact on elements of the Egyptian officer corps, but that impact had little to do with a reanalysis of the balance of capabilities, as realist theories would expect. Colonel Nasser and his colleagues among the Free Officers held King Farouk and his corrupt regime responsible for the military defeat. Indeed, the defeat was a powerful impetus to the coup against the monarchy, which took place in 1952. The corruption of the regime and the poorly paid and trained army were identified as the major reasons for the humiliating defeat. There was, however, very little serious analysis either of the fighting or of the relative balance of capabilities. Little attention was paid to the military advantages that Israel had been able to exploit successfully during the war (Safran 1969: 28–36). The expectation was that, under the leadership of the new regime, Egyptian military assets would soon be determining. There was little incentive to end the conflict.

1956: preventive war

A campaign of harassment across Israel's borders by Palestinian *feda'iyin* operating from Gaza began in 1954. In response to Palestinian pressure, President Nasser approved the formation of small, lightly armed Palestinian border guard and police units. The president thought that these units would be a useful way both to channel Palestinian protest and control infiltration (Sayigh 1991). The low-level challenge to Israel was the beginning of a process that culminated in reprisal raids by Israel and, through a process of escalation, in a preventive attack by Israel, in coordination with Britain and France, and an Egyptian military defeat in the Sinai in 1956.

Structural arguments of the balance of power and relative military capabilities have difficulty in explaining both Egypt's enabling of a low-level challenge and Israel's attack. Nasser's tolerance of raids across Israel's border began before the arms deal with Czechoslovakia in 1955, which could have changed the military balance in Egypt's favour. The challenge to Israel originated not in response to the 'pull' of a favourable change in the balance of capabilities, but rather to the 'push' of Palestinian pressure.

Israel's escalating reprisal raids were designed to compel Egypt to restrain Palestinian irregulars from crossing the border. This kind of strategy is consistent with theories of compellence that model a targeted use of force and a willingness to escalate in an attempt to compel the other to do something that it does not wish to do. The evidence suggests that the reprisal raids, rather than compelling the Egyptian government to restrain Palestinian forces, created a climate that made it more difficult for Egypt to restrain forces from crossing the border, even though Nasser did not want war with Israel. Although Egypt had not moderated its intentions toward Israel in the wake of the defeat in 1949, Israel was nevertheless a relatively low priority on Nasser's agenda during this period. The president was preoccupied with consolidating his regime against domestic opponents (Stein 1985a). We need to look beyond the relative military balance and inside Egyptian politics to understand Nasser's strategy.

Israel's preventive attack is also a puzzle for structural theories. The military balance and its meaning were disputed then and after the fact. The mobilisable forces of Egypt and Israel were about 200,000. Some analysts considered that Egypt had an advantage in heavy equipment, while others maintained that Israel had decisive superiority over Egypt (Safran 1969: 225; Jabber 1981: 115–21; Dupuy 1978: 3–19). It was the 'opportunity' provided by Egypt's nationalisation of the Suez Canal and the certainty of Anglo-French support that tipped the decision to launch a preventive war. That decision could not have been predicted from the ambiguous trends in the military balance.

Initiated as a preventive attack to establish deterrence and demonstrate resolve, the attack in Suez changed the trajectory of the modern Middle East. The Arab world now associated Israel with the 'imperial powers' and that association became part of the broader struggle against imperialism within the Arab world. After the war, accommodation became more, not less, difficult.

1957–67: the limits of learning

For eleven years, from 1956 until 1967, there was no war between Israel and Egypt. This was the longest period of quiet along the armistice lines until a serious process of negotiations began in the wake of the war in 1973. This period of 'stability' has been explained as a result of the credible reputation for offense that Israel developed in 1956 through its preventive attack and its enhanced capacity to deter. Despite the considerable political and economic pressures that Nasser faced, the argument goes, the Egyptian president resisted the temptation to challenge because he feared the consequences of escalation. Deterrence was created by the credibility of Israel's reputation forged in the crucible of war in 1956.

The argument hinges on evidence of what Nasser learned from the defeat in 1956. The military defeat in the Sinai in 1956—notwithstanding the considerable political victory that followed—did lead to considerable tactical learning. There was, this time, considerable re-evaluation of the relative balance of capabilities, but not in the way realists would expect. President Nasser explained the military defeat largely as a consequence of the collusion of imperialist powers. It was neither superior Israeli military capability nor performance but British and French participation in the attack against Egypt which provided the decisive margin. Egypt had faced the combined forces of Britain and France as well as Israel alone, without Arab military assistance. The logical implication was that if Israel could be isolated from its international supporters and subjected to a multifront Arab attack, it could be defeated (Dupuy 1978: 217–18 and Safran 1969: 56). Throughout much of this period, moreover,

Nasser was preoccupied with economic restructuring at home and the assertion of his leadership in the Arab world. Although he ruled out any accommodation, renewed confrontation with Israel was not a priority.

On several occasions, the Egyptian president came under pressure from Arab leaders to attack Israel. In November 1959, when Israel announced its plan to use the waters of the Jordan River for a national water carrier; in 1960, after a raid by Israel against Syria, then formally united with Egypt in the United Arab Republic; in early 1964, when the plan for the Jordan waters was completed; again in 1965 when Israel destroyed the equipment Syria intended to use to divert the waters of the Jordan; and most heavily in December 1966, in the wake of a retaliatory raid by Israel against the village of el-Samu in Jordan, when Nasser was criticised by Syrian, Saudi and Jordanian leaders for his failure to expel the UN force that had been stationed in the Sinai in 1957. In this last case, in the face of taunting from Arab leaders, Field Marshal Abd'ul al-Hakim Amir recommended that Egypt send forces to Sharm el-Sheikh on the Straits of Tiran, but President Nasser rejected the advice. In none of these cases was it likely that President Nasser would receive either unified Arab support or that Israel would be isolated from its western allies.

Even more important were regional and domestic challenges the president confronted. By 1962, after a coup in Damascus, the union with Syria had fractured and an embattled Nasser launched an ideological assault on conservative 'reactionary' governments throughout the Arab world. The president was convinced that reactionary forces had prompted the coup and that they were organising to defeat the 'progressive' forces. An intense 'cold war' broke out within the Arab world, and in the autumn of 1962, following a coup in Yemen, Egypt committed approximately 50,000 troops to the civil conflict that followed (Kerr 1971: 96; Dawisha 1976: 38–9; Gerges 1994: 166–80). By 1964, Egypt was deeply involved in a long and frustrating proxy war in Yemen against Saudi Arabia. Arab pressure on Egypt was high and building. During this period, Nasser was also deeply preoccupied not only with the challenge that he perceived from 'reactionary' monarchies to his leadership of the Arab world, but also with the restructuring of the Egyptian economy (Parker 1992, 1993, 1996). In a phrase frequently used by Egyptian diplomats in conversation with their American counterparts, Egypt's conflict with Israel 'was in the icebox and could remain there'. The Arab–Israeli conflict was not a priority for President Nasser and his motivation to mount any kind of challenge was low. The president was preoccupied with Arab adversaries and the Egyptian economy.

Analysis of Egyptian thinking from 1957 to the spring of 1967 provides considerable support for the realist proposition that tactical learning from military defeat induces caution. The evidence shows that President Nasser repeatedly counseled patience until the conditions that he had learned from the defeat in 1956 were necessary were in place. From 1964 to 1967, he actively restrained the PLO and imposed sharp constraints on the formation of Palestine Liberation Army units in Gaza in an attempt to limits their autonomy of action across the border (Sayigh 1991).

Caution, however, does not ensure 'stable deterrence' predicated on a favourable balance of military power. Realists expect that deterrence will become stable over time as a would-be challenger learns 'the hard way' about the capability of a defender through repeated failures of deterrence and military defeat and consequently reduces the scope of its challenges and gradually changes its goals (Lieberman 1994, 1995). War that results from the failure of deterrence, the argument goes, provides a valuable learning experience. Evidence from the critical case of the Egyptian-Israeli conflict lends very limited support to one of the core proposition of realist theories.

After almost two decades of 'learning' about the military balance, Nasser threw caution to the winds in the spring of 1967 as pressures from Arab leaders mounted. Leaders dissatisfied with the status quo tend to attribute the unsuccessful outcome of the last war not to the capability of the other side but to correctable shortcomings in their own military organisations. In short, psychological factors rather than a rational calculation of the balance of power best explains why learning from defeat is so limited for so long.

1967: a miscalculated war

Nasser's decision to blockade the Straits of Tiran on 22 May 1967 precipitated a war he did not want because he knew that Egypt was not yet prepared. This war is a puzzle for rational deterrence theory augmented by simple learning models. If cumulative learning over time had created an Israeli reputation for superior capabilities and had thereby reinforced deterrence stability, then Nasser should not have blockaded the Straits unless the balance of capabilities had changed significantly. There is no evidence either that it had or that Nasser had changed his estimate of the balance of capability until after he had blockaded the Straits. Contrary to the expectations of rational deterrence theory, policy drove estimates rather than estimates driving policy. We have seen the same pattern in the US and British intelligence estimates prior to the attack against Iraq in 2003.

No 'objective' changes in the balance of capabilities justified the radical and rapid upward revision of estimates of Egypt's capacity to go to war. Egyptian military commanders overrode the caution that Nasser had expressed just a few months earlier. Their optimism cannot be explained as a rational calculation under conditions of uncertainty. Why did Egypt's leaders miscalculate the balance of capabilities so badly?

Some of Nasser's close associates speculated after the war that the president was deliberately misled by Field Marshal Amir who strongly favoured a military confrontation with Israel. Indeed, after the war Nasser acknowledged that Amir had misled him about the strength of the Egyptian armed forces (Mutawi 1987: 96). Amir exercised strong control over the armed forces through the promotion of officers who were loyal to him personally, and relations between the president and Amir were badly strained. While institutional politics undoubtedly contributed to the decision,

Nasser's extensive military background should have limited the credibility of Amir's optimistic predictions.

Far more important were the overwhelming impact of an aroused public opinion in Egypt and, particularly, the challenge to his leadership from Syria and Jordan. Pressure from Saudi Arabia, Jordan and Syria had been building in intensity over time. President Nasser had withstood the pressure from Jordan and Syria over the waters of the Jordan. More damning—and more difficult—for Nasser were the charges hurled at him when Egypt failed to respond to Israel's retaliation for an el-Fatah raid by attacking the Jordanian village of el-Samu in November of 1966. Jordanian officials bitterly criticised the Egyptian president's failure to meet his obligations under the Unified Arab Command established in Cairo in 1964 to come to the assistance of Arab states attacked by Israel (Mutawi 1987: 58). A full-scale propaganda war broke out between Egypt and Jordan that raged until the crisis in May. Still worse were the acerbic attacks by the government in Damascus when Egypt failed to come to assistance of Syria, its declared ally, after the humiliating outcome of an air battle with Israel in April 1967. Ambassador Lucius Battle, in his last cable from Cairo to Washington in the spring of 1967, warned that Nasser was in such political trouble in the Arab world that he would have to do something 'dramatic' to restore his prestige (Parker 1993: 92, 104–7).

Pressure can cumulate, as can learning. President Nasser, with his forces embattled in Yemen, the economy increasingly in difficulty at home, and subject to the repeated and growing taunts not only from Arab adversaries, but from an Arab ally as well, succumbed. Emboldened in part by misleading signals from the Soviet Union, and unable any longer to resist the clamour coming from the Arab world, Nasser chose to blockade the Straits, despite the pessimism of his estimates just a few weeks before. He then worked hard to ensure the coordination of Arab military support and the isolation of Israel that he had learned he needed and refused repeatedly his commanders' request to strike first. The president provoked a crisis not, as realists expect, because he was confident of Egypt's military strength but rather because of political weakness. Theories of deterrence focused attention in the wrong place.

The miscalculated war changed the face of the modern Middle East as Israel preempted and occupied the Golan Heights, the Sinai Peninsula, the West Bank and Gaza. More than three decades later, the Middle East is still living with the consequences of the catastrophic decisions made by Arab political leaders in those few weeks, decisions that no realist theory of war focused on the balance of military capabilities can adequately explain.

1967–70: defeat and learning to fight

Egypt suffered a massive military defeat in the war in 1967. The defeat was so overwhelming that Israel's leaders expected Egypt to moderate its political objectives in the absence of any conceivable military option and seek a political accommodation. This expectation is consistent with the evidence that even though leaders can deny ambiguous results, they do learn from unambiguous and catastrophic events. Anticipating this kind of correction, within days of the ceasefire, Israel offered to return the Sinai to Egypt in exchange for full diplomatic recognition and peace (Korn 1992: 13). Nasser, humiliated by defeat and pressed by Arab allies, categorically rejected the offer and began almost immediately to plan for war. Even though the Sinai was under military occupation, Egypt's leaders refused to entertain the option of its recovery through political accommodation. Until Anwar Sadat succeeded Nasser as president, Egyptian leaders saw no option but war to recover the Sinai.

In the wake of the defeat in 1967, Egyptian leaders learned that they could not eradicate Israel in a military campaign from the prevailing lines behind the Canal. Since they were not willing to regain the Sinai at the cost of the recognition of Israel and they could not tolerate the status quo, they faced a painful dilemma. This dilemma stimulated a search for military options that would impose unsustainable costs on Israel so that it would be forced, either directly or indirectly, to return the Sinai to Egypt. Indeed, as early as November 1967, even before Egyptian defences had been rebuilt, Nasser had determined that he would go to war again. Late in 1967, Nasser instructed his officers to press forward with plans for the liberation of Sinai (Korn 1992: 87, 93). Defeat made the prevention of yet another round of war significantly less, not more, likely.

Immediately after the war, Egyptian planners began for the first time in the history of their rivalry to analyse the performance of Israel's army. Egypt began to probe for Israel's weaknesses and to develop plans that could exploit Egyptian strengths in artillery and firepower and Israel's thin deployment along the Suez Canal. In short, Egyptian officers were learning in order to design around Israel's military superiority and craft a viable military option. Contrary to realist expectations, they were learning in order to fight, not to avoid war.

In the wake of defeat, the Soviet Union became heavily involved in the training and resupply of the Egyptian army. Soviet personnel on the ground advised strongly against any resumption of a strategy of attrition, anticipating that Israel would escalate in return (Korn 1992: 54). The Soviet presence was a restraint, rather than an inducement to Egyptian military action and Israel's military response. Unable to tolerate the status quo, President Nasser nevertheless ignored the advice and decided to launch an intensive war of attrition along the Suez Canal in January of 1969 that lasted until August 1970.

President Nasser wanted to impose heavy costs on Israel and expected that Israel would not retaliate with its air force behind Egyptian lines. He expected the visible Soviet involvement to deter Israel. Yet, twice after Egypt had begun intermittent shelling across the Canal, Israel had already struck behind Egyptian lines. Israel indeed was not anxious to escalate the fighting to the point where the United States and the Soviet Union would feel compelled to intervene. Nevertheless, as the static war continued along the Canal, it was predictable from Israel's emphasis on deterrence and resolve that it would seek to reduce casualties by taking the war behind Egyptian lines (Shueftan 1989; Shlaim and Tanter 1978).

The War of Attrition is instructive as a learning experience. Egypt's leaders, trapped in a painful dilemma, learned that it could not launch a full-scale attack, but risked escalation in an attempt to inflict heavy casualties on Israel even though they knew that the balance of capabilities was inferior and had suffered Israeli retaliation in the past. Dissent within the Egyptian senior leadership after the defeat of 1967, the anger of the public and intense pressure from the officer corps, which insisted that the army must avenge the defeat and redeem its honour, led Nasser to reject any diplomatic option and push for military action, almost as soon as the guns fell silent in June 1967 (Korn 1992: 88). Israel, reluctant to escalate because of the adverse political consequences, nevertheless chose to engage in deep penetration bombing because of its unwillingness to tolerate mounting casualties that were heavier on the Egyptian front than they had been in 1967. Egypt was not deterred and Israel was not restrained.

1970–73: who learned what from stalemate?

Egypt and Israel drew radically different lessons from the War of Attrition. After the Soviet Union engaged actively on the ground and in the air on behalf of Egypt and the United States intervened to arrange a ceasefire, both Israel and Egypt claimed victory and each insisted that it had defeated the other. Israel's leaders insisted that they had withstood a war of attrition designed to exact political concessions while Egypt claimed that, with Soviet assistance, they had stopped Israel's deep penetration raids. Neither acknowledged the stalemate that had resulted. The 'lessons' to be learned from battle were far from obvious to those who fought.

Anwar Sadat, who assumed the presidency of Egypt after Nasser's death in the autumn of 1970, changed Egypt's political strategy fundamentally. It is important to note that the political strategy changed before he decided to use military force. In February 1971, in an initiative discounted at the time by Israel's leaders, Sadat offered for the first time to sign a peace treaty with Israel in exchange for a complete withdrawal from the territories occupied in the 1967 war (Sadat 1977: 279–80). His initiative marked an important change in Egyptian objectives that his predecessor had never been willing to make during his years in office. For the first time, an Egyptian leader signaled his willingness to accept Israel's existence, albeit in a limited way and with specified conditions. The terms of the debate about legitimacy changed.

Sadat's political strategy has been explained solely as a function of learning from the balance of capabilities. This explanation is not convincing. The president, of course, understood the sharp military constraints that Egypt faced in recovering the Sinai, but so had his predecessor. President Nasser had refused adamantly to enter into any kind of negotiation with Israel, even in the wake of military defeat. Almost all of Sadat's colleagues adamantly opposed his initiative and the new president did not have the public support that his predecessor had enjoyed. Nor, as we have seen, were the 'lessons' of the War of Attrition so compelling that Sadat was led ineluctably to the conclusion that acceptance of Israel was unavoidable.

President Sadat was deeply troubled by the burden of heavy defence spending on the Egyptian treasury, by the urgency of economic reform and by the restiveness of the Egyptian population as the almost continual war footing of the Egyptian economy dragged on (Stein 1985a: 49–51). He was also less interested in asserting Egyptian leadership of the Arab world and more comfortable than Nasser had been with the conservative monarchies and sheikhdoms that controlled Arab wealth. In short, Sadat's priorities were different from those of Nasser. Anxious to reform and open the Egyptian economy, to escape the constraints of a Soviet embrace, and to consolidate his domestic political authority, Sadat attempted an accommodation with Israel. The relative balance of capabilities with Israel was one, but only one, of the factors that led him to change his objectives (Stein 1993).

The attempt at accommodation failed, largely because Israel's leaders did not consider the signal credible. Nor had they learned, despite its repeated failures, that deterrence was unstable. On the contrary, they expected that deterrence would hold at least until 1975, when Egypt would have augmented its military capability in the air, and, consequently, saw no reason to enter into political negotiations. Paradoxically, their optimism about the stability of deterrence, an optimism that was consistent with the theoretical expectations of deterrence, helped to reinforce the conditions for its instability (Stein 1985b).

When it became apparent to Sadat that the prospects for an accommodation were poor, he determined to go to war. Sadat argued that Israel's confidence in the stability of deterrence was the core problem preventing an accommodation, rather than part of the solution. His political objective was to destroy Israel's confidence in deterrence through military means. The political purposes of the attack, rather than the military objectives, were paramount in his planning.

Egyptian military leaders told President Sadat repeatedly that Egypt was still incapable of a general attack across the Canal (Sadat 219–21; Badri, Magdoub and Zhody 1978; Shazli 1980). President Sadat, despite the opposition of his generals, nevertheless began to plan for a large-scale attack as early as mid-1971. The president wanted, actively considered, and pushed his generals to prepare as quickly as possible for an attack against Israel, despite an unfavourable military balance of power. It is difficult to conclude that deterrence was 'stable' during this period. At best, we can conclude that deterrence held for a short time as Sadat waited for a more favourable international constellation and pressed Soviet leaders for advanced weaponry. The active search for a military option and his commitment to military attack, however, were constants in Sadat's thinking and planning. He pushed his generals to develop a military option that would maximise Egyptian advantage, in order to create the political conditions necessary to recover the Sinai and for his broader economic strategy of opening Egypt to the West.

Egyptian generals 'designed around' Israel's military advantages to create a military option for a limited attack across the Suez Canal. They planned a large-scale crossing of the Suez Canal and a ground offensive that would not exceed the range of a dense anti-aircraft system. In short, an unfavourable estimate of the balance of capabilities was not a long-term barrier to military action. Egyptian military leaders learned, but not in the way realist theories expect. From 1971 to 1973 in the enduring rivalry between Egypt and Israel, deterrence was acutely unstable as need trumped opportunity. Political incentives drove military calculations in Egypt.

Who learned what and how?

The conflict between Egypt and Israel was driven by a fundamental disagreement about what constituted a legitimate status quo. From 1948 on, Egypt saw itself first as the defender of Palestinian rights and then, after 1967, as driven to recapture its lost territory. It was seeking constantly to restore a lost status quo. Israel saw itself as the defender against Arab states determined to eradicate its existence. The repeated use of force can best be understood as an attempt to define an acceptable status quo in a relationship where it was essentially contested. Each side framed the problem differently and, consequently, both found themselves in the domain of losses (Levy 1992a, 1992b). It is precisely when both parties anticipate significant losses that the use of force becomes most likely and most difficult to prevent.

At the beginning of the rivalry, learning from defeat was very limited. Only partial lessons were drawn as successive defeats were explained away. This pattern of learning is consistent with the expectations of cognitive theories; people cling to core beliefs and adjust at the margins until the disconfirming evidence is overwhelming. The longest period without war, from 1957 to 1967, was due largely to the low priority Nasser gave to the conflict with Israel throughout most of this period. As pressures cumulated over time, however, the lessons that were learned in the first twenty years of the rivalry were overwhelmed in intense frustration in the spring of 1967. Pressure, rather than learning, culminated to destabilise deterrence. Updated estimates of the balance of capabilities did not drive policy; rather, policy drove the revision of estimates.

After the overwhelming disaster in 1967, Egyptian leaders learned much more intensively about the military constraints that they faced. That was not all, however, that they learned. Deterrence was most unstable after Egypt experienced its worst defeat. As pressure to challenge deterrence continued to intensify once the Sinai was occupied, they were strongly motivated to learn how they could design around their adversary's strengths and impose heavy costs on a militarily superior adversary.

Learning about the relative balance of capabilities was only part of what Egyptian leaders learned in the course of the enduring rivalry. A new president, freed of the commitments of his predecessor, and motivated not only to regain the Sinai but also by a different set of political and economic objectives, learned that agreement on a legitimate status quo was essential to end the rivalry and allow Egypt to achieve other important objectives. Sadat was almost alone among his colleagues in learning this lesson; other members of his Cabinet and most of his principal advisers opposed any accommodation with Israel. Clarification of the relative balance of capabilities through defeat was at best an inconsistent teacher.

In the epidemiology of enduring rivalries, it is as important to examine what leaders learn from victory, as it is to explore what they learn from defeat. This question is largely outside the scope of deterrence theories that assume learning only by the would-be attacker. Learning from victory was a critical element in reaching the accommodation that ultimately ended this enduring rivalry. Israel's leaders were generally badly over-confident of the stability of deterrence throughout the enduring rivalry. They learned little from repeated failures of deterrence. Only after the war in 1973, when Egypt fought a war for limited purposes and simultaneously imposed heavy casualties on Israel's forces, did Israel's leaders finally learn about the costs of repeated victories. They began to moderate their confidence in the relative balance of capabilities as a sufficient deterrent to war, and experimented with political concessions even in the wake of 'victory'. Shared learning about the political conditions of accommodation created the necessary conditions for the first trial-and-error experimentation with a process of negotiation that ultimately ended their rivalry a decade later.

The Israel–Palestine Conflict

This pattern of repeated wars followed by only partial learning by both parties helps to explain the enduring Israel–Palestine conflict (Stein 1994; Sitkin 1992). The long-lasting Israel-Palestine conflict has been driven by many of the same dynamics that drove the conflict between Egypt and Israel. For more than a hundred years, they have not been able to agree on what constitutes a legitimate status quo and on the rights of both peoples. Their conflict is much deeper, since both lay claim to part or all of mandated Palestine. It is more acute, because Palestinians and Israelis live in close proximity to one another, with their populations increasingly intermingled. The Palestine–Israel conflict is not only an 'interstate' conflict, but also a conflict between and within the two civil societies.

From 1948–67, the Palestinian movement refused to normalise the loss of more than half of mandated Palestine to the state of Israel. It had considerable difficulty in asserting its own voice in an attempt to change the status quo and undo the creation of Israel. The Hashemite Kingdom of Jordan annexed what remained of mandated Palestine in 1950, and the Palestinian national movement in exile had great difficulty in shaping a coherent voice, independent of Arab governments. Palestinians resorted to armed attacks across Israel's borders, but in mounting these attacks, they were hostage to Arab governments that sought to control the use of force. Israel responded with a mixed strategy of deterrence and compellence. It built up its military capabilities in the expectation that its military superiority would deter attack and when the raids continued, responded with escalating reprisals in an attempt to compel Arab governments to restrain Palestinian irregulars from operating across Israel's borders. The evidence is clear: Palestinian attacks, far from breaking Israel's resolve, led to an intensification of its military capabilities and response, and Israel's military response often provoked rather than deterred and culminated in at least two rounds of all-out war between Israel and Arab states, in 1956 and 1967.

The outcome of the war in 1967 changed the trajectory of Palestinian politics and strategy. A significant part of the Palestinian population was now directly under Israeli occupation, but it was simultaneously freed of control and restraint by the governments of Jordan and Egypt. In the wake of the defeat of Arab armies, the Palestinian national movement in exile began to reorganise to craft a strategy of low-intensity warfare to compel Israel to end the occupation by increasing its costs. It also began to develop a political strategy that initiated the painful process of coming to terms with Israel's existence. As the Palestinian national movement grew, divisions between those under occupation and those in exile deepened. When Egypt reached a separate accommodation with Israel, Palestinian resolve to rely on their capacity to obstruct and harass deepened.

In 1982, Israel launched an all-out war against Palestinian bases in Lebanon in an effort to destroy Palestinian capability to launch cross-border attacks, to decimate the Palestinian leadership in exile and to compel the government of Lebanon to assert control of the southern areas. The Palestinian leadership was expelled to Tunis, but Israel's gains were short-lived. The conflict expanded as the population in southern Lebanon mobilised and Israel's public eventually turned against the government as the casualties mounted over time. Compellence achieved only limited success in stabilising the Lebanese–Israeli lines. Even though compellence had failed, ironically many Palestinians and Israelis concluded that Israel's unilateral withdrawal from Lebanon had weakened Israel's reputation for resolve.

In 1987, the Palestinian *intifada* broke out, fueled by frustration and grievance by those under occupation. This was the first time in fifty years that Palestinians living within Palestine took leadership in challenging Israel. Very quickly, the Palestine Liberation Organisation (PLO) in Tunis appropriated leadership of the *intifada*. Violence quickly escalated, imposing serious costs on Israel and decimating Palestinian society. A cycle of attack and reprisal moved neither party closer to accommodation. The cycle was broken only in the aftermath of the Gulf War in 1991, when the United States convened a peace conference in Madrid that put bilateral Arab-Israel and multilateral issues on the table. Despite the enormous asymmetry in military capabilities, Israeli and Palestinian leaders had begun to 'learn' that neither side could defeat the other.

It is not difficult to understand why the PLO was anxious to begin a process of negotiation, given the severe diplomatic, economic and political losses it had suffered as a result of its support for Saddam Hussein during the Gulf War in 1990–91. More perplexing is why Israel, with its position more secure in the region than it had been in decades—its concern about Iraq allayed and the Arab coalition fractured in the wake of the war—should have chosen to reverse a long-standing position and entered into secret negotiations with the PLO. No conceivable analysis of the balance of capabilities would expect such an outcome.

Despite its unquestioned military superiority, Israel's new leadership, particularly Prime Minister Rabin, emphasised the instability of the status quo and the looming threat from unconventional weapons. Iraq's bombardments of Israel with Scuds during the Gulf War, though the cause of relatively little damage, were, in his estimate, early indicators of the kind of threat Israel could face. The *intifada* had proven very costly to Palestinian society but, like the October War in 1973, had also punctured Israel's confident expectations that the status quo could continue indefinitely. To varying degrees, in 1991–92, the PLO and Israel shared a sense of loss, although not equally or with comparable intensity. The sense of loss grew out of a stalemate that they both, for quite different reasons, considered unstable and deteriorating. When the opportunity for a secret 'unofficial' dialogue with PLO officials arose, Prime Minister Rabin approved the Oslo process but distanced himself from it so that, if necessary, he could deny any involvement (Makovsky 1996: 19). The prime minister was deeply sceptical but curious to see what, if anything, the process would produce. Agreement on general principles came surprisingly quickly. The process, which quickly became official, produced the Declaration of Principles, the first framework agreement between Israel and the PLO.

Despite the significant differences in the scope of the two conflicts, the far greater tractability of the geostrategic environment between Egypt and Israel when compared to the environment between Israel and the PLO, and the strength of the Egyptian state in comparison to the fragile structure of Palestinian institutions, the parallels between the Egypt–Israel process and the Israel–PLO negotiations fifteen years later are striking. Like the Egypt–Israel process, the leaders of both Israel and the PLO were in the domain of loss as they each—for different reasons—saw an unstable and deteriorating stalemate. Irrespective of the relative balance of power, both had learned about the costs of the use of force, and were sceptical of the benefits that a use of force could provide. Both had also learned from past experience in negotiation. The relevant experience was not only their own brief history, but also the experience of Israel with Egypt as they broke out of established channels to clear a bilateral track for a comprehensive settlement. Very quickly, the United States became intimately involved as facilitator, guarantor, insurer and monitor of the process between Israel and the PLO, as it had between Egypt and Israel. The critical importance of the United States to both parties was telling.

The presence over time of all these four factors—the losses from continuing conflict, an unstable and deteriorating stalemate, learning from past attempts at negotiation, and the intervention of a powerful outsider pushing a negotiated accommodation—engaged Israel and Palestine for the first time in their history in a discussion of legitimacy and rights.

The negotiations dragged on throughout the decade as both parties attempted to make gains and avoid the difficult concessions that would be necessary to bridge the deep divides. Indeed, both manipulated the process to justify their failure to comply with commitments they had made. Prime Minister Ehud Barak came to office in 1999 committed to reaching a full and comprehensive settlement with the Palestine

Authority. He was determined to break through the process of interim agreements, which were exhausting political capital within Israel and in Palestine, and engage in a process that could end the conflict. Barak insisted on putting all the issues on the table so that the broad outlines of the trades across the remaining issues would become clear.

The push to a comprehensive agreement came at the summit at Camp David, convened by President Clinton in the summer of 2000. Clinton agreed to Barak's request for a summit, despite warnings from Arafat that adequate preparations had not been made, and that he was not ready for a negotiation of a comprehensive agreement. Arafat was persuaded that the gaps between the two sides on the critical issues of Jerusalem, refugees, borders and settlements were still too wide. Under intense political pressure from Palestinian leaders who had seen no change on the ground, a continuation of settlement and a sharp deterioration of the Palestinian economy, Arafat was deeply concerned about the risks of failure. Barak nevertheless pushed hard for the summit, convinced that further interim agreements were impossible. In the drive toward a comprehensive agreement, however, Barak fractured his coalition and lost the support of the majority of the Knesset. A pressured Palestinian leader and a politically weak Israeli prime minister came to Camp David to discuss, for the first time, the contours of a final settlement. The two leaders put forward proposals to resolve the outstanding issues, but failed to reach firm agreements on any.

The creation of an independent Palestinian state was not in dispute, but its borders were. Barak proposed that the Palestinian state include almost 90 per cent of the territory of the West Bank and all of Gaza. Territory adjacent to the borders of 1967, which included approximately two thirds of Israeli settlers, would be annexed to Israel. The principle of a 'swap' was discussed, but the parties disagreed both on the ratio of territory that would be exchanged and the location of the territory that would be added to the Palestinian state.

The issue of the Palestinian refugees proved far more difficult. Barak and Arafat again agreed on the broad principles to govern a settlement of the refugee issue, but could not reach a settlement on two critical issues: the number of Palestinian refugees that would have the right to return to Israel within its 1967 borders, and the declaration that Israel would make about its role in the creation of the refugees. The future of the Palestinian refugees was a critical constituency issue for Arafat and a fundamental—in all likelihood the most fundamental—issue of security for Israel's negotiating team.

The final issue, Jerusalem, was politically explosive in both communities. The two leaders agreed in principle on the return of Palestinian communities in the 'outer ring' of Jerusalem to the new Palestinian state. Barak offered Palestinian communities in the 'inner ring' autonomy, rather than sovereignty, and for the first time, asserted Israel's sovereignty over the Temple Mount, including Haram al-Sharif. In the past, although Israel had annexed East Jerusalem in 1967, it had been officially silent on the issue of sovereignty over Islamic Holy Places; in practice, the Muslim Waqf had controlled and managed the two mosques. Arafat rejected out of hand any solution that did not give the new state of Palestine full sovereignty over East Jerusalem, including Haram al-Sharif.

Despite the failure of the summit, violence did not erupt in its immediate aftermath. Negotiations continued quietly through back channels in an effort to bridge the gaps and made considerable progress at their final meeting in Taba. Barak and Arafat, for the first time, had put the most difficult issues on the table, had explored the gaps, and had positioned the negotiations so that the painful trade-offs across the remaining issues could be identified. The political weakness of both leaders, however, made open discussion of possible trades so risky that neither leader would reveal publicly what had been accomplished at Camp David. Indeed, there is significant disagreement between Palestinians and Israelis as to what had been 'understood' at Taba.

In this context of frustration and political weakness, Ariel Sharon visited the Temple Mount in September 2000, accompanied by hundreds of armed policemen as guards. Violence exploded as Palestinians inferred that the visit was an intentional plan to assert Israeli sovereignty over Islamic holy places. A day after the visit, nine Palestinians were killed in the violence, and a cycle of escalation began that radicalised both communities and reduced support for further negotiations. The ensuing violence, far more lethal than the *intifada* from 1987–92, would continue for years, wreaking devastating destruction on Palestinian society and huge costs on Israel's economy and its social cohesion.

The escalating violence and the breakdown of negotiations challenges the central argument that learning by both the 'winner' and 'loser' about the costs and consequences of violence is a necessary but insufficient condition of the willingness to enter into negotiation. Israelis and Palestinians had suffered five years of violence in the *intifada* that began in 1987, had negotiated for a decade, and yet found themselves again trapped in the 'Al-Aksa *intifada*'. The violence can be explained paradoxically by the second proposition: leaders had learned about the costs of failed structures and strategies of negotiation. The process of phased interim agreements had extended for seven years, yet Palestinians had experienced little improvement in their daily lives: settlements continued to expand, entry and exit remained under Israel's control, occupation continued and time seemed to be working against a final settlement. Prime Minister Barak too had learned about the costs of failed structures and strategies of negotiation: the process of interim agreements had produced no closure to the conflict, led to unremitting pressure for further concessions and produced no map of an end to the conflict. Third, as I have argued, the domestic politics of both parties worked against, rather than for, an agreement that required far more difficult concessions than they had made in the interim phase. In this context, Prime Minister Barak chose a risk-acceptant strategy of a comprehensive negotiation to achieve a final resolution of the conflict. Learning led to a large gamble that failed in the first round.

The failure and the ensuing violence should not, however, obscure the learning that has taken place. Even in the midst of escalating violence, of atrocities against civilians, and a large number of killed and wounded, leaders on both sides recognise that they cannot achieve security through force and violence. They have learned that neither an imbalance of power resources nor violence can extract concessions in the field that would not be made at the table. Each has learned that it cannot defeat the other. Each has learned that the status quo, without progress to accommodation, is unstable and will deteriorate into violence that imposes heavy costs on both. The relative balance—or imbalance—of capabilities insures neither against these costs. Both have learned that the final issues cannot be delayed indefinitely.

Conclusion

I have argued that for enduring rivalries to reach a critical turning point from war and violence to conflict management requires that:

- the parties be in the in the domain of loss: they see an unstable and deteriorating stalemate and/or they face economic or political pressures, which may be linked to security issues;
- they have learned about the costs of the use of force, and are sceptical of the benefits that a use of force could provide. Parties need not be optimistic about the prospects of negotiation but they must be deeply pessimistic about the gains from a use of force;
- the parties have learned from past successes and failures in negotiation; and
- often, though not necessarily, a powerful third party facilitator, guarantor, insurer and monitor be available to map and steer the negotiating process.

Critics can justifiably point to weaknesses in this argument. It is difficult if not impossible to specify *a priori* thresholds along some of these dimensions. How deeply, for example, do the parties have to be in the domain of loss? How sceptical do they have to be of the benefits of a use of force? Although no precise thresholds can be established, the analysis does suggest that if the parties are moving in these directions over time, the rivalry may shift direction away from war.

It should be clear as well that the relative military balance explains only a small part of the epidemiology of war and conflict. It has been relatively static throughout the modern history of the Arab–Israeli conflict and cannot explain the shift in trajectory in the Egypt–Israel and Israel–Palestine rivalries. Nor does it explain three decades of war in the Gulf. What is important is learning by leaders about the heavy costs of the use of force, irrespective of who is superior and who is inferior. Nor can military superiority insure against attack. Theories of war and conflict management need to capture dynamic learning over time by leaders, learning that is shaped by domestic politics. Finally, theories need to encompass the social construction of legitimacy and rights, issues that go to the core of the enduring rivalries that have shaped—and bedeviled—the modern Middle East.

These are cautionary tales for a Middle East in the throes of fundamental change at the beginning of the twenty-first century. The United States used force to eliminate the government of Saddam Hussein but now must develop political strategies to reconstruct Iraqi society. Its superior military force, as we have seen in the two enduring rivalries we examined, is no guarantee against ongoing violence that erupts from grievance and frustration. Spurred by the challenge of Islamicists, governments throughout the region are just beginning to come to grips with the challenges of governance and development. Legitimacy and rights will be as important in constructing security in the rest of the Middle East as they have been in the Arab–Israeli conflict. Security from war and violence can be built only through political strategies that create legitimacy and embed rights. The 'old' security agenda cannot be separated from the 'new' security agenda of human development and human security.

Further Reading

EVANS, P., JACOBSEN, H. and PUTNAM, J. (eds.), *Double-Edged Diplomacy: International Bargaining and Domestic Politics* (Berkeley: University of California Press, 1993). The authors examine the complex interactions between domestic and international politics and the challenges of bargaining simultaneously at two tables.

JERVIS, R., LEBOW, R. N. and STEIN, J. G., *Psychology and Deterrence* (Baltimore: Johns Hopkins University Press, 1985). This collection of essays challenges rational models of deterrence and examines the dynamics of spiraling escalation that can result from threat-based strategies.

MAKOVSKY, D., *Making Peace with the PLO: The Rabin Government's Road to the Oslo Accord* (Boulder, Colo.: Westview Press, 1996). Makovsky draws on interviews of the participants to analyse the bargaining that culminated in the Oslo agreements.

MUTAWI, S., *Jordan in the 1967 War* (Cambridge: Cambridge University Press, 1987). Mutawi brilliantly examines the complex pressures that operated in Jordan as leaders struggled with the decision whether or not to go to war.

PARKER, R., *The Politics of Miscalculation in the Middle East* (Bloomington: Indiana University Press, 1993). Parker assembled many of the participants in key decisions in the Middle East and reconstructs the politics of miscalculation and misunderstanding.

RABINOVICH, I., *Waging Peace: Israel and the Arabs 1948–2003* (Princeton, NJ: Princeton University Press, 2004). Rabinovich provides a superb analysis of the many failed attempts at peacemaking, punctuated by the few successes, in the long and bitter Arab-Israeli conflict.

SAYIGH, Y., *Armed Struggle and the Search for a State: A History of the Palestinian National Movement, 1949–1993* (Oxford: Clarendon Press, 1991). Sayigh has written a magisterial overview of the history and struggles of the Palestinian national movement.

WALT, S., *The Origins of Alliances* (Ithaca, NY: Cornell University Press, 1987). Walt challenges conventional balancing and bandwagoning theories of alliances and emphasises the importance of perceptions of threat rather than the balance of power.

PART 3

KEY ISSUES AND ACTORS

10

The Arab–Israeli Conflict

Charles Smith

OVERVIEW

The term 'Arab–Israeli Conflict' refers to a condition of belligerency between the Arab states and Israel. The first Arab–Israeli war began immediately after the proclamation of the state of Israel on 14 May 1948 with assaults by Egypt, Jordan, Syria and elements from the Iraqi and Lebanese armies. Subsequent wars in this conflict were the 1956 Suez Crisis where Israel, Britain and France attacked Egypt, the 1967 and 1973 Wars and the Israeli invasion of Lebanon in 1982. In addition, border tensions and armed clashes between Israel and Arab neighbours were frequent in the early 1950s, and in the mid-1960s, the latter contributing to the 1967 War. Two Arab states, Egypt (1979) and Jordan (1994) have signed peace treaties with Israel, but tensions remain high because of the Palestinian question and Israeli settlement expansion in the occupied territories.

Introduction

The Arab–Israeli conflict is a direct outgrowth of the Palestinian question that resulted from the inclusion of the Balfour Declaration (1917) in the mandate for Palestine. This obliged Britain to support Zionist aspirations to create a Jewish state against the wishes of the Palestinian Arab inhabitants. These two conflicts, the Arab–Israeli and the Palestinian-Israeli, have frequently intersected, with the Palestinian question often serving as a major factor in Arab state rivalries as well as Arab–Israeli tensions.

The Arab–Israeli conflict has taken many forms. Most obviously the clash has been *military* but it also has been a *political* and *economic* conflict. Arab states refused to give diplomatic recognition to the state of Israel. Through the League of Arab States (established in 1945), Arab countries organised a boycott of international companies that traded with Israel. Conversely Israeli diplomats and pro-Israeli lobbyists strove to persuade American policymakers to deny arms and economic aid to Arab states considered friendly to the United States during the Cold War era.

However, Arab–Israeli hostility did not create alignments that paralleled the Cold War rivalry between the United State and the Soviet Union. The major dividing lines were among Arab states which either aligned with the United States or Great Britain during the 1950s and 1960s, or pursued a policy of non-alignment. Non-alignment permitted its adherents to deal with the West and the Soviet bloc, but often resulted in major arms deals with the Soviets and their Eastern European satellites. This split frequently coincided with one between states such as Egypt and Syria that were governed by young, more radical military officers or politicians set against more conservative monarchies with close Western ties, such as Saudi Arabia, Jordan and Iraq until the 1958 Revolution.

Cold War allegiances saw Jordan and Israel identified with Western powers whereas Egypt and Syria were often linked to the Soviet Union. With respect to the Arab–Israeli conflict, Jordan, Egypt and Syria, whatever their mutual animosities, were considered to be aligned against Israel.

A key element in examining the Arab–Israeli conflict is asking what conditions are required to resolve it. Realist theory has come to assume a certain uniformity in states' calculations of their own interests based on their judgments of their power relative to that of their rivals. Such criteria may encourage peace, but can also foster alliances aimed at neutralising if not breaking the might of rival states, as occurred on the eve of the First World War.

A more salient approach for the Middle East, and the subject of Chapter 7, is to consider the question of identity politics as key to the definition of nationality, and to ask whether such a definition corresponds to the perceived basis of the state and its security. Can conflicting visions of what constitutes the identity of the state and what factors should guarantee its security, based on religion, ethnicity or language, block efforts for peaceful resolution of differences? The following examples consider, under separate headings, the utility of realism as opposed to identity politics as applicable to an examination of the history of the Arab–Israeli conflict.

Realism

Many proponents of realism assume that policymakers in a given state share a common view of what constitutes the security of the state and will act in concert to fulfill shared goals, which include military actions as well as political approaches to resolution of conflicts. The following examples challenge that assumption.

Israel

Major differences emerged in the early 1950s as to what was required for the security of the state. There were two options: A. An 'activist', aggressive policy that assumed that Arabs would only seek peace once they had been crushed militarily. This was the doctrine known as the 'Iron Wall' espoused by Revisionists but held also by the Labour Zionist leadership centered in the first prime minister, David Ben-Gurion; B. a 'Weizmannist' policy that did not eschew force but advocated seeking to resolve disputes initially by diplomacy and reliance on outside agencies if necessary, such as the United Nations. This approach was linked to Moshe Sharett, first foreign minister of Israel who succeeded Ben-Gurion briefly as prime minister in 1954–55.

Officials loyal to Ben-Gurion undertook military reprisals and activated a spy ring in Egypt in 1954 without informing the then prime minister, Moshe Sharett. Egyptian discovery of the spy ring played a role in Israeli reprisal actions in early 1955 against Egypt; the Israeli public was never informed at the time that the Egyptian charges were true.

In 1982, Ariel Sharon lied to the Israeli cabinet, and possibly to his prime minister, Menachem Begin. He assured them that the planned invasion of Lebanon was a limited one, when he intended to proceed to Beirut, destroy the PLO infrastructure there, and instigate a war with Syrian forces to oust them from Lebanon. The Israeli government thus approved a major venture on the basis of false information provided by its defence minister.

Egypt

Accounts suggest that Gamal Abd al-Nasser did not control his leading military advisers in the weeks leading up to the 1967 war, especially the Chief of Staff, Abd al-Hakim Amir, and Minister of Defence, Shams al-Din Badran. They pursued a more aggressive military posture than Nasser may have intended, creating the opportunity and justification for an Israeli attack.

United States

During the Nixon administration, major differences emerged over the conduct of Middle East policy between the Secretary of State, William Rogers, and National Defense Secretary Henry Kissinger and President Richard Nixon. Rogers backed United Nations efforts to induce a ceasefire between Egypt and Syria in 1969–70 which would result in negotiations over the Sinai Peninsula, occupied by Israel in the 1967 War. Israel opposed Rogers' efforts, and was encouraged to do so by Kisssinger and Nixon. They objected to UN involvement in a peace process which they believed the US should control to the exclusion of its Cold War rival, the Soviet Union. Cold War rivalry on a global scale, 'beating' the Soviets by controlling peace efforts, counted more than seeking resolution of regional disputes through international cooperation.

Identity politics: nationalism, religion and the state

Arab nationalism

The Arab national idea in the twentieth century defined itself on the basis of language and culture, seeking to establish a unity of Arab peoples from Morocco to the Arabian peninsula. Though it failed and has been replaced by identification with individual states and their boundaries, its symbolic power and rhetoric caused Western powers to seek to undermine it. But rivalry for leadership of the movement, especially between Egypt and Syria, would prove destructive and ultimately become a major factor inciting the 1967 War.

Israel: religion and identity

Factions have always differed on what lands were essential to constitute the state of Israel. Menachem Begin's Herut Party consistently advocated during the 1950s an immediate Israeli takeover of not only the West Bank but Jordan as well to fulfill Revisionist Zionist expansionist principles. For Revisionists, Israel as a nation was incomplete until its state boundaries embraced those attributed to ancient Israel. Similarly, the Likud Party platform today calls for inclusion of the West Bank as essential to the fulfillment of Israel's destiny, whereas a majority of Israelis accept, with some territorial adjustments, a return to the pre-1967 War state, granting the Palestinians a state of their own. These conflicting approaches to the identity of Israel directly affect the peace process and call attention to the question of state security also.

Would Israel be more secure with the absorption of the West Bank and its Palestinian Arab population, thus weakening the nature and identity of a Jewish state? By the year 2020, it is predicted that the Palestinian Arab populations of the West Bank and Gaza, with the Israeli Arabs, will equal if not surpass the Jewish population of Israel. Or would Israel be more secure by withdrawing to boundaries resembling those of 1967, thus preserving its character as a Jewish state and entering into peace treaties with its Arab neighbours? In both cases, competing considerations of security are bound up with conflicting visions of what borders are required to constitute Israeli identity.

A complicating factor is that right-wing Israeli ambitions, whether religious or secular in origin, acquire great support from the worldwide Christian evangelical movement, and especially Christian fundamentalists in the United States. These Christian Zionists openly back Israeli retention of the West Bank and ouster of the Palestinians to fulfill Old Testament prophecy. They are a major factor in current US Middle East policy with strong representation in Congress. In short, definitions of what constitutes the legitimate identity of Israel go beyond the views of their citizens to acquire backing from ardent believers of a different religion in another country. Christian fundamentalist identity, to these believers, requires fulfillment of scripture through Israeli expansion, with major policy implications for resolution of Palestinian–Israeli problems.

Hamas/Islamic Jihad

Whereas official Palestinian policy recognises Israel and supports a two-state solution, the major Islamic groups call for eradication of Israel and return of all of former Palestine to Palestinian rule, preferably under an Islamic government. This definition of a Palestinian state, based on an Islamic identity, clearly conflicts with that offered by the Palestinian Authority and, as with Likud in Israel, establishes competing visions of the ideal state based on differing calculations of identity, full control of the homeland as opposed to compromise.

1948–67: From the Creation of Israel to the 1967 War

Great Britain handed over responsibility for Palestine to the United Nations in February 1947, setting the stage for the General Assembly's partition decision of November. Fighting quickly erupted between Zionist forces and Palestinians. Zionist military superiority enabled Jewish forces to gain control of the territory awarded them in the 1947 partition plan, resulting in the declaration of Israeli independence on 14 May 1948.

The Arab state assault on Israel immediately following this declaration of independence indicated rejection of that claim. Nevertheless the Arab states were not united in their objectives. Most backed the creation of a Palestinian state to be led by the former mufti of Jerusalem, Hajj Amin al-Husseini, who then lived in Egypt. Transjordan, to become the Hashemite Kingdom of Jordan in 1948, opposed Palestinian self-determination as did the Zionists, and accepted the idea of partition, hoping to divide Palestine with the new state of Israel. Jordan's Arab Legion fought mainly to preserve control of already occupied territory, to be known as the West Bank, and clashed with Israeli forces only when challenged for control of the city of Jerusalem, which was divided. Jordan's King Abdullah was assassinated in 1951 because of his negotiations with Zionists over the partition of Palestine.

This disarray, accentuated by the lack of Arab military coordination, led to defeat with Israel acquiring more land than that allotted under the 1947 partition proposal. Israel and the combatant Arab states signed armistice agreements between January and June 1949 but a state of war still existed and the Arab–Israeli conflict took shape.

Arab states refused to recognise Israel, although behind-the-scenes discussions occurred during the first decade of Israel's existence that included at times Egypt and Syria as well as Jordan. Arab states established economic boycotts and Egypt forbade Israeli ships from transiting the Suez Canal although it permitted passage of foreign ships destined for Israel. Between 1948 and 1956, border tensions were strong with frequent clashes between Israel and its neighbours, Syria, Jordan and Egypt.

Most clashes involving armed forces were instigated by Israel in retaliation for border crossings and attacks by individual Palestinians who had lived in what was now Israel. However, Israel often initiated clashes without provocation from the Arab side in order to impress Arabs with their military prowess and to enhance combat readiness. This strife was particularly intense along the Jordanian-Israeli frontier until 1955; Jordan was unable to control its Palestinian refugees but was held responsible by Israel for their incursions (Morris 1996).[1]

The Suez Crisis of 1956—background

During 1955 the focus of Arab–Israeli animosity shifted from the Jordanian front to the Egyptian, influenced by rivalries among the Great Powers and the inauguration of Cold War competition between the Soviet Union and the West for paramountcy in the region. Washington wanted Egypt to be the linchpin of a Middle Eastern alliance to form part of the West's containment policy toward the Soviet Union and world communism. However, Egypt's Gamal Abd al-Nasser, the young colonel who had taken over in a coup in July 1952, espoused the doctrine of neutrality or nonalignment between the Cold War rivals. Though willing to consider a Middle East security sphere independent of official Western ties, he rejected any appearance of links to former imperial powers. When Britain arranged a security pact with Nuri al-Said of Iraq in February 1955 (the Baghdad Pact), this ignited severe inter-Arab rivalries and regional tensions.

At the same time, February 1955, Nasser suddenly found himself confronted by a military crisis with Israel. This stemmed from an agreement he had reached with Great Britain during the summer of 1954 for British withdrawal of forces from their two hundred-square-mile military base in the Suez Canal Zone, to be completed by June 1956. News of this pact led Israeli officials to activate a spy ring in Egypt without the knowledge of the prime minister, Moshe Sharett. The reason given was to buttress Israel's future security by forcing Britain to remain in the Suez Canal Zone, thus blocking the possibility of Egyptian troop movements into the Sinai. This would be done by having the spies blow up installations frequented by Westerners, forcing Britain to conclude that it should remain to protect its citizens.

Its logic doubtful from inception, the spies were soon captured and placed on trial. The hanging of two spies and imprisonment of others gave the Israeli public the impression of Egyptian discrimination against Israel since Sharett, once aware of Israeli responsibility for the ring, could not openly admit it. Popular alarm at Israel's inability or unwillingness to counter Egypt's actions led to calls for Ben-Gurion's return to government, rewarded when he took over as Minister of Defence in January 1955, officially under Sharett's control but in reality independent.

In February 1955, Israel undertook a masssive raid into Gaza that resulted in major Egyptian casualties. Justified as a reaction to Egyptian border attacks, the raid was primarily intended to reassure Israeli citizens of their government's military superiority in the face of Egyptian provocations in the aftermath of the spy trials. It proved to be a landmark in the Arab–Israeli conflict within the Cold War context. Concerned about Egyptian military weakness, Nasser signed an arms pact with the Soviet Union in September 1955, causing Israel to seek more arms from its supplier, France.

Tensions mounted in July 1956 when the United States and Britain refused to finance the building of the Aswan Dam. Nasser retaliated by nationalising the Suez Canal the same month.

As a result, Britain, France and Israel, for different reasons, collaborated to attack Egypt. Israel sought to destroy the Egyptian blockade of shipping through the Tiran Straits into the Gulf of Aqaba, and to force Nasser's overthrow if possible, the latter goal shared by France. Humiliated by its forced withdrawal from Vietnam in 1954, French officials were determined to retain control of Algeria which they had invaded in 1830 and colonised, making it a *department* of France. Convinced that Nasser was sustaining the Algerian Revolt which had erupted in 1955, France saw Nasser's ouster as ensuring their position in Algeria. The British government viewed the canal's nationalisation as an intolerable affront by a former imperial possession and a threat to international order.

The Suez War and its legacy

The Suez war of late October 1956 ended in political failure for France and Great Britain despite the military defeat suffered by the Egyptians. Nasser's defiance in the face of aggression by the Western imperial powers, Britain and France, allied with Israel which Arabs considered to be the product of British imperialism, reinforced his reputation as a defender of Arab nationalism. The war brought Israel ten years of peace on her Egyptian frontier with open passage for Israeli shipping into the Gulf of Aqaba. United Nations Emergency Forces (UNEF) were stationed in the Sinai to serve as buffers betweeen Israel and Egypt; Israel warned that Egyptian reimposition of the blockade of the Tiran Straits from the Sinai promontory of Sharm al-Shaykh would be a *casus belli*, a legitimate cause for war.

The Suez crisis was the last Middle Eastern war in which former imperial powers were involved as combatants striving to retain or reassert an imperial presence. Henceforth the Arab–Israeli conflict involved only regional forces although the US and the Soviets, along with European countries, were heavily involved in supplying arms to Arab states and Israel.

The 1967 War, Arab Nationalist Rivalries and the Re-emergence of the Palestinian Factor

Introduction

In contrast to the causes of the Suez crisis, the preliminaries to the 1967 Arab–Israeli war directly involved Palestinian factions; Palestinians served competing Arab state interests while seeking to define their own objectives. The war's aftermath introduced a new stage in the Arab–Israeli conflict whose territorial ramifications remain unresolved to this day.

Arab rivalries

Although the war marks a major turning point in the Arab–Israeli conflict, its causes were rooted as much in Arab nationalist debates and rivalries as in direct Arab–Israeli hostilities.

Following its secession from the United Arab Republic (1958–61), Syria strove to impugn Nasser's Arab nationalist credentials and strengthen their own by accusing him of evading further confrontations with Israel. These charges and countercharges became a staple of Egyptian–Syrian–Iraqi invective as did similar accusations hurled by Jordan's King Hussein; both leftist and conservative governments used the same propaganda, inspired by Egyptian claims of being in the vanguard of the Arab liberation movement. The symbols of Nasser's supposed fear of challenging Israel were the UNEF forces stationed in the Sinai as a buffer to prevent a recurrence of tensions that had led to the Suez war of 1956. Syria especially accused Egypt of hiding behind the UNEF because of Syrian–Israeli confrontations in 1963 over Syrian development of a water diversion system that Israeli attacked and destroyed.

Palestinians and a concern for the Palestinian question became embroiled in these inter-Arab disputes. At an Arab League meeting in Cairo in January 1964 that had been called to discuss Syrian–Israeli clashes, Egypt's Nasser agreed to back the formation of an official organisation that represented the Palestinians, the Palestinian Liberation Organisation (PLO). Nasser saw the PLO as a body that would focus Palestinian attention on political concerns under Egyptian control. Backing the PLO in propaganda and organisational efforts would counter Syrian charges of being unconcerned with Israel and with the Palestinians, while defusing Syrian calls for war with Israel.

Syria, on the other hand, was determined to incite tensions with Israel, if only to bolster its own Ba'thist image as the leader of Arab nationalism. With Egypt controlling the PLO, Syria turned to a small, revolutionary group dedicated to the destruction of Israel, Fatah. Founded in 1959 in Kuwait by young Palestinians who included Yasser Arafat, Fatah rejected links to the PLO which Fatah leaders saw as a tool of Egypt. In 1965 Syria began to sponsor Fatah raids into Israel, frequently launched from Jordan, not Syria. These incursions and Israeli reprisals against Jordan and later Syria inflamed Arab–Israeli and inter-Arab tensions throughout 1966 and into 1967, especially once Syria became directly involved in skirmishes with Israel in early 1967.

The 1967 War

In May Israel warned Syria of posssible major retaliatory strikes, leading the Soviets to warn Nasser that Israel was massing forces on the Syrian border, information later judged to be false. Seizing the chance to boost his anti-Israeli image, Nasser responded by sending Egyptian troops into the Sinai Peninsula on 14 May 1967. They ousted UNEF forces from the Sinai, including Sharm al-Shaykh which controlled the Straits of Tiran, and, in response to taunts from Jordan and Syria—with whom Egypt was allied when war erupted, reimposed a blockade of those straits to Israeli shipping. Nasser thus recreated the circumstances previous to the Suez War of 1956. Egypt's actions, motivated primarily to demonstrate its primacy in Arab affairs against Syrian claims, established the *casus belli* for Israel that it had proclaimed in 1957.

Israel attacked Egypt on 5 June 1967 after receiving information from the United States that Egypt would not attack but was going to try to extricate itself from the Sinai with a propaganda victory (Neff 1984; Quandt 1992). With the entrance of Jordan and Syria into the war, Israel erased the 1948 armistice lines separating them as well. The war resulted in Israel's conquest and occupation of the Gaza Strip, the Sinai Peninsula, the West Bank and the Golan Heights. East Jerusalem, with its religious sites holy to Judaism, Islam and Christianity and formerly under Jordanian control, was immediately annexed to Israel with the declaration that unified Jerusalem would remain forever the capital of the Israeli state. Hundreds of thousands of West Bank and Gaza Palestinians now fell under Israeli rule.

The 1967 war and its legacy: Security Council Resolution 242

The consequences of the 1967 War have defined the parameters of negotiations to resolve the Arab–Israeli conflict ever since. Israel declared that it would return territories in exchange for full peace agreements, the extent of the lands involved left undefined. Arab countries, meeting at Khartoum, Sudan, in August 1967, issued a document that called for full Israeli withdrawal but without entering negotiations with that country.

The contradictions found in the Khartoum Declaration reflected those found in the Arab alliance on the eve of the 1967 war. Nasser favoured a diplomatic resolution of the crisis and sided with Jordan's King Hussein in seeking international intervention via the United Nations. Syrian refusal to consider negotiations was consistent with Syrian hostility toward Israel prior to the war as was Palestinian rejection of talks. For the Palestinians, however, the situation was more complicated. To have had Arab states recognise Israel would have meant acceptance of refugee status for Palestinians as a result of the wars following 1948, a condition in which there was no Palestinian political entity.

Palestinians sought to regain all of pre-1967 Israel or former Palestine, a position proclaimed in the modified 1968 PLO charter that referred to the attainment of this goal by 'armed struggle'. Palestinian groups and the PLO, with Arafat as its head from 1969 onward, constantly opposed international efforts to resolve the results of the 1967 War unless the Palestinian political objective—self determination—was considered. This explains their attempts to undermine or later modify the document considered the basis of negotiations to resolve the changes brought by that war, Security Council Resolution 242.

Security Council Resolution 242 (SCR 242), passed by the United Nations in November 1967, called for Arab–Israeli settlement of the consequences of the war based on exchanges of occupied land in return for peace. Its deliberate ambiguity led to conflicting interpretations at the Arab–Israeli state level, but none at all for the Palestinians.

Declaring its intent to achieve 'a just and lasting peace' for the region, the resolution condemned 'the acquisition of territory by war' and called for all states 'to live in peace in secure and recognized boundaries'. SCR 242's key statement was its clause stating that Israel should withdraw 'from territories occupied in the recent conflict.' This expression deliberately excluded the article 'the' before the word 'territories', owing to Israel's insistence that it should not be required to withdraw from *all* the territories it had occupied. Israel argued that the resolution's statement that all states should live 'within secure and recognized boundaries' required that it retain some territories acquired in the war in order to establish those secure boundaries it had lacked prior to the war.

As for the Palestinians, they were referred to in SCR 242 solely as refugees whose condition would be resolved through these Arab–Israeli state negotiations. As they had feared, the Palestinians were not considered to be a people with legitimate political aspirations. The PLO from this time onward strove to block any settlement that enshrined their refugee status while working to modify SCR 242 to permit Palestinian access to negotiations as a people with acknowledged political rights.

1967–79: From the 1967 War to the Egyptian–Israeli Peace Treaty

In the aftermath of the 1967 war Arab states worked to recover lands taken by Israel in that conflict by both military and diplomatic means. Their strategies differed according to their perceptions of their interests.

The war of attrition

Egypt undertook a war of attrition from 1968–70, combating Israel across the Suez Canal. Although the victor militarily, Israel's triumph was marred by significant casualties and ultimate setback. Its military advantage, especially air superiority, led Israel to bomb targets inside Egypt, not just on the canal, raids designed to humiliate Nasser and discredit him, possibly causing his downfall. Instead these attacks brought the Soviet Union more directly into the Arab–Israeli conflict. Nearly fifteen thousand Soviet troops and pilots were shifted to Egypt to bolster her defences.

This massive Soviet presence altered the Cold War equation in the Arab–Israeli conflict. It also caused the United States under the Nixon administration to pursue a contradictory policy. Its Secretary of State, William Rogers, backed United Nations' efforts to institute a cease fire between Israel and Egypt, achieved in August 1970, a regionalist approach. At the same time National Security Adviser Henry Kissinger, with Nixon's approval, acted to undermine Rogers' efforts; he objected to any international effort, preferring to establish American domination of the peace process, and exclude the Soviets, viewing the problem in the context of a global rivalry between the two great powers (Hersh 1983; Morris 1977).

The Jordanian civil war, September 1970

For their part, the Palestinians were alarmed by the August 1970 cease-fire, fearing it might lead to negotiations where they would be excluded. Arafat, now head of the PLO, could not dominate that organisation, challenged by groups such as the Popular Front for the Liberation of Palestine (PFLP) headed by George Habash and the Popular Democratic Front for the Liberation of Palestine (PDFLP) led by Nayif Hawatmah. Both called for the overthrow of conservative Arab regimes as a precondition for an assault on Israel whereas Arafat and Fatah focused on Israel and endeavoured to distance the PLO from Arab state politics. Following the August 1970 cease-fire, the PFLP and PDFLP attempted to overthrow Jordan's King Hussein as the first step in creating a more radical Arab front that would challenge Israel. This led to the Jordanian civil war of September 1970 where King Hussein's Jordanian army crushed Palestinian forces with a major Arab–Israeli crisis barely averted.

The Palestinian–Jordanian clashes of August–September 1970 altered Arab state involvement in the Arab–Israeli conflict. The Palestinian defeat, and subsequent losses in later engagements with Jordanian forces, forced the PLO to move its command structure in 1971 from Jordan to Lebanon. From that time onward, PLO actions against Israel engaged Lebanon more directly in the Arab–Israeli conflict and become a major factor in instigating a Lebanese civil war in the mid-1970s.

The Jordanian civil war had another casualty: Nasser of Egypt died shortly after negotiating a ceasefire. He was succeeded by Anwar Sadat who, from 1971–73, sought unsuccessfully to negotiate with Israel for a settlement involving Israeli withdrawal from the Sinai, and failed to gain American backing for his efforts.

Henry Kissinger, by now Secretary of State as well as National Security Adviser, controlled all aspects of American foreign policy. He rejected Egyptian overtures, refusing to act while Soviet forces remained in Egypt. Then when Sadat expelled them, a Cold War victory for Washington, the US did not act because Kissinger was diverted by scandals pertaining to Nixon's reelection campaign in 1972. American inaction contributed to the 1973 War.

The 1973 war and its consequences

In 1973 Egypt and Syria decided to attack Israeli forces in the Golan Heights and Sinai Peninsula if no new diplomatic initiatives were forthcoming. Expectations of continued diplomatic stalemate were furthered when Israel decided to annex a large area of the Sinai in defiance of SCR 242. Minister of Defense Moshe Dayan proposed this plan as a condition of his remaining part of the Labour Party (formed in 1968) in forthcoming elections scheduled for November.

Egypt and Syria attacked Israel on 6 October 1973. Israeli forces fell back in the Golan Heights but ultimately stopped the Syrians. Egyptian troops crossed the Suez Canal and overwhelmed the Israeli defences, advancing into the Sinai before being checked. Initial Egyptian successes were thwarted by Israeli counter-attacks that led to Israeli forces crossing the Canal and occupying its west bank. Technically Israel had won the war against Egypt but Egyptian forces held out in pockets in the Sinai against fierce Israeli efforts to oust them and to restore the *status quo ante.*

Whereas the 1967 war had completely overturned the political-military parameters of the Arab–Israeli conflict existing since 1948, the 1973 war created a modified territorial framework within which the changes wrought by 1967 might be resolved. Henry Kissinger intervened to form a ceasefire between Israel and Egypt that left Egyptian forces in the Sinai, creating a situation that required negotiations. Kissinger believed that limited agreements between Israel, Syria and Egypt, involving minor withdrawals from lands occupied by Israel, could create a climate of confidence and trust whereby full peace treaties might ensue. Kissinger negotiated Israeli pullback accords in the Sinai and the Golan Heights with Egypt and Syria during 1974, pursuant to Security Council Resolution 338, passed on 22 October 1973, the last day of the war; it called for full implementation of SCR 242.

Ever more eager to pursue talks and to recover the Sinai, Sadat agreed to a second limited agreement with Israel in September 1975. To Arab leaders this signalled Egypt's willingness to seek a separate agreement, a possibility that had also occurred to Israeli politicians, including Yitzhak Rabin who had succeeded Golda Meir as prime minister in the summer of 1974.

Rabin, like most Israeli leaders, was primarily concerned with retaining the Golan Heights and the West Bank for Israel regardless of SCR 242. From this perspective, a separate peace with Egypt would not signify the first step toward a total resolution of the Arab–Israeli conflict by diplomacy. Rather, it would remove Egypt from the military equation of the Arab–Israeli conflict, enabling Israel to concentrate its forces against Syria and Jordan in order to impose its terms on them. Here, Rabin was reassured by Kissinger that the US would not push for any limited withdrawal agreements between Israel and Jordan over the West Bank.

The American-sponsored peace efforts of 1974–75 and Israeli disinterest in any agreement with Jordan over the West Bank had important repercussions for Palestinians and the PLO within the framework of the Arab-Israeli conflict.

Jordan and the Rabat Declaration

Jordan's King Hussein had been humiliated by his exclusion from the pullback agreements of 1974, the product of Israel's refusal to negotiate over the West Bank. His inclusion would have reaffirmed Jordanian claims to the area and undercut PLO calls for Palestinian self-determination and claims to represent all Palestinians.

Further humiliation awaited Hussein. In October 1974 Arab heads of state met in Rabat, Morocco. There they recognised 'the right of the Palestinian people to establish an independent national authority under the command of the Palestinian Liberation Organization, the sole legitimate representative of the Palestinian people, in any Palestinian territory that is liberated' (Cobban 1984: 60). The Rabat Declaration remains a landmark in the history of Palestinian efforts for self-determination within the framework of the Arab–Israeli conflict. Its terms declared that Hussein and Jordan had no right to represent Palestinian interests in any international forum. Hussein appeared to accept this decision which acquired international recognition when Arafat spoke at the United Nations General Assembly in November 1974 and the PLO was awarded observer status over the strong objections of Israel and the United States.

Henceforth, advocates of a diplomatic resolution of the Arab–Israeli conflict were divided. Most countries, including America's European allies, called for inclusion of the PLO and discussion of Palestinian political rights in any negotiations based on SCR 242. In contrast the United States and Israel rejected PLO inclusion in talks, calling it a terrorist organisation.

The Camp David talks and the Egyptian–Israeli peace accord

The election of Jimmy Carter as US president in November 1976 initiated a new approach to the Arab–Israeli conflict. Carter abandoned Kissinger's scheme of limited agreements and American control of peace efforts. He decided to seek a comprehensive Arab–Israeli accord, to be negotiated at an international conference that included the Soviet Union. In addition he believed that the Palestinian question had to be considered and that the PLO should be invited to an international conference if it accepted SCR 242, apparently willing to reconsider its clause relegating the Palestinian question to that of refugees.

Carter failed to gain his objectives. The Camp David Agreement of September 1978 between Egypt and Israel was a last gasp effort to salvage something out of his search for a comprehensive peace. There were many reasons for Carter's inability to achieve his broader objectives.

Arab states which might have attended such a conference had no common policy agenda. The PLO would not openly acccept SCR 242 unless their right to a state was acknowledged beforehand, a condition Carter could not meet. Moreover, Israel opposed an international conference, preferring American sponsorship. Finally, Israeli opposition to negotiations involving territory or the Palestinians was now intransigent. Menachem Begin had succeeded Rabin as prime minister of Israel in June 1977. Leader of the right-wing Likud Party and a pillar of Revisionist Zionism, he had continually advocated since 1948 the need for Israel to invade and capture the West Bank (ancient Judea and Samaria) to fulfill the Zionist goal of governing ancient Israel; the Likud Coalition official platform (1977) proclaimed its rejection of the idea of a Palestinian state and stated that Israel would rule eternally over the land between the Mediterranean and the Jordan River.

Carter's difficulties convinced Sadat to approach Israel on its terms, those of a separate peace. This arrangement could serve his interests, hopefully bringing economic development to Egypt in the form of Western, especially American assistance. On 9 November 1977 Sadat announced to the Egyptian National Assembly that he would go to Jerusalem in search of peace if invited, leading to his visit to that city the same month. The search for an Egyptian–Israeli peace had been set in motion.

The most tangible result of the Camp David accord was the Egyptian–Israeli peace treaty of March 1979, the first between an Arab state and Israel and a milestone in the history of the Arab–Israeli conflict (Quandt 1986: 256). But the Egyptian–Israeli peace treaty did not suggest any progress toward resolution of the broader conflict by further negotiation. Sadat's willingness to conclude a separate peace led to Egypt's being ostracised from the Arab League, whose headquarters were transferred from Cairo to Tunis.

Arab censure of Sadat seemed justified by the official Israeli interpretation of the agreements: consolidation of Israel's hold over the other occupied territories and greater Israeli military freedom to confront other Arab states and impose her will. Anger focused on the conflicting interpretations of what Camp David promised with respect to the Palestinians. The agreement referred to the 'legitimate rights of the Palestinian people'. Begin interpreted that to mean their non-political rights under Israeli occupation while Carter and Sadat believed it meant political rights under Arab rule, possibly Jordanian. Disputes also arose over the supposed moratorium on Israeli settlement building after Camp David; Israel undertook such activity after three months whereas Sadat and Carter thought they had an oral agreement for five years. From Begin's perspective, 'the Sinai had been sacrificed but Eretz Israel had been won', meaning that removing Egypt as a hostile neighbour would enable Israel to impose its will elsewhere and retain the West Bank. The task now was to establish firmer control over the area and to prove to the one million Palestinians living there that they had no hope of true self-determination.

The legacy of Camp David went beyond the achievement of an Egyptian–Israeli peace. The document's clauses for the West Bank envisaged a transition period of five years during which gradually implemented electoral and administrative procedures, including Israel's withdrawal from many areas, would lead to final status negotiations. Never attempted as part of the Camp David accord, this scheme nonetheless would become the basis for the Oslo process following the first Oslo accord in 1993.

From Camp David to the White House Lawn, 1978–93

Introduction

With Egypt removed from Arab–Israeli hostilities, the conflict assumed new dimensions which included state sponsorship of proxies, notably in Lebanon, ultimately leading to the Israeli invasion of that country in 1982.

Lebanon: civil war and foreign intervention

Lebanon had long been an unwilling base for PLO attacks into Israel, dating back to the later 1960s when hijackings of El Al planes by Palestinian factions based in Lebanon resulted in an Israeli assault on the Beirut airport in 1968. The shift of the PLO command from Jordan to camps outside Beirut in 1971 further destabilised an already fragile Lebanese political structure and inspired the formation of Maronite Catholic militias independent of government control, as was the PLO. The Maronites in particular resented Lebanon being drawn into the Arab–Israeli conflict, but this confrontation became embroiled in local political tensions. Lebanese Muslim and leftist anger at Maronite political dominance, expressed in the 1957–58 civil war, again erupted in the mid-1970s.

The clashes this time were far more destructive and involved state sponsors, Israel and Syria. In addition to arming and training the Maronites, Israel facilitated Maronite infiltration into southern Lebanon via Israel to seek to block Palestinian attacks. The Syrians briefly supported the Palestinians before allowing them to be crushed by the Israeli-backed Maronites, fearing that Palestinian dominance in Lebanon might lead to a Syrian confrontation with Israel. A truce in the civil war in 1976 permitted PLO groups to again attack Israel from the south, leading to a major Israeli invasion into southern Lebanon in March 1978 in response to a terrorist attack into Tel Aviv.

In the wake of Camp David and the Egyptian–Israeli peace treaty, Prime Minister Menachem Begin and his chief adviser, Ariel Sharon, reconsidered their strategy regarding the PLO. The treaty with Egypt seemed to ensure Israeli domination of the West Bank. What then to do with the allegiance of most West Bank Palestinians to the PLO? Destruction of the PLO command in Lebanon would both relieve Israel of border strife and, in Likud's view, remove any hope among West Bank Palestinians that they could escape Israeli rule.

Israeli ambitions meshed with those of Bashir Gemayel, leader of the Phalange, the premier Maronite militia; Gemayel had wiped out his leading Maronite rivals. With close ties to Israel he, like Begin and Sharon, hoped to oust if not destroy the PLO in Lebanon, with the goal of installing himself in power with Israeli assistance; this would ensure Maronite dominance of Lebanon despite their minority status, and for Israel give it an ally on their northern border.

These calculations resulted in the Israeli invasion of Lebanon in June 1982, when Ariel Sharon misled the Israeli cabinet which had been briefed for a limited incursion similar to that of 1978. The Israeli army encircled Beirut where repeated asssaults caused many civilian casualties but did not destroy the Palestinian community or command. International intervention resulted in the PLO agreeing to leave Lebanon for Tunisia in August with guarantees that the Palestinians who remained would be protected. Once the PLO left Lebanon, American military contingents were with-drawn. Almost simultaneously, Bashir Gemayel was assassinated. As a result the Israeli army permitted Maronite Phalangists to enter the Sabra and Shatila refugee camps where nearly a thousand Palestinians were slaughtered (Schiff and Ya'ari 1984; Khalidi 1986).

The massacres in the camps brought the return of American forces who remained until early 1984, though increasingly caught up in Lebanese factional disputes as US policy seemed to favour the Maronites. In 1983 when the Reagan administration called for naval bombardments of Druze positions, over the strong objections of the marine commander in Beirut, opposition forces retaliated with the suicide bombing of the marine barracks in October, causing 241 deaths. After a further show of force, Reagan ordered the withdrawal of American troops, leaving Lebanon to its regional competitors.

The 1982 Israeli invasion of Lebanon proved in restrospect to be an undertaking whose short-term triumphs masked long-term liabilities, in particular the incitement of Lebanese Shi'ite hostility toward Israel. The Lebanese–Israeli frontier remained a zone of conflict, notably the enclave in the south where Israel retained control. There Lebanese Shi'ites, often members of the Iranian-backed Hizballah (Party of God) forces, undertook assaults against Israeli troops and client forces in a war of attrition that ultimately ended with Israel voluntarily withdrawing from most of the enclave in May 2000.

Israel and the intifada

These difficulties did not deter Israeli Likud prime ministers of the 1980s, Menachem Begin and later Yitzhak Shamir, from pursuing the real goal of the Lebanese venture, consolidation of the Israeli position in the West Bank. The decade saw the vast expansion of Israeli settlements in the area, sponsored by Likud in the hope of creating facts that would bar any future Israeli withdrawal. Arab–Israeli state tensions were muted with Egypt sidelined, Iraq involved in a protracted and costly war with Iran (1980–88), and Syria monitoring its position in Lebanon. Jordan sought entry into negotiations with American support and that of Labour politicians in Israeli coalitions, continually stymied by Likud objections. No major change in the diplomacy of the Arab–Israeli conflict occurred until December 1988 when the US agreed to talk to the PLO, declaring that it had satisfactorily renounced terrorism and accepted Security Council Resolution 242.

The American decision, taken with more reluctance than enthusiasm, appeared to be a major stepping stone toward resolution of issues within the framework of the broader Arab–Israeli conflict. But the impetus for the decision had nothing to do with diplomacy. Rather it was the actions of Palestinians in the West Bank and especially in the Gaza Strip who had rebelled against Israeli occupation. The rebellion, known as the *intifada*, began in December 1987 and lasted into 1991. The intensity of Palestinian protests and the brutality of the Israeli response forced international attention on the nature of Israel's role as occupiers of these lands and called into question the future of the territories. In addition, the *intifada* gave legitimacy, if only indirectly, to PLO claims to represent the Palestinians in the territories. But American agreement to discuss matters with Arafat did not mean a willingness to negotiate with him; the Jordanian solution remained the favoured option. Matters remained stalemated with Likud, guided by Yitzhak Shamir, ever more determined to resist pressures to compromise, despite American encouragement to do so.

The Gulf War, 1990–91

The catalyst for an apparent breakthrough toward resolution of Arab-Israeli matters was a factor indirectly related to the Arab–Israeli conflict: the decision of Saddam Hussein to invade Kuwait in August 1990 and the counter decision of President George Bush that the United States would forge a military coalition that included Arab armies to drive Iraqi forces out of that country. These developments, coupled with the disintegration of the Soviet Union, removed the Cold War justification of American–Soviet rivalry for control of Arab–Israeli negotiations. Arab states such as Syria, long a recipient of Soviet aid but a foe of Iraq, now had incentives to join an American-led force. These incentives were not limited to defeat of an Arab rival; they included American promises to seek to broaden Arab–Israeli negotiations at the conclusion of the war and to confront more directly the militancy of Yitzhak Shamir.

The Madrid conference

Herein lay the basic irony of the Gulf War. The ultimate though not immediate beneficiary of the Gulf War was to be Arafat and with him the PLO, despite the fact that he had sided with Saddam against the American-led coalition and had as a result lost his funding from Saudi Arabia and Kuwait, his principal sources of revenue.

With the US now in full command of the Arab–Israeli talks, it behooved Washington to pressure Israel in order to fulfill promises made to Arab leaders to gain their inclusion in the coalition against Saddam Hussein. Secretary of State James Baker's efforts resulted in an international conference in Madrid, convened in October 1991. The Arab states represented were Syria, Jordan and Lebanon. In addition, the Palestinians were for the first time permitted to attend such a conference although the PLO was excluded and the Palestinian delegation was, officially, part of the Jordanian contingent.

The Madrid talks included several rounds of negotiations from October 1991 to the summer of 1993. Arab states and Israel negotiated directly for the first time as did Israelis and Palestinians. No formal agreements emerged during these talks, although Israel and Jordan drafted a peace accord which Jordan would not acknowledge until progress on the Israeli–Palestinian front appeared; the Israeli–ordanian peace treaty would be signed in October 1994 following the 1993 Oslo Accord (see Chapter 11). Exchanges between other delegations led nowhere, especially those between Palestinian delegates and their Israeli counterparts during a period of increasing violence in the territories and suicide bombings in Israel, undertaken by the Islamic groups, Hamas and Islamic Jihad. These attacks reflected anger at Israel's settlement expansion and at Arafat's failure to represent Palestinian interests. Although Arafat had benefited from the Gulf War to the extent that Palestinians were invited to the Madrid talks, albeit unconnected to the PLO, his reputation among rank and file Palestinians had been severely tarnished because of his apparent acquiescence in the continuing settlement process in the occupied territories.

The election of Yitzhak Rabin as Israeli prime minister in 1992 gave momentum to peace efforts, if only because he and foreign minister Shimon Peres saw the Islamic-inspired violence as a greater threat to Israeli security than Arafat and the PLO. They decided to resurrect Arafat and instill a sense of hope among Palestinians to undermine the appeal of the Islamists, a decision that led to the historic Oslo Accord of August–September 1993, the subject of the following chapter in this volume.

Conclusion

The Oslo Accord had significance beyond the scope of Israeli–Palestinian relations. As noted, it legitimised Jordan's right to reach its own peace treaty with Israel, long a goal of the late King Hussein. The treaty, signed in October 1994, created within a few months more normalisation of relations than that achieved in the fifteen years spanned by Israel's treaty with Egypt.

Nonetheless, the Arab–Israeli conflict remains an unresolved question whose configuration has altered in the aftermath of the Cold War, the failure of the Israeli–Palestinian peace talks of 2000, and the impact of 11 September 2001 on American interpretations of events, leading them to decide to attack Iraq and remove Saddam Hussein from power.

The first two decades of the conflict, though marked by armed hostilities, were notable also for Arab refusal to recognise Israel's existence. Following the 1967 War, that political equation changed, particularly once Revisionist Zionists gained power in Israel from 1977 onward. Most Arab states, notably Syria and Saudi Arabia, have displayed willingness to recognise Israel and two, Egypt and Jordan, have signed peace treaties; the Palestinians recognised Israel's right to exist in the 1993 Oslo Agreement.

This recognition has been premised on a two-state solution to the Palestinian-Israeli question with Israel ceding the Gaza Strip and most of the West Bank. Revisionist Zionism, in the form of the Likud Party, rejects that notion, insisting on either full control of the West Bank or granting a Palestinian state with no contiguity or sovereignty on approximately 42 per cent of the West Bank. This stance, linked to continued Israeli settlement growth, undermines further resolution of Arab state relations with Israel and encourages the growth of Islamist movements in Arab states opposed to Israel's right to exist.

These developments suggest that the resolution of the Arab–Israeli conflict is now affected more by Israeli state militancy than Arab as was formerly the case. Likud expansionism to achieve fulfillment of its image of a true Jewish state, with the apparent tolerance of the United States, embraces ideological perspectives requiring the subjugation of neighbours. This replaces the search for peace through diplomacy based on negotiation and compromise, an approach that until now has been the norm, even in the immediate aftermath of war.

In this regard, most Arab states have adopted a realist approach to the Arab-Israeli conflict, seeking co-existence based in part on acceptance of Israel's military supremacy. In contrast, Israel, backed by American pro-Likud ideologues in the George W. Bush administration, appears to insist on security through regional domination, coupled with retention of the West Bank as Greater Israel. Here one finds no homogeneity of state interests as realist theory sometimes assumes but, rather, assertion of identity based both on power and on claims to historic territory, the West Bank, that confronts Hamas's search for total victory, not that of Arafat and the Palestinian Authority.

This stalemate will likely serve to prolong the Arab–Israeli conflict given the centrality of the Palestinian question to the possible normalisation of relations between Arab states and Israel. Indeed, in the aftermath of the al-Qaida terrorist attacks of September 11, 2001 and the subsequent American occupation of Iraq, this stalemate may increase the possibility that the conflict, heretofore one of states, could be interpreted more fully in religious terms as well.

Further Reading

KERR, M., *The Arab Cold War: Gamal 'Abd al-Nasir and his Rivals, 1958–1970* (New York: Oxford University Press, 1971). A classic account of Arab infighting and tensions building to the 1967 War.

LEBOW, R. N. and STEIN, J. G., *We All Lost the Cold War* (Princeton, NJ: Princeton University Press, 1994). A clear, unsentimental examination of the Cold War and its impact on global stability and diplomacy.

LUSTICK, I., *Unsettled States, Disputed Lands: Britain and Ireland, France and Algeria, Israel and the West Bank-Gaza* (Ithaca, NY: Cornell University Press, 1993). A path-breaking comparative study of the impact of colonisation on considerations of state security and stability when confronting national independence movements.

QUANDT, W. B., *Peace Process: American Diplomacy and the Arab–Israeli Conflict Since 1967* (Washington, D.C.: Brookings Institution, 1993). The best one-volume overview of American policy, though deserving of an update.

SAYIGH, Y., *Armed Struggle and the Search for State: the Palestinian National Movement, 1949–1993* (New York: Oxford University Press, 1997). The basic study of Palestinian nationalism, its politics and factional disputes. Highly detailed it can be mined for its bibliographical information as well as its data.

SEALE, P., *The Struggle for Syria: A Study of Post-War Arab Politics, 1945–1957* (Oxford: Oxford University Press, 1966). The classic study of Arab politics to 1957,

recently reissued. Can be read as pre-
liminary to Kerr's *Arab Cold War*.

SHEFFER, G., *Moshe Sharett: Biography of a Political Moderate* (New York: Oxford University Press, 1996). Rivaling Sayigh in detail, it provides the best account of Israeli political relationships, disputes and views of Arab neighbours in the first decade of Israel's existence.

SHLAIM, A., *The Iron Wall: Israel and the Arab World* (New York: W. W. Norton, 2000). A challenging, incisive examination of the basic Israeli approach to dealing with the Arab world. Can be read in tandem with Sheffer's biography of Sharett (see above).

SMITH, C. D., *Palestine and the Arab-Israeli Conflict* (Boston: Bedford/ St. Martin's Press, 5th edn., 2004). A highly regarded, comprehensive synthesis of the subject.

TELHAMI, S. and BARNETT, M. (eds.), *Identity and Foreign Policy in the Middle East* (Ithaca, NY: Cornell University Press, 2002). Excellent introduction to the question of identity politics and its relationship to realist theory, with useful case studies.

Chronology

Box 10.1 Important events

DATE	EVENT.
14 May 1948	Declaration of State of Israel.
May–July 1948	First Arab–Israeli War: Arab states attack Israel.
October–November 1956	Suez Crisis: Israel, France and Great Britain attack Egypt.
1964	Formation of Palestine Liberation Organisation.
June 1967	Six-Day War. Israel Attacks Egypt, Jordan and Syria in response to incitements and encirclement—occupies Sinai Peninsula, Golan Heights, Gaza Strip and West Bank.
October 1973	1973 War. Egypt and Syria Attack Israel in Golan Heights and Sinai Peninsula.
September 1978/March 1979	Camp David Talks establish basis for an Egyptian–Israeli Peace Treaty.
December 1987	Outbreak of First Palestinian *intifada*.
February–March 1991	First Gulf War.
September 1991	Convening of Madrid Conference.
August–September 1993	First Oslo Accord.

Box 10.1 Continued

May 1994	Palestinian self-rule begins in Gaza Strip (excluding Jewish settlements) and in Jericho, West Bank.
26 October 1994	Jordan–Israeli Peace Treaty signed.
24 September 1995	Oslo 2, the 'Interim Agreement' proposed in the 1993 Oslo Accord, is initialed by Yitzhak Rabin and Yasser Arafat; official signing is September 28 in Washington, D.C. News of the pending agreement inspires massive right-wing Israeli protest demonstrations, led by Binyamin Netanyahu and Ariel Sharon.
October 1995	Islamic Jihad head Fathi Shiqaqi is assassinated in Malta by Israel.
4 November 1995	Yitzhak Rabin is assassinated by right-winger opposed to Oslo 2 Accord. Rabin succeeded as prime minister by Shimon Peres.
December 1995	Israeli forces withdraw from Zone A and Zone B areas outlined in Oslo 2.
5 January 1996	Hamas bomb maker Yayha Ayyash assassinated by Israel, breaking five month Hamas–Israel truce.
20 January 1996	Palestinian Self-Governing Authority (Council) elected.
11 February 1996	Peres advances Israeli elections from November to May.
25 February–4 March 1996	Four suicide bombings, avenging Ayyash killing, kill at least 59 Israelis, woundover 200.
March–April 1996	Operation 'Grapes of Wrath'—Israel attacks into Lebanon, responding to Hizballah attacks in Israeli enclave in south Lebanon. One hundred Lebanese killed while seeking shelter in UN camp.
May 1996	Binyamin Netanyahu elected prime minister by less than one percent of vote. Takes office in June.
January 1997	Hebron Redeployment Agreement signed.
23 October 1998	Wye Memorandum between Israel and Palestinians signed.
December 1998	Palestinian National Council officially removes clauses from 1968 Palestine National Charter calling for Israel's destruction.

Box 10.1 Continued

February 1999	Jordan's King Hussein dies, succeeded by his son who takes title Abdullah II.
4 May 1999	Official deadline for conclusion of Israeli–Palestinian final status talks, as stipulated in Oslo Agreements; deadline passes without talks ever having begun.
18 May 1999	Ehud Barak of One Israel Party, which includes Labour, elected prime minister, takes office in July.
January–March 2000	Syrian–Israeli peace talks end in failure.
June 2000	Syrian President Hafiz al-Asad dies, succeeded by son, Bashar.
11–25 July 2000	Camp David Israeli–Palestinian summit (final status talks).
28 September 2000	Ariel Sharon visits Temple Mount/Haram al-Sharif to undermine ongoing negotiations. Triggers second *intifada*.
November 2000	George W. Bush elected president of the United States; takes office in January 2001.
December 2000–January 2001	Positive Israeli–Palestinian talks building on Camp David end inconclusively in midst of Israeli election campaign.
6 February 2001	Likud candidate Ariel Sharon elected prime minister. Takes office in March.
30 April 2001	Sharm al-Sheikh Fact Finding Committee (Mitchell Committee) authorized by President Clinton submits report to President George W. Bush on outbreak of second intifada. One of its findings is that Palestinians used weapons in 27.6% of clashes from September 28–December 31 2000; Israeli troops used live ammunition from the outset.
11 September 2001	Al-Qaida terrorist attacks on the United States destroy World Trade Center in New York City and damage Pentagon, killing over 3,000.
October 2001	US initiates attacks on Afghanistan in response to 9/11 assaults.
January 2002	Israel isolates Yasser Arafat in his Ramallah compound where he still remains.

Box 10.1 Continued

18 February 2002	Saudi Arabia offers peace initiative where Israel will withdraw from occupied territories in return for peace accords with Arab world. Sharon rejects initiative.
24 June 2002	President Bush delivers Rose Garden address at White House calling for removal of Yasser Arafat as Palestinian leader as condition for US intervention in Palestinian–Israeli conflict. Also refers to need for a Palestinian state.
16 July 2002	First Quartet statement, based on President Bush's Rose Garden address.
28 January 2003	Ariel Sharon reelected prime minister. Initiates construction of Israeli 'security fence' to block Palestinian suicide bombings; barrier designed to incorporate at least 14% more West Bank Palestinian land.
March 2003	US begins assault on Iraq to remove Saddam Hussein from power after build-up of troops and supplies of seven months
19 March 2003	Yasser Arafat appoints Mahmud Abbas prime minister of Palestinian Authority after the post is created by Palestinian legislature.
30 April 2003	Official issuance of the Road Map in response to Abbas's appointment as Palestinian prime minister.
September 2003	Mahmud Abbas resigns as Palestinian prime minister.
April 2004	Ariel Sharon announces a disengagement plan whereby all Israeli settlements in Gaza Strip will be evacuated. Plan arouses furor among Likud. The plan indicates that Sharon intends to keep nearly all of West Bank, evacuating only four settlements in far north where Palestinian communities would have contiguity. No contiguity for Palestinian areas in rest of region. Reference to a 'Palestinian state' is removed in second version of plan issued in May.
11 November 2004	Death of Yasser Arafat.

Note

1. Morris's text and evidence contradict his title and conclusion, giving ample proof of Israeli unilateral activity without Arab provocation.

11

The Rise and Fall of the Oslo Peace Process

Avi Shlaim*

OVERVIEW

One of the salient strands in the International Relations of the Middle East in the aftermath of the 1991 Gulf War was the American-sponsored peace process between Israel and the Arabs. On the Arab side the principal participants were Syria, Jordan and the Palestinians. This chapter focuses on the two principal parties to the Arab–Israeli conflict—Israel and the Palestinians. It traces the emergence, the development and the breakdown of the peace negotiations between Israel and the PLO from 1991 to 2001. The main landmarks in this process are the conclusion of the Oslo accord, the implementation of the accord, Oslo II, the

* The author would like to thank the United States Institute of Peace for supporting his research on the Middle East peace process.

Camp David summit and the return to violence. The main conclusion is that the Oslo accord was not doomed to failure from the start: it failed because Israel, under the leadership of the Likud, reneged on its side of the deal.

Introduction

The Middle East is the most penetrated sub-system of the international political system. Ever since Napoleon's expeditionary force landed in Egypt in 1798, it has been an object of rivalry among the great powers. The strategic value of the Middle East was considerable as the gateway between Europe and the Far East. The discovery of oil, in the early part of the twentieth century, enhanced the region's importance for the global economy. After the Second World War, the Middle East became one of the major theatres of the Cold War. It was constantly caught up in superpower rivalry for political influence, power and prestige. External sources of conflict combined with internal ones to produce frequent crises, violence and wars. One of the most destabilising factors in the affairs of the region is the dispute between Israel and the Arabs.

The Arab–Israeli conflict is one of the most bitter, protracted and intractable conflicts of modern times. It is also one of the dominant themes in the International Relations of the Middle East. There are two principal levels to this conflict: the inter-state level and the Israeli–Palestinian level. In origin and in essence this is a clash between the Jewish and Palestinian national movements over the land of Palestine. The Palestine problem therefore remains the core of the conflict. But the search for a settlement is complicated by inter-Arab relations and by the involvement of outside powers. The purpose of this chapter is to examine the peace process that got under way in the aftermath of the Gulf War and, more specifically, the quest for a settlement between Israel and the Palestinians.

The Peace Process

The United States took the lead in convening an international conference to address the Arab–Israeli dispute following the expulsion of Iraq from Kuwait. The conference was held in Madrid at the end of October 1991. At the conference the US adopted an even-handed approach and pledged to promote a settlement that would provide security for Israel and justice to the Palestinians. Negotiations were to be based on UN resolution 242 of November 1967 and the principle of land for peace that it incorporated.

All the parties to the conflict were invited to Madrid but the PLO was excluded on account of its support for Iraq following its invasion if Kuwait on 2 August 1990.

The Palestinian delegation was made up of residents of the West Bank and the Gaza Strip who went to Madrid not as an independent delegation but as part of a joint delegation with Jordan. Jordan thus provided an umbrella for Palestinian participation in the peace talks. Although the PLO leadership in Tunis was formally banned from attending this major international gathering, the Palestinian negotiators kept in close touch with their colleagues in Tunis.

The Israeli delegation to Madrid was headed by Prime Minister Itzhak Shamir, the leader of the right-wing Likud party. Whereas Labour is a pragmatic party committed to territorial compromise, the Likud is an ideological party committed to maintaining the West Bank as part of the ancestral Land of Israel. At Madrid, Shamir struck a tough and uncompromising posture. By arguing that the basic problem was not territory but the Arab denial of Israel's very right to exist, he came close to rejecting the principle of swapping land for peace.

Two tracks for negotiations were established in Madrid: an Israeli–Arab track and an Israeli–Palestinian track. Stage two of the peace process consisted of bilateral negotiations between Israel and individual Arab parties. These bilateral talks were held under American auspices in Washington, starting in January 1992. Several rounds of negotiations were held in the American capital, but as long as the Likud remained in power little progress was made on either track. It was only after the Labour's victory over the Likud in June 1992 that the Israeli position began to be modified, at least on the Arab track. On the Palestinian issue the Israeli position displayed more continuity than change following the rise of the Labour government under the leadership of Itzhak Rabin. Consequently, the official talks between the Israeli and Palestinian delegations in Washington made painfully slow progress.

The Road to Oslo

Stalemate in the official talks led both Israel and the PLO to seek a back channel for communicating. The decision to hold direct talks with the PLO was a diplomatic revolution in Israel's foreign policy and paved the way to the Oslo accord of 13 September 1993. Three men were primarily responsible for this decision: Yitzhak Rabin, Shimon Peres, the foreign minister and Yossi Beilin, the youthful deputy foreign minister. Rabin held out against direct talks with the PLO for as long as he could. Peres took the view that without the PLO there could be no settlement. Expecting the PLO to enable the local Palestinian leaders to reach an agreement with Israel, he said on one occasion, was like expecting the turkey to help in preparing the Thanksgiving dinner. As long as Yasser Arafat, the chairman of the PLO, remained in Tunis, he argued, he represented the 'outsiders', the Palestinian diaspora, and he would do his best to slow down the peace talks (Peres 1995: 323–4).

Yossi Beilin was even more categorical in his view that talking to the PLO was a necessary condition for an agreement with the Palestinians. Beilin had always belonged to the extreme dovish wing of the Labour Party. He was the real architect behind the Israeli recognition of the PLO. Peres backed him all the way and the two of them succeeded in carrying their hesitant and suspicious senior colleague with them.

The secret talks in Oslo got under way in late January 1993 with the active encouragement of Yossi Beilin who kept Shimon Peres fully informed. Altogether, fourteen sessions of talks were held over an eight-month period, all behind a thick veil of secrecy. Norwegian foreign affairs minister Johan Joergen Holst and social scientist Terge Rød Larsen acted as generous hosts and facilitators. The key players were two Israeli academics, Dr Yair Hirschfeld and Dr Ron Pundik, and PLO treasurer Ahmad Qurei, better known as Abu Ala. Away from the glare of publicity and political pressures, these three men worked imaginatively and indefatigably to establish the conceptual framework of the Israel–PLO accord. Their discussions ran parallel to the bilateral talks in Washington but they proceeded without the knowledge of the official Israeli and Palestinian negotiators.

The unofficial talks dealt initially with economic cooperation but quickly broadened into a dialogue about a joint declaration of principles. In May, Peres took a highly significant decision: he ordered Uri Savir, the director-general of the foreign ministry, and Yoel Singer, a high-flying attorney who had spent twenty years in the IDF legal department, to join Hirschfeld and Pundik on the weekend trips to Oslo. At this point Peres began to report to Rabin regularly on developments in the Norwegian back-channel. At first Rabin showed little interest in this channel but he raised no objection to continuing the explorations either. Gradually, however, he became more involved in the details and assumed an active role in directing the talks alongside Peres. Since Abu Ala reported directly to Arafat, an indirect line of communication had been established between Jerusalem and the PLO headquarters in Tunis.

Another landmark in the progress of the talks was the failure of the tenth round of the official Israeli–Palestinian negotiations in Washington. To tempt the Palestinians to move forward, Peres floated the idea of 'Gaza first'. He believed that Arafat was desperate for a concrete achievement to bolster his sagging political fortunes and that Gaza would provide him with his first toehold in the occupied territories. Peres also knew that an Israeli withdrawal from Gaza would be greeted with sighs of relief among the great majority of his countrymen. Arafat, however, did not swallow the bait, suspecting an Israeli plan to confine the dream of Palestinian independence to the narrow strip of territory stretching from Gaza City to Rafah. The idea was attractive to some Palestinians, especially the inhabitants of the Gaza Strip, but not to the politicians in Tunis. Rather than reject the Israeli offer out of hand, Yasser Arafat came up with a counter offer of his own: Gaza and Jericho first. His choice of the small and sleepy West Bank town seemed quirky at first sight but it served as a symbol of his claim to the whole of the West Bank.

Rabin did not balk at the counter offer. All along he had supported handing over Jericho to Jordanian rule while keeping the Jordan Valley in Israeli hands. But he had one condition: the Palestinian foothold on the West Bank would be an island inside

Israeli-controlled territory with the Allenby Bridge also remaining in Israeli hands. Jordan, too, preferred Israel to the Palestinians at the other end of the bridge. Arafat therefore had to settle for the Israeli version of the 'Gaza and Jericho first' plan.

Rabin's conversion to the idea of a deal with the PLO was clinched by four evaluations which reached him between the end of May and July. First was the advice of Itamar Rabinovich, the head of the Israeli delegation to the talks with Syria, that a settlement with Syria was attainable but only at the cost of complete Israeli withdrawal from the Golan Heights. Second were the reports from various quarters that the local Palestinian leadership had been finally neutralised. Third was the assessment of the IDF director of military intelligence that Arafat's dire situation, and possibly imminent collapse, made him the most convenient interlocutor for Israel at that particular juncture. Fourth were the reports of the impressive progress achieved through the Oslo channel. Other reports that reached Rabin during this period pointed to an alarming growth in the popular following of Hamas and Islamic Jihad in the occupied territories. Both the army chiefs and the internal security chiefs repeatedly stressed to him the urgency of finding a political solution to the crisis in the relations between Israel and the inhabitants of the occupied territories. Rabin therefore gave the green light to the Israeli team and the secret diplomacy in Oslo moved into higher gear.

Rabin and Peres also believed that progress towards a settlement with the Palestinians would lower the price of a settlement with Syria by reducing the latter's bargaining power. Peres reduced the link between the two sets of negotiations to what he called 'the bicycle principle': when one presses on one pedal, the other pedal moves by itself. His formula was not directed at reaching a separate agreement with the Palestinians but at gradual movement towards a settlement with the Palestinians, the Syrians and the Jordanians.

On 23 August, Rabin stated publicly for the first time that 'there would be no escape from recognising the PLO.' In private, he elaborated on the price that Israel could extract in exchange for this recognition. In his estimate, the PLO was 'on the ropes' and it was therefore highly probable that the PLO would drop some of its sacred principles to secure Israeli recognition. Accordingly, while endorsing the joint declaration of principles on Palestinian self-government in Gaza and Jericho and mutual recognition between Israel and the PLO, he insisted on changes to the Palestinian National Charter as part of the package deal.

Peres flew to California to explain the accord to the US Secretary of State, Warren Christopher. Christopher was surprised by the scope of the accord and by the unorthodox method by which it had been achieved. He naturally assumed that America had a monopoly over the peace process. His aides in the State Department had come to be called 'the peace processors'. Now their feathers were ruffled because they had been so thoroughly upstaged by the Norwegians. All the participants in the Oslo back-channel, on the other hand, had the satisfaction of knowing that they had reached the accord on their own without any help from the State Department. Their success showed that the fate of the peace process lay in the hands of the protagonists rather than in the hands of the intermediaries.

The Oslo Accord

The Declaration of Principles on Interim Self-Government Arrangements was essentially an agenda for negotiations, governed by a tight timetable, rather than a full-blown agreement. The Declaration laid down that within two months of the signing ceremony, agreement on Israel's military withdrawal from Gaza and Jericho should be reached and within four months the withdrawal should be completed. A Palestinian police force, made up mostly of pro-Arafat Palestinian fighters, was to be imported to maintain internal security in Gaza and Jericho, with Israel retaining overall responsibility for external security and foreign affairs. At the same time, elsewhere in the West Bank, Israel undertook to transfer power to 'authorised Palestinians' in five spheres: education, health, social welfare, direct taxation and tourism. Within nine months, the Palestinians in the West Bank and Gaza were to hold elections to a Palestinian Council to take office and assume responsibility for most government functions except defence and foreign affairs. Within two years, Israel and the Palestinians agreed to commence negotiations on the final status of the territories, and at the end of five years the permanent settlement was to come into force (Medzini 1995: 319–28). In short, the Declaration of Principles promised to set in motion a process that would end Israeli rule over the two million Palestinians living in the West Bank and Gaza.

The shape of the permanent settlement was not specified in the Declaration of Principles but was left to negotiations between the two parties during the second stage. The Declaration was completely silent on vital issues such as the right of return of the 1948 refugees, the borders of the Palestinian entity, the future of the Jewish settlements on the West Bank and Gaza and the status of Jerusalem. The reason for this silence is not hard to understand: if these issues had been addressed, there would have been no accord. Both sides took a calculated risk, realising that a great deal would depend on the way the experiment in Palestinian self-government worked out in practice. Rabin was strongly opposed to an independent Palestinian state but he favoured an eventual Jordanian–Palestinian confederation. Arafat was strongly committed to an independent Palestinian state, with East Jerusalem as its capital, but he did not rule out the idea of a confederation with Jordan.

Despite all its limitations and ambiguities, the Declaration of Principles for Palestinian self-government in Gaza and Jericho marked a major breakthrough in the century-old conflict between Arabs and Jews in Palestine. On Monday, 13 September 1993, the Declaration was signed on the South Lawn of the White House and sealed with the historic handshake between Prime Minister Rabin and Chairman Arafat.

The Oslo accord consisted of two parts, both of which were the product of secret diplomacy in the Norwegian capital. The first part consisted of mutual recognition between Israel and the PLO. It took the form of two letters, on plain paper and without letterheads, signed by chairman Arafat and Prime Minister Rabin respectively on 9 and 10 September. Nearly all the publicity focused on the signing of the

Declaration of Principles, but without the mutual recognition there could have been no meaningful agreement on Palestinian self-government.

In his letter to Rabin, Arafat observed that the signing of the Declaration of Principles marked a new era in the history of the Middle East. He then confirmed the PLO's commitment to recognise Israel's right to live in peace and security, to accept United Nations Security Council Resolutions 242 and 338, to renounce the use of terrorism and other acts of violence and to change those parts of the Palestinian National Charter which were inconsistent with these commitments. In his terse, one-sentence reply to Arafat, Rabin confirmed that in the light of these commitments, the Government of Israel decided to recognise the PLO as the representative of the Palestinian people and to commence negotiations with the PLO within the Middle East peace process.

Taken together, the two parts of the Oslo accord seemed at the time to merit the over-worked epithet 'historic' because they reconciled the two principal parties to the Arab–Israeli conflict. The clash between Jewish and Palestinian nationalism had always been the heart and core of the Arab–Israeli conflict. Both national movements, Jewish and Palestinian, denied the other the right to self-determination in Palestine. Their history was one of mutual denial and mutual rejection. Now mutual denial made way for mutual recognition. Israel not only recognised the Palestinians as a people with political rights but formally recognised the PLO as its representative. The handshake between Rabin and Arafat at the signing ceremony, despite the former's awkward body language, was a powerful symbol of the historic reconciliation between the two nations.

The historic reconciliation was based on a historic compromise: acceptance of the principle of the partition of Palestine. Both sides accepted territorial compromise as the basis for the settlement of their long and bitter conflict. By accepting the principle of partition, the two sides suspended the ideological dispute as to who is the rightful owner of Palestine and turned to finding a practical solution to the problem of sharing the cramped living space between the Jordan River and the Mediterranean sea. Each side resigned itself to parting with territory that it had previously regarded not only as its patrimony but as a vital part of its national identity. Each side was driven to this historic compromise by the recognition that it lacked the power to impose its own vision on the other side. That the idea of partition was finally accepted by the two sides seemed to support Abba Eban's observation that men and nations often behave wisely once they have exhausted all the other alternatives (Eban 1993).

The breakthrough at Oslo was achieved by separating the interim settlement from the final settlement. In the past the Palestinians had always refused to consider any interim agreement unless the principles of the permanent settlement were agreed in advance. Israel on the other hand, had insisted that a five-year transition period should begin without a prior agreement about the nature of the permanent settlement. At Oslo the PLO accepted the Israeli formula. In contrast to the official Palestinian position in Washington, the PLO agreed to a five-year transition period without clear commitments by Israel as to the nature of the permanent settlement (Beilin 1997: 152).

Reactions to Oslo

The Israeli–PLO accord had far-reaching implications for the interstate dimension of the Arab–Israeli conflict. Originally, the Arab states got involved in the Palestine conflict out of a sense of solidarity with the Palestine Arabs against the Zionist intruders. Continuing commitment to the Palestinian cause had precluded the Arab states, with the notable exception of Egypt, from extending recognition to the Jewish state. One of the main functions of the Arab League, which was established in 1945, was to assist the Palestinians in the struggle for Palestine. After 1948, the League became a forum for coordinating military policy and for waging political, economic and ideological warfare against the Jewish state. In 1974 the Arab League recognised the PLO as the sole legitimate representative of the Palestinian people. Now that the PLO had formally recognised Israel, there was no longer any compelling reason for the Arab states to continue to reject her.

Clearly, an important taboo had been broken. PLO recognition of Israel was an important landmark along the road to Arab recognition of Israel and the normalising of relations with her. Egypt, which was first to take the plunge back in the late 1970s, felt vindicated and elated by the breakthrough. When Rabin stopped in Rabat on his way home after attending the signing ceremony in Washington, he was received like any other visiting head of state by King Hassan II of Morocco. Jordan allowed Israeli television the first ever live report by one of its correspondents from Amman. A number of Arab states, like Tunisia and Saudi Arabia, started thinking seriously about the establishment of diplomatic relations with Israel. And the Arab League began discussions on the lifting of the economic boycott which had been in force since Israel's creation. Nothing was quite the same in the Arab world as a result of the Israel–PLO accord. The rules of the game in the entire Middle East had changed radically.

The change was no less marked in Israel's approach to her Arab opponents than in their approach to her. Zionist policy, before and after 1948, proceeded on the assumption that agreement on the partition of Palestine would be easier to achieve with the rulers of the neighbouring Arab states than with the Palestine Arabs. Israel's courting of conservative Arab leaders, like King Hussein of Jordan and President Anwar Sadat of Egypt, was an attempt to bypass the local Arabs, and avoid having to address the core issue of the conflict. Recognition by the Arab states, it was hoped, would help to alleviate the conflict without conceding the right of national self-determination to the Palestinians. Now this strategy was reversed. PLO recognition of Israel was expected to pave the way for wider recognition by the Arab states from North Africa to the Persian Gulf. Rabin expressed this hope when signing the letter to Arafat in which Israel recognised the PLO. 'I believe', he said, 'that there is a great opportunity of changing not only the relations between the Palestinians and Israel, but to expand it to the solution of the conflict between Israel and the Arab countries and other Arab peoples' (International Herald Tribune, 11–12 Sept. 1993).

On both sides of the Israeli–Palestinian divide, the Rabin–Arafat deal provoked strong and vociferous opposition on the part of the hardliners. Both leaders were accused of a betrayal and a sell-out. Leaders of the Likud, and of the nationalistic parties further to the right, attacked Rabin for his abrupt departure from the bipartisan policy of refusing to negotiate with the PLO and charged him with abandoning the 120,000 settlers in the occupied territories to the tender mercies of terrorists. The Gaza-Jericho plan was denounced as a bridgehead to a Palestinian state and the beginning of the end of Greater Israel. A Gallup poll, however, indicated considerable popular support for the prime minister. Of the 1,000 Israelis polled, 65 per cent said they approved of the peace accord, with only 13 per cent describing themselves as 'very much against' (Guardian, 16 Sept. 1993).

Within the Palestinian camp the accord also encountered loud but ineffective opposition. The PLO itself was split, with the radical nationalists accusing Arafat of abandoning principles to grab power. They included the Popular Front for the Liberation of Palestine, led by George Habash, and the Damascus-based Democratic Front for the Liberation of Palestine, led by Nayef Hawatmeh. Arafat succeeded in mustering the necessary majority in favour of the deal on the PLO's eighteen-member Executive Committee but only after a bruising battle and the resignation of four of his colleagues. Outside the PLO, the deal aroused the implacable wrath of the militant resistance movements, Hamas and Islamic Jihad, who regarded any compromise with the Jewish state as anathema.

Opposition to the deal from rejectionist quarters, whether secular or religious, was only to be expected. More disturbing was the opposition of mainstream figures like Farouk Kaddoumi, the PLO 'foreign minister' and prominent intellectuals like Professor Edward Said and the poet Mahmoud Darwish. Some of the criticisms related to Arafat's autocratic, idiosyncratic and secretive style of management. Others related to the substance of the deal. The most basic criticism was that the deal negotiated by Arafat did not carry the promise, let alone a guarantee, of an independent Palestinian state.

This criticism took various forms. Farouk Kaddoumi argued that the deal compromised the basic national rights of the Palestinian people as well as the individual rights of the 1948 refugees. Edward Said lambasted Arafat for unilaterally cancelling the *intifada*, for failing to coordinate his moves with the Arab states, and for introducing appalling disarray within the ranks of the PLO. 'The PLO', wrote Said, 'has transformed itself from a national liberation movement into a kind of small-town government, with the same handful of people still in command'. For the deal itself, Said had nothing but scorn. 'All secret deals between a very strong and a very weak partner necessarily involve concessions hidden in embarrassment by the latter', he wrote. 'The deal before us', he continued, 'smacks of the PLO leadership's exhaustion and isolation, and of Israel's shrewdness' (Said 1995: 2). 'Gaza and Jericho first . . . and last' was Mahmoud Darwish's damning verdict on the deal.

Arab reactions to the Israeli–Palestinian accord were rather mixed. Arafat got a polite but cool reception from the nineteen foreign ministers of the Arab League who met in Cairo a week after the signing ceremony in Washington. Some member states of the League, especially Jordan, Syria and Lebanon, were dismayed by the PLO chairman's solo diplomacy which violated Arab pledges to coordinate their negotiating strategy. Arafat defended his decision to sign the accord by presenting it as the first step towards a more comprehensive peace in the Middle East. The interim agreement, he said, was only the first step towards a final settlement of the Palestinian problem and of the Arab-Israeli conflict which would involve Israeli withdrawal from all the occupied territories, including 'Holy Jerusalem'. He justified his resort to a secret channel by arguing that the almost two years of public negotiations under US sponsorship had reached a dead end. Some of the Arab foreign ministers agreed with the PLO chairman that the accord was an important first step, even if they were not all agreed on the next step or the final destination.

Implementing the Declaration of Principles

Two committees were set up in early October 1993 to negotiate the implementation of the lofty-sounding declaration signed in Washington. The first committee was chaired by Shimon Peres and Mahmoud Abbas, the leader who signed the declaration on behalf of the PLO. This ministerial-level committee was supposed to meet in Cairo every two or three weeks. The other committee, the nuts and bolts committee, consisted of experts who were supposed to meet for two or three days each week in the Egyptian resort of Taba on the Red Sea. The heads of the delegations to these talks were Nabil Sha'ath and Major-General Amnon Lipkin-Shahak the number-two man in the IDF and head of its military intelligence. The two sides managed to hammer out an agenda and formed two groups of experts, one to deal with military affairs, the other with the transfer of authority.

The IDF officers took a generally tough line in the negotiations. These officers had been excluded from the secret talks in the Norwegian capital and they felt bitter at having not been consulted about the security implications of the accord. Chief of staff Ehud Barak believed that in their haste to secure their place in history, the politicians had conceded too much to the PLO and that when the time came to implement the agreement, it would be the responsibility of the army to tackle the security problems.

Underlying the labyrinthine negotiations at Taba, there was a basic conceptual divide. The Israeli representatives wanted a gradual and strictly limited transfer of powers while maintaining overall responsibility for security in the occupied territories in their own hands. They wanted to repackage rather than end Israel's military occupation. The Palestinians wanted an early and extensive transfer of power to enable them to start laying the foundations for an independent state. They were anxious to get rid of the Israeli occupation and they struggled to gain every possible symbol of sovereignty. As a result of this basic conceptual divide the Taba negotiations plunged repeatedly into crisis and took considerably longer to complete than the two months allowed for in the original timetable.

After four months of wrangling, an agreement was reached in the form of two documents, one on general principles, and the other on border crossings. The two documents were initialled by Shimon Peres and Yasser Arafat in Cairo on 9 February 1994. Although the Cairo agreement was tactfully presented as a compromise solution, it was a compromise that tilted very heavily towards the Israeli position. The IDF had managed to impose its own conception of the interim period: specific steps to transfer limited powers to the Palestinians without giving up Israel's overall responsibility for security. The IDF undertook to redeploy rather than withdraw its forces in the Gaza Strip and Jericho. The Cairo agreement gave the IDF full authority over Gaza's three settlement blocs, the four lateral roads joining them to the Green Line and 'the relevant territory overlooking them'. The outstanding feature of the agreement was thus to allow the IDF to maintain a military presence in and around the area earmarked for Palestinian self-government and to retain full responsibility for external security and control of the land crossings to Egypt and Jordan. Despite these serious limitations, the Cairo agreement formed a first step in regulating the withdrawal of the Israeli Civil Administration and secret services from Gaza and Jericho.

Another round of negotiations resulted in an agreement which was signed by Yitzhak Rabin and Yasser Arafat in Cairo on 4 May. The Cairo agreement wrapped up the Gaza-Jericho negotiations and set the terms for expanding Palestinian self-government to the rest of the West Bank. Expansion was to take place in three stages. First, responsibility for tourism, education and culture, health, social welfare and direct taxation was to be transferred from Israel's Civil Administration to the Palestinian National Authority. Second, Israel was to redeploy its armed forces away from 'Palestinian population centres'. Third, elections were due to take place throughout the West Bank and the Gaza Strip for a new authority.

The Cairo document was billed by both sides as an agreement to divorce after twenty-seven years of unhappy coexistence in which the stronger partner forced the weaker to live under its yoke. This was true in the sense that Israel secured a separate legal system and separate water, electricity and roads for the Jewish settlements. It was not true in the sense that the document gave the stronger party firm control over the new relationship.

The Cairo document stressed repeatedly the need for cooperation, coordination and harmonisation in the new relationship. A large number of liaison committees, most of which were to have an equal number of representatives from the two sides, gave a superficial appearance of parity. But this parity was undermined in favour of the stronger partner by the fact that Israeli occupation laws and military orders were to remain in force unless amended or abrogated by mutual agreement. What this meant in practice was that any issue that could not be resolved by negotiation would be subject to the provisions of Israeli law rather than that of international law. This was a retreat from the Palestinian demand that international law, particularly the Fourth Geneva Convention, should be the source of legislation and jurisdiction during the transition period.

A week after the Cairo document was signed, a token force of thirty Palestinian policemen entered the Gaza Strip from Egypt to assume control for internal security from the retreating Israelis. This was the first tangible evidence that Israeli occupation was winding down. Until this point all the movement had been unilateral as the Israeli army redeployed its forces so as to provide continuing protection for the tiny community of Jewish settlers in the strip. Now a new Palestinian police force was to take charge of the nearby Palestinian population centres in accordance with a pre-arranged division of labour. The Israeli withdrawal was greeted with a sigh of relief at home and great joy and jubilation among the Gazans. As the last Israeli soldiers pulled out of their military camps in Rafah and Nusairat to a final barrage of stones, the Israeli flag was replaced by the flag of Palestine. A twenty-seven year old experiment in imposing Israeli rule over two million recalcitrant Arabs was symbolically and visibly nearing the end of its life.

The government's policy of controlled withdrawal from Gaza and Jericho enjoyed broad popular support. Hard as they tried, the leaders of the opposition failed to arouse the nation against the decisions of the government. As far as the government was concerned, the real paradox was that it needed a strong PLO to implement the Gaza-Jericho settlement, but a strong PLO could only reinforce the determination of the Palestinians to fight for a state of their own.

The government maintained its commitment to peace with the Palestinians despite the protests from the right and despite the terrorist attacks launched by Hamas and Islamic Jihad with the aim of derailing the peace talks. On 29 August 1994, the Agreement on Preparatory Transfer of Powers and Responsibilities was signed by Israel and the Palestinians. This agreement transferred powers to the Palestinian Authority in five specified spheres: education and culture, health, social welfare, direct taxation and tourism.

Oslo II

Negotiations on the Syrian track proceeded in parallel to those on the Palestinian track. Rabin's strategy was to decouple the Syrian track from the Palestinian, Jordanian and Lebanese tracks. He controlled the pace of the negotiations with Syria according to what was happening on the other tracks. The Americans offered their good offices in trying to broker a settlement with Syria. For Syria the key issue was full Israeli withdrawal from the Golan Heights by which they meant a return to the armistice lines of 4 June 1967. The Israelis preferred withdrawal to the 1923 international border which was more favourable to them. In the second half of 1993 Rabin came close to accepting the Syrian condition if Syria met his demands, the four legs of the table as he used to call them. Besides withdrawal, the other three legs of the table were normalisation, security arrangements and a timetable for implementation. The Syrian response on these other points did not satisfy Rabin. Consequently, although considerable progress was achieved by the two sides in narrowing down the differences, it was not sufficient to secure a breakthrough on the Syrian track.

Jordan was more directly affected by the Israel–PLO accord than any other Arab country because of its close association with the West Bank and because over half of its population is of Palestinian origin. A day after the accord was presented to the world, in a much more modest ceremony in the State Department, the representatives of Jordan and Israel signed a common agenda for negotiations aimed at a comprehensive peace treaty. Its main components were borders and territorial matters, Jerusalem, water, security and refugees. The document bore the personal stamp of King Hussein who had been deeply involved in the quest for peace in the Middle East for the preceding quarter of a century. A year of intensive negotiations culminated in the signature of a peace treaty in the Arava desert on 26 October 1994. This was the second peace treaty concluded between Israel and an Arab country in fifteen years and the first to be signed in the region. The treaty between Israel and Egypt had been signed in 1979. But whereas Egypt had offered a cold peace, King Hussein offered Israel a warm peace.

On 28 September 1995, the Israeli–Palestinian Interim Agreement on the West Bank and the Gaza Strip was signed in Washington by Yitzhak Rabin and Yasser Arafat in the presence of Bill Clinton, Hosni Mubarak and King Hussein of Jordan. It became popularly known as Oslo II. This agreement, which marked the conclusion of the first stage in the negotiations between Israel and the PLO, incorporated and superseded the Gaza-Jericho and the early empowerment agreements. The Interim Agreement was comprehensive in its scope and, with its various annexes, stretched to over 300 pages. From the point of view of changes on the ground, it was highly significant. It provided for elections to a Palestinian Council, the transfer of legislative authority to this Council, the withdrawal of Israeli forces from the Palestinian centres of population, and the division of territories into three areas—A, B and C. Area A was under exclusive Palestinian control, area C under exclusive Israeli control and in area B the Palestinians exercised civilian authority while Israel continued to be in charge of security. Under the terms of this agreement, Israel yielded to the Palestinians control over nearly a third of the West Bank. Four per cent of the West Bank (including the towns of Jenin, Nablus, Kalkilya, Tulkarem, Ramallah, Bethlehem and Hebron) were turned over to exclusive Palestinian control and another 25 per cent to administrative-civilian control. Oslo II marked the point of no return in the process of ending Israel's coercive control over the Palestinian people.

On 5 October, Yitzhak Rabin gave the Knesset a comprehensive survey of Oslo II and of the thinking behind it. His speech was repeatedly interrupted by catcalls from the benches of the opposition. Two Likud MKs opened black umbrellas, the symbols of Neville Chamberlain's appeasement of Adolf Hitler at Munich. In the course of his speech, Rabin outlined his thinking for the permanent settlement: military presence but no annexation of the Jordan Valley; retention of the large blocks of settlements near the 1967 border; preservation of a united Jerusalem with respect for the rights of the other religions; and a Palestinian entity which would be less than a state and whose territory would be demilitarised. The fact that Rabin sketched out the principles of the permanent settlement in a session devoted to the interim settlement suggested a strong interest in proceeding to the next stage.

The day that Knesset endorsed Oslo II by a majority of one, thousands of demonstrators gathered in Zion Square in Jerusalem. Binjamin Netanyahu, the leader of the Likud, was on the grandstand while the demonstrators displayed an effigy of Rabin in SS uniform. Netanyahu set the tone with an inflammatory speech. He called Oslo II a surrender agreement and accused Rabin of 'causing national humiliation by accepting the dictates of the terrorist Arafat'. A month later, on 4 November 1995, Rabin was assassinated by a religious-nationalist Jewish fanatic with the explicit aim of derailing the peace process. Rabin's demise, as the murderer expected, dealt a serious body blow to the entire peace process. Shimon Peres followed Rabin down the pot-holed road to peace with the Palestinians but his efforts were cut short by his electoral defeat in May 1996.

Declaration of War on the Peace Process

The return of power of the Likud under the leadership of Binyamin Netanyahu dealt another body blow to the Oslo peace process. From the very beginning the Likud had been bitterly opposed to the Labour government's land-for-peace deal with the PLO. Netanyahu himself repeatedly denounced the accord as a violation of the historic right of the Jewish people to the Land of Israel and as a mortal danger to their security. The foreign policy guidelines of his government expressed firm opposition to a Palestinian state, to the Palestinian right of return and to the dismantling of Jewish settlements. They also asserted Israel's sovereignty over the whole of Jerusalem and ruled out withdrawal from the Golan Heights. In the Arab world this programme was widely seen as a declaration of war on the peace process.

Netanyahu spent his two and a half years in power in a relentless attempt to arrest, freeze and subvert the Oslo accords. He kept preaching reciprocity while acting unilaterally in demolishing Arab houses, imposing curfews, confiscating Arab land, building new Jewish settlements and opening an archaeological tunnel near the Muslim holy places in the Old City of Jerusalem. Whereas the Oslo accord left Jerusalem to the final stage of the negotiations, Netanyahu made it the centrepiece of his programme in order to block progress on any other issue. His government waged an economic and political war of attrition against the Palestinians in order to lower their expectations.

Intense American pressure compelled Netanyahu to concede territory to the Palestinian Authority on two occasions. The Hebron Protocol was signed on 15 January 1997, dividing the city into a Palestinian zone and a Jewish zone. This was a milestone in the Middle East peace process, the first agreement signed by the Likud government and the Palestinians. The second agreement was brokered by President Bill Clinton at Wye Plantation in Maryland on 23 October 1998. By signing the Wye

River Memorandum, Netanyahu undertook to withdraw from a further 13 per cent of the West Bank in three stages over a period of three months. But a revolt of his ultra-nationalist and religious partners brought down the government after only one pullback. The fall of the government was inevitable because of the basic contradiction between its declared policy of striving for peace with the Arab world and its ideological makeup, which militated against trading land for peace.

Under the leadership of Ehud Barak, the Labour Party won a landslide victory in the May 1999. Labour's return to power was widely expected to revive the moribund peace process. During the election campaign Barak presented himself as Rabin's disciple, as a soldier who turned from fighting the Arabs to peace-making. He was given a clear mandate to resume the quest for peace with all of Israel's neighbours. Within a short time, however, Barak dashed the hopes that had been pinned on him. He lacked the vision, the political courage and the personal qualities that were necessary to follow through on the peace partnership with the Palestinians. During his army days Barak used to be called Little Napoleon. In politics, too, his style was arrogant and authoritarian and he approached diplomacy as the extension of war by other means.

The greatest barrier on the road to peace with the Palestinians raised by Barak was the expansion of Jewish settlements on the West Bank. Settlement activity is not contrary to the letter of the Oslo accord, but it is contrary to its spirit. True, settlement activity had gone on under all previous prime ministers, Labour as well as Likud. But under Barak settlement activity gathered pace: more houses were constructed, more Arab land was confiscated, and more access roads were built to isolated Jewish settlements. For the Palestinian population these settlements are not just a symbol of the hated occupation but a source of daily friction and a constant reminder of the danger to the territorial contiguity of their future state.

Another reason for the slowdown on the Palestinian track was the clear preference articulated by Barak for a deal with Syria first on the grounds that Syria was a serious military power whereas the Palestinians were not. During his first six months in power Barak concentrated almost exclusively on the Syrian track, leaving the Palestinians to twist in the wind. When the late Syrian President, Hafiz al-Asad, rejected his final offer, Barak turned, belatedly and reluctantly, to the Palestinian track. His reservations about the Oslo accord were well known. He argued that the step-by-step approach of trading land for peace does not serve Israel's interests because the Palestinians will always come back for more. This made him wary of further interim agreements and prompted him to insist that the Palestinian Authority commit itself to an absolutely final end to the conflict.

Camp David

One more interim agreement was necessary, however, before taking the plunge to the final settlement. It took ten months to break the deadlock created by the Likud government's failure to implement the Wye River Memorandum. Once again, Barak proved to be a tough negotiator, applying intense pressure on the Palestinians. His method was described as 'peace by ultimatum'. The accord that he and Yasser Arafat signed at Sharm el-Sheikh, on 4 September 1999, reflected the underlying balance of power between the two parties. It put in place a new timetable for the final status talks, aiming at a 'framework agreement' by February and a fully fledged peace treaty by 13 September 2000.

The February deadline fell by the wayside, fuelling frustration on the Palestinian side and prompting Arafat to threaten to issue a unilateral declaration of independence if no agreement could be reached. To forestall this eventuality, Barak persuaded President Clinton to convene a trilateral summit in the United States. With the announcement of the summit, Barak's chaotic coalition fell apart. Three parties quit the government, robbing him of his parliamentary majority on the eve of his departure for the summit. In a defiant speech, Barak told the Knesset that although he no longer commanded a majority, as the directly elected prime minister he still had a mandate to make peace. But Barak's domestic political weakness inevitably reduced the diplomatic room for manoeuvre that he enjoyed. Once again, as so often in the past, the peace process was held hostage to the vagaries of the Israeli political system.

Negotiations at Camp David started on 11 July 2000 and lasted fourteen days. Barak approached the summit meeting in the manner of a soldier rather than that of a diplomat. He dismissed Arafat's plea for more time to prepare the groundwork, believing that with the help of the American 'peace processors' he would be able to impose his terms for the final settlement on the opponent. In fairness to Barak it must be said that he crossed his own 'red lines' and put on the table a package which addressed all the issues at the heart of the conflict: land, settlements, refugee rights and Jerusalem.

Basically, Barak envisaged an independent Palestinian state over the whole of the Gaza Strip and most of the West Bank, but with the large settlement blocs next to the 1967 border being annexed to Israel. The Jordan Valley, long cherished as Israel's security border, would eventually be turned over to exclusive Palestinian sovereignty. Altogether, 20.5 per cent of the West Bank was to remain in Israel's hands: 10.5 per cent to be annexed outright and 10 per cent to be under Israeli military occupation for twenty years. Barak agreed to the return of Palestinian refugees but only in the context of family reunification involving 500 people a year. On Jerusalem he went further than any previous Israeli prime minister, and indeed broke a taboo by agreeing to the partition of the city. But his offer fell well short of the Palestinian demand for exclusive sovereignty over all of the city's Arab suburbs and over Haram al-Sharif/Temple Mount (Enderlin 2003: 213, 270, 324). The problem with this package was that it was presented pretty much on a 'take it or leave it' basis. Moreover, Barak insisted that an agreement would mark the final end of the conflict, with the Palestinians formally renouncing any further claim against the State of Israel.

The Palestinian delegation was divided in its response to the package. Some saw in it a historic opportunity for putting the conflict behind them. Others felt that it would compromise their basic national rights, and in particular the right of return of the

1948 refugees. In addition, the Palestinian delegation came under pressure from Egypt and Saudi Arabia not to compromise Muslim rights over the Muslim holy places in the Old City of Jerusalem. At this critical juncture in his people's history, Yasser Arafat displayed neither courage nor statesmanship. His greatest mistake lay in rejecting many of the proposals put to him without putting forward any counter-proposals of his own. Consequently, when the summit ended in failure, Barak and Clinton were able to put all the blame on Arafat. Arafat returned home to a hero's welcome, but he returned empty-handed.

The question of responsibility for the failure of the summit became the subject of heated controversy, not surprisingly given the serious consequences of failure. Both sides of the argument were forcefully presented over the pages of the *New York Review of Books* in articles and letters to the editor. Robert Malley and Hussein Agha launched the debate with a long revisionist article based on first-hand knowledge. They believe that Bill Clinton consistently sided with Ehud Barak leading Yasser Arafat to suspect that there was a conspiracy afoot against him and causing him to dig his heels in (Malley and Agha 2001). Ehud Barak repeatedly asserted that at Camp David he made a most generous offer and that Arafat made a deliberate choice to abort the negotiations and to resort to violence in order to extract further concessions from Israel (Morris 2002 and Morris and Barak 2002). Dennis Ross, Clinton's special envoy to the Middle East, also laid all the blame at Arafat's door, arguing that at no point during Camp David or in the six months after it did the Chairman demonstrate any capability to conclude a permanent status deal (Ross 2001). Jeremy Pressman, an academic with no axe to grind, examined in depth both the Israeli and the Palestinian versions of the Camp David summit and concluded that the latter is significantly more accurate than the former (Pressman 2003).

The Al-Aqsa *Intifada*

With the collapse of the Camp David summit, the countdown to the outbreak of the next round of violence began. On the Palestinian side there was mounting frustration and deepening doubt that Israel would ever voluntarily accept a settlement that involved even a modicum of justice. Israel's apparent intransigence fed the belief that it only understands the language of force. On the Israeli side, there was growing disenchantment with the Palestinians and disillusion with the results of the Oslo accord. Ehud Barak succeeded in persuading virtually all his compatriots that there is no Palestinian peace partner.

It was against this background that Ariel Sharon, the leader of the Likud, chose to stage his much-publicised visit to al-Haram al-Sharif, the Noble Sanctuary which the Jews call Temple Mount. On 28 September 2000, flanked by a thousand security men and in deliberate disregard for the sensitivity of the Muslim worshippers, Sharon walked into the sanctuary. By embarking on this deliberately provocative walkabout,

Sharon in effect put a match to the barrel of gun-powder. His visit sparked off riots on the Haram al-Sharif that spread to other Arab areas of East Jerusalem and to other cities. Within a very short time, the riots snowballed into a full-scale uprising—the Al-Aqsa *intifada*.

Although the uprising happened spontaneously, the Palestinian security services became involved and played their part in the escalation of violence. The move from rocks to rifles on the Palestinian side and the resort to rockets, tanks and attack helicopters by the Israelis drove the death toll inexorably upwards. As so often in the past, the sound of gunfire drowned the dialogue of the diplomats. Violence is, of course, no stranger to the region. Even after the signing of the Oslo accord, diplomacy was sometimes interspersed with bursts of violence. Now fierce fighting was interspersed with small doses of ineffectual diplomacy. Positions hardened on both sides and the tit-for-tat gathered its own momentum.

Neither side wanted to be seen as willing to back down. Yasser Arafat saw no contradiction between the *intifada* and negotiations. On the contrary, he hoped that the *intifada* would give him more leverage in dealing with the Israelis. Ehud Barak insisted that the incitement and the violence had to end before he would return to the negotiating table. His announcement of 'time out' signaled the abandonment of the political track until further notice. In the absence of talks, the security situation steadily deteriorated, clashes became more frequent and lethal and the death toll increased at an alarming rate. Trust between the two sides broke down completely. The two societies became locked in a dance of death. The Oslo accords were in tatters.

Conclusion

Why did the Oslo peace process break down? One possible answer is that the Oslo accord was doomed to failure from the start because of its inherent shortcomings, and in particular because it did not address any of the core issues in the conflict between Israel and the Palestinians. The foregoing account of the rise and fall of the Oslo accord, however, suggests a different answer. It suggests that the basic reason for the failure of Oslo to resolve the conflict is that Israel, under the leadership of the Likud, reneged on its side of the deal. By resorting to violence, the Palestinians contributed to the breakdown of trust without which no political progress is possible. But the more fundamental cause behind the loss of trust and the loss of momentum was the Israeli policy of expanding settlements on the West Bank which carried on under Labour as well as Likud. This policy precluded the emergence of a viable Palestinian state without which there can be no end to the conflict.

The breakdown of the Oslo peace process suggests one general conclusion about the International Relations of the Middle East, namely, the importance of external intervention for the resolution of regional conflicts. According to a no doubt apocryphal story, Pope John Paul believes that there are two possible solutions to the

Arab–Israeli conflict—the realistic and the miraculous. The realistic would involve divine intervention, the miraculous a voluntary agreement between the parties. For the reasons explained in this chapter, the PLO and Israel were able to negotiate the Oslo accord without the help of a third party. But the imbalance in power between them made it exceedingly difficult to carry this agreement to a successful conclusion. America's role as the manager of the peace process was therefore essential to the success of the whole enterprise. In the final analysis, only America could push Israel into a settlement. And in the event, America's failure to exert sufficient pressure on Israel to withdraw from the occupied territories was one of the factors that contributed to the breakdown of the Oslo peace process.

Further Reading

EISENBERG, L. Z. and CAPLAN, N., *Negotiating Arab-Israeli Peace: Patterns, Problems, Possibilities* (Bloomington: Indiana University Press, 1998). A useful comparative survey of peace negotiations between Israel and its neighbours.

ENDERLIN, C., *Shattered Dreams: The Failure of the Peace Process in the Middle East, 1995–2002* (New York: Other Press, 2003). A detailed but readable account of the breakdown of the peace process based on extensive research and interviews, and on minutes of conversations taken by the participants themselves.

GUYATT, N., *The Absence of Peace: Understanding the Israeli–Palestinian Conflict* (London: Zed Books, 1998). A highly critical analysis of the nature of the Oslo accord and of its political and economic consequences for the Palestinians.

MAKOVSKY, D., *Making Peace with the PLO: The Rabin Government's Road to the Oslo Accord* (Boulder, Colo.: Westview Press, 1996). A detailed account of the politics and diplomacy of the Rabin government by a well-informed Israeli journalist.

RABINOVICH, I., *Waging Peace: Israel and the Arabs at the End of the Century*

(New York: Farrar, Straus and Giroux, 1999). An overview of Israel's relationship with the Arab world by an academic who headed the Israeli delegation to the talks with Syria.

SAID, E. W., *Peace and its Discontents: Gaza-Jericho, 1993–1995* (London: Vintage Books, 1995). A collection of essays by a prominent Palestinian academic with severe strictures on the PLO leadership and the peace it made with Israel.

SAID, E. W., *The End of the Peace Process: Oslo and After* (London: Granta Books, 2000). A subsequent collection of articles by the same author that deal with the peace process and other aspects of Palestinian life.

SHLAIM, A., *War and Peace in the Middle East: A Concise History* (London: Penguin Books, 1995). A brief and basic introduction to the international politics of the Middle East since the First World War.

SHLAIM, A., *The Iron Wall: Israel and the Arab World* (New York: W. W. Norton, 2000). A detailed and highly critical study of Israel's policy in the conflict with the Arabs during the first fifty years of statehood.

OSLO CHRONOLOGY

2 Aug. 1990	Iraq invades Kuwait.
16 Jan.–28 Feb. 1991	The Gulf War.
30–31 Oct. 1991	Middle East peace conference convenes in Madrid.
10 Dec. 1991	Bilateral Arab–Israeli peace talks begin in Washington.
23 June 1992	Labour defeats Likud in Israeli elections.
19 Jan. 1993	Knesset repeals ban on contacts with the PLO.
10 Sept. 1993	Israel and PLO exchange letters formally recognising each other.
13 Sept. 1993	Israel–PLO Declaration of Principles on Palestinian self-government is signed in the White House.
4 May 1994	Israel and PLO reach agreement in Cairo on the application of the Declaration of Principles.
25 July 1994	Washington Declaration ends state of war between Israel and Jordan.
26 Oct. 1994	Israel and Jordan sign a peace treaty.
28 Sept. 1995	Israeli–Palestinian Interim Agreement on the West Bank and the Gaza Strip (Oslo II) is signed.
4 Nov. 1995	Yitzhak Rabin is assassinated and Shimon Peres succeeds him as prime minister.
21 Jan. 1996	First Palestinian elections.
24 April 1996	The Palestinian National Council amends the Palestinian National Charter.
29 May 1996	Binyamin Netanyahu defeats Shimon Peres in Israeli elections.
15 Jan. 1997	The Hebron Protocol is signed.
23 Oct. 1998	Binyamin Netanyahu and Yasser Arafat sign the Wye River Memorandum.
17 May 1999	Ehud Barak defeats Binyamin Netanyahu in Israeli elections.
4 Sept. 1999	Ehud Barak and Yasser Arafat sign the Sharm el-Sheikh accord.
11–25 July 2000	Camp David summit.

28 Sept. 2000	Ariel Sharon visits Temple Mount. Outbreak of the Al-Aqsa *intifada*.
23 Dec. 2000	President Clinton presents his 'parameters'.
18–28 Jan. 2001	Israeli-Palestinian negotiations at Taba in Egypt.
6 Feb. 2001	Ariel Sharon defeats Ehud Barak in Israeli elections.

12

The International Politics of the Gulf

F. Gregory Gause, III

OVERVIEW

The international politics of the Gulf region are defined by the interplay of the local states and by the increasingly direct role of the United States in the region. The local states deal with each other not simply on the basis of balance of power concerns, though those concerns are certainly present. With Arab nationalist, Islamic and ethnic identities transcending Gulf borders, domestic security and stability concerns are as important in the foreign policies of the region's states toward each other and outside powers. The Gulf's strategic role as the source of two-thirds of the world's known petroleum reserves has given it enduring importance in global American strategy; its central role in the Islamic resurgence of past decades has increased Washington's interest in the area. From the Iranian Revolution in 1979 Washington has taken an increasingly direct military and political role there, culminating with the American invasion and occupation of Iraq in 2003.

Introduction

Two almost contemporaneous events in the early 1970's created the international politics of the Persian/Arabian Gulf region as we know them today: the British withdrawal of its protectorate over the Arab states of the lower Gulf, and the dramatic increase in oil world prices. This is not to say that there were no international relations in the Gulf before 1971. The Gulf had an important role in British imperial strategy from the outset of the nineteenth century, reinforced in the early twentieth century by the increasing importance of oil. The oil resources of the region made it important to both super-powers in the Cold War. The strong American relationship with both Saudi Arabia and monarchical Iran is a testament to that fact. Iran and Iraq, Iraq and Kuwait, Bahrain and Qatar, Saudi Arabia and the smaller Gulf states all had 'open files' of contentious issues among them, including but not limited to border disputes. However, the early 1970's marks a dramatic change in the structure of power in the area.

Before that time, the states of the region were limited in their abilities to project their power and influence beyond their borders, and checked by what remained of British power in the area should they try to do so. After that time, the three major regional states—Iran, Iraq and Saudi Arabia—all had vastly increased amounts of military and economic power. They could, and did, imagine themselves playing major roles in Gulf security issues. Their foreign policies became much more ambitious. At the same time, the restraint of great power presence in the area was removed, at least temporarily. Britain had left; the United States, mired in Vietnam and unwilling to take on new obligations, did not 'fill the vacuum'. The field was open for the regional states to take more forward and aggressive roles.

To some extent these new ambitions on the part of the regional powers can be understood in classical realist, balance of power terms. The desire for regional dominance is not unique to the Gulf. Balance of power motivations have proved as powerful for Iran, Iraq, Saudi Arabia and other local states as they have for states in other regions and other time periods. However, classical realism and balance of power politics do not provide a perfect template for understanding the Gulf regional system; they are necessary but not sufficient.

The security agenda in the Gulf is complicated by the fact that the local states were, at the same time that they were competing with each other for power and influence regionally, also confronting difficult domestic issues of state building. The social dislocations brought on by great oil wealth brought down the Shah's regime in Iran. Centrifugal forces threatened the integrity of the Iraqi state. The Gulf monarchies were buffeted by challenges to their domestic stability. The importance of trans-national identities in the Gulf states exacerbated the sense of threat that rulers faced. Ba'thist Iraq's Arab nationalism was deployed at various times to encourage opposition to rulers in Iran (in Khuzistan) and the Gulf monarchies. Revolutionary Shi'i Islam was an important threat to domestic stability in Iraq, Kuwait, Bahrain and, to a lesser extent, Saudi Arabia. Kurdish ties cut across borders, and were exploited by one regime to pressure another on various occasions.

So it is not simply the balancing of power, or the desire to extend one's power internationally that has driven calculations of war and alliance in the Gulf. Threats are not simply military; they are also political. The Shah and the ayatallahs governed the same country, but the Arab states have viewed the nature of the threat emanating from different Iranian regimes in very different ways, and those views have affected the way they have dealt with the different Iranian regimes. Whether the Gulf states viewed Iraq as a threat or a protector had more to do with their perceptions of Iraqi intentions toward their regimes than with estimates of Iraqi military power. Regime security—the ability of the ruling élites to stay in power domestically—was as important, if not more important, in determining foreign policy choices than more traditional state security concerns, though they have been present as well.

I hope to demonstrate these points by considering two sets of issues: 1) Iraqi war decisions, in 1980 and 1990, and also in 1975 (Algiers Agreement) when Iraq chose not to go to war, and 1991, when Iraq chose not to withdraw from Kuwait in the face of superior power and almost certain defeat; and 2) the alliance choices made by Saudi Arabia at various times since 1971 in regional politics.

The regional security picture is not complete, however, without consideration of a third issue, the changes in American policy toward the region. American interest in the Gulf has been a constant, because of the strategic importance of oil, but the tactics that the United States has pursued have changed significantly over time, as a result of changes within the American political system—the 'Vietnam syndrome' and its aftermath; changes in the Gulf itself, such as the Iranian Revolution of 1979 and the Iraqi attack on Kuwait in 1990; and changes in the international distribution of economic and political power, such as the oil price revolution of the early 1970's and the end of the Cold War in 1991. These changes have brought the United States into a much more direct role in the security picture of the Gulf from the late 1980's, constraining the freedom of action that the local states had enjoyed and presenting them with new challenges to regime and state security. With the American occupation of Iraq after its successful war in March–April 2003 to bring down the regime of Saddam Hussein, the United States has become not merely an international actor in the region, but a local actor. The effects of this new level of American involvement in Gulf politics both in Iraq and regionally remain, as of 2004, to be seen.

Regime Security, Political Identity and Iraqi War Decisions

In both 1980 and 1990 the regime of Saddam Hussein launched wars against foes who were, or seemed to be, considerably weaker than Iraq. It is tempting to conclude that the ambitious Iraqi president attacked a militarily weakened Iran and a practically defenseless Kuwait because he thought he would win. Undoubtedly, the prospect for victory was an important element in Saddam's war calculations. However, the sequence of events and evidence from Iraqi sources indicate that these war decisions were driven as much, if not more, by fears about the prospects for regime security within Iraq itself, fears that were based on a belief that outside actors could manipulate Iraqi domestic politics against the Ba'thist regime. In each case, also, Iraqi calculations about the prospects of victory were inflated by the belief that the invasion would be met with at least some support both in the target state and in the larger region. Transnational connections inspired both the fears and hopes that lay behind the Iran-Iraq War of 1980–88 and the first Gulf War of 1990–91. (For a fuller account of this argument, see Gause 2002.)

The Iran–Iraq War

The Iranian Revolution is the starting point for understanding the Iraqi war decision of 1980. The Shah's Iran and Ba'thist Iraq were never on particularly good terms. There were border crises between the countries that raised the prospect of war in 1969 and 1975. The 1975 crisis led to the Algiers Agreement, signed by then Vice-President Saddam Hussein and the Shah at an OPEC meeting in the Algeria capital. Iraq agreed to accept the Iranian definition of their common border along the Shatt al-Arab river. In turn, Iran ceased supporting the Iraqi Kurdish rebellion that was raging in northern Iraq. While not close, relations between the two states after 1975 were not overtly hostile.

The weakening of Iran in conventional power terms, which began in late 1977 as the revolutionary movement gathered steam, did not immediately excite Iraqi ambitions. On the contrary, Baghdad expelled Ayatollah Khomeini from Iraq in October 1978 and engaged in security consultations with the Shah's government. When the monarchical regime fell in February 1979, Iraq's first reactions were mildly welcoming to the new regime. Relations soon deteriorated, however. In June 1979 Ayatollah Muhammad Baqir al-Sadr, the most politicized of the major Iraqi Shi'i religious leaders, was arrested on the eve of a scheduled trip to Teheran. Violent demonstrations ensued in Iraqi Shi'i areas. Several prominent Iranian ayatollahs, including Khomeini, condemned the Iraqi regime as 'despotic' and 'criminal,' warning Iraq's rulers of 'the wrath of God and the anger of the Muslim people' (Menashri 1990: 101). Border clashes in the Kurdish areas ensued. In July 1979 Mas'ud and 'Idris Barazani, the sons of Iraqi Kurdish leader Mustafa Barazani, crossed the border into Iran and received support from the revolutionary government (Hiro 1991: 35).

In the midst of these events, Saddam Hussein became president of Iraq on 16 July 1979. An explanation that focused purely upon Saddam's ambitions would expect a militant change in Iraqi policy toward Iran from that time. That did not happen. On the contrary, the two governments sought in the short term to deescalate tensions. Border skirmishes subsided. This did not, however, lead to any lessening of political ferment among Iraq's Shi'i majority. In July 1979, while under house arrest, Ayatollah Muhammad Baqir al-Sadr called for violent opposition to the regime. Shortly thereafter the major Iraqi Shi'i political groups announced the formation of the 'Islamic Liberation Movement,' ready to 'resort to all means' to bring down the Ba'thist regime. In October 1979 the organisation of the Iraqi 'ulama, which previously had been leery of overt political opposition, declared its support for the use of violence against the government. Al-Da'wa, the major Iraqi Shi'i party, formed a military wing by the end of the year (Wiley 1992: 54–5; Tripp 2000: 229). In May 1980 the Iraqi interior minister told an interviewer that, while there were fewer than 1,000 members of al-Da'wa, 'the number of misguided supporters and religious sympathizers is considerable' (Foreign Broadcast Information Service-MEA-80-097, 16 May 1980: E2).

In the midst of this rising tide of Shi'i opposition in late 1979, Iranian politics took a militant turn. Prime Minister Mehdi Bazargan resigned in November 1979, in the wake of the take-over of the American embassy in Teheran. Statements about the need to export the Iranian revolutionary model around the region became more frequent, and by 1980 there were explicit calls by Iranian government officials for the Iraqi people to overthrow the Ba'th regime (Menashri 1990: 157–8; Khadduri 1988: 82; Chubin and Tripp 1988: 34). On 1 April 1980 a member of one of the Shi'i opposition groups attempted to kill Deputy Prime Minister Tariq Aziz. During the funeral procession for some of those killed in that attempt, according to the Iraqi media, a bomb was thrown from a window of an 'Iranian school' in Baghdad as the procession went past (FBIS-MEA-80-068, 7 April 1980: E5–7). In retaliation the Iraqi government executed Ayatollah Muhammad Baqir al-Sadr and his sister and began to expel tens of thousands of Iraqi Shi'a of Iranian origins from the country.

These events were the final straw for Saddam Hussein, and the spur for the Iraqi war decision. His rhetoric underwent an immediate change. He began to threaten Iran in the most obvious way. By late July 1980 Saddam was all but promising a war: 'We are not the kind of people to bow to Khomeini. He wagered to bend us and we wagered to bend him. We will see who will bend the other' (FBIS-MEA-80-144, 24 July 1980: E4–5). When news of Ayatollah Baqir al-Sadr's execution reached Iran, in mid-April 1980, the Iranian reaction matched the hostility now being exhibited by Saddam. Ayatollah Khomeini reiterated his previous calls to the Iraqi people and the Iraqi army to overthrow the regime, accusing the Ba'th of launching a 'war against Islam' (Hiro 1991: 35). Border clashes resumed.

Sources that have reported on the timing of the Iraqi decision to go to war almost unanimously place the decision in the spring of 1980, after the events of April (Gause 2002: 68). The gap between the war decision and the actual initiation of conflict in September 1980 is attributable to two factors. The first is planning and organisation, which would take some months to achieve. The second is the effort by Iranian exiles in Iraq to organise a military coup to overthrow the Islamic regime in Tehran. That effort, termed the 'Nuzhih plot' for the airforce base from which it was launched, was fully supported by Iraq and planned on Iraqi territory. Begun on 9 July 1980, it was a spectacular and immediate failure (Gasiorowski 2002). The failure of the coup served as confirmation to the Baghdad leadership the durability of the Islamic revolutionary regime on its border.

The Iraqi war decision of 1980 is best explained by the change in Saddam Hussein's framing of the issue of how to deal with Iran. With the changes in Iran after

November 1979 and the more open calls for the export of the Islamic Revolution, domestic unrest in Iraq came to be seen as orchestrated by Tehran. Saddam's regime could only look forward to further Iranian efforts to foment revolution against it, if nothing changed in Tehran. Facing that prospect, Saddam chose the risky path of war. He certainly thought he and Iraq would gain by victory, but the elements that made victory likely had been in place for some time. What had changed was his belief that a continuation of the status quo would only bring him more domestic problems.

Iraq's attack on Iran was spectacularly unsuccessful, both in destabilising the revolutionary regime in Tehran and in securing Iraqi control of southwestern Iran. By the summer of 1982 Iranian counterattacks had driven Iraqi forces out of Iranian territory. The Khomeini regime was then faced with a decision: declare victory over Iraq and accept a ceasefire, or continue the war in Iraqi territory. Ayatollah Khomeini decided the issue with a call to continue the war until the downfall of the Ba'thist regime in Baghdad. Tehran hoped that an effort to spread the Islamic revolution would be met with support among Iraqi Shi'is. That support was not forthcoming in any substantial way. The war dragged on for six more years. During most of that time, Iran was on the offensive and made occasional, limited gains, but was unable to break the Iraqi forces. Iraq turned the tide in 1988, recapturing lost territory in southern Iraq and demoralising Iran with missile attacks on Tehran. From 1987 the United States navy became directly involved in the war, protecting oil tankers from Kuwait and Saudi Arabia against Iranian attack. After an American naval vessel shot down an Iranian civilian airliner in July 1988, Iran accepted UN Security Council resolution 598, calling for a ceasefire. Khomeini liked this decision to 'drinking poison', but even he had become convinced that Iran could not win the war. Eight years of bloody war, with hundreds of thousands of casualties on each side, ended with the two sides basically in the same position as when the war began.

The Gulf War

Establishing with certainty when Saddam Hussein decided to attack Kuwait is a difficult task. There are indications from Iraqi sources themselves that the decision was made only a few months before the actual invasion. Other sources place the decision to invade slightly earlier in 1990 (Gause 2002: 53–4). No source that refers specifically to the timing of the decision places it earlier than the spring of 1990. The haste with which the decision was made was reflected indirectly in some of the (very mild) self-criticism exercised by Iraqi leaders after the invasion. At a meeting of the Iraqi Revolutionary Command Council and Ba'th party leadership on 24 January 1991 Taha Yasin Ramadan told his colleagues 'I am not saying that August 2, 1990 [the date of Iraq's attack on Kuwait] was the best day for the mother of battles. We had not studied the situation for a year, or even for months, preparing for the mother of battles. But it was the will of God that decided the date' (al-Bazzaz 1996: 200, quoting from minutes of the meeting). There is every indication that the decision to invade Kuwait was made relatively shortly before the invasion, under feelings of time pressure. What had happened in the period leading up to the decision to trigger it?

Saddam Hussein's regime made it clear, before and after its invasion of Kuwait, that it saw an international conspiracy against it, meant to weaken Iraq internationally and destabilise it domestically. Its economic problems were blamed on lower oil prices, which were in turn blamed on 'overproduction' by Kuwait and the UAE, clients of the United States. Small shifts in American policy (like limits on US credits for Iraqi purchases of US rice exports and Congressional resolutions condemning Iraq for human rights violations) and damaging revelations (like Iraq's use of the Atlanta branch of an Italian bank to launder arms purchase money) after the end of the Iran–Iraq war were read as evidence that the United States had adopted a hostile attitude toward Iraq. Media attention to the Iraqi nuclear programme, and subsequent British and American efforts to block the export of dual-use technology to Iraq, were seen as part of a concerted effort to build a case against Iraq as a prelude to more severe measures.

Lurking behind many of these efforts, in the Iraqi view, was Israel, seen as preparing for a strike on the Iraqi nuclear establishment similar to the one it conducted in 1981 (Freedman and Karsh 1993: Chapters 2–3; Heikal 1993: 158–231; Baram 1993). Wafiq al-Samara'i, then deputy director of Iraqi military intelligence, says that at the beginning of 1990 his office began receiving a wave of warnings from Saddam's office about Israeli plans to strike at Iraqi nuclear, chemical and biological weapons facilities (al-Samara'i 1997: 365). Sa'ad al-Bazzaz, editor at the time of a major Baghdad daily newspaper, reports that the Iraqi leadership fully expected an Israeli military attack sometime in August 1990 (al-Bazzaz 1993: 345).

Saddam himself bluntly described this 'conspiracy' to al-Samara'i in March 1990 (al-Samara'i 1997: 222–3): 'America is coordinating with Saudi Arabia and the UAE and Kuwait in a conspiracy against us. They are trying to reduce the price of oil to affect our military industries and our scientific research, to force us to reduce the size of our armed forces... You must expect from another direction an Israeli military airstrike, or more than one, to destroy some of our important targets as part of this conspiracy'.

There was also an internal aspect to the Iraqi regime's fears. In either late 1988 or early 1989 scores of officers, many decorated for heroism in the war with Iran, were arrested and executed on the charge of membership in a secret organisation working to bring down the government. Hundreds of high-ranking officers indirectly connected to the accused were forced to retire (Baram 1993: 8; al-Bazzaz 1996: 36–7, 89–90; al-Samara'i 1997: 184–5; Tripp 2000: 249–50). Iraqi ruling circles came to believe during 1989 that they had evidence that a number of foreign powers, including Iran, Saudi Arabia and the United States, were attempting to infiltrate Iraqi society to collect intelligence and pressure the government (al-Bazzaz 1993: 159–60, 210–13). Other sources report a failed coup attempt in September 1989 and the exposure of a coup attempt, coupled with a plan to assassinate Saddam, in January 1990 (Freedman and Karsh 1993: 29–30; al-Samara'i 1997: 185; Baram 1997: 5–6).

While Saddam Hussein increasingly saw his domestic political and economic situation in 1989 deteriorate, events in the larger world during that year reinforced his growing sense of crisis. The fall of the Soviet client states in Eastern European increased his fears about the future of his own regime (al-Bazzaz 1993: 392). Saddam's sense that international and regional forces were conspiring with his domestic opponents against him had reached the point that, in October 1989, Tariq Aziz raised this issue in his meeting with Secretary of State Baker in Washington (Baker 1995: 265).

By early 1990 Saddam Hussein was convinced that his regime was being targeted. This belief was reflected in the changes in his rhetoric and the tone of Iraqi foreign policy. In February 1990 Saddam launched an attack on the United States military presence in the Gulf at the founding summit of the Arab Cooperation Council and devoted much of the speech to criticism of Israel (Bengio 1992: 37–49). This was followed by Saddam's threat in April 1990 to 'burn half of Israel', if the Israelis attacked Iraq. The rhetorical temperature escalated from there. At the same time, Iraqi rhetoric toward Kuwait and the other Gulf states hardened, and in January 1990 Iraq first proposed that Kuwait 'loan' it $10 billion, as well as write off Iraqi debts incurred during the war with Iran (Heikal 1993: 209). At the Arab summit of May 1990 Saddam likened overproduction of OPEC quotas to an act of war against Iraq (Freedman and Karsh 1993: 46–8).

This shift in Iraqi foreign policy, the beginning of the process that led to the invasion of Kuwait, came when Saddam concluded that there were international efforts afoot to destabilise him domestically. (Comments by Saddam himself and one of his chief aides at a meeting of the Iraqi leadership during the war confirm this analysis. See al-Bazzaz 1996: 198–99, 227–28.) It culminated with the Iraqi occupation of Kuwait in August 1990. Saddam's unwillingness to accept a negotiated solution to the Kuwait crisis, which would have required him to withdraw from Kuwait but spared his country and military the devastating attack of American and coalition forces, provides further evidence for the hypothesis that it was fear of domestic destabilisation that was the most important factor prompting his decision to invade.

The Iraqi leadership did not believe that withdrawal from Kuwait would end what it saw as the international conspiracy against it. On the eve of the ground war, after enduring a month of air attacks, Saddam told Soviet envoy Yevgeny Primakov, 'If America decided on war it will go to war whether I withdraw from Kuwait or not. They were conspiring against us. They are targeting the leadership for assassination. What have the Iraqis lost? They might yet gain!' (al-Bazzaz 1993: 399). After the war, Tariq Aziz was asked on the PBS documentary *The Gulf War* why Iraq did not withdraw when defeat seemed inevitable. He replied: 'Iraq was designated by George Bush for destruction, with or without Kuwait. Inside Kuwait or outside Kuwait. Before the 2nd of August or after the 2nd of August' (www.pbs.org/wgbh/pages/frontline/gulf/oral/aziz/2.html).

The contrast with Iraqi acceptance of the Algiers Agreement in 1975 is instructive. Then, Saddam Hussein (who personally signed the agreement and continued to defend that decision, even after he himself had abrogated it at the outset of the Iran-Iraq War) believed that retreat internationally would strengthen the regime's domestic position. Saddam's belief that withdrawal from Kuwait in 1991 would not end the pressures on his domestic position emanating from abroad explains the different outcome in 1991.

The Gulf War ended with Iraq's defeat on the battlefield, its humiliating withdrawal from Kuwait and American dominance of the Gulf. However, Saddam Hussein for over a decade claimed victory in what Iraq termed the 'mother of battles' because his regime remained in power after the war.

Regime Security, Regional Balancing and Saudi Arabian Alliance Decisions

The importance of domestic regime security concerns in the foreign policies of Gulf states is highlighted by the alliance choices of Saudi Arabia during the different Gulf wars. Saudi maneuvering between Iraq and Iran during the 1980's was dictated as much by the ideological threat posed by the Iranian Islamic revolution as by simple balance of power concerns. The different Saudi reactions during the first and second Gulf Wars reflects the level of threat—both military and ideological—posed by Saddam Hussein's regime to the Saudi leadership, and by the different public opinion reactions in Saudi Arabia to American military moves against Iraq. While the Saudis acted in both cases within the broad confines of their long-standing security relationship with the United States, in the first they cooperated enthusiastically and publicly with the American military. In the second their cooperation was much less extensive and largely hidden from their population.

Saudi Arabia and the Iran–Iraq War

The Iranian Revolution changed the strategic picture dramatically for the Saudis. The new Islamic Republican government presented an open challenge to the legitimacy and stability of the Saudi regime, both as an example of Islamic revolution and as a promoter of discontent within Saudi Arabia and the other monarchical states of the Gulf. Driving home the threat posed by the new revolutionary regime, a wave of unrest, concentrated mostly in Shi'i communities, swept Kuwait, Bahrain and Saudi Arabia from 1978 through 1980 (Kostiner 1987: 179; Ramazani 1986: 39–40). While the intensity of Iranian pressure on Saudi Arabia declined during the 1980's, the revolutionaries in Tehran continued to challenge the al Saud's Islamic credentials. Central to this challenge was Iranian behaviour during the annual pilgrimmage to Mecca. Iranian pilgrims held political demonstrations, expressly forbidden by the Saudi authorities, during the 1982 and 1983 pilgrimages. In 1987 Saudi security forces clashed with Iranian pilgrims, resulting in over 400 deaths. In contrast, during the 1980's Saddam Hussein's Iraq assiduously courted the Saudis, emphasising their common interest in checking the Iranian threat.

The beginning of the Iran–Iraq War presented the Saudis with a serious dilemma. They were concerned about the ultimate intentions of Saddam Hussein, if he emerged victorious against Iran. However, forced to choose between the two combatants, Saudi Arabia aligned with Iraq. Immediately upon the beginning of hostilities, Saudi Arabia permitted Iraqi planes to use Saudi bases (to hide them from Iranian counter-attack) and Saudi ports were opened for the trans-shipment of goods to Iraq (Safran 1986: 369). Contemporary sources report substantial Saudi financial aid to Iraq in 1980 and 1981 (Nonneman 1986: 96–7). Once Iranian forces entered Iraqi territory in 1982, Saudi support became more substantial. Billions of dollars of Saudi financial support helped Iraq fund the war. That support included direct aid, loans, military equipment and the sale of oil from the Saudi-Kuwaiti neutral zone with profits going to Iraq, theoretically as a 'loan' (King Fahd listed Saudi support for Iraq in a speech during the first Gulf war, *al-Sharq al-Awsat*, 17 January 1991: 4). After Syria cut the Iraqi pipeline to the Mediterranean in 1982, the Saudis permitted Iraq to build an oil pipeline into the Kingdom, connecting to an existing Saudi line from the Gulf to the Red Sea. Saudi Arabia also publicly supported Iraq in various diplomatic fora. During the Iran–Iraq War, Saudi Arabia was squarely in Iraq's camp.

The Saudis were not immune to exploiting the opportunities that the Iran–Iraq War presented. With Iran and Iraq consumed by their war, and the smaller states exposed to the myriad threats that war presented, the Saudis were able to organise in 1981 the Gulf Cooperation Council. The Council brought together the smaller monarchies (Kuwait, Bahrain, Qatar, United Arab Emirates and Oman) under Saudi leadership.

Saudi Arabia and the Gulf War

With the Iraqi invasion of Kuwait, the Saudi threat perception changed dramatically. Iraq was now an immediate military threat, moving troops up to the border of the oil-rich Eastern Province of Saudi Arabia. It was also an immediate ideological/domestic threat to the Saudi regime. Iraq had overthrown a fellow monarchy. Shortly after the invasion, Iraq openly called, on both Islamic and Arab nationalist bases, for citizens in Saudi Arabia to revolt against their government. One Iraqi source reported that Saddam was confident that this propaganda barrage would destabilise the Saudi domestic scene so thoroughly that Riyadh would have no choice but to reverse its course and accept the new realities (al-Bazzaz 1996: 112).

The dire threat posed by Iraq, on both balance of power and domestic security levels, led the Saudis to overcome their hesitations about an open military alliance with the United States. In the past, Riyadh preferred to keep the American military 'over the horizon', worried that too public an embrace of the United States could lead to a domestic and regional public opinion backlash against the Al Saud regime.

The Saudis chose to run the risk of alienating their own public, and welcomed hundreds of thousands of American forces into the kingdom.

With the success of the American campaign to eject Iraqi forces from Kuwait, a new period in American–Saudi relations began. Riyadh was much more willing than in the past to cooperate openly with the American military, allowing it to use Saudi bases throughout the 1990's and into the 2000's to patrol the 'no-fly' zone in southern Iraq. This seemingly permanent American military presence excited domestic political opposition. It was one of the prime complaints leveled by Osama bin Laden against the Saudi rulers in his campaign against them. American facilities were attacked in Saudi Arabia in November 1995 in Riyadh and June 1996 in the Eastern Province. The former attack killed five Americans; the latter killed nineteenth and wounded hundreds.

As the Saudis continued to see Saddam Hussein as a major threat after the first Gulf War, their relations with Iran slowly began to improve. This trend was facilitated by changes in Iran itself. The death of Ayatollah Khomeini in 1989 dissipated some of the fervor to 'export' the revolution, reducing at least one element of the threat the Saudis perceived from Iran. The collapse of oil prices in the mid-1990's brought Riyadh and Tehran closer together, as they cooperated within OPEC and with major non-OPEC producers to push prices up. Riyadh still looked upon Tehran with suspicion, both as an ideological competitor in the Muslim world and as a major regional power. Tehran was equally mistrustful of Saudi–American relations, which it saw in the context of Washington's anti-Iranian policy. However, the hard edge of ideological hostility that characterised relations in the 1980's had been replaced by more normal and businesslike ties.

Saudi Arabia and the Iraq War

Riyadh was much less willing to cooperate with the United States in its attack on Iraq in 2003 than it was in 1990–91. The Saudis officially opposed the American war. American ground troops and air forces were not permitted to use Saudi bases, with some exceptions that the Saudi government kept secret from its own population. The Saudi hesitancy to be publicly linked to this US attack on Iraq stemmed from two factors: 1) Saddam Hussein was not nearly the threat to the Saudi rulers that he was in 1990; and 2) Saudi public opinion had taken a dramatic anti-American turn. Publicly backing the United States ran the risk of fomenting a domestic backlash against the ruling regime. However, the Saudi rulers also did not want to alienate their American allies, whom they continued to see as their long-term security guarantors. The Saudis therefore cooperated with Washington militarily when such cooperation could be kept relatively quiet, and removed from the glare of publicity.

Saudi public opinion, by the beginning of 2003, was extremely anti-American. The upsurge in Israeli–Palestinian violence in the second *intifada*, which began in the autumn of 2000, was one factor increasing the level of anti-Americanism in the kingdom. The American reaction to the attacks of 11 September 2001 was another.

The debate in the United States over Saudi complicity in the attack was seen by many in Saudi Arabia as an attack on their country and their religion. The Saudi response, on both the governmental and popular levels, in the immediate aftermath was defensive and hostile to the United States. The American attack on the Taliban and al-Qaida in Afghanistan was depicted by many in Saudi as a super-power attack on a defenseless civilian population. A Gallup poll, conducted in late January–early February 2002, reported that 64 per cent of Saudi respondents viewed the US either very unfavourably or most unfavourably. Majorities in the poll associated America with the adjectives 'conceited, ruthless and arrogant'. Fewer than 10 per cent saw the US as either friendly or trustworthy (Burkholder 2002). Even though the Saudi government had begun, by the spring of 2002, to signal its public that it sought to preserve the Saudi–American relationship, anti-Americanism still ran high. A Zogby International poll conducted in February–March 2003 found that 95 per cent of the Saudis polled had either a very unfavourable or a somewhat unfavourable attitude toward the United States (Zogby International 2003).

In the face of this considerable public opinion rejection of American policy in the region, and without the perception of an immediate threat from Saddam Hussein, the Saudi leadership made every effort to separate itself publicly from American policy toward Iraq. However, the importance of the Saudi–American security relationship was such that Riyadh sought to cooperate with Washington where that cooperation could be kept out of their public's eye. The Saudis increased their oil production in the lead-up to the war, to try to prevent price spikes in world oil market. They permitted the United States to coordinate air attacks on Iraq from the command and control center at Prince Sultan Airbase south of Riyadh. They allowed American special forces access to an isolated Saudi bases in the northwest corner of the country, near the Iraqi border (*Financial Times*, 9 March 2003; *New York Times*, 18 March 2003).

The Saudis walked a tightrope in the second Gulf War, trying to do enough to keep Washington happy but not so much as to alienate their own public. It is a tightrope they had walked successfully before. The interesting point about their behaviour in this episode was not their cooperation with Washington, which could be expected both from their long-standing ties with the US and their hostility to Saddam Hussein. Rather, it was the way that Saudi public opinion put serious limits on the extent of that cooperation. Saudi anti-Americanism in this episode was based, at least in part, on transnational Arab and Muslim ideological solidarity with Palestinians and Iraqis.

American Policy in the Gulf

For the United States, the strategic significance of the Gulf region has been a constant since the Second World War because of its oil resources. During the period between the end of the Second World War and 1971, the United States developed close political, economic and military relations with both Iran and Saudi Arabia, to safeguard its interests and check the possibilities of Soviet moves in the area. Since the British withdrawal from the Gulf in 1971, American policy in the region has gone through a number of stages, reflecting changes in the United States itself, in the Gulf, and in the world economic and strategic picture. Those stages have seen progressively greater American military involvement in the area, culminating in the second Gulf War of 2003.

The 1970's: oil revolution and the twin pillar policy

The end of British military responsibilities in the smaller Gulf states in 1971 could have been an opening for the United States to take on the British mantle directly, as it had in many other parts of the region since the Second World War. However, the British withdrawal occurred at the height of the American involvement in Vietnam, and there was no public or Congressional support for new foreign military obligations. Consistent with the 'Nixon Doctrine' of supporting friendly regional powers, Washington sought to safeguard its interests in the Gulf by supporting the military build-up of its two local allies, Iran and Saudi Arabia (Gause 1985: 258–66). The Soviet Union responded by strengthening its relations with Iraq, signing a treaty of friendship and cooperation with Baghdad in 1972, providing a Cold War justification for continued American military support for the 'twin pillars' of Iran and Saudi Arabia.

The oil revolution of the early 1970's, culminating in the Saudi-led embargo by many Arab states of the sale of oil to the United States in 1973–74 (in reaction to American support for Israel in the 1973 Arab–Israeli War), could have been seen as a direct challenge to America's 'twin pillar' policy in the Gulf. Saudi Arabia led the embargo against the US. Iran took advantage of the situation to push oil prices to their highest levels in history. By the time the dust settled, oil prices had increased from around \$3.00 per barrel to over \$12.00 per barrel, sending the US and much of the rest of the world into a recession that lasted through the decade. Paradoxically, the oil revolution strengthened the 'twin pillar' policy. The importance of the Gulf region for American foreign policy increased dramatically, but Washington was unable to take a direct military role there. With vast new oil revenues, Iran and Saudi Arabia were able to drastically increase their military spending, with most of their purchases coming from the United States. The 1970's saw an intensification of military, economic and political relations between the United States and its Gulf partners (Safran 1986: Chapter 12; Bill 1988: Chapter 6).

The Iranian Revolution and the Iran–Iraq War

America's 'twin pillar' policy in the Gulf came crashing down in 1979, as the Islamic revolution swept the Shah of Iran from power. The new Islamic Republic of Iran was intensely hostile toward the United States, a hostility both signified and magnified by what in the US came to be known as the 'Iranian hostage crisis'.

From November 1979 to January 1981 Iranian revolutionaries, with the support of Iran's leader, Ayatollah Ruhollah Khomeini, detained American diplomatic personnel in Iran. President Jimmy Carter attempted to free the hostages through a military raid in April 1980, which failed spectacularly, pointing up the weakness of the US military position in the area. Almost contemporaneously with the hostage crisis, the Soviet Union in December 1979 invaded Afghanistan in order to prop up a failing Communist regime there. The Iranian Revolution, the Soviet invasion of Afghanistan and the subsequent Iraqi attack on Iran in September 1980 all further destabilised the world oil market, with oil prices increasing to over $30 per barrel in 1980–81.

The American reaction to this set of strategic challenges was to reconfirm its commitment to its remaining Gulf ally, Saudi Arabia, and to begin a reconfiguration of American military power to focus more resources on the Gulf region. In the State of the Union address in January 1980, President Carter declared that the United States would use all of the military means at its disposal to confront any 'hostile power' trying to dominate the Gulf. The Reagan Administration, coming to power in January 1981, vastly increased the US military budget, fleshing out operationally the ambitious plans laid out at the end of the Carter Administration for a 'Central Command' devoted to the Gulf region. Over intense Congressional objections, it sold Airborne Warning and Control System aircraft (AWACS) to Saudi Arabia in 1981, re-establishing what had by the late 1970's become a slightly frayed US-Saudi security relationship. The Reagan Administration also continued efforts begun by Carter to negotiate basing rights in the region, most notably with Oman. Other Gulf states were more reluctant in the early 1980's to open their territory to the American military (Kupchan 1987: Chapters 4–6).

While the United States increased its regional military capabilities in the early and mid-1980's, it did not find it necessary to use them, even though war raged between Iraq and Iran. As damaging as the Iran–Iraq War was to the combatants, it had surprisingly few spillover effects in the region as a whole, at least until its last years. Though the fortunes of war ebbed and flowed, neither side achieved a military breakthrough that might have drastically altered the regional power situation. Moreover, the price of oil, after spiking to over $40 per barrel at the beginning of the war, began to decline markedly from 1982. In 1986, prices briefly fell below $10 per barrel, less in real terms than they were before the 1973 oil price revolution. With the war generally stalemated and oil prices declining, the United States saw no need for direct military intervention in the region.

From 1982, when Iraqi forces withdrew from Iran and the Iranians took the fight across the border into Iraq, Washington began to support Iraq directly. The US shared intelligence with Baghdad, encouraged (or did not discourage) allies from supplying Iraq with weapons, sold Iraq 'dual use' technologies like helicopters and extended economic credits for the Iraqi purchase of American agricultural goods (Jentleson 1994: Chapter 1). In 1985–86 the Reagan Administration also conducted secret diplomacy with Iran in what became known as the 'Iran-contra scandal'. The US arranged for Israeli arms to be sold to Iran, in an effort to secure the release of

American hostages from Lebanon and channel funding to the American-supported Nicaraguan opposition forces, the 'contras'. Some in the Administration hoped that this opening would lead to a renewal of a strategic partnership with Iran, but public revelation of these dealings led both sides to repudiate the initiative.

Seeking to pressure the Gulf monarchies to cut their support for Iraq, Iran in 1986 began to attack oil tankers shipping Kuwaiti, and occasionally Saudi, oil through the Gulf (Iraq had been striking at Iranian tankers for some time). Kuwait requested both the United States and the Soviet Union to protect their ships. The combination of Washington's interest in balancing the Soviets and desire to restore its *bona fides* with the Arab states after the revelation of the 'Iran-contra scandal' in November 1986 brought the American navy into the Gulf in early 1987, where it engaged with Iranian forces on numerous occasions. In July 1988 an American ship shot down an Iranian civilian airliner over the Gulf, mistaking it for an Iranian air force jet. Days later, Iran accepted UN Security Council Resolution 598, calling for a ceasefire in the Iran–Iraq War.

The Gulf War and the 1990's

The American naval deployment at the end of the Iran–Iraq War represented a new level of military cooperation between the Gulf monarchies and the US. Kuwait opened up its ports to American naval vessels. Saudi Arabia, which had preferred that the US military be 'over the horizon' rather than in the Gulf itself, granted American forces new levels of access to Saudi facilities. This was the beginning of what would become an open security alliance with the United States in the wake of the Iraqi attack on Kuwait in August 1990.

The end of the Cold War had removed the global strategic threat that had, in part, driven American policy toward the Gulf over the previous decades. However, the first Gulf War demonstrated to Washington that local actors could challenge America's oil interests and America's allies in the region as well. With Saddam Hussein still in power in Iraq after the war, and the Islamic Republic of Iran still at odds with the United States, Washington looked to the Gulf monarchies to provide bases for the American forces which took up a long-term station in the region. The monarchies, still traumatised by the Iraqi invasion of Kuwait and wary of Iranian intentions, welcomed the security cover that the American forces provided. American military bases (though they were not officially called bases) were established in Kuwait and Qatar. The command of America's Gulf naval force, renamed the Fifth Fleet, moved onshore in Bahrain. Oman and the UAE provided regular access to their facilities for American forces. An American air wing operated out of Saudi airbases to patrol southern Iraq. There were some negative public reactions to this new level of American military presence, most notably the June 1996 bombing of an apartment complex in eastern Saudi Arabia called Khobar Towers housing American air force personnel. However, these events did not alter the course of American policy.

That policy was based on the containment of both Saddam's Iraq and Islamic Iran—what the Clinton Administration called 'dual containment.' Containment of Iraq was legitimated by UN Security Council resolutions that maintained severe economic and military sanctions on the country as long as Saddam's regime failed to comply fully with the requirement that it disarm. While the sanctions were altered at times during the 1990's to try to alleviate the sufferings it imposed on the Iraqi population, their cumulative effect was to impoverish the country while not destabilising Saddam's regime (Graham-Brown 1999). American containment of Iran was unilateral, and largely ignored by the rest of the world.

11 September 2001 and the Iraq War

The attacks of 11 September 2001 by Osama bin Laden's al-Qaida group on New York and Washington marked an important turning point in American policy in the Gulf. There was a sense as the new Bush Administration came to power in January 2001 that US Gulf policy had reached an impasse. Sanctions on Iraq were losing international support and showed no prospect of unseating Saddam Hussein's regime. Increasing anti-Americanism in Saudi Arabia made the American military deployment there increasingly difficult. Neither containment nor inducements seemed to change the hostile status-quo of Iranian–American relations. September 11 drove American policy in new directions toward all three countries.

The most important change was toward Iraq. The new US 'war on terrorism' was not limited to al-Qaida and its direct state supporter, the Taliban regime in Afghanistan. In his State of the Union address in January 2002, President Bush defined the terrorist threat to include unfriendly states seeking to develop weapons of mass destruction, because they could pass those weapons on to terrorist groups seeking to use them against the United States. Iraq was named by the president as the centre of this new 'axis of evil' threatening American security. The Administration succeeded in garnering American public and Congressional approval for war, but failed to receive the kind of UN mandate that legitimated the first Gulf War. With limited international support, the US launched a war against Iraq in March 2003. In a matter of weeks Saddam's regime crumbled and American forces occupied the country.

The contention that Iraq had large stockpiles of weapons of mass destruction, readily deployable and able to be passed on to terrorists—the centrepiece of the Bush Administration's public case for war—proved to be unfounded. The causes of this intelligence failure, and the extent to which the Bush Administration knowingly exaggerated this threat, will be the subject of considerable investigation and debate. However, it is clear that the WMD issue was not the only factor in the American war decision. The belief that an American-reconstructed Iraqi polity could be a beacon of moderation and pro-Western democracy in the region, exerting pressure for reform on neighbouring states that would then reduce the chances of terrorist groups developing in those states, was strongly held by some in the Administration. The strategic benefits of increased American power in the centre of world oil production, and in an area directly connected to Arab-Israeli issues, also had to be part of the decision calculus. The reconstruction of the Iraqi political system, a task far from complete as 2004 began, will determine whether the Bush Administration's ambitious gamble in Iraq will yield the results it hoped.

The September 11 attacks also altered the American–Saudi relationship. The mastermind of the attacks, Osama bin Laden, and fifteen of the nineteen perpetrators were from Saudi Arabia, focusing American public anger against the kingdom in a way unprecedented since the 1973–74 oil embargo. Many in America saw Saudi Arabia as, at best, an ambivalent ally in the 'war on terrorism', and, at worst, through its funding of Islamic groups and causes around the world, a supporter of terrorism. Anti-Americanism in Saudi Arabia, growing in the 1990's for reasons discussed above, increased even further in reaction to what was seen by many Saudis as an American effort to blame them specifically, and Islam in general, for the attacks (Gause 2002). While both the Saudi and American governments stressed that the bilateral relationship remained sound, it quickly became clear that the close military cooperation developed after the first Gulf War could not be sustained. At the end of the second Gulf War, the American combat personnel who had been stationed in Saudi Arabia since 1991 were withdrawn. The two governments continued to cooperate on oil and regional political issues, but the American strategic presence in the region came to be concentrated in the smaller Gulf states and in Iraq. Tensions over 'war on terrorism' issues looked to become an enduring part of the Saudi–American relationship.

September 11 also brought to an end the tentative steps, at the end of the Clinton Administration, to re-engage with the Islamic Republic of Iran. Paradoxically, the 'war on terrorism' pitted the US against two Iranian adversaries: the Taliban regime in Afghanistan and Saddam Hussein in Iraq. Iran remained neutral in both wars, a stance which helped the United States. However, Iran fell into the category of states targeted in the expansive definition the Bush Administration gave to the 'war on terrorism', in that it was suspected of developing nuclear weapons and had links to groups identified by the US as terrorist. It was named by President Bush in his January 2002 State of the Union address as one of the members of the 'axis of evil'. With Washington concentrating on Iraq throughout 2002 and the first half of 2003, Iran policy was put on hold. There were even discussions between American and Iranian representatives on Afghan and Iraqi issues. After the second Gulf War, however, indications emerged of a new American policy of pressure on Iran. Confrontation rather than rapprochement seemed more likely.

Conclusion

During the 1970's and the 1980's, up to the first Gulf War, the driving force behind international political events in the Gulf was the regional states themselves: the oil embargo of 1973–74, the Iranian Revolution, the Iraqi war decisions of 1980 and

1990. The United States played an important, but largely reactive, role in that period. It was constrained by its own domestic politics, with the Vietnam legacy preventing it from playing a more direct military role in the Gulf. It was constrained by the super-power competition of the Cold War, where American actions could be met by Soviet reactions. The first sections of this chapter thus dealt with the motivations behind regional state behaviour—Iraqi war decisions and Saudi alliance decisions—because it was the regional states that set the agenda. That agenda was greatly influenced by the importance of transnational Arab, Muslim and ethnic (Kurdish) identities in the region. Regime security concerns, the desire to stay in power and thwart domestic opponents, drove regional states' foreign policy behaviour as much as, if not more than, classic balance of power considerations.

The initiative in Gulf international politics passes from the regional states to the United States during the Gulf War of 1990–91. The constraints of domestic public opinion and Cold War competition on American freedom of action were removed, and the Gulf monarchies were willing to associate themselves with the US military in an unprecedented way during the 1990s. 11 September 2001 marks a further esca-lation of American regional involvement, as the 'war on terrorism' becomes both the motive and the justification for the United States to shed the last international constraint on its behaviour in the Gulf—the need for international legitimation provided by the United Nations. With the United States occupying Iraq, con-solidating its protectorate status in the smaller Gulf monarchies, pushing Saudi Arabia to cooperate more actively in the 'war on terrorism' and pressuring Iran for major changes in its foreign policy, the driving force in Gulf politics is now Washington. How successful this ambitious American effort to remake the politics of the region will be is an open question. It was a domestic political event, the Iranian Revolution, which scuttled an earlier American security policy in the Gulf. Whether domestic political trends in Iraq, Iran and Saudi Arabia will work for or against American ambitions in the future remains to be seen.

Further Reading

AL-RASHEED, M., *A History of Saudi Arabia* (Cambridge: Cambridge University Press, 2002). A re-interpretation of the coun-try's history that emphasises power and domination.

KEDDIE, N. R., *Modern Iran: Roots and Results of Revolution* (New Haven: Yale University Press, 2003). The best single volume history of modern Iran.

LIPPMAN, T. W., *Inside the Mirage: America's Fragile Partnership with Saudi Arabia* (Boulder, Colo.: Westview Press, 2004). A balanced approach to a complicated rela-tionship.

MARR, P., *The Modern History of Iraq*, 2nd edn. (Boulder, Colo.: Westview Press, 2004). A comprehensive and readable one volume history.

PURDUM, T. S. and the Staff of the *New York Times*, *A Time of Our Choosing: America's War in Iraq* (New York: Henry Holt/Times Books, 2003). The politics in Washington and the battles in Iraq, according to the *New York Times* correspondents.

SIFRY, M. L. and CERF, C. (eds.), *The Iraq War Reader: History, Documents, Opinions* (New York: Touchstone Books, 2003). A useful collection of various points of view and background material on the war.

13

The United States in the Middle East

Michael C. Hudson

OVERVIEW

This chapter reviews and analyses American foreign policy in the Middle East. It begins with an historical sketch of US involvement in the area, discussing the traditional American interests as well as Washington's response to new regional tensions and upheavals since the late 1970s. It then describes the structure of Middle East policymaking and its domestic political context. The chapter concludes with an analysis of the 'neoconservative revolution' in American policy and its implications for US–Middle East relations. Among the questions raised are the following: are traditional US interests compatible with one another? What challenges do the social, economic and political tensions within the region pose for American policymakers? How have the attacks of September 11 affected America's position and policies in the Middle East? Is the US, under the neoconservatives' influence, embarked on an imperial project in the Middle East? What is the relation between American domestic politics and its Middle East policies?

Introduction

The United States today dominates the Middle East to an unprecedented extent. In a region historically penetrated by competing Western powers, there are no longer any serious challengers to American hegemony. Yet, paradoxically, American policymakers see the Middle East as posing an unprecedented threat to national security. This is because they believe it is a breeding ground for terrorist movements that are hostile to the US and able to strike violently against the American homeland as well as American interests overseas.

In this chapter we seek to explain this paradox. We will do so, first, by presenting in two parts an historical sketch of the US involvement in the area. This narrative focuses initially on the traditional trio of American interests: anti-Communism, oil and Israel. In the second part we discuss how new regional tensions and upheavals since the late 1970s have challenged American interests and how US policy has sought to cope with them. The third section describes the structure of Middle East policy-making, emphasising both the instruments of policy and the effects of domestic politics on policy. Finally, we look at what some observers call the 'neoconservative revolution' in US foreign policy in the Administration of President George W. Bush, which has laid out a far more ambitious political agenda for the region coupled with a new emphasis on preemptive military actions.

The Roots of American Involvement

There was a time—very different from the present period—when the United States was popular and respected throughout the Middle East. That benign image began to dissipate around the period of the Second World War, when America as an emergent Great Power became directly involved in a region which itself was undergoing great internal upheavals. Washington's concern about the Soviet Union, access to oil and the project for a Jewish state in Palestine—concerns which clashed with the rising nationalism in the region—eroded the earlier positive image.

The age of innocence

America's first encounters with the Middle East and North Africa date back to the founding of the republic (Bryson 1977). Relations revolved mainly around trade and missionary activity. In the late nineteenth and early twentieth centuries, as France, Britain and Russia established an imperial presence in North Africa, Egypt, the Levant, Iran and the periphery of the Arabian peninsula, the United States by contrast eschewed a colonial role in the Middle East. Indeed, in the aftermath of World War I—that watershed event in which European countries replaced Ottoman Turkish administration in much of the Arab world—the Arabs indicated that if they could not have the independence which they most wanted they would rather be governed by the United States than by Britain or France. These were the findings of the King–Crane Commission, sent by President Wilson in 1919 to ascertain the wishes of 'the people' in the former Ottoman territories. Americans were seen as good people, untainted by the selfishness and duplicity associated with the Europeans. As nationalist and religious movements reorganised to roll back European imperialism in the 1920s and 1930s they spared the US from their anger.

Coming of age

World War II marked what America's veteran 'Arabist' ambassador Raymond Hare called 'the great divide' in US relations with the Middle East, 'between our traditional national position of rejecting political responsibility in the Middle East and our postwar acceptance of responsibility on a global or great power basis'. Three issues drove America's new 'great-power' policies in the Middle East: communism, oil and Israel.

Containing Soviet Communism

In October 1947, as Hare (1993: 20) tells it, American and British officials met at the Pentagon to sketch out a geopolitical blueprint for the Middle East in light of the new threats of Soviet expansionism and Communist ideology. Gone was the 'reverse Monroe doctrine' of the interwar period in which the US left the Middle East to Britain (in contrast to President Monroe's insistence on keeping Britain out of Latin America in the nineteeth century). Already President Truman had extended aid to Greece and Turkey to help those governments stave off communist or Soviet challenges. While still conceding Britain 'primary responsibility' for the Middle East and the Mediterranean, Secretary of State Marshall already was contemplating an eventual leadership role for the United States in the region.

A decade later John C. Campbell, with the help of a study group from the Council on Foreign Relations, published *Defense of the Middle East* (1958)—a revealing account of the concern with which the foreign policy establishment viewed trends in the region. The fundamental problem was the Soviet threat to the security, even the survival, of the United States in the face of the global Soviet challenge. As for the Middle East: 'The entrenchment of Soviet power in that strategic region would bring a decisive shift in the world balance, outflanking NATO. Soviet control of Middle Eastern oil could disrupt the economy of the free world. And the triumph of communism in the heart of the Islamic world could be the prelude to its triumph through Asia, Africa and Europe' (Campbell: 4–5). The study group asserted that the Arab-Israeli conflict 'hangs like a poisonous cloud over the entire Middle East . . . Time has not solved the problem of the Arab refugees. Something must be done about it . . . The American commitment to Israel is to its continued independent existence, not to its existing boundaries or policies' (Campbell: 351–2).

On the geostrategic level American policy sought to contain the Soviets in the Middle East through military alliances, as in Europe through NATO. But this approach largely failed, as the examples of the Middle East Command proposal, the Middle East Defense Organization in 1951–52 indicate (Bryson 1997: 179–81). Even the Baghdad Pact (1955), generated more animosity than security in the Arab world (see Chapter 8). Nor were looser political/economic umbrella projects such as the Eisenhower Doctrine (1957), under which Washington promised financial aid and security assistance to Middle Eastern governments requesting American protection from 'international communism', any more successful. Lebanon was the only Arab state to take up the offer, a decision that brought more instability than security to that small country. Indeed, under Stalin's less doctrinaire successors, the Soviet Union and its satellites succeeded in leaping over the Baghdad Pact into the Arab heartland through its arms deals with Syria and Egypt of 1954–56. To these governments, the real geostrategic threat was Israel, not the Soviet Union; and therein lay a real problem for American diplomacy. The US–Soviet 'game' was not being played exclusively on the geostrategic level. It was also being played on the volatile ideological terrain of Middle East domestic politics.

The waning of European imperialism in the Middle East after World War II coincided with a powerful current of national assertiveness in Iran and the Arab countries, which were rapidly modernising. Ascension to great power status and close wartime cooperation with colonialist European allies had not extinguished American liberal idealism. Accordingly, there was great curiosity and not a little sympathy with the emergence of independent states in what came to be called the Third World. With these trends in mind, leading US government officials, had correctly prophesied that support for a Zionist state in Palestine would set the US at odds with the emerging Arab nationalist currents. They were equally right in predicting that the Soviet Union would try to associate itself with this trend in order to advance its own interests throughout the region. Regimes friendly to Washington would be weakened. Developments during the 1950's and 1960's revealed the extent of the problem: nationalist coups or upheavals took place in Egypt, Iran, Iraq, Jordan, Lebanon, Libya, North Yemen, South Yemen, the Sudan; and Syria suffered major instability. Ongoing eruptions (1956, 1967, 1969–70) in the unsolved Arab–Israeli conflict did not help matters.

If the American response to all this was often improvised and contradictory, the results were not altogether negative. American diplomats tried to avoid a head-on confrontation with nationalist forces—US efforts to deal with Nasser are a fascinating case in point. Even American presidents occasionally made a supportive gesture: for example, Dwight Eisenhower in the 1956 war, and John F. Kennedy, who, as a senator, had spoken positively on Algeria and, as president, initiated a dialogue with Nasser and supported the republican revolution in Yemen. On the other hand, the US worked to suppress Iranian nationalism by organising the overthrow of Prime Minister Muhammad Mussadiq's government in 1953, and it opposed the nationalist upheavals in Syria and Iraq. While Kennedy had some temporary doubts about supporting a 'traditional' regime in Saudi Arabia he did not hesitate to support the Saudis when they were challenged by Nasser in the 1960s.

US diplomacy in the field, and the respected non-governmental American presence, somewhat blunted the US confrontation with Arab nationalism, but it could hardly eliminate it. The Palestine problem lay at the heart of the pan-Arab cause, and American support for Israel was too massive to allow for healthy relationships with most Arab states, let alone with Arab public opinion. The Soviet Union, therefore, had a clear field to plow. But the Soviets had their own problems and weaknesses. Communism and Arab nationalism did not mix well together, and the Soviets were often clumsy in their military and aid relationships. Nationalist Arab regimes complained about the low level and poor quality of Soviet support. Nevertheless, Soviet patronage enabled the nationalist, anti-Israel camp to pose a serious challenge to US interests in the region.

The enfeeblement of the Soviet Union vis-à-vis the United States was increasingly evident from the 1970s even to Arab governments heavily dependent on Moscow for arms and diplomatic support. Following Israel's smashing victory over the Arabs in the 1967 'Six-Day War' an Arab 'rejectionist bloc' emerged which, with Moscow's support, had refused American and international plans for a negotiated settlement that would require recognition of Israel. But gradually this bloc began to disintegrate, and with it the influence in Arab public opinion of the pan-Arab nationalist movement. Egypt's President Anwar Sadat was the first Arab leader to recognise Moscow's decline, and he drew the logical *Realpolitik* conclusion by throwing out his Soviet military advisors and dramatically turning toward Washington in search of a negotiated solution to the Arab–Israel conflict. Later, Iraq and Syria would engage in their own more cautious flirtations with the US. By the time of the Soviet Union's collapse in 1990, the US was able to enlist the one-time rejectionist governments in Egypt and Syria in the international coalition to remove Iraq as a threat to Kuwait and Saudi Arabia. The US–Soviet cold war in the Middle East was over, and the Arab nationalist camp (what was left of it) no longer had a superpower patron to constrain the US and Israel.

Oil

US commercial interest in Middle East oil predates Hare's 'great divide'. American companies got their foot in the door of the Middle East oil cartel with the Red Line Agreement of 1928. Under the Red Line Agreement the major international oil companies—including now an American group—pledged in a 'self-denying' clause to share proportionally the future oil discoveries in the former Ottoman Turkish territories, including the Arabian peninsula (except for Kuwait), Iraq, the Levant (except for Sinai), Cyprus and Anatolia. A decade later in Saudi Arabia, having outmaneuvered their British rivals in Saudi Arabia, a subsidiary of Standard of California made a stupendous find at 'Dammam No. 7' which, over the next 45 years, was to produce over 32 million barrels of oil. But oil did not acquire a strategic security dimension until World War II. Just as the British at the beginning of the century had seen the military and economic value of Middle East oil, so too did the Americans, not only for prosecuting World War II but also as a cheap supplement to declining US reserves, and the West's oil-driven post-war economic development. With the price of Middle East oil a mere $2 per barrel up until 1971 it is hardly surprising that western Europe and even the US would become dependent on it.

While European and Japanese dependency was well over two-thirds of total consumption, Americans in the 1970's found that half their oil was imported and half the imports were from the Middle East. Given, then, the importance of a secure supply of cheap Middle East oil, US policymakers determined that their main tasks were to exclude Soviet influence from the region and prevent any internal force from nationalising Western companies, restricting production and/or raising prices and overturning established regimes. Clandestine involvement by the CIA and the British in a coup codenamed 'Operation Ajax' which returned the young Shah to his throne in Iran in 1953 was an effective object lesson for would-be nationalist challengers (Bill 1980: 86–94). As for the US-Arab oil relationship, ARAMCO (the Arabian-American Oil Company, a consortium of US companies active in Saudi Arabia) had mounted a remarkably effective, indeed amicable, working relationship that has endured up to the present, weathering even the transfer to Saudi ownership.

In 1960, following an abrupt decision by the oil companies on a price cut, outraged governments of oil-producing states established the Organization of Petroleum Exporting Countries (OPEC). OPEC, inexperienced and weakened by internal rivalries, had little success in defending the price of oil during its first decade. But the situation was about to change. Growing world demand, the proliferation of small independent companies, and domestic nationalist pressures in several oil producing countries set in motion the 'oil revolution' of the 1970s which by the end of the decade had lifted the price to around $35 per barrel. It also led to a shift in the balance of oil power from the companies to the producing countries, by breaking the cohesion of the producer cartel at a time when world oil demand was growing. Libya, following Colonel Mu'ammar al-Qadhafi's nationalist revolution in 1969, led the charge, followed by Iran. Then, during the 1973 Arab-Israeli war, King Faisal of Saudi Arabia, did what Americans had thought was unthinkable: he imposed a partial boycott on the US and on European consumers. Suddenly the Arabs had 'the oil weapon' and, stung by America's emergency war aid to Israel, they had used it.

The shock in the United States and Europe was palpable, and it lent urgency to Secretary of State Kissinger's mediation of the war. In the long term it also led to a comprehensive new energy policy designed to blunt the oil weapon in the future through the Strategic Petroleum Reserve, a vast underground oil storage facility, and conservation measures. Thus, by the time of the second major price hike in 1979, due to the Iranian revolution of 1979–80, and the Iraq–Iran war of 1980–88, the global oil market was far more stable. Moreover, Saudi Arabia was both able and willing to cushion these shocks. With the collapse of world oil prices in 1986, OPEC and non-OPEC producers alike lost their collective effectiveness, and 'the Arab oil weapon' basically disappeared. For US policymakers the main oil problem now was ensuring that the newly formed (1981) Arab Gulf Cooperation Council (GCC) be 'protected' from regional (Iranian) or exogenous (Soviet) inroads. Fortunately for Washington, the Iraqi president, Saddam Hussein, shared American concern over Ayatollah Rouhollah Khomeini's regional system-challenging proclivities. Iraq provided the military shield, the GCC states the money, and the US the intelligence data to beat back the Iranian Islamist challenge.

Israel

So firm—indeed, fervent—has American support for Israel become since 1967 that it is easy to forget how bitter the policy debate in the US was over Palestine in the 1940s and how evenly matched the antagonists. On the one side were the pro-Zionists in the domestic political arena; on the other, the Executive Branch officials concerned with the global and regional implications of a US-supported Jewish state. In a well-known article published in *The Middle East Journal* in 1948, Kermit Roosevelt, an American intelligence expert on the Middle East, described (and criticised) the Zionist lobbying effort, observing that '[A]lmost all Americans with diplomatic, educational, missionary, or business experience in the Middle East protest fervently that support of political Zionism is directly contrary to our national interests, as well as to common justice' (Roosevelt 1948: 1).

But President Harry Truman, influenced by Zionist friends and desirous of Zionist political support in the 1948 election campaign, decided that the US would support the establishment of a Jewish state in Palestine. Had he not taken that stand (and he himself wavered at one point), the Zionist enterprise in Palestine might have taken a weaker form and, indeed, might not have ultimately succeeded. It was not until 1967 that the Executive Branch diplomatic and defense establishment, impressed with Israel's military prowess and Arab weakness, was finally persuaded that Israel might be something more than a burden on the national interest. Since then the deeply committed supporters of Israel have managed not only to mobilise most of the American Jewish community but have helped win American public opinion, in general, to support Israel and its policies in the region almost without reservation. Perhaps the best evidence for the political clout of Israel's supporters is the size of the annual US aid package—upwards of $3 billion.

Israel today is not only an established part of the Middle East landscape but has become a regional superpower: its GNP is more than twice that of the largest Arab state, Egypt; and it has a world-class military establishment. Yet the naysayers of the 1940s were not entirely wrong in their assessment. Indeed, they were right in forecasting that the US relationship with the Arab world would deteriorate, that repeated wars and immense suffering would result from the creation of a Jewish state, and that the Soviets would take advantage of this rancour and instability. America's political leadership was prepared to accept these costs and insist that the Arabs accept them too. For American leaders the costs were bearable because they did not include loss of access to Arab oil nor the complete loss of the Middle East to the Soviet Union.

For that, they may thank the Arabs, who failed to respond collectively to the challenges facing them, and the Soviets who proved incapable of sustaining their empire.

As midwife at the birth of Israel in 1948, the US faced the task of helping arrange a settlement that would see it through infancy and ensure it a prosperous life. To that end the United States has supported over the years a variety of diplomatic initiatives and projects to normalise the new state's relations with its neighbours. But owing to the manner in which Israel had been established—basically by force of arms which led to the displacement of some 750,000 Palestinians into neighbouring countries—these efforts were largely unsuccessful until 1978. Only then, at Camp David did the American government finally make a significant dent in the problem.

The Camp David Accord is a milestone (see Chapter 10): one of two pivotal events for American policy in securing the 'normalisation' of Israel in the Middle East; the other is the Madrid/Oslo 'peace process' that began in September 1991. But the road from Camp David to Madrid was, to say the least, bumpy. The presidency of Ronald Reagan (1980–88) proved sterile with respect to the Middle East. Reagan's officials maintained a quixotic and unrealistic fixation on 'strategic consensus', by which they meant agreement between Israel and its Arab neighbours to cooperate in rolling back what they saw as Soviet inroads in the Middle East. Reagan's first Secretary of State Alexander Haig is widely believed to have given 'an amber light' for Israel's invasion of Lebanon, a bloody adventure that only intensified Israeli–Palestinian hostility. The Reagan administration also sought to resuscitate the perennial 'Jordanian option' as a solution to the Palestine problem, even though Jordan's King Hussein was no longer in a position to represent Palestinian nationalism. So ill-equipped were the Reaganites to understand, let alone deal with, the Middle East, that they allowed valuable years to go by during which the Arab-Israeli situation only worsened. This paralysis of policymaking set the stage for the Palestinian *intifada*, a mass uprising of young, stone-throwing Palestinians in the occupied territories, that began in December 1987 and refocused world attention on Palestinian national grievances as the heart of the Arab–Israeli conflict.

New Regional Tensions and Challenges

While the United States was growing in power and its interests in the Middle East were deepening, the region itself was not standing still. In fact, it was and still is in the process of far-reaching social, economic and political upheavals. It has been experiencing rapid population growth and suffering from uneven and sluggish economic development. Oil wealth is mainly concentrated in a just a few small, thinly populated countries; and it has not been successfully deployed to promote region-wide sustainable development. Moreover, the collapse of oil prices in the mid-1980s has continued to generate socioeconomic strains on governments. Poor educational systems and a growing pool of unemployed young people pose a constant challenge to largely inefficient, authoritarian regimes. The three *Arab Human Development Reports*, prepared by Arab social scientists in 2002–04, highlight these issues, which constitute important underlying factors behind several emerging political challenges to America's role in the region.

1979: the beginning of a watershed decade

These challenges were dramatically illustrated in 1979. That year was marked by five landmark events. (1) the peace treaty between Egypt and Israel; (2) the Islamist revolution in Iran; (3) The takeover of the Grand Mosque in Mecca, Saudi Arabia, by Islamist militants; (4) the Soviet invasion of Afghanistan; and (5) the emergence of Saddam Hussein as the sole ruler of Iraq. Each in its way posed new challenges for American policymakers.

On the surface, the Egypt–Israel treaty of 26 March 1979 represented a positive development, with the United States playing the crucial role in bringing it about thanks to the diplomacy of President Carter in the Camp David meetings the previous year. Momentous as it was, this breakthrough failed to address the heart of the Arab–Israeli problem—the conflict between Israel and the Palestinians. Indeed, because the 'Palestinian dimension' had not been successfully dealt with at Camp David, new pressures began to build up within the Palestinian community (both inside and outside historical Palestine) to confront the Israeli occupation. Scarcely had Israel's withdrawal from the Egyptian Sinai peninsula been completed, Israel's right-wing government, strongly influenced by Defense Minister Ariel Sharon, launched its ill-fated invasion of Lebanon with the aim of liquidating the Palestine Liberation Organization and establishing a regime in Lebanon that would be friendly (and compliant) toward Israel. Greatly weakened, the PLO, under Chairman Yasser Arafat, tried to move toward a stance more acceptable to the international community, but the Palestinians remained diplomatically isolated. The onset of the *intifada* helped to re-engage American diplomacy, but as we have seen the once promising Madrid and Oslo 'peace processes' ultimately collapsed, and the ensuing brutal conflict between Israel and the Palestinians greatly weakened US stature in the Arab and Islamic worlds.

Farther to the east, in Iran, an even greater challenge had emerged. Iran's pro-American leader, Shah Muhammad Reza Pahlavi, had been forced to leave Tehran in January 1979 and the Islamic revolution was fully under way a month later. The coming to power of Ayatollah Rouhollah Khomeini undermined a 'pillar' of US security interests in the region dating back to the early 1950s. Decades of Iranian popular resentment at the American intervention erupted, symbolised by the seizure of the American embassy on 4 November 1979, and the holding of US hostages for over a year. The hostage crisis traumatised American public opinion and contributed to the defeat of President Carter in 1980. It also reignited negative perceptions of Islam among Americans and of America among Muslims. During the first phase of the Islamic revolution from 1979 until Khomeini's death in 1989 the Iranian regime waged an ideological campaign against the traditional (and pro-American) oil monarchies on the Arab side of the Gulf. So, when Iraq's leader, Saddam Hussein, decided to attack Iraq in 1980 he was able to count on financial support from the Arab gulf regimes and military intelligence support from the United States. But the Iranian challenge extended well beyond the Gulf: Tehran also helped develop and support the Islamist militant organisation Hizballah in Lebanon, elements of which were responsible for the murder and kidnapping of Americans and other westerners, and for the disastrous bombings of the US embassy and Marine barracks in Beirut.

As if the 'fall' of Iran were not enough of a problem for Washington, the Soviet invasion of Afghanistan in December 1979 triggered fears among some American strategists that the Soviets would use Afghanistan as a springboard for extending their influence into the Persian Gulf area and perhaps beyond. Such fears revealed an ignorance of geography and topography as well as of Soviet capabilities. To prevent a new Russian march toward warmer waters, the Carter administration warned that Washington regarded the Gulf (on the Arab side at least) as vital to American interests, and it also undertook an energetic effort, with the support of Pakistan and Saudi Arabia, to roll back the Soviets in Afghanistan by mobilising Islamist militants called *mujahideen*. Armed with American shoulder-launched Stinger missiles, the mujahideen were able to inflict severe damage on Soviet military helicopters and entrap their ground forces in the rugged Afghan terrain. But the defeat of the Soviets, which led in part to the collapse of the Soviet Union itself, not only failed to bring security to Afghanistan and the Gulf area, it also left a chaotic 'failed state' of warring Islamist militias. Worse still, with the battle against the Soviets won, many thousands of these militants, who had come from Arab and other Muslim states, left Afghanistan in a mood to promote puritanical Islamic reform by force of arms against the American presence in their home countries.

Meanwhile, an ominous event had occurred on the Arab side of the Gulf: on 20 November 1979 a well-organised group of Islamist radicals seized the Grand Mosque in Mecca—the holiest site in the Islamic world. It took three weeks for the Saudi authorities, reportedly with help from French commandos, to quell the rebellion. While the militants were executed forthwith, the incident suggested that the Saudi regime—notwithstanding its conservative Islamic credentials—was vulnerable to Islamist opposition. Around the same time there was an uprising by Shi'ite militants, perhaps inspired by the Iranian revolution, in Saudi Arabia's heavily Shi'ite eastern province. It was also quickly put down. But these events presaged the emergence of a much more serious threat from other religious dissidents in the 1990s (Fandy 1999: 47 ff). Shi'ite protest, mostly from Saudis abroad, reappeared. More significantly, a small number of radical *salafi* clerics, both inside and outside the Kingdom, began to agitate for reforms of what they saw as a regime corrupted by Western—especially American—influences. Among these activists was a young man from one of Saudi Arabia's most successful business families whose name was Osama bin Laden.

Finally, on 16 July 1979 Saddam Hussein consolidated his personal authority in Iraq, upon the resignation of President Ahmad Hassan Al-Bakr, a decade after their

Ba'th nationalist party had taken power in a military coup. At this juncture Iraq was well-placed to assume the leadership of the Arab world, especially since Egypt had been ostracised after President Anwar Sadat signed the peace treaty with Israel without having achieved any gains for the Palestinians. Iraq's abundant oil revenues were actually used quite effectively to build the country's socioeconomic infrastructure as well as support an ambitious military programme. Saddam Hussein's ambition and ignorance of political realities led him to go to war with Khomeini's Iran. In Washington the Reagan Administration (some of whose officials resurfaced in the administration of George W. Bush), attempting to play *Realpolitik*, offered military intelligence assistance to Saddam in hopes of preventing an Iranian takeover of the vulnerable pro-Western Arab oil monarchies; but they also were pleased that the war lasted a long time (from 1980 to 1988), giving Iraq a Pyrrhic victory and weakening both of these big and unfriendly Gulf countries. But Washington's satisfaction was short-lived, for in 1990 Iraq suddenly overran its small and oil-rich neighbor Kuwait. The administration of George H. W. Bush refused to countenance Saddam's takeover, and the United States armed forces led an international coalition to expel the Iraqis from Kuwait. It was the first—but not the last—major US military action in the Arab world. Following Iraq's expulsion, for just over a decade Washington sought to maintain Gulf security through a strategy of 'dual containment' of both Iraq and Iran, with the emphasis on pervasive and debilitating sanctions against Iraq intended to diminish its military threat potential against its neighbours and to eliminate its capabilities to produce or deploy weapons of mass destruction.

The emergence of Islamist transnational networks

Perhaps the most important and disturbing development in the period after 1979 was the emergence of a new kind of phenomenon, one that was not readily comprehensible in terms of traditional state-oriented approaches to international relations. This was the phenomenon of transnational Islamist networks prepared to utilise terrorist tactics against the United States especially and the West in general. Although its political discourse was couched in Islamic terms, it took two fairly distinct forms. The dominant one was Shiite-driven movements sponsored by the revolutionary Iranian regime. It manifested itself most dramatically in Lebanon, which was in the throes of a civil war. Americans and other Westerners were taken hostage in Beirut, and some were killed. Groups affiliated with what would become Hizballah twice bombed the American embassy and, in a suicide truck-bombing, killed 241 US Marines on a peacekeeping mission in 1983. Other such incidents occurred outside Lebanon. Veteran American journalist John Cooley has chronicled these developments in his books, *Payback* (1991) and *Unholy Wars* (2002).

The second strand, marked by fundamentalist *salafi* and *wahhabi* Sunni Islam, traced its lineage to the anti-colonial struggles between the two World Wars but then was overshadowed by the relatively secular nationalist movements of the 1950s and

1960s. Inspired by radical offshoots from the Egyptian Muslim Brotherhood, it resurfaced in Egypt and Syria in the 1970s and caused the assassination of Egypt's President Anwar Sadat in 1980 and a bloody confrontation with the Syrian regime of President Hafiz al-Asad in the late 1970s and early 1980s. Islamist organisations also began to play a major role in Palestinian politics. In the 1990s Islamist movements successfully mobilised large numbers of followers in many Arab countries, leading in some cases, such as Algeria, Tunisia and Egypt, to violent confrontations. The movement assumed a transnational aspect, inasmuch as its leading ideologues, such as the Sudanese activist Dr. Hassan al-Turabi, sought to build a loose, broad-based front across the entire Arab world. All of these developments were deeply worrying to American officials, because of the anti-Israeli and anti-American tone of their discourse.

America's missed opportunities in the 1990s

At the beginning of the 1990s there were many reasons to suppose that the United States had achieved much in the Middle East. Yet these successes were shadowed by negative after-effects. The Americans had played the leading role in defeating Soviet communism in Afghanistan. And then of course the Soviet Union itself had collapsed. But success in Afghanistan was achieved by utilising the militant mujahideen Islamists. When many of these 'Arab Afghan' fighters returned home, they turned their attention to combating pro-American regimes.

In Iraq, Washington reacted quickly to Saddam Hussein's invasion of Kuwait. Immediately, sensing a direct threat to its oil and security interests in the Gulf, the US determined that it had to go to war to evict the Iraqis. The war was quick, inexpensive and relatively painless for the victors. President George H. W. Bush effectively mobilized an international coalition, including several Arab states, to liberate Kuwait, but he lacked an international mandate to occupy Iraq to bring down the Saddam Hussein regime. Instead, a decade-long sanctions regime was imposed, which wreaked devastating effects on the Iraqi civilian population without undermining the regime. Along with its support for Israel's occupation of the Palestinian territories, the US-led sanctions on Iraq contributed to the growing hostility toward America in Arab and Muslim public opinion. The American policy of 'dual containment' of Iraq and Iran seemed at best a palliative, not a cure for Gulf insecurity. A small but influential group of hawkish officials, former officials and policy analysts—later to be known as 'neoconservatives'—fervently believed that Iraq under Saddam Hussein was so dangerous to American (and Israeli) interests that merely 'containing' him was insufficient. With the election of George W. Bush as president in 2000, this group would be catapulted into power.

In the Arab–Israeli theatre, President Clinton, elected in 1992, inherited a promising new 'peace process' from his defeated predecessor. The mechanisms laid down by former Secretary of State James Baker which led to the Madrid Conference in 1991, had brought together the conflicting parties, and created an elaborate multi-track structure of negotiations. By the time Clinton took office early in 1993, the initial momentum of Madrid had flagged, and the subsequent bilateral talks in Washington between Israel and its neighbours had got bogged down. But then Clinton received an even better gift from Israel and the Palestine Liberation Organization themselves. The secret negotiations in Oslo led to the breakthrough 'Declaration of Principles' in September 1993 on the White House lawn and the beginning of the 'Oslo peace process' that appeared initially to be the best hope ever for Arab–Israeli peace (see Chapter 11). But Washington's failure at the highest levels to prod the parties into keeping to the Oslo timetable, and its failure to stop new Israeli settlement construction, finally led to the collapse of the Oslo process, ironically at Camp David, in August 2000. And so the vision of a 'new Middle East' articulated by Israel's Shimon Peres (1993) never materialised.

Meanwhile, the second strand of networked Islamist terrorism—exemplified by fundamentalist Sunnis like Osama bin Laden, was gaining ground. In the 1990s there were several terrorist attacks on American targets, including one on New York's World Trade Center in 1993. In the late 1990s American personnel in Saudi Arabia and embassies in Africa were also targeted. Although increasingly aware of this serious new threat, the Clinton Administration responded in a relatively ad hoc manner (Gerges 1999). After the bombing of American embassies in Kenya and Tanzania in 1996, President Clinton ordered limited military strikes in Afghanistan and on what turned out to be a legitimate pharmaceutical factory in Khartoum. Following the bombing of American military facilities in Saudi Arabia in 1998 administration officials became even more alarmed but were unable to fashion an effective counter-terrorism strategy. And President Clinton made no military response at all to the bomb attack on the USS Cole in Aden harbor in October 2000, just a few months before the end of his term. To its credit, Washington undertook efforts to reassure the Islamic world that America was not anti-Islamic. For example, American Muslim leaders were invited to the White House for the *iftar* (fast-breaking meal) in the month of Ramadan. But such gestures were mainly symbolic, and America's attitude toward rising political Islam remained ambivalent at best, if not hostile.

The promise of the early 1990s—the removal of Soviet threat from the region; the expulsion of Saddam Hussein from Kuwait; the Oslo peace process; President George H. W. Bush's talk of a 'new world order'—by the end of the decade had turned to ashes, and America found itself more deeply disliked throughout the region than it ever had been.

Policymaking: Structures and Process

An examination of the internal workings of American Middle East policy is essential in trying to explain why the US consistently pursues policies that elicit such hostility from people in the region and even exasperate traditional European allies.

One key point emerges: Middle East policy is decisively shaped by domestic American politics.

Unlike other major US foreign policy issue areas, the Middle East is deeply embedded in American domestic politics. The process of Middle East policymaking involves interaction between the following key structures:

The White House: The President, as Quandt (1993) has observed, is by far the key actor in the shaping of Middle East policy. He is driven by an awareness that what he does in the Middle East can have a significant positive or negative effect on his political future, owing to the influence of the pro-Israel forces on the electoral process. He is also influenced by a panoply of policy experts in the Executive branch and in the 'think tank' and academic communities, who shape his understanding of what is going on in the region and how this affects American security and economic interests.

The Executive Branch: The State Department is not the only organisation in the vast Executive Branch of the US government that helps shape Middle East policy. It must compete with other bureaucracies which often have divergent views. It must also contend with influential lobbies and elements in the Congress who see the State Department as 'anti-Israel'. The Defense Department has an important voice, especially at present since the US military has a significant presence in almost every country in the region. The 'intelligence community' consists not only of the Central Intelligence Agency (CIA) but several other similar organisations, such as the National Security Agency (NSA) which monitors electronic communications worldwide. Increasingly the Federal Bureau of Investigation (FBI) plays an important role overseas, especially since the rise of transnational terrorist networks.

The Legislative Branch: Both houses of the US Congress—the Senate and the House of Representatives—play an important role in Middle East policy formation. Each body has well-staffed committees on foreign relations, security issues, intelligence and finance. These committees hold hearings on Middle East policy issues, mobilising both the research arm of the Congress, but also outside experts and lobbyists. Because the pro-Israel lobbies, and the voting constituencies behind them, exert such pervasive influence over members of Congress, who fear and respect the influence they exert in elections, the Congress regularly authorises massive US financial aid to Israel (now over $3 million annually) and occasionally passes resolutions that even the White House finds excessively pro-Israel. Congressmen generally go along with the policy advice disseminated by pro-Israel think tanks on other Middle East issues, such as arms sales to Arab governments or criticism of the Palestinian leadership. It should also be noted, however, that Congress does offer a limited opportunity for opponents of US policies in the Middle East to be heard.

The Political Parties: In general, Middle East policy issues have been considered 'above partisan politics', at least by the politicians. Indeed, there is a bipartisan consensus that Israel's security and prosperity is a fundamental American priority. Similarly, the importance of access to oil and (until the demise of the Soviet Union) the need to contain communist influence in the region has been shared by both Democrats and Republicans. That said, it is generally believed that the Democratic Party has been more pro-Israel than the Republicans, and that the Republicans have been more pro-oil interests than the Democrats. Recently, however, the two parties have sought to invoke the Middle East to promote their own partisan interests over the other. In the 2004 presidential campaign, for example, Democratic candidates accused President Bush of needlessly invading Iraq and failing to advance in the 'war on terrorism'.

The 'Opinion Makers': Within the policy community, a variety of private research organisations (often called 'think tanks') attempt to influence the Middle East policy debates. Those debates are heavily shaped at the present time by think tanks with a pro-Israel and neoconservative agenda: the Washington Institute on Near Eastern Affairs, a spinoff from one of the key pro-Israel lobbies; the Heritage Foundation, the American Enterprise Institute and the Hudson Institute. It is an exaggeration to assert, as some have done, that the news media are controlled by pro-Israel elements that dictate their coverage of the Middle East; if anything, news coverage in the American press has improved markedly, in terms of reporting Arab as well as Israeli perspectives. On the editorial and opinion pages, however, anti-Arab and pro-Israeli commentary is abundant. But on Middle East issues not directly involving Israel there is considerably greater diversity of opinion. Liberal and left-wing media outlets certainly exist (*The Nation* magazine, for one), but their voices are relatively weak.

The Lobbies: There is a consensus among observers of American politics (whatever their views on the Middle East) that the network of organisations that make up 'the Israel lobby' is one of the two or three most powerful lobbies in Washington (Tivnan 1987). The American-Israel Public Affairs Committee (AIPAC) is perhaps the most visible of these groups, and it has decades of experience in influencing both Congress and the White House, but it is only the tip of an iceberg of state and local organisations with a well-deserved reputation for being able to channel money and votes in election campaigns. The Israel lobby is thought to have more influence with the Democrats than with the Republicans, although it assiduously cultivates both. Democratic candidates typically win a large majority of 'the Jewish vote'. While American Jews make up less than five per cent of the population, they are concentrated in key states, and they are politically active in terms of campaign contributions and voter turnout. It is also important to note that support for Israel is not at all confined to Jewish Americans. Many Christians, especially the increasingly influential Christian fundamentalists, also enthusiastically support the hawkish elements that dominate Israeli politics.

The other major lobbying force, less focused than the Israel lobby but still influential, is the oil and business lobby. Big oil companies, and construction and financial firms with major Middle East interests are concerned that the United States be able to do business in the region. The business lobby is generally closer to the Republicans than the Democrats. To a certain extent this pits them against the 'Israel lobby' but not always. In the Republican administration of Ronald Reagan, the secretary of state, George Shultz, an executive of Bechtel Corporation (a construction company with strong Middle East connections) turned out to be strongly pro-Israel. Many Arabs praised the election of George W. Bush in 2000, because they thought the Arab oil and business connections of his family and key officials (such as Vice President Dick Cheney) would lead to greater 'understanding' by Washington of Arab points of view; but this did not happen.

Given the apparent structural complexity of the decision-making process on Middle East policy, and the amount of information and expert opinion that is theoretically available to decisionmakers, an academic observer is struck by the narrow, uninformed, and ad hoc nature of some policy outcomes. The decisionmaking on Palestine-Israel seems not to comprehend the dysfunctional side-effects of American policy. In the decision to invade Iraq, the Administration's contentions about the danger of weapons of mass destruction and Iraqi collaboration with al-Qaida terrorists were largely incorrect. And its post-invasion policy planning and implementation seem to have been utterly uninformed by any understanding of Iraq's history, culture, politics, or its place in the region.

The 'Neoconservative Revolution'

In less than two years after 11 September 2001, the administration of George W. Bush had launched three wars: (1) the war in Afghanistan to effect 'regime change', removing the Taliban and their al-Qaida collaborators; (2) the larger 'war on terrorism' to disrupt Islamist networks and cells around the globe, from Germany to Indonesia to the United States itself, utilising law enforcement and intelligence capabilities; and (3) the invasion and occupation of Iraq, ostensibly to neutralise a regime with significant weapons of mass destruction and the will to use them, and one that actively supported al-Qaida terrorism. The President allowed himself to be persuaded that there was still another front in the new struggle: the terrorism practiced by Palestinian Islamist organisations against Israel. To that end, he undertook to effect 'regime change' (as he had in Afghanistan and Iraq) among the Palestinians by trying to sideline President Yasser Arafat with a more 'moderate' Palestinian leadership. He redoubled traditional American support for Israel by embracing Israeli Prime Minister Ariel Sharon as 'a man of peace' and a fellow-struggler against the common terrorist enemy. While professing an 'honest broker' role in breaking the Palestinian–Israeli impasse with a diplomatic agenda called 'the road map', the President made it clear that the real problem was on the Palestinian side, not the Israeli.

With over 130,000 American troops occupying Iraq and the Administration declaring 'a generational commitment to helping the people of the Middle East transform their region' (Rice 2003), it was obvious that the United States has moved away from its traditional stance of upholding the regional status quo toward a proactive, interventionist policy. In what was widely hailed as a landmark speech, President Bush himself committed the US to the goal of actively promoting liberal democracy and free market economic reforms, not just in Iraq but throughout the region (Bush speech, 6 November 2003). The 'neoconservative' network of hawkish policymakers who had fashioned the new approach justified America's new boldness as Manifest Destiny, on the one hand, and the ineluctable workings of Realism in international politics, on the other. The term 'neoconservative' thus seems problematical: a more accurate label might be 'radical interventionists'. As one of the more thoughtful neoconservatives, Robert Kagan, wrote, it was a policy driven by two imperatives: security in the post 11 September 2001 era and an ideological sense of moral mission whose origins can be traced to the very beginnings of the American republic (Kagan 2003: 85–8).

The greater Middle East became the testing ground for the new American project, and within it the Arab world was 'ground zero'—the source of what the US administration insisted was the new danger, a danger even worse than the old Soviet threat. Islamist terrorists, irrational and therefore undeterrable, possessed of low-tech portable weapons of mass destruction and therefore uncontainable, could and would strike at the American heartland unless they are preemptively liquidated. The Middle East and indeed the vaster Islamic world was, in its view, a breeding ground for terrorism. Not only must terrorist organisations be rooted out but the 'swamp' in which they breed must be drained. The new task of American foreign policy was not just to use force proactively but also to reshape the domestic environment of the several 'failed states' in the Middle East whose educational systems, religious organisations, incompetent governments and stagnant economies nurtured anti-American terrorism.

How it happened

How could this 'neoconservative revolution' have happened? The short answer is that a network of radical 'hawks', supported by right-wing Israeli circles, was able to seize a particular historical moment to impose its interventionist agenda. The moment was September 11, but it was preceded by decades of preparation. The origins of today's neoconservatives can be traced to the Cold War, represented by groups like the Committee on the Present Danger, established in 1950 to support the US military build up against the Soviet threat, and in the mid-1970s by the Jewish Institute for National Security, which was passionately concerned about Israel, and alarmed by the soft stance of the Carter Administration.

During the 1990s it would appear that the neoconservatives belatedly shed their historic core concern about the Soviet threat and began to search for other enemies. Despite the end of the Soviet Union, the US, in their view, still faced fundamental threats from various directions, not very clearly specified. As an undersecretary of defense, Paul Wolfowitz drafted an internal strategy document for the Pentagon in 1992, which some have suggested prefigures the G. W. Bush administration's national security document of 2002 (Gellman 1992). Although the final draft was substantially softened by senior Clinton administration officials, who rejected its unilateralist tone, Wolfowitz's draft called for a major increase in Pentagon funding to 'establish and protect a new order' from the possible emergence of a rival superpower that could threaten eastern or western Europe, east Asia, the former Soviet Union's territories and Southwest Asia. Japan, Germany and even India appeared to be potential adversaries; oddly, there was no mention of China. Odd too, and very significant in retrospect, was that 'terrorism' had not yet emerged as a tangible threat. Nor was the Middle East or the Islamic world given any prominence, apart from one of several scenarios that envisages a war against Iraq should it attack its 'southern neighbor', presumably Saudi Arabia. Wolfowitz's early draft included no reference to Israel, but in the revised version a clause was added making a specific commitment to the security of Israel.

But Israel was very much on the minds of other neoconservatives. In 1996 an Israeli think tank called The Institute for Advanced Strategic and Political Studies (1996) convened a study group, whose members included prominent American Zionist neoconservatives. It issued a policy memorandum called 'A Clean Break: A New Strategy for Securing the Realm'—for the edification of the incoming right-wing Israeli prime minister, Benjamin Netanyahu. Echoing the muscular theses of American neoconservatives, it preached self-reliance and the balance of power as the keys to Israel's security. 'Israel has no obligations under the Oslo agreements if the PLO does not fulfill its obligations', it asserted; and it proposed cultivating alternatives to Yasser Arafat's rule. A preponderance of power would enable Israel to roll back the Syrian threat, establish a right of hot pursuit against Palestinian resistance to the occupation, and work with Jordan to destabilise Syria and reinstall a Hashemite monarchy in Iraq. The memo also called for a new relationship with the United States based on a philosophy of peace through strength.

Neoconservatives created yet another organisation in 1997, the Project for the New American Century, which issued a clarion call for return to 'a Reaganite policy of military strength and moral clarity' in order to 'build on the successes of this past century and our greatness in the next' (Statement of Principles 1997). A year and half later the New American Century group sent a letter to President Clinton criticising his policy of 'containing' Saddam Hussein's regime in Iraq: '. . . if Saddam does acquire the capability to deliver weapons of mass destruction, as he is almost certain to do if we continue along the present course, the safety of American troops in the region, of our friends and allies like Israel and the moderate Arab states, and a significant portion of the world's supply of oil will all be put at hazard'. It called for 'removing Saddam Hussein and his regime from power' (Letter to President Clinton 1998). The letter was signed by a group that would become the 'Who's Who' of George W. Bush's foreign and security policy inner circle. Once in power, and well before September 11, the network was well-placed to advance its plans for Iraq and the Middle East. But it needed a catalyst to implement them. Like most others, the neoconservatives seem to have discovered the dangers of global terrorism only belatedly; but as al-Qa'ida stepped up its attacks on US interests overseas, finally striking the American homeland on September 11, the catalyst appeared. The trauma of September 11 paralyzed the formal structures of policy debate, and it is only two years later that Americans are beginning critically to assess the performance of the neoconservatives.

What it meant

Having achieved power in Washington in 2000, the neoconservatives faced the task of transforming their dreams into realities. The policy debates fell along two dimensions: (1) the relatively short-term practical question of establishing a viable 'security architecture' for the region, and (2) the larger, long-term goal of reshaping the domestic politics, economics and culture of the region, through liberal reforms that would 'drain the swamp' of anti-American Islamist extremist and terrorist elements. The pursuit of these goals was undertaken in a unilateral, indeed abrasive, manner that led to a weakening of the traditional transatlantic alliance.

A new 'security architecture'

Had matters in Iraq after the US conquest gone as the neoconservatives expected, that country might have become the foundation of America's security architecture for the region as a whole. But the immediate post-war consequences were not promising. Nevertheless, influential policy analysts, such as Kenneth Pollack (2003) imagined among their scenarios a 'GCC + 1' solution in which an Americanised Iraq allied with the six countries of the Arab Gulf Cooperation Council comprise an alliance under direct or indirect American tutelage. Variations of this idea envisaged a formal pact, along the lines of NATO, or less intrusively, a return to an 'over-the-horizon' posture that characterised America's position from the 1970s through the 1990s. The most sophisticated version ('GCC + 2') proposed some kind of American 'condominium' over Iraq, the GCC countries and Iran, modeled along the Commission on Security and Cooperation in Europe (Pollack 2003: 13). Assuming a stable and pro-American Iraq, the main sticking point in these schemes was Iran; they presumed that the present or future Iranian government might want, to engage. Another sticking point, however, was Saudi Arabia. As apprehensions mounted as to the stability of the Al Saud dynasty, and in light of the strong negative perceptions of Saudi Arabia in the United States following September 11, a question arose as to how comfortably Saudi Arabia might fit in America's security architecture.

But some neoconservatives argued that a relatively permanent US military presence in Iraq would make an American occupation of the oil fields in eastern Saudi Arabia easier in the event of a disintegration of political authority in the Kingdom.

Turning to the other flash-point in the region, the Palestinian–Israeli conflict, the Bush administration neoconservatives argued, implausibly, that regime change in Iraq would facilitate a solution to this, the oldest active conflict in the region. It is probable that American concentration on reviving the Palestine/Israel 'peace process' might have eased the path for Washington in post-war Iraq, but the converse does not hold. The record of this administration on this issue, indeed, has been a catalogue of blunders from the beginning. It began by trying to ignore the matter. When, belatedly, it recognised its importance it sent Secretary of State Colin Powell on a fruitless mission to persuade the Israelis from re-occupying the Palestinian areas. Despite President Bush's commendable commitment in principle to a Palestinian state alongside a secure Israel, he was unwilling to devote the energy—including pressure on the Israeli government to stop settlement activity and ease Israel's pressures on the Palestinian population. At the same time he became increasingly persuaded by Prime Minister Ariel Sharon's argument that Palestinian resistance—or 'terrorism'—was of a piece with the terrorism inflicted on the US in September 2001. As for the Palestinians, the President, following Sharon, declared the elected Palestinian president—Yasser Arafat—unacceptable as a negotiating partner, lumping the Palestinian National Authority together with Hamas and other militant organisations as terrorists. In Washington's view, without positive 'regime change' (as the US had forcefully accomplished in Afghanistan and Iraq), the Palestinians would once again be sidelined.

In the George W. Bush administration, like its predecessors, US policymaking relating to Israel was controlled essentially by the political operatives in the White House, not by the normal foreign and security offices of the Executive Branch; so the idea that America might pressure the Israeli government to ease its policies (strongly advocated within the State Department and parts of the intelligence community and uniformed military) failed to gain acceptance at the level of the President and his neoconservative advisors, many of whom (as we have noted above) were themselves ideologically committed to Israel as a regional superpower. A domestic 'triple entente' of neoconservatives, the Israel lobby, and Christian fundamentalists ensured that Israel, 'right or wrong', would not be seriously challenged by Washington. In the spring of 2004, as the US presidential election campaign got underway, President Bush endorsed Sharon's plan for an Israeli withdrawal from most of the Gaza Strip, and—in a major shift in American policy—accepted the legitimacy of the major Israeli settlements in east Jerusalem and the West Bank. Equally anxious to court Jewish and non-Jewish pro-Israeli voters, his Democratic Party rival, Senator John Kerry, also endorsed the Sharon plan.

The most hawkish of the neoconservatives believed that America by virtue of its overwhelming military power (and what they also considered to be its indisputably superior moral mission) was in a position to be the sole architect of regional security. Perhaps this is a correct assumption. But it ignored (and indeed was probably ignorant of) indigenous ideas of regional 'security architecture'. It dismissed the struggle of emerging countries in the region since the First World War to fashion their own security architecture, independent of Western domination. It was contemptuous of indigenous experiments in collective security such as the League of Arab States, the GCC, and other regional organisations. It could not accept Iran's long-standing position that Gulf security should be the sole concern of the littoral countries of the Gulf on both the Arab and Iranian sides. And it rejected transnational projects, whether under Arab nationalist or Islamist banners. Considering the significant American military presence in nearly every Arab country and the enormous economic-financial leverage that Washington could exert, one can understand the neoconservatives' conviction that they could be the exclusive architects of regional security. But if the lessons of history are worth anything, they should have noted that previous efforts by Western powers to dominate this area proved both costly and temporary.

Transforming Middle Eastern societies

The second dimension in the neoconservative project for 'operationalizing American hegemony' was to win the 'battle for hearts and minds' in the Middle East. President Bush himself, as well as his senior officials, repeatedly spoke of the need to make a generational commitment to transform the political systems of the Middle East toward some sort of democracy and to jump-start their economies in a liberal direction as well. Hard-core neoconservatives (including Bush himself when he was campaigning for the presidency in 2000) were leery of 'nation-building', but their own analysis of the security challenge emanating from the Middle East seemed to require nothing less. If forcible regime change was the agreed-on first step toward nation-building (or re-building), there was less clarity in neoconservative thinking about the subsequent steps, and perhaps less enthusiasm in committing resources too. The hawks, claiming to be realists, actually turned out to be naïve idealists in supposing that our getting rid of bad regimes in Afghanistan and Iraq would almost automatically lead grateful, 'liberated' local populations, thirsting for 'freedom', into establishing stable democracies. Warnings from regional specialists were sometimes dismissed as patronising to the indigenous cultures insofar as they suggested that democracy might not be achieved easily or quickly. As President G. W. Bush neared the end of his term in 2004, the process of democratising Afghanistan and Iraq was proving to be far more difficult than expected; and there was little sign that the American military interventions had initiated a benign 'domino effect' of democratisation in neighboring countries, as the neoconservatives had predicted. If anything, the regional insecurities engendered by America's war on terrorism had made the neighbouring regimes more repressive.

Conclusion

As future historians look back on the present era, would they conclude that September 11 triggered an imperial era for America in the Middle East? If so, would they find that Washington had achieved a permanent, liberal 'pax Americana' in this troubled region; or instead that its policies had led to deeper tension, instability and violence? Alternatively, would their verdict on September 11 be that the neoconservative project was a short-term aberration carried out by a network of radical-conservative ideologues whose influence evaporated owing to the growing unpopularity of their policies and the countervailing forces of the American political system? Would it be seen as a *thawra* (revolution) or as a mere *inqilab* (coup)?

Lacking the luxury of historical hindsight, and with the neoconservatives having been in power for only a few years, analysts are at an obvious disadvantage. On the one hand, the administration's dramatic interventions seem to carry a logic of their own which precluded any reversal of course. Considering the way in which the administration conceptualised the 'war on terror' then the 'enemy' would be with us for a very long time. Furthermore, assuming that this enemy could strike at the very homeland of the United States, the idea of abandoning the struggle would appear untenable. Despite 'victories' in Afghanistan and Iraq the wars still go on. And despite a half-hearted, unbalanced diplomatic stab at solving the Palestinian–Israeli conflict, it too goes on. In all of these places the neoconservatives see 'terror' at work. In his speeches, including a televised address to the nation on 7 September 2003, President Bush conflated the terror perpetrated by Palestinians and the terror perpetrated in Iraq and Afghanistan with the ultimate terror perpetrated by al-Qaida against the United States. The United States, he insisted, would never abandon Iraq until terrorism has been extirpated and a stable, democratic, and friendly political order has been established. And the larger commitment to transform Middle Eastern societies was a 'generational' one. The costs, though mounting, could be borne, considering the immense economic and military power of the United, States. Moreover, the neoconservative reading of US history—as Kagan and others have argued—has been interventionist: from Barbary to the Philippines to Central America and the Caribbean to Korea, Vietnam, Lebanon, Somalia, Bosnia and Kosovo—not to mention the two world wars (Ignatiev 2003). Finally, one could not see the prospect of any international coalition forming to check American assertiveness. Neither 'old Europe', Russia, China, India or Brazil—let alone any regional coalition of Arab governments, most of which are completely dependent on the US—had the capabilities to undertake such a challenge.

On the other hand, American domestic politics has a way of generating countervailing pressures on any administration in power. As the administration's conduct of its 'war on terrorism' faltered, important internal opposition currents began to stir. The Democratic Party, largely mute following September 11, began to find its critical voice. The steady resistance against the American-led coalition in Iraq, and also in Afghanistan, was continually on view to the American public through satellite television, even if often filtered through hyper-patriotic commentary. No less significant were the debates being initiated within policy-making circles both inside and close to the government. Advocates of the pragmatic realist tradition, emphasising multilateral approaches and 'soft' power (as Nye (2004) defines it) began to raise their voices with increasing vigour against the neoconservative approach to the Middle East. Were they to gain ascendancy, one might envisage a return to America's traditional approach to the Middle East, as discussed at the beginning of this chapter. That approach relied less on military interventions and more on a variety of policy instruments—traditional diplomacy, cultural and 'public' diplomacy, foreign aid, educational exchanges and security assistance. Commercial interests (especially oil) and qualified support for Israel would remain constants of American policy, but a certain respect for the sovereignty and internal affairs of Middle Eastern countries would also reappear as a feature of the traditional approach.

In the final analysis, then, American domestic opposition would be the main factor that could might cut short the neoconservative foreign policy revolution in the Middle East. But the strength of that opposition would likely depend significantly on the strength of indigenous Middle Eastern resistance to the neoconservative project.

Further Reading

BILL, J. A., Jr. *The Eagle and the Lion: The Tragedy of American-Iranian Relations* (New Haven: Yale University Press, 1980). A well researched and informative study of US–Iran relations from the Second World War until the Revolution.

COOLEY, J. K., *Unholy Wars: Afghanistan, America and International Terrorism*, Revised edition (London: Pluto Press, 2002). A journalist's account which links US responses to the Soviet invasion of Afghanistan to the expansion of international terror and drugs networks.

GERGES, F. A., *America and Political Islam: Clash of Cultures or Clash of Interests?*

(Cambridge: Cambridge University Press, 1999). An analysis of US policy and thinking on the role of Islam in the political process.

LESCH, D. W. (ed.), *The Middle East and the United States: A Historical and Political Reassessment.* (Boulder, Colo., Westview Press, 1996). Useful collection of essays on different aspects of US policy during the last century.

NYE, J. S., Jr., *Soft Power: The Means to Success in World Politics* (New York: Public Affairs Press, 2004). Argues that 'soft' power as well as 'hard' or coercive power is needed to persuade others in international politics.

14

Europe in the Middle East

Rosemary Hollis

OVERVIEW

The early twentieth century saw Europe literally take over the Middle East, turn 'the Arab world' into a system of separate states and facilitate the establishment of a Jewish homeland which became the state of Israel, before retreating in the face of independence movements and competitive superpower clientelism. By the end of the century the United States was unrivalled power-broker across the region, but the Europeans had turned old imperialist relationships into commercial ones. Economic interdependence and migration flows now knit Europe into the Middle East, in a manner which the European Union has sought to address through a Common Foreign and Security Policy, with mixed results. Latterly, the EU has been seeking a new form of region-to-region relationship with its Middle Eastern neighbours. This chapter traces this evolution in relations between the two contiguous regions, noting the interplay between changes in both, and concludes with some thoughts on how the Middle East has become caught up in fractious transatlantic relations post 11 September 2001.

Introduction

There are three discernible phases to the story of Europe and the Middle East in the twentieth century. The first, spanning the First World War and collapse of the Ottoman Empire to the 1950s, is the era of European imperialism in the Middle East out of which was born the contemporary state system in the region. The second coincides with the Cold War, during which Europe was part of the Western camp, but the United States unilaterally increased its power and influence in the Middle East as Britain and France retracted their colonial reach. While superpower rivalry was the dominant motif during the Cold War, with newly independent and in most cases militaristic regional states playing off one against the other to achieve room for manoeuvre, the subtext was rivalry between the Western powers for commercial gain.

The third, post Cold War, period dates from the beginning of the 1990s, by which time the European Union comes into being as an actor both comparable to and contrasting with the United States. Increasingly the vehicle through which individual European member states, including Britain and France, interact with the Middle East and pursue common diplomatic and economic policy initiatives, the EU is still not a unified actor. It does, however, have a totally different orientation to that of the United States, which has been characterised simplistically as the difference between advocacy of an international system based on international law and institutions versus one defined by US hegemony.

This dichotomy was laid bare in the transatlantic divide over Iraq, with the Bush administration in Washington effectively embarking on a new era of interventionism in the Middle East, and the EU, about to expand to encompass the newly independent East European states of the former Soviet bloc, internally riven over how to respond. In effect, the Middle East has become the focus for a struggle within the West and beyond, over the future shape of the international system. Neither in Europe nor in the developing world is there acceptance of the US line that the organising principle is a war between 'civilisation', championed by the United States, and transnational terrorism associated primarily with violent Islamism.

These developments have been cause for consternation across the Middle East on various grounds. Hopes among Arabs and Iranians that Europe could serve as a counterweight to the United States are tempered by perceptions that both are components of 'the West' and thus, in some senses, 'the other', which must be resisted if the indigenous states and peoples are to assert their own distinctive identities and place in the world.

The United Nations, itself created by and frequently the instrument of the Western powers, is distrusted for applying double standards, particularly with respect to the Muslim 'East'. So Arab élites may celebrate when the French foreign minister faces down his US counterpart at the Security Council over Iraq, but the powerlessness of European and other opponents of the war to avert the US-led invasion of March 2003 has concentrated minds on a new East-West, Muslim-Christian, liberationist versus imperialist confrontation, with Iraq the battlefront.

The literature on imperialism and neo-imperialism is thus instructive for understanding not only early twentieth century European relations with the Middle East but also subsequent US dealings with the region. Realism comes into its own during the Cold War period, not least in the cynical commentaries of Arab columnists, as a predictor of not only superpower but also US–European competition for clients, access to resources and military sales as well as the paramountcy of military force.

However, the realist and neo-realist paradigms are hopelessly limiting in so far as they reinforce the perception that states are rational actors calculating and acting upon their interests in a global competition. Issues of identity do not feature in the realist paradigm, yet they help explain the resistance to and nature of anti-imperialism and latterly anti-Americanism. Meanwhile, theories of regionalism in world politics are instructive in identifying how regions take shape, not just internally, but in relation to one another.

The contention here is that while imperialism was *done to* the Middle East by Europe, the experience has shaped Europe as well as the regions colonised. The contemporary identity of the EU is being defined in relation to neighbouring regions, as well as in juxtaposition to the United States. Its culture and politics are also informed by the presence within of Muslim émigré communities alongside Jewish Europeans with links including family ties to Israel.

By the same token, initiatives to develop regional institutions and consciousness in the Middle East, as discussed in Chapter 8, have met with limited results. Unresolved conflicts are part of the explanation, but so too are the interventions of external players operating with their own notions of what constitutes the region and which cut across indigenous conceptions.

In economic terms, the Middle East is in many ways the periphery and Europe the core. In the 1990s, when globalisation became the fashionable paradigm, theorists puzzled over whether the Middle East region as a whole and the Arab economies in particular, had somehow been left behind in a global liberalisation trend. European policy initiatives, especially in the Mediterranean, were informed by the espousal of liberal market capitalism.

Resistance in the Arab world to the medicine dealt out under 'the Washington consensus' has been explained as somehow to do with culture. As the debate about a 'clash of civilizations' raged, a new tranche of theories has emerged, especially in the United States, which burgeoned in the wake of the attacks of 11 September 2001. Some of these echo the exceptionalism of the old Orientalists, even though they claim to be universalist, espousing democracy and capitalism for all. Perhaps because of proximity, the colonial legacy, migration, economic interdependence and cultural interchange, the European depiction of the Middle East and its travails does not accord with that championed by the 'neoconservatives' in the United States.

Social theory is of use here in explaining how depictions of the problems can vary so profoundly from region to region, across and within societies. It helps alert the scholar to the coexistence of contrasting world views which serve a purpose for their proponents but cannot be reconciled. Encountering difficulties in their quest to liberalise the Middle East economies, the Europeans placed more emphasis on the promotion of civil society and human rights in Middle Eastern polities. Now they are talking of forging a 'strategic partnership' with the region. And so the story goes on.

Phase I: The Imperial Carve Up and Birth of the State System

Early twentieth century European imperialism in the Middle East was almost entirely a British and French endeavour, but the legacy of this period informs contemporary thinking about Europe's role in the region. Both countries left their mark on the societies they either colonised or controlled as protectorates and League of Nations Mandates. More importantly, these powers were responsible between them for devising the map of the contemporary Middle East state system in the aftermath of the First World War and collapse of the Ottoman Empire.

Imperial interests

Without dwelling on the details of how the British and French gradually made inroads into the Ottoman imperial domains, which are recounted in Chapter 1, what matters here are the consequences of their progressive encroachment. Also of note is that their policies were derivative of their global ambitions and interests, quite apart from any fascination with the region for its own sake.

Britain initially sought access to coastal ports along the Persian Gulf, Indian Ocean and Red Sea littorals, to protect the communication routes to its imperial possessions in India and beyond. The building of the Suez Canal, which opened a new sea route from the Mediterranean to the Red Sea, was a French, and later, a British business venture. It presaged progressive British interference in Egypt and protection of the Canal was cited as a reason for British designs on Palestine in the early twentieth century.

Britain's decision to convert its navy from steam to oil was made at the beginning of the twentieth century and prompted its quest to control access to the oil resources of Iran and the Ottoman-controlled province of Mosul (subsequently part of Iraq). Even before the collapse of the Ottoman Empire, therefore, the scene was set for a century of competition between the major oil companies and thus the governments of Britain, France and the United States.

The French presence was initially concentrated in North Africa. Here their objective was more about extending the Francophone empire than just securing trade routes. French colonisation of Algeria, begun in 1830, lasted until 1962: leaving the

Algerians with an identity crisis post-independence. Morocco and Tunisia were made protectorates for several decades. The French interest in the Levant, meanwhile, had in part to do with proprietorial connections to the Christian community in the Lebanon as well as competition with the British.

Wheeling and dealing

The way in which the British and French manoeuvred and schemed to carve up Ottoman domains even before that empire had collapsed gave them a reputation for subterfuge and double-dealing. Three sets of documents, also discussed in Chapter 1, bear witness to the machinations that took place[1] and are important because they are cited by Arabs to this day as evidence of European interference and perfidy.

First, the exchange of letters between Sir Henry McMahon, British High Commissioner in Egypt and Sherif Hussein of Mecca, from July 1915 to January 1916 (the Hussein–McMahon correspondence) encouraged Hashemite leadership of an Arab revolt in return for British recognition and support for Arab independence, including in areas which eventually came under British and French Mandatory rule in 1920.

Second, in January 1916, a secret agreement negotiated during the previous year between Sir Mark Sykes for the British and François Georges-Picot for the French (the Sykes–Picot Agreement) provided for British and French spheres of influence and control across whole swathes of the Ottoman Empire, including in those areas that subsequently became their League of Nations Mandates of Syria/Lebanon, Iraq and Palestine. In its specifics, this deal undercut the British understandings reached with Sherif Hussein.

Third, in a letter dated 2 November 1917, from the British Foreign Secretary Lord Balfour to Lord Rothschild, the British minister stated:

Her Majesty's Government views with favour the establishment in Palestine of a national home for the Jewish people, and will use their best endeavours to facilitate the achievement of this objective, it being clearly understood that nothing shall be done which may prejudice the civil and religious rights of existing non-Jewish communities in Palestine, or the rights and political status enjoyed by Jews in any other country.

The 'Balfour Declaration', and by extension the British, are still held responsible among Arabs for enabling the creation of the state of Israel at the expense of the Palestinians, and thus generating the Arab–Israeli conflict. The records suggest that the British did not foresee the difficulties they would encounter in managing Jewish immigration to Palestine or the eventual outcome.

The lines on the map

More broadly, the European imperialists are held responsible for devising the lines on the map that shaped the contemporary Arab state system. Palestine and Iraq were

Box 14.1 European imperialism and emergence of the state system

Maghreb (North Africa)

1830–1902—*Algeria* turned into colony of France (won independence in 1962)

1881—France made *Tunisia* a protectorate (independence came in 1956)

1911—Italy took *Libya* from the Ottomans (made independent, with extended British involvement, in 1951)

By 1904—*Morocco* under French and Spanish areas of control; 1912 made a French protectorate, with administration in north ceded to Spain (gained independence in 1956)

Mashreq (Levant/Arabia)

Nineteenth century Britain established semi-colonial role (responsible for external relations) in Arab *Gulf Sheikhdoms* (Kuwait, the last to join the British 'Trucial system' was first to gain independence in 1961; others—United Arab Emirates, Qatar, Bahrain gained independence in 1971)

Separate arrangements in *Sultanate of Oman* (replaced with Treaty in 1971) and *South Arabia* (Yemen), with *Aden* a British colony (until left South Arabia and Aden in 1967)

1882—Britain took control of *Egypt* (officially ended role in 1936, but retained their presence until 1950s)

1899—*Sudan* made an 'Anglo-Egyptian condominium'

1920—France received the League of Nations Mandate for *Syria* (independent in 1946) from which it separated *Lebanon* (officially independent in 1943, French left in 1946)

1920—Britain gained Mandates for *Palestine* and Mesopotamia (*Iraq*); established Hashemite monarchies in *Transjordan* (separated from Mandatory remit) and *Iraq* (independent in 1932; monarchy overthrown in 1958); ruled Palestine as a colony, within which a 'Jewish homeland' took shape on the basis of the Balfour Declaration of 1917 as stipulated under the mandate

1948—Britain withdrew from the Palestine Mandate—establishment of the state of *Israel*; *West Bank* incorporated in Jordan; *Gaza Strip* under Egyptian administration until both captured by Israel in 1967 war

Iran

1906—Discovery of oil in Iran, foundation of the Anglo-Persian Oil Company

1919—Attempted imposition of Anglo-Persian Agreement

1941—Allied invasion of Iran: Britain in south, Soviets in north; abdication of Reza Shah, succession of Mohammed Reza Shah

1945/6—British and Soviets withdraw

Box 14.1 Continued

1951—Nationalisation of Iranian oil

1952—Diplomatic relations with Britain severed

1953—Britain assists CIA instigated coup to overthrow Mussadiq/National Front government, re-instate Shah and reverse oil nationalisation

established as separate entities, administered by the British as League of Nations Mandates on the way to independent statehood. France took responsibility for what became the states of Syria and Lebanon. British acquiescence enabled the emergence of the Kingdom of Saudi Arabia in the 1920s, at the expense of the Hashemite emirate in the Hijaz. By way of partial recompense, the British installed Hashemite monarchs in what became Transjordan and Iraq.

These arrangements meant that the Arabs of the Levant and Mesopotamia transited from subjects of the Ottoman caliphate to citizens in the client states of the European victors of 'the Great War'. Arab input in the process was limited to lobbying the imperialists who decided the outcome. The United States attempted some mediation but soon withdrew to concentrate on its own domestic affairs and regions closer to home. Russia was in the throes of establishing the Soviet Union on the back of the Bolshevik Revolution.

The new borders cut across pre-existing age-old lines of communication, administration, kinship and association. Iraq had previously been three Ottoman provinces, not one entity. In the Eastern Mediterranean economic links had grown up that tied a string of port cities to the towns in the interior rather than to each other. Thus, Tripoli served as the trading outlet for the cities of Homs, Hama and Aleppo; Beirut was the port for Damascus; Haifa, Acre and Sidon were the coastal outlets for the fertile Hauran plane, and Jaffa operated as the port for Jerusalem.

The Mandate system separated coastal communities from those in the interior. Residents in the north and centre of what became Jordan (initially Transjordan) for example, had traditionally related to their neighbours to the east (in the new Iraq) and the west (in the newly separate Syria and Palestine), in keeping with east-west trade routes from interior to coast. All of a sudden these people had to develop a common national identity along a north–south axis instead, interlinked with those in the south of the new state who themselves had traditionally had more day to day interchange with their Hijazi neighbours to the south-east, along the Red Sea coast. The latter found themselves part of another new state, the Kingdom of Saudi Arabia.

Thus it was that European imperialism came to take the blame for dividing up the Arab world and setting up a competitive state system that undercut Arab unity and produced militarist, undemocratic and client regimes thereafter. In the popular Arab narrative, this was an imperial plot to divide and rule which the Americans are accused of mimicking in the twenty-first century.

Phase II: Imperial Retreat and Cold War Rivalries

The end of colonialism

In all the new Arab states the rallying cry became Arab nationalism and independence. The resulting struggle to end imperial rule and residual British and French interference across much of the Arab world became an essential ingredient of national pride and identity in the individual states. In the circumstances it is not surprising that the European retreat from empire in the mid twentieth century was followed by a 'cooling off' period in relations between the two regions.

Post-independence governments espoused anti-imperialist credentials to bolster their legitimacy. In Algeria, for example, the Front de Libération Nationale (FLN) based decades of political dominance on its leadership of the liberation from France. The Ba'th Party in Syria still lambasts the French at independence day celebrations to stir national sentiment and unity. The republicans who murdered the Iraqi king in 1958 were overthrowing the vestiges of British influence as well as the monarchy.

The British retreated from Mandate Palestine in 1948 in the face of two nationalist movements whose aspirations they had failed to reconcile. They had repressed Arab opposition to Jewish immigration but also fell foul of the Zionist movement by attempting to limit the inflow of Jewish migrants. The rise of Nazism and thence the Holocaust in Europe meant that British attempts to block the entry to Palestine of Jews fleeing systematic extermination was indefensible and widely criticised, not least in Washington. Various formulae were mooted for partitioning Palestine between Jews and Arabs, culminating in the United Nations partition plan of 1947 (Resolution 181). This was accepted by the Jewish leadership but rejected by the Arabs.

Lacking the will and probably the means, in the aftermath of the Second World War, to implement the UN plan by force, the British simply announced their intention to leave. As they did so, the first Arab–Israeli war, resulting in the establishment of the state of Israel in 1948, decided the issue. For the Palestinians, the legacy of the British Mandate was a catastrophe. For the Israelis, there was little appreciation and much cause for resentment of the policies of the British Mandatory authority.

The ultimate humiliation for the British and French came in 1956, when they secretly colluded with the Israelis to seize control of the Suez Canal, nationalised by Egyptian President and hero of Arab nationalism, Gamal Abd al-Nasser, and overthrow his government. Concealing their plans from the Americans, the British and French pretended that their deployment to Egypt was necessary to separate advancing Israeli forces from the Egyptians. The US administration was outraged and ordered their immediate withdrawal. To press home the point, the Americans triggered a run on the pound sterling which was so serious as to force the British to comply, leaving the French and Israelis with no choice but to follow suit.

France saw Nasser as the inspiration behind opposition to French rule in Algeria. The British encountered opposition to their colony in Aden from rebels assisted by Nasser. In both cases the imperialists were ultimately driven out. In Britain's case, the subsequent departure from the Arab sheikhdoms of the lower Gulf was achieved relatively peacefully, by negotiation, in 1971. That finally was the last step in Europe's imperial retreat from the Middle East.

Oil wealth and commercial competition

This was also the moment at which the oil producing states of the region began nationalising their oil industries, ending a half century of predominance of the Western oil companies in the energy sector and their control over price levels. The ensuing rise in oil prices, coupled with the Arab embargo on oil sales to Western countries supporting Israel in the 1973 Arab–Israeli war delivered a profound shock to the developed economies. Meanwhile, the oil booms of the mid 1970s and early 1980s fuelled a spending spree in the oil producing states from which European contractors and suppliers of consumer goods and arms competed to benefit. The international banking system absorbed surplus Arab capital.

Cold War rivalry between the United States and the Soviet Union encompassed both the Persian Gulf and the Arab–Israeli confrontation zone (Reich 1987). Even though the United States came to Nasser's rescue during the Suez war, its reluctance to finance the Aswan High Dam project, or supply arms, led Egypt to turn to the Soviet bloc. Thus began a period of superpower rivalry in the Arab–Israeli conflict which saw the Americans take over from the French as the principle arms supplier to Israel as of the 1967 war, and the Soviets siding with the Arab republics of Egypt, Syria and Iraq.

The Shah of Iran, who owed his throne to British and American connivance in the coup of 1953 that ended both the republican government of Mohammed Mussadiq and his strategy to nationalise Iranian oil, became America's principle ally and proxy policeman in the Gulf. After the British withdrew their forces from the Persian Gulf in 1971, Washington built up the Shah's Iran as a bulwark against Soviet expansion and sold him whatever arms he asked for. Saudi Arabia was the other pillar in US Gulf policy.

In the shadow of America

Since the Israelis were effective in lobbying against the US sale of some high tech weaponry sought by the Saudis, Britain had Washington's blessing to make up the difference. This arrangement was behind the British *Al Yamamah* defence sales project in Saudi Arabia, which kept production lines of the British Tornado aircraft running pending the development of a Eurofighter in partnership with Germany and Italy. The British–Saudi deal was worth billions of pounds over several years and formed the bedrock of bilateral relations in the 1980s and into the 1990s.

In fierce competition with the Americans and British, French arms manufacturers ranked third as suppliers to the Arab Gulf states, and alongside the Soviets they were the principle suppliers to Iraq in the 1980s. By this stage Iraq was at war with Iran. The Iranian revolution that toppled the Shah in 1979 had brought to an end Iran's special relationship with the United States and also presaged an upset in relations with Europe, especially with the British. Even though Iraq was the instigator of the 1980–88 Iran–Iraq war and a number of states instituted a ban on arms sales to both countries, the Iraqis continued to receive supplies, including covert help from both the Americans and the British over time.

With the fall of the Shah and prompted by the Soviet invasion of Afghanistan, in 1978, Washington moved away from a policy of securing its interests in the Gulf, including protection of the free flow of oil, by relying on proxies, and became directly involved in patrolling Gulf waters. Washington also gave its backing and support to the *mujahedin* and Arab volunteers fighting the Soviets in Afghanistan.

Meanwhile, in the Arab-Israeli sector, Washington became the principle architect of moves towards peace. The treaty between Egypt and Israel of 1979, presaged by the Camp David Accords of 1977, was bankrolled and sustained by US aid to both parties. That cemented Egypt's shift from the Soviet camp and into alignment with Washington. Europe was very much on the sidelines of the Middle East peace process in the 1970s and 1980s. As will be seen, the members of the European Community, including Britain and France, developed a common stance on the conflict, which was not to the liking of Israel and, although more palatable to the Arabs, could not match the leverage of the United States or continued influence of the Soviets.

In the background, the identity of Europe was itself developing, with plans to move from an Economic Community to a Union of member states by 1992. As this project progressed the Arabs began to cherish hopes that Europe could serve as a counterweight to the United States, as its influence and visibility in the region grew. In particular, the Arabs apparently thought that Europe might replace the Soviet Union as a defender of the Palestinian cause against the US–Israeli alliance. Those Arabs have since professed their disappointment that Europe does not seem to operate as the kind of power they had hoped it would be.

Phase III: The EU, Globalisation and the New Security Agenda

As the transition from the EC to EU drew nigh, Europe was overtaken by the momentous events surrounding the collapse of the Soviet Union, symbolised by the tearing down of the Berlin Wall. In foreign policy terms this meant a complete rethink of defence and security issues, as well as a preoccupation with forging new relationships with former Soviet bloc states to the east. The new security agenda was also influenced by globalisation.

Setting the agenda

Economists will argue that globalisation is not a new phenomenon, however, the Cold War divide between the capitalist West and communist or centrally planned economies of the East kept it limited in scope for decades. The collapse of the Soviet system gave free rein to capitalism and liberal market philosophies became the consensus approach to economic growth and development. East European states embraced the creed, in most cases spurred on by the prospect of EU membership as a reward and safety net.

For the developing and rentier states of the Middle East the same incentives were not made available. However, this did not stop the Europeans, as too the Americans, advocating liberalisation and privatisation to Iran and the Arab states as the way to cope with globalisation and economic interdependence (Dodge and Higgott 2002). Iran was open to discussion on the significance of globalisation, granting that in terms of new technologies at least it could be considered a descriptive concept rather than a Western plot. In the Arab states there was some resistance to treating it as a phenomenon to which they might have to adapt, as opposed to a new form of imperialism to be resisted.

Economic links between Europe and the Middle East are of greater significance than US trade ties to the region. The EU is the most important destination for exports from North Africa and the Gulf and the overall trade balance is in Europe's favour although Europe is heavily dependent on Middle Eastern energy supplies and more so than the United States. Israel's primary market is Europe not the United States.

These economic ties, together with geographic proximity and inward migration from the Arab countries, Turkey and Iran to Europe make for a totally different relationship between the two regions which contrasts with that between the more distant and militarily unrivalled United States and the Middle East. Reflecting this difference, European policies in the Middle East have placed much greater emphasis on so-called 'soft security' issues and socioeconomic strategies to deal with these (Behrendt and Hanelt 2000).

Thus, in their dealings with each other in the 1990s, the Europeans and the Arabs have both manoeuvred around the imperatives of economic interdependence and attendant security issues in a way that suggests both parties remain as much influenced by political considerations as any economic wisdom.

The Balkan wars of the 1990s made manifest the security problems that can result from the resurgence of ethnic and sectarian tensions within states. Concerns about 'failed states', refugee flows, gun running, the drug trade and all aspects of international crime supplanted the old preoccupations of the Cold War and the strategic nuclear threat. Yet the transition to a new world order began with another war in the Middle East, triggered by the Iraqi invasion of Kuwait in August 1990.

European policies and the Gulf

The US-led campaign to liberate Kuwait has been dubbed the first US war in the Middle East or alternatively the first NATO out-of-area campaign in all but name. In any case, unlike the subsequent US-led invasion of Iraq in 2003, the 1991 Gulf War had UN blessing. Iraq had blatantly violated international law by taking over another sovereign state and not only the Western allies but many Arab states could sign on to the liberation effort. The EC imposed sanctions on Iraq and its members provided military and financial support to the coalition. After the war most of the forces went home, though a US security presence was retained in order to contain both Iraq and Iran (Long and Koch 1997).

For a time the Europeans went along with the containment of Iraq, including sanctions and weapons inspections. Britain and France joined the United States in imposing so called no-fly zones over both the Kurdish region of northern Iraq and in the south, ostensibly to protect the Shi'i population there, but arguably more to defend Kuwait. The French eventually stopped their engagement in this effort. Only the British stayed the course and assisted the Americans in a bombing operation against the Iraqis in 1998, Operation Desert Fox, purportedly to force Iraqi compliance with weapons inspections.

The EU made more progress in pursuing a common strategy toward Iran. The European approach, which has espoused dialogue over isolation, was initially dubbed 'critical dialogue' in the early 1990s, and after the election of reformist Iranian President Mohammed Khatami in 1997, progressed to 'comprehensive engagement'. Khatami made official visits to a number of European capitals, cementing diplomatic, trade and cultural links. At the end of 2002, negotiations began for an EU–Iran trade and cooperation agreement and a dialogue on human rights was initiated.

Throughout, in their dealings with Iran, the Europeans have been at odds with the United States, which has continued to subject the Islamic Republic to economic sanctions, including secondary boycott measures to deter others from investing there. Barred by sanctions from competing for business, US companies, especially in the energy sector, had to watch from the sidelines as the Europeans signed contracts with Tehran. US critics of the Iranian regime deplored what they deemed European materialism in contrast to their own 'ethical' stance. For their part the Europeans argued that engagement can be more effective than confrontation.

However, in 2003, the EU itself resorted to pressuring Tehran, urged on by Washington, to sign up to a new protocol to the Nuclear Non-Proliferation Treaty. This shift reflects the precedence accorded in Europe to the non-proliferation agenda over pure economic interests in Iran. Even so, Tehran's reluctance to cooperate fully with inspectors from the International Atomic Energy Agency (IAEA) has led Washington to assume that the Iranians are set on developing a nuclear weapons capability and the Europeans to fear that they may not have enough leverage with Tehran to stop them, whether they present a united EU stance or not.

With respect to the Arab Gulf states, the Europeans have pursued independent and competitive commercial agendas. However, during the 1990s the EU instituted a dialogue with the Gulf Cooperation Council (GCC), the alliance that links Saudi Arabia, Kuwait, Bahrain, Qatar, the United Arab Emirates and Oman. With the introduction of a GCC customs union, the EU–GCC dialogue is expected to deliver a Free Trade Agreement and in 2004 the European Commission was planning broader engagement.

Most effective has been the formulation of a collective EU policy on the Arab–Israeli conflict, as discussed below. Equally expressive of a common European approach is the Euro-Mediterranean Partnership Programme.

Regionalism and the Euro-Mediterranean Partnership Programme

A new initiative for relations between the EU and its Mediterranean neighbours was launched in Barcelona in November 1995. The central objective was the creation of a Euro-Mediterranean Economic Area, to come into effect by 2010. The intention was to dismantle tariff and non-tariff barriers to trade in manufactured products between the EU and neighbouring states on the southern and eastern shores of the Mediterranean. Taking into account traditional trade flows and existing agricultural policies, trade in agricultural produce was also to be progressively liberalised; as too provision of cross-border services and capital movements.

The Barcelona Declaration

In the Barcelona Declaration,[2] the fifteen member states of the EU and Morocco, Algeria, Tunisia, Egypt, Israel, Jordan, Syria, Lebanon, Turkey, the Palestinian Authority, Cyprus and Malta, embraced a three-tier agenda for economic, political and cultural, and security cooperation that would turn the Mediterranean into a more integrated region, complementing existing north–south trade and cultural ties with new south–south links. The EU allocated funds to promote new communication and trade links between the Maghreb and the Levant and by 2004 was spending about 1 billion Euros a year on the programme.

It was counted a notable achievement of the Euro-Mediterranean Partnership (EMP) that Syria and Lebanon were involved as well as Israel, not withstanding the unresolved conflict between them. In the mid-1990s, progress in Middle East peacemaking through the Oslo process was expected to deliver an end to the conflict and the Barcelona initiative was intended both to compliment and capitalise on that process, but not directly interact with it. As it transpired, the EMP survived the demise of the Oslo process, but not without some stormy encounters at ministerial meetings of the participants, and the collapse of early efforts at security cooperation across the Arab–Israeli divide.

What remains is the economic dimension and some aspects of the cultural and human rights agenda embodied in the initiative. A series of bilateral Association Agreements have been concluded between the EU and Morocco, Algeria, Tunisia, Egypt, Jordan, Lebanon, Israel and the Palestinian Authority. As of this writing, negotiations with Syria are still in progress, held up in part because of a new requirement for partner states to renounce weapons of mass destruction. Libya, initially excluded from the EMP, pending resolution of the Lockerbie issue and sanctions, has since become an observer and potential full participant.

Reshaping regions

By 2003 the broad parameters and shortcomings of the EMP were apparent. Instead of an integrated region around the Mediterranean, what has emerged is a hub and spokes arrangement, with the EU as the hub connected to each partner state by separate bilateral trade links or spokes (Xenakis and Chryssochoou 2001). No one of the partner states has the capacity to match the European Commission in managing the bureaucratic complexities of the relationship. This has enabled the latter to set the pace, at least in terms of trade relations, but not much more than that.

The Maghreb states and Egypt have voiced complaints that they are disadvantaged, especially in the agricultural sector, because the southern European member states have lobbied effectively in Brussels to protect their farmers from competition from North African producers. All the partner states fear exposure of fragile domestic industries to European competition. The intensification of the Arab–Israeli conflict has impeded cooperation across this divide.

For their part the Europeans are disappointed that provisions in the Barcelona process to combat corruption, promote accountability and transparency and export European norms for human rights protection have not achieved the results for which they hoped. They contend that Arab élites have proved adaptive at maintaining their relatively privileged positions in the partner states and governments have resisted European efforts to support civil society, democracy and human rights movements in the partner states on the grounds that these interfere with indigenous culture and sovereignty.

There are, however, some more positive indicators for the aspirations of Barcelona. Conscious of their relative weakness in relation to the EU, Morocco, Tunisia, Egypt and Jordan decided to join forces, in the Agadier Agreement of 2003, to dismantle trade barriers between them and thence qualify for EU aid in support of south-south cooperation. In addition, human rights campaigners in the partner states have begun to report that pressures from the EU can help their cause.

Even so, the limited achievements of the EMP have led to calls for a rethink and re-launch of the programme as part of a new 'EU Neighbourhood Policy'. This reflects a decision, in the wake of EU enlargement from fifteen to twenty-five members, to develop a comprehensive formula to embrace non-candidate countries around the periphery, the better to enhance their stability and prosperity, to mutual benefit. The new policy was also developed in response to a US initiative to promote economic and political reform in what Washington called 'the Wider Middle East' (including Pakistan and Afghanistan).

The core concept of the EU policy is a 'strategic partnership' with neighbours in the Middle East, to encompass the EMP as well as Iran and the Arabian Peninsular states.[3] The focus is on dialogue and the EU undertakes to assist with indigenously-generated reform programmes but not impose its ideas from outside.

Conflict Mediation: Europe and the Middle East Peace Process

Individually and collectively, the Europeans have championed the view that the land-for-peace formula that underpinned the Egypt–Israel Peace Treaty of 1979 is the appropriate formula for a comprehensive peace deal. The concept was adopted by the UN Security Council in the aftermath of the 1967 war in Resolution 242, and repeated in Resolution 338 after the 1973 war. In those days, reflecting their historical involvement in the region, Britain and France were in the forefront of European diplomacy with respect to the Arab–Israeli conflict.

All European Community and Union statements on the Arab–Israeli conflict thereafter have kept to the basic principle of implementing UN resolutions. By contrast, the United States has been less faithful to the letter of international law, on the grounds that, if the actual parties to the conflict can agree on a formula for a deal, that should be supported, irrespective of how it squares with UN pronouncements and precedents. While the United States can claim that its position is actually the more practical and responsive to realities on the ground (including the fact that Israel is not prepared to concede all the territory it captured from the Arabs in 1967 in return for peace with either the Palestinians or Syria), the Europeans essentially tend to the view that the more land handed back, the more sustainable the peace.

Two observers of the differences between the European and US approaches to the conflict (Allin and Simon 2003) contend that both share an interest in its resolution, but differ in their identification of the problem. While the United States holds the Palestinians responsible for the collapse of the Oslo process, resumed violence and failure of new peace initiatives; the Europeans see Israel as the party most to blame. In any case, as of 2002, both have identified a two-state solution, with a Palestinian state alongside Israel, as the solution to the core conflict.

However, in March 2004, US President Bush went beyond the usual US emphasis on pragmatism when he gave support to a unilateralist initiative of Israeli Prime Minister Ariel Sharon, in which the Palestinians had not been consulted and which would compromise their rights under international law. British Prime Minister Tony Blair's statement that the plan could constitute the first step toward a negotiated peace between the parties, lacked credence for many observers, and set the scene for internal European as well as transatlantic tension.

European leverage

The Europeans led the way in coming round to espousal of Palestinian statehood as the goal. In the Venice Declaration of 1980[4] they stated that the Palestinian problem was not simply one of refugees, which is how it was framed in 1948 and in UN Resolutions 242 and 338, and that the Palestinian people must be able 'to exercise fully their right to self-determination'. The Declaration also broke new ground by stating that the Palestine Liberation Organization (PLO) would have to be involved in peace negotiations—a view which caused outrage at the time, in Israel and the United States, but was eventually adopted in the Oslo process.

For several years the Venice Declaration was the basis of the European stance on the conflict, but the United States was the peace broker. Meanwhile, Israel's invasion of Lebanon in 1982 shifted the focus to that arena, where again the United States was in the forefront of mediation efforts, including the evacuation of the PLO leadership from Beirut to Tunis. Europe's stance was condemnation of the occupation and to call for unconditional withdrawal in accordance with UN Resolution 425 (of 1978). When the Palestinian uprising or *intifada* erupted in Gaza and the West Bank in December 1987, European opinion was shocked by television coverage of Israel's military response to stone-throwing Palestinians.

The European Parliament debated how to respond in March 1988 and voted to deny finalisation of three protocols on Israel's trade and financial relations with the EC. The Parliament also criticised conditions set by Israel for implementation of an EC provision for direct dealings between Palestinian exporters and European importers. The move achieved an alleviation of those conditions prior to passage of the protocols later in the year.[5]

The tactic of delaying approval of bureaucratic instruments affecting trade with Israel was to be used on subsequent occasions, as a way to convey European disapproval of Israeli policies in relation to the Palestinians. For example, ratification of Israel's partnership agreement with the EU, reached in 1995 under the EMP, was held up the following year to signal dissatisfaction with the policy of the Netanyahu government (which took office in 1996), with respect to the peace process.

The Europeans were only given observer status at the November 1991 Madrid conference that launched the peace process following the Gulf War. That gave birth to both bilateral and multilateral tracks and the EC was made convenor of the working group dealing with regional economic development. For the duration of the multilaterals process—which eventually went into abeyance because of problems on the bilateral tracks—the EU used this platform to take a number of initiatives, including commissioning a World Bank report that laid the basis for an economic aid and development plan for the West Bank and Gaza.

The EU took overall responsibility for monitoring the elections of the Palestinian Authority (PA). Under the framework of Oslo the EU became the largest single donor to the PA (though initially the United States and Japan headed the league table for individual country aid). Member states of the EU also had their own aid programmes and projects in the Occupied Territories designed to bolster Palestinian self-determination and anticipated statehood. Unilateral and collective European projects were also aimed at building up Palestinian civil society institutions.

Even before it became an issue of the Israelis and the US Congress and administration, in the late 1990s the European Commission funded a major inquiry into the functioning of the PA, identified sources of corruption, questionable procedures and overlapping mandates, and initiated measures for reform.[6] The US administration kept to itself management of actual peace negotiations, but acknowledged that the whole process was facilitated by the EU role. For their part, the Europeans remained critical of some Israeli policies, particularly under Netanyahu, but worked more to support than to impede US mediation efforts.

When the official end of the five-year interim phase envisaged in Oslo drew near in 1999, the EU had Washington's unofficial blessing to head off a Palestinian threat to declare statehood unilaterally. The Israeli government was thought likely to react by annexing all the territory not under Palestinian autonomous rule, thereby undercutting negotiations and rendering the self-declared state nonviable. To dissuade the Palestinian President Yasser Arafat from this course, the EU issued a formal declaration envisaging Palestinian statehood as the expected outcome of the peace process.

This move helped pave the way for a resumption of more serious negotiations under the Israeli government of Ehud Barak. Nonetheless, the make-or-break summit at Camp David in July 2000 collapsed without agreement and the following September the outbreak of the second *intifada* and Israel's tough response derailed the peace process. Under the premiership of Ariel Sharon, who replaced Barak in February 2001, the conflict became ever more bitter, with Palestinian suicide attacks in Israel reaching unprecedented levels and the Israelis re-occupying Palestinian autonomous areas in Spring 2002.

The EU did not support the decision of the Bush administration to boycott and sideline Yasser Arafat, or bracket the Palestinian resistance with the transnational terrorist threat that took the world by storm on 11 September 2001. Emergency aid from the EU kept the PA afloat, when US assistance was suspended. Responding pragmatically to US President George Bush's endorsement of a two-state solution to the conflict, in Spring 2002, the EU worked through the mechanism of 'the Quartet' (the EU, US, UN and Russia) to produce the 'Road Map', formally launched in 2003, spelling out steps to reach that goal.

This, as other initiatives before it, was nonetheless dependent on US leverage and when this is lacking, Europe is seemingly powerless to resolve the conflict. When President Bush announced his support for Sharon's unilateral 'disengagement' plan in March 2004, most commentators saw it as contradictory to the Road Map if not actually damaging to the cause of peace. Meanwhile, Europe's new 'Neighbourhood Policy' can have only limited success without Arab–Israeli peace.

The Transatlantic Relationship and Iraq

More by default than design, the Middle East has become the testing ground for the shape of the post-Cold War, post September 11 world order. The fault lines in that order were laid bare by the crisis surrounding the Iraq war. Iraq was after all chosen by the US administration of George W. Bush as the laboratory in which to try out its new strategic doctrine of pre-emptive defence and the lynch-pin in its counter-terrorism strategy across the Middle East.

The reaction of key European governments and European public opinion to the US approach to Iraq demonstrated their attachment to international law and institutions, and above all the United Nations, as precious guarantors of an international order which they do not want to see cast aside by the sole remaining superpower. Consequently, as the United States flexed its muscles and called for loyalty, its European allies adopted various approaches that they hoped would either prevent the Americans from going completely out on a limb or at least preserve the credibility of international mechanisms for preserving world order the day after. The result was disunity and a severe setback for the EU's goal of a Common Foreign and Security Policy (CFSP).

In any case, Europe did not approach the Iraq crisis as one and dealt with it not as an isolated issue but within the broader context of transatlantic relations (Gordon 2002; Ortega 2003). For the duration of the crisis Europe was in reactive mode, but not to developments in the Middle East so much as to the policy of the United States. It is to be expected that hereafter the EU and its member states will weigh policy options in the Middle East within this broader frame of reference and not purely in terms of bilateral relations with states in the region.

In the months preceding the war France and Germany led the effort to avert military action through renewed UN weapons inspections. Britain sought UN cover for what the United States seemed set on doing, but itself sided so closely with the Americans, in an attempt to exert maximum influence in Washington, that in the event British forces joined in the US military action without UN endorsement. European public opinion was largely opposed to the war, though the governments of the East European states, lined up to become new EU members, were torn between their European ambitions and their support for America. Ultimately, the fallout for European unity and EU expansion was damaging but not fatal.

The implications for European relations with the Middle East have yet to be determined. Arab governments were generally fearful that a US success in Iraq could portend a more ambitious US agenda for regime change in the region and some countries, for example Iran and Syria, looked to Europe to counter this. But when the occupation met increasing Iraqi opposition in early 2004 there was greater fear that Iraq could turn into a maelstrom akin to Lebanon during its civil war, if not worse. Such European support as had been forthcoming for the rebuilding effort in Iraq began to peel away.

More portentous for Europe was a terrorist bombing in Madrid in early 2004, which appeared to be inspired by al-Qaida. Faced with the very real prospect of more such incidents inside Europe, the need for close cooperation between Europe, the United States and the governments of the Middle East to counter the transnational threat seemed imperative. However, the general European view was that US policy in Iraq and support for Israel were part of the problem not the solution. The chances of effective cooperation were therefore moot.

Arab élites meanwhile may still make a distinction between Europe and America in their understanding of 'the West' but are nonetheless disappointed in the EU for failing to counter the US superpower now deployed in their very midst. Arab public opinion appears to be radicalised and sympathetic to the anti-Western rhetoric of the Islamists. The Israeli government, by contrast, claims to be in the forefront of the global war on terrorism and scoffs at European calls for addressing the causes as well as the symptoms of terrorism, especially in their defence of the Palestinian quest for statehood. Europe's leverage in the region will therefore remain linked to its relative influence in Washington.

Conclusion

Europe has undergone profound transformation since the end of the Second World War. The Europeans have turned their back on centuries of internal competition and conflict to build a regional club that binds the members into structures which completely reorient them away from the old balance of power game into a new collective endeavour.

Thus, while the United States is exploring the possibilities of a Pax Americana across the globe—and expecting its allies to get in line—Europe is preoccupied with enlargement and adapting its decision-making structures accordingly. The whole project is now either misunderstood or viewed with ambivalence if not hostility in the United States (Kagan 2002).

The EU is now, as it were, integrated into the economic fabric of the Middle East, both as aid donor and supplier of arms, infrastructure projects and consumer goods. There is interdependence, with Europe serving as the principle market for exports from the Middle East and itself dependent on energy supplies from North Africa and the Persian Gulf. Europe is the beneficiary of inward investment and the holiday destination of many Middle Easterners. European tourists help keep Middle Eastern economies afloat.

Europe's colonial history in the Middle East and migration flows, of Jews from Europe into Israel and of Arabs, Iranians and Turks into Europe, bind the populations and politics of these two contiguous geographic regions. European efforts to promote Arab–Israeli peace are an expression of Europe's own security interests and ties on both sides of the divide. Yet this is not just a simple tale of harmonious interchange, there is ambivalence and friction with clear historical roots.

The Arabs thought they had managed to emerge from colonialism for good by the mid-twentieth century, but now wonder if the United States intends to revive the imperial era or simply create chaos and instability. The Israelis rely more on Europe as a trade partner than on the United States, but distrust European thinking on their conflict with the Arabs and look to the United States to back them up. How the Europeans handle the fallout from the US–UK occupation of Iraq and the vicious cycle of violence on the Israeli-Palestinian front will determine how Europe and European initiatives are viewed in the region. For their part the Europeans have no option but to balance their policies in the Middle East with EU internal priorities and the transatlantic agenda.

Further Reading

DOSENRODE, S. and STUBKJAER, A., *The European Union and the Middle East* (London and New York: Sheffield Academic Press, 2002). Useful chronological account of policies of the European Community and thereafter the European Union on the Middle East.

EHTESHAMI, A. (ed.), *From the Gulf to Central Asia: Players in the New Great Game* (Exeter: University of Exeter Press, 1994). Shows how, with the demise of the Soviet Union, Central Asia became a new regional focus for competition among the power brokers of the Persian Gulf.

FAWCETT, L. and HURRELL, A., *Regionalism and World Politics: Regional Organisation and International Order* (Oxford: Oxford University Press, 1995). A discussion of regionalism in theoretical and historical perspective and its application in different contexts, including Europe and the Middle East, thereby providing a context within which to understand relations between the two.

FROMKIN, D., *The Peace to End All Peace: The Fall of the Ottoman Empire and the Creation of the Modern Middle East* (New York: Henry Holt & Co., 1989). A compelling account of the role of the Europeans in the formation of the contemporary state system of the Middle East.

LUDLOW, P. (ed.), *Europe and the Mediterranean* (London and New York: Brasseys, for the Centre for European Policy Studies, 1994). A set of essays which give a flavour of European thinking about interdependence and relations across the Mediterranean in the period following the end of the Cold War and preceding the formulation of the Euro-Mediterranean Partnership Programme.

OWEN, R., *State, Power and Politics in the Making of the Modern Middle East* 2nd edn. (London and New York: Routledge, 2000). Gives pointers to how the European colonial legacy in the Middle East affected state building and politics in the region.

WENDT, A., *Social Theory of International Politics* (Cambridge: Cambridge University Press, 1999). An exposition of social theory from which to derive applications to the Middle East, and useful specifically for understanding competing narratives about identity, states, regions, and society in this context.

Notes

1. For the texts of these documents see Laqueur, W., and Rubin, B. (eds.), *The Arab-Israeli Reader: A Documentary History of the Middle East Conflict*, 5th edn. (New York: Penguin Group, 1995).

2. Barcelona Declaration, 28 November 1995, *http://europa.eu.int/en/comm/dg1b/en/den-barc.htm*.

3. See 'Interim Report on an EU Strategic Partnership with the Mediterranean and the Middle East' *Euromed Report*, Issue No. 73, 23 March 2004, *http://europa.eu.int/comm/eexternal_relations/euromed/publications.htm*.

4. Venice Declaration 1980, *Bulletin of the EC*, 6–1980: 10–11, point 1.1.6.

5. For sources see Hollis, R., 'Europe and the Middle East: Power by Stealth?' (1997) 73:1 *International Affairs* 15–29.

6. Council on Foreign Relations, Task Force Report, 'Strengthening Palestinian Public Institutions' available at: *http://www.cfr.org/public/pubs/palinstfull.html*.

Bibliography

AARTS, P. (1999), 'The Middle East: A Region without Regionalism or the End of Exceptionalism?', *Third World Quarterly* 20/5: 911–25.

AJAMI, F. (1978/9), 'The End of Pan-Arabism', *Foreign Affairs*, 57/2: 355–73.

ALBRIGHT, M. K. (2003), Bridges, Bombs or Bluster?, *Foreign Affairs* 82/5: 2–19.

AL-BAZZAZ, S. (1993), *harb tulid 'ukhra* [One War Gives Birth to Another] (Amman, Jordan: al-àhliyya lil-nashr wa al-tawzi').

AL-BAZZAZ, S. (1996), *al-janaralat àkhr man ya'lam* [The Generals Are the Last to Know] (Amman, Jordan: al-àhliyya lil-nashr wa al-tawzi').

ALLIN, D. and SIMON, S. (2003), 'The Moral Psychology of US Support for Israel', *Survival*, 45/3: 123–44.

AL-SAMARA'I, W. (1997), *hatam al-bawaba al-sharqiyya* [The Destruction of the Eastern Gate] (Kuwait: dar al-qabas).

AL-SAYYID, M. K. (1991), Slow Thaw in the Arab World, *World Policy Journal*, 8/4, 711–38.

AMIN, S. (1978), *The Arab Nation: Nationalism and Class Struggles* (London: Zed Press).

ANDERSON, L. (1986), *The State and Social Transformation in Tunisia and Libya, 1830–1980* (Princeton, NJ: Princeton University Press).

ANDERSON, L. (1991), 'Legitimacy, Identity and the Writing of History in Libya' in E. Davis and N. Gavrielides (eds.), *Statecraft in the Middle East* (Miami: Florida International University Press).

ANSCOMBE, F. (1997), *The Ottoman Gulf: The Creation of Kuwait, Saudi Arabia and Qatar* (New York: Columbia University Press).

ASHRAF, A. (1988), Bazaar-Mosque Alliance: 'The Social Bases of Revolts and Revolutions', *Politics, Culture, and Society*, 1/4: 558–67.

ASHRAF, A. (1990), 'Theocracy and Charisma: New Men of Power in Iran', *International Journal of Politics, Culture and Society*, 4/1: 113–52.

AYOOB, M. (1995), *The Third World Security Predicament, State Making, Regional Conflict and the International System* (Boulder, Colo.: Lynne Rienner Press).

AYUBI, N. (1995), *Overstating the Arab State: Politics and Society in the Middle East* (London: I. B. Tauris).

BADRI, H., MAGDOUB, T. and ZHODY, M. DIA EL-DIN (1978), *The Ramadan War* (Dunn Loring, VA: T. N. Dupuy Associates).

BAKER, J. A., III (1995), *The Politics of Diplomacy* (New York: G. P. Putnam's).

BAKER, R. W. (2004), *Islam without Fear: The New Islamists* (Cambridge: Harvard University Press).

BARAM, A. (1993), 'The Iraqi Invasion of Kuwait: Decision-Making in Baghdad' in Amatzia Baram and Barry Rubin, *Iraq's Road to War* (New York: St. Martin's Press).

BARAM, A. (1997), 'Neo-tribalism in Iraq: Saddam Hussein's Tribal Policies, 1991–1996', *International Journal of Middle East Studies*, 29/1: 1–31.

BARNETT, M. (1996), 'Identity and Alliances in the Middle East', in Peter J. Katzenstein (ed.) (1996), *The Culture of National Security. Norms and Identity in World*

Politics, (New York: Colombia University Press).

BARNETT, M. N. (1998), *Dialogues in Arab Politics: Negotiations in Regional Order* (New York: Columbia University Press).

BARNETT, M. and GAUSE, G. F. (1998), 'Caravans in Opposite Directions: society, state and the development of a community in the Gulf Cooperation Council, in E. Adler and M. Barnett, *Security Communities* (Cambridge: Cambridge University Press).

BATATU, H. (1978), *The Old Social Classes and the Revolutionary Movements of Iraq: a Study of Iraq's Old Landed and Commercial Classes and of its Communists, Ba'thists and Free Officers* (Princeton, NJ: Princeton University Press).

BEBLAWI, H. (1987), 'The Rentier State in the Arab World' in Beblawi and Luciani; Beblawi, H. and Luciani, G. (eds.) (1987), *The Rentier State* (London: Croom Helm).

BEBLAWI, H. and LUCIANI, G. (eds.) (1987), *The Rentier State.* (London & New York: Croom Helm).

BEHRENDT, S. and HANELT, C. (eds.) (2000), *Bound to Cooperate: Europe and the Middle East* (Guetersloh: Bertelsmann Foundation Publishers).

BEILIN, Y. (1997), *Touching Peace* (Hebrew), (Tel Aviv: Yediot Aharonot).

BELLIN, E. (2004), 'The Robustness of Authoritarianism in the Middle East: Exceptionalism in Comparative Perspective', *Comparative Politics*, 36/2, 139–57.

BENGIO, O. (ed.) (1992), *Saddam Speaks on the Gulf Crisis: A Collection of Documents* (Tel Aviv: Dayan Center for Middle Eastern and African Studies).

BERMAN, S. (1997), Civil Society and the Rise of the Weimar Republic, *World Politics*, 49/3, 401–29.

BERMAN, S. (2003), 'Islamism, Revolution, Civil Society', *Perspectives on Politics*, 1/2, 257–72.

BILL, J. A. (1988), *The Eagle and the Lion: The Tragedy of American-Iranian Relations* (New Haven: Yale University Press).

BILL, J. (1996), 'The Study of Middle East Politics 1946–1996: A Stocktaking', *Middle East Journal*, 50/4: 501–12.

BOTMAN, S. (1998), 'The Liberal Age, 1923–1952', in Daly, M. W. (ed.), *The Cambridge History of Egypt*, vol. 2 (Cambridge: Cambridge University Press).

BOUTROS-GHALI, B. (1992), *Agenda for Peace* (New York: United Nations).

BP Statistical Review of World Energy 2002: http://www.bp.com/centres/energy2002/index.asp (5 October 2002).

BRECHER, M. (1972), *The Foreign Policy System of Israel: Setting, Images, Process* (Oxford: Oxford University Press).

BROWN, L. C. (1984), *International Politics and the Middle East: Old Rules, Dangerous Game* (Princeton, NJ: Princeton University Press).

BROWN, L. C. (ed.) (1996), *Imperial Legacy: The Ottoman Imprint on the Balkans and the Middle East* (New York: Columbia University Press).

BROWN, L. C. (ed.) (2001), *Diplomacy in the Middle East: The International Relations of Regional and Outside Powers* (London: I. B. Tauris).

Bryson, Thomas A. (1977), *American Diplomatic Relations With the Middle East, 1784–1975: A Survey* (Metuchen, NJ: The Scarecrow Press).

BRZEZINSKI, Z. K. (1998), *The Grand Chessboard: American Primacy and Its Geostrategic Imperatives* (New York: Harper Collins).

BUDEIRI, M. (1997), 'Palestinians' Nationalist religious identities,' in Jankowski and Gershoni (1997).

BULL, H. (1977), *The Anarchical Society* (London: Macmillan).

BULL, H. (1984), 'The Emergence of a Universal International Society', in Bull and Watson (1984).

BULL, H. and WATSON, A. (eds.) (1984), *The Expansion of International Society* (Oxford: Oxford University Press).

BURKHOLDER, R. (2002), 'The U.S. and the West—Through Saudi Eyes', Gallup Tuesday Briefing, 6 August 2002, www.gallup.com/poll/tb/goverpubli/20020806.asp.

BUSH, G. W. (2003), 'President Bush Discusses Freedom in Iraq and the Middle East', Remarks by the President at the 20th Anniversary of the National Endowment for Democracy, U.S. Chamber of Commerce, 6 November 2003. http:/www.whitehouse.gov/news/releases/2003/11/print/20031106-2.html.

BUZAN, B. and WAEVER, O. (2003), *Regions and Powers. The Structure of International Security* (Cambridge: Cambridge University Press).

CAMPBELL, J. C. (1958), *Defence of the Middle East: Problems of American Policy* (New York: Council on Foreign Relations).

CARR, E. H. (1961), *What is History?* (London: Macmillan).

CARRÈRE D'ENCAUSSE, H. (1975), *La Politique Soviétique au Moyen Orient, 1955–1975* (Paris: Presses de la Fondation Nationale des Sciences Politiques).

CHAQUEIRI, C. (1995), *The Soviet Socialist Republic of Iran, 1920–1921: Birth of the Trauma* (Pittsburgh and London: Pittsburgh University Press).

CHOUCRI, N. and NORTH, R. (1975), *Nations in Conflict* (San Francisco: Freeman).

CHUBIN, S. and TRIPP, C. (1988), *Iran and Iraq at War* (Boulder, CO: Westview Press).

CLAPHAM, C. (1996), *Africa and the International System: The Politics of State Survival* (Cambridge: Cambridge University Press).

CLAUDE, I. (1968), 'The OAS, the UN and the United States', in Nye (1968).

COBBAN, H. (1984), *The Palestine Liberation Organization: People, Power, and Politics* (Cambridge, England: Cambridge University Press).

COLDWELL, D. (2003), 'Egypt's Autumn of Fury: the Construction of Opposition to the Egyptian-Israeli Peace Process', (Oxford: St. Anthony's College Masters Thesis).

COOLEY, J. K. (1991), *Payback: America's Long War in the Middle East* (Washington: Brassey's (US)).

COOLEY, J. K. (2002), *Unholy Wars: Afghanistan, America and International Terrorism.* Revised edn. (London: Pluto Press).

CORDSMAN, A. (2001), *Economic, Demographic, and Security Trends in the Middle East* (Washington, D.C.: Centre for Strategic and International Studies).

CROCE, B. (1941), *History as the Story of Liberty* (New York: W. W. Norton).

DANN, U. (1984), *Studies in the History of Transjordan, 1920–1949: The Making of a State* (Boulder, Colo.: Westview Press).

DARWIN, J. (1981), *Britain, Egypt and the Middle East: Imperial policy in the aftermath of war, 1918–1922* (London and Basingstoke: Macmillan).

DAWISHA, A. I. (1976), *Egypt in the Arab World: The Elements of Foreign Policy* (New York: Wiley, 1976).

Declaration of Principles on Interim Self-Government, Washington, 13 September 1993, Meron Medzini, ed., *Israel's Foreign Relations: Selected Documents, 1992–1994*, volume 13, Ministry of Foreign Affairs, Jerusalem, 1995, 319–28.

DEUTSCH, K. (1953), *Nationalism and Social Communication* (Cambridge, Mass.: MIT Press).

DEUTSCH, K. (1957), *Political Community and the North Atlantic Area* (Princeton, NJ: Princeton University Press).

DODGE, D. and HIGGOTT, R. (eds.) (2002), *Globalization and the Middle East: Islam, Economy, Society and Politics* (London: Royal Institute of International Affairs).

DODGE, T. (2003), *Inventing Iraq: The Failure of Nation Building and a History Denied* (New York: Columbia University Press).

DRYSDALE, A. and BLAKE, G. H. (1985), *The Middle East and North Africa: A Political Geography* (Oxford: Oxford University Press).

DUPUY, T. (1978), *Elusive Victory: The Arab-Israeli Wars, 1947–1974* (New York: Harper & Row).

EBAN, A. (1993), 'Building Bridges, Not Walls', *The Guardian*, 10 September.

ENDERLIN, C. (2003), *Shattered Dreams: The Failure of the Peace Process in the Middle East, 1995–2002* (New York: Other Press).

ESPOSITO, J. L. (1995), *The Islamic Threat. Myth or Reality*, (Oxford: Oxford University Press).

FANDY, M. (1999), *Saudi Arabia and the Politics of Dissent* (New York: St. Martin's Press).

FARAH, T. and FEISAL, S. (1980), 'Group Affiliations of Children in the Arab Middle East (Kuwait)', *Journal of Social Psychology* 111.

FAROUK-SLUGLETT, M. (1982), '"Socialist" Iraq 1963–1978—towards a reappraisal', *Orient*, 23, 206–19.

FAROUK-SLUGLETT, M. (1994), 'Power and Responsibility: U.S. Hegemony and the Arab States in the Post-Gulf War Middle East' in O'Loughlin, J., Mayer, T. and Greenberg, E. S. (eds.), *War and its Consequences: Lessons from the Persian Gulf Conflict* (New York: HarperCollins College Publishers).

FAROUK-SLUGLETT, M. and SLUGLETT, P. (1983), 'Labor and National Liberation: the Trade Union Movement in Iraq, 1920–1958', *Arab Studies Quarterly*, 5: 139–54.

FAROUK-SLUGLETT, M. and SLUGLETT, P. (2001), *Iraq since 1958; from Revolution to Dictatorship* 3rd edn. (London: I. B. Tauris).

FAWCETT, L. (1992), *Iran and the Cold War: the Azerbaijan Crisis of 1946*, (Cambridge: Cambridge University Press).

FAWCETT, L. (2003), 'The Evolving Architecture of Regionalization' in Pugh, M. and Suidhu W.P.S. (eds.), *The United Nations and Regional Security. Europe and Beyond* (Boulder, Colo.: Lynne Reinner).

FAWCETT, L. and HURRELL, A. (1995), *Regionalism and World Politics* (Oxford: Oxford University Press).

FEIS, M. (1947), *Seen from E. A.; Three International Episodes* (New York: A. A. Knopt).

FIELD, J. A., Jr. (1969), *America and the Mediterranean World, 1776–1882.* (Princeton, NJ: Princeton University Press).

FINDLEY, C. V. (1989), *Ottoman Civil Officialdom: A Social History* (Princeton, NJ: Princeton University Press).

FRANKEL, J. (1988), *International Relations in a Changing World*, 4th edn. (Oxford: Oxford University Press).

FREEDMAN, L. and KARSH, E. (1993), *The Gulf Conflict, 1990–91* (Princeton, NJ: Princeton University Press).

FUKUYAMA, F. (1992), *The End of History and the Last Man* (London: Penguin and New York: St. Martin's).

FULLER, G. and LESSER, I. (1995), *A Sense of Siege: The Geopolitics of Islam and the West* (Boulder, CO: Westview Press).

GASIOROWSKI, M. J. (2002), 'The Nuzhih Plot and Iranian Politics', *International*

Journal of Middle East Studies, 34/4: 645–66.

GAUSE, F. G., III (1985), 'British and American Policies in the Persian Gulf, 1968–1973', *Review of International Studies*, 11/4: 247–73.

GAUSE, F. G., III (1992), 'Sovereignty, State-craft and Stability in the Middle East', *Journal of International Affairs*, 45/2: 441–67.

GAUSE, F. G. (1999), 'Systemic Approaches to the International Relations of the Middle East', *International Studies Review*, 1/1: 11–31.

GAUSE, F. G., III (2002), 'Iraq's Decisions to Go to War, 1980 and 1990', *Middle East Journal*, 56/1: 47–70.

GAUSE, F. G., III (2002), 'Be Careful What You Wish For: The Future of U.S.–Saudi Relations', *World Policy Journal*, 49/1: 37–50.

GELLMAN, B. (1992), 'Pentagon Would Preclude a Rival Superpower', *Washington Post*, March 11.

GELVIN, J. L. (1998), *Divided Loyalties: Nationalism and Mass Politics in Syria at the Close of Empire* (Berkeley and Los Angeles: University of California Press).

GEORGE, D. (1996), 'Pax-Islamica: an Alternative New World Order?' in Sidahmad, A. and Ehteshami, A. (eds.), *Islamic Fundamentalism* (Boulder, Colo.: Westview Press).

GERGES, F. (1994), The *Superpowers and the Middle East: Regional and International Politics, 1955–1967* (Boulder, Colo.: Westview Press).

GERGES, F. A. (1999), *America and Political Islam: Clash of Cultures or Clash of Interests?* (Cambridge: Cambridge University Press).

GILPIN, R. (1989), *The Origins and Prevention of Major Wars* (Cambridge: Cambridge University Press).

GÖÇEK, F. (1987), *East Encounters West: France and the Ottoman Empire in the Eighteenth Century* (New York: Oxford University Press).

GOLAN, G. (1992), *Moscow and the Middle East: New Thinking on Regional Conflict* (London: Royal Institute of International Affairs, Washington: Council on Foreign Relations Press).

GOMAA, AHMED (1977), *The Foundation of the League of Arab States* (London: Longman).

GORDON, P. (2002), *Iraq: the Transatlantic Debate*, Occasional Papers No.39 (Paris: Institute for Security Studies).

GRAHAM-BROWN, S. (1999), *Sanctioning Saddam: The Politics of Intervention in Iraq* (London: I. B. Tauris).

GRAY, J. (1998), *False Dawn: The Delusions of Global Capitalism* (New York: New Press).

HAASS, R. (2003), 'Toward Greater Democracy in the Muslim World', *The Washington Quarterly*, 26/3 137–48.

HALLIDAY, F. (1997), 'The Middle East, the Great Powers and the Cold War' in Sayigh and Shlaim, A. (eds.), *The Cold War and the Middle East* (Oxford: Clarendon Press).

HALLIDAY, F. (1999), *Nation and Religion in the Middle East* (London: Saqi Books).

HALLIDAY, F. (2001), 'The Foreign Policy of Yemen', in Hinnebusch and Ehteshami (2001).

HALLIDAY, F. (2002), *Arabia Without Sultans* 2nd edn. (London: Saqi).

HALLIDAY, F. (2004), *The Middle East in International Relations. Power Politics and Ideology* (Cambridge, Cambridge University Press (forthcoming)).

HAMMOUDI, A. (1997), *Master and Disciple: The Cultural Foundations of Moroccan Authoritarianism* (Chicago: University of Chicago Press).

HARE, P. J. (1993), *Diplomatic Chronicles of the Middle East: A Biography of Raymond Hare* (Washington, D. C.: The Middle East Institute).

HARIK, I. (1987), 'The Origins of the Arab State System' in Salame', G. (ed.), *The Foundations of the Arab State* (London: Croom Helm); reprinted in Luciani (1990).

HEARD-BEY, F. (1999), 'The United Arab Emirates: A Quarter Century of Federation' in Hudson (1999).

HEIKAL, M. (1993), *Illusions of Triumph: An Arab View of the Gulf War* (London: HarperCollins).

HELMREICH, P. C. (1974), *From Paris to Sèvres: The Partition of the Ottoman Empire at the Peace Conference of 1919–1920* (Columbus: Ohio State University Press).

HENRY, C. M. (1996), *The Mediterranean Debt Crescent*, (Gainesville, Fla.: University Press of Florida).

HENRY, C. M. and SPRINGBORG, R. (2001), *Globalization and the Politics of Development in the Middle East* (Cambridge: Cambridge University Press).

HERSH, S. (1983), *The Price of Power: Kissinger in the Nixon White House* (New York: Summit Books).

HERZIG, E. (2004), 'Regionalism, Iran and Central Asia', *International Affairs*, 80/3: 503–172.

HEYDEMANN, S. (1993), Taxation without Representation: Authoritarianism and Economic Liberalization in Syria in *Rules and Rights in the Middle East: Democracy, Law, and Society* Goldberg, E., Kesaba, R. and Migdal, J. (eds.) (Seattle: University of Washington Press).

HINNEBUSCH, R. (1982), 'Children of the Elite: Political Attitudes of the Westernised Bourgeoisie in Contemporary Egypt', *Middle East Journal*, 36/4: 535–61.

HINNEBUSCH, R. (2002), 'The Middle East Regional System', in Hinnebusch and Ehteshami (2002).

HINNEBUSCH, R. (2003), *The International Politics of the Middle East*, (Manchester: Manchester University Press).

HINNEBUSCH, R. and ANOUSHIRAVAN, E. (2002), *The Foreign Policies of Middle Eastern States* (London: Lynne Reinner).

HIRO, D. (1991), *The Longest War: The Iran-Iraq Military Conflict* (New York: Routledge).

HOFFMANN, S. (1995), 'The Crisis of Liberal Internationalism', *Foreign Policy*, 98 (spring), 159–77.

HOFFMANN, S. (2002), 'The Clash of Globalizations', *Foreign Affairs* 81/4: 104–115.

HOURANI, A. H. (1962), *Arabic Thought in the Liberal Age, 1789–1939* (Oxford: Oxford University Press).

HOURANI, A. (1991), *A History of Arab Peoples* (London: Faber and Faber).

HOWARD, HARRY N. (1963), *The King-Crane Commission: An American Inquiry into the Middle East* (Beirut: Khayat's).

HUDSON, M. (1977), *Arab Politics: The Search for Legitimacy* (New York: Yale University Press).

HUDSON, MICHAEL (ed.) (1999), *The Middle East Dilemma. The Politics and Economics of Arab Integration* (London: I. B. Tauris).

HUNTINGTON, S. (1996), *The Clash of Civilizations* (New York: Simon and Schuster).

HUREWITZ, J. C. (1975, 1979), *The Middle East and North Africa in World Politics: A documentary record, Second Edition, vol. 1, European Expansion, 1535–1914 and vol. 2, British-French Supremacy, 1914–1945* (New Haven and London: Yale University Press).

HUREWITZ, J. C. (1976), *The Struggle for Palestine* (New York: Schocken Books).

IBRAHIM, S. E. (1995), 'Civil Society and the Prospects for Democratization in the Arab World' in Norton, A. R., ed., *Civil Society in the Middle East*, Vol. I (Leiden: E. J. Brill).

IGNATIEV, M. (2003), 'The Burden', *The New York Times Magazine*, 5 January.

INDYK, M. (2002), Back to the Bazaar, *Foreign Affairs*, 81/1: 75–88.

Institute for Advanced Strategic and Political Studies (1996), 'A Clean Break: A New Strategy for Securing the Realm', reproduced at http://www.israeleconomy.org/strat1.htm.

ISMAEL, T. Y. (1986), *International Relations of the Contemporary Middle East: A Study in World Politics* (Syracuse, NY: Syracuse University Press).

ITZKOWITZ, N. and MOTE, M. (1970), *Mubadele: An Ottoman-Russian Exchange of Ambassadors* (Chicago: University of Chicago Press).

JABBER, P. (1981), *Not by War Alone: Security and Arms Control in the Middle East* (Berkeley: University of California Press).

JANKOWSKI, J. and GERSHONI, I. (eds.) (1997), *Rethinking Nationalism in the Arab Middle East* (New York: Columbia University Press).

JENTLESON, B. W. (1994), *With Friends Like These: Reagan, Bush and Saddam, 1982–1990* (New York: W. W. Norton).

KAGAN, R. (2002), 'The Power Divide', *Prospect*, August.

KAGAN, R. (2003), *Of Paradise and Power: America and Europe in the New World Order* (New York: Knopf).

KANOVSKY, E. (1968), 'Arab Economic Unity', in Nye (1968).

KARAWAN, I. (1997), *Islamic Impasse* (London: IISS, Adelphi Paper 314).

KARAWAN, I. (2002), 'Identity and Foreign Policy: the Case of Egypt', in Telhami and Barnett (2002).

KEDOURIE, E. (1992), *Democracy and Arab Political Culture* (Washington, D.C.: Washington Institute for Near East Policy).

KEOHANE, R. O. (1984), *After Hegemony: Cooperation and Discord in the World Political Economy* (Princeton: Princeton University Press)

KERR, M. (1971), *The Arab Cold War: Gamal abd al-Nasir and His Rivals, 1958–1970* (London: Oxford University Press).

KHADDURI, M. (1988), *The Gulf War: The Origins and Implications of the Iraq-Iran Conflict* (New York: Oxford University Press).

KHALIDI, R. (1986), *Under Siege: PLO Decisionmaking during the 1982 War* (New York: Columbia University Press).

KHALIDI, R. (1997), 'The Formation of Palestinian Identity 1917–23', in Jankowski and Gershoni (1997).

KHOURY, P. S. (1987), *Syria and the French Mandate: The Politics of Arab Nationalism, 1920–1945* (Princeton: Princeton University Press).

KHOURY, P. S., and KOSTINER, J. (1990), *Tribes and State Formation in the Middle East* (Berkeley: University of California Press).

KIENLE, E. (1990), *Ba'th vs. Ba'th: The Conflict between Syria and Iraq* (London: I. B. Tauris).

KLIEMAN, A. S. (1970), *Foundations of British Policy in the Arab World: The Cairo Conference of 1921* (Baltimore and London: The Johns Hopkins Press).

KOBRIN, S. J. (1998), 'The MAI and the Clash of Globalizations', *Foreign Policy*, 112 (Fall): 97–109.

KORANY, B. (1987), 'Alien and besieged yet here to stay: the contradictions of the

Arab territorial state', in Ghassan Salame, *The Foundations of the Arab State* (London: Croom Helm).

KORANY, B. (1999), 'International Relations Theory: Contributions from Research in the Middle East', in Tessler et al, (1999).

KORANY, B. and HILLAL DESSOUKI, A. E. (1991), *The Foreign Policies of Arab States.* (Boulder, Colo.: Westview Press).

KORANY, B., NOBLE, P., and BRYNEN, R. eds. (1998), *The Many Faces of National Security in the Arab World* (New York: St Martin's).

KORN, D. A. (1992), *Stalemate, The War of Attrition and Great Power Diplomacy in the Middle East, 1967–1970* (Boulder, Colo.: Westview Press).

KOSTINER, J. (1987), 'Shi'i Unrest in the Gulf', in Kramer, M. (ed.), *Shi'ism, Resistance and Revolution* (Boulder, Colo.: Westview Press).

KUNIHOLM, B. (1980), *The Origins of the Cold War in the Near East: Great Power Conflict and Diplomacy in Iran, Turkey and Greece* (Princeton, NJ: Princeton University Press).

KUNZ, D. B. (2002), 'The Emergence of the United States as a Middle Eastern Power, 1956–1968', in Louis, W. R. and Owen, R. (eds.), *A Revolutionary Year: the Middle East in 1958* (London and Washington, D.C.: I. B. Tauris and Woodrow Wilson Center Press).

KUPCHAN, C. A. (1987), *The Persian Gulf and the West: The Dilemmas of Security* (Boston: Allen and Unwin).

LAIDI, Z. (1994), *Power and Purpose After the Cold War* (Oxford: Berg Publishers).

LAQUEUR, W. (2003), *No End to War. Terrorism in the Twenty-First Century* (New York: Continuum).

LAQUEUR, W. and RUBIN, B. (eds.), (1985), *The Israel-Arab Reader: A Documentary History of the Middle East Conflict* (Harmondsworth: Penguin Books).

LEENDERS, R. and SFAKIANAKIS, J. (2003), 'Middle East and North Africa', *Global Corruption Report 2003*, Transparency International (London: Profile Books).

LENCZOWSKI, GEORGE (1990), *American Presidents and the Middle East* (Durham, N.C.: Duke University Press).

LERNER, D. (1958), *The Passing of Traditional Society: Modernizing the Middle East* (Glencoe, Ill.: Free Press).

LEVY, J. (1992a), 'An Introduction to Prospect Theory' *Political Psychology* 13: 171–86.

LEVY, J. (1992b), 'Prospect Theory and International Relations: Theoretical Applications and Analytical Problems' *Political Psychology* 13 (June): 283–310.

LIEBERMAN, E. (1994), 'The Rational Deterrence Theory Debate: Is the Dependent Variable Elusive' *Security Studies* 3/3: 384–427.

LIEBERMAN, E. (1995), 'What Makes Deterrence Work? Lessons from the Egyptian-Israeli Rivalry?' *Security Studies* 4/4: 851–910.

LONG, D. and KOCH, C. (eds.) (1997), *Gulf Security in the Twenty-First Century* (London: British Academic Press for Emirates Center for Strategic Studies and Research).

LOUIS, W. R. (1984), *The British Empire in the Middle East 1945–1951: Arab Nationalism, The United States and Postwar Imperialism* (London: Oxford University Press).

LOUIS, W. R. (1986), 'British Imperialism and the end of the Palestine Mandate', in Louis, W. R. and Stookey, R. W. (eds.), *The End of the Palestine Mandate* (Austin: University of Texas Press).

LOUIS, W. R. (ed.) (1988), *Musaddiq, Nationalism and Oil* (Austin: University of Texas Press).

Louis, W. R., 'The Dissolution of the British Empire in the Era of Vietnam', *The Guardian*, 16 September 1993.

Luciani, G. (1987), 'Allocation vs. Production States: A Theoretical Framework' in Beblawi and Luciani (1987).

Luciani, G. (1990), *The Arab State* (Berkeley: California University Press).

Luciani, G. (1994), 'The Oil Rent, the Fiscal Crisis of the State and Democratization', in Salamé, G. ed., *Democracy without Democrats? The Renewal of Politics in the Muslim World* (London: I. B. Tauris).

Luciani, G. and Salame, S. (eds.) (1988), *The Politics of Arab Integration* (New York: Croom Helm).

Lustick, I. (1997), 'The Absence of Middle Eastern Great Powers: Political "Backwardness" in Historical Perspective', *International Organization* 51/4: 653–83.

Lynch, M. (1999), *State Interests and Public Spheres: the international politics of Jordan's Identity* (New York: Columbia University Press).

Mahdavy, H. (1970), 'The Patterns and Problems of Economic Development in Rentier States: the case of Iran' in Cook, M. (ed.), *Studies in the Economic History of the Middle East* (Oxford: Oxford University Press).

Makiya, K. (1998), *Republic of Fear; the Politics of Modern Iraq*, 3rd edn. (Berkeley and Los Angeles: University of California Press).

Makiya, K. (1993), *Cruelty and Silence: War, Tyranny, Uprising and the Arab World* (London: Jonathan Cape).

Makovsky, D. (1996), *Making Peace with the PLO: The Rabin Government's Road to the Oslo Accord.* (Boulder, CO: Westview Press).

Malley, R. and Agha, H. (2001), 'Camp David: The Tragedy of Errors', *New York Review of Books*, 9 August.

Maoz, Zeev (ed.) (1997), *Regional Security in the Middle East. Past, Present and Future* (London: Frank Cass).

McGhee, G. (1990), *The US-Turkish-NATO Middle Eastern Connection; How the Truman Doctrine and Turkey's NATO Entry Contained the Soviets* (Houndmills, Basingstoke: Macmillan).

Medzini, M. (ed.) (1995), *Israel's Foreign Relations: Selected Documents, 1992–1994.* volume 13, Ministry of Foreign Affairs, Jerusalem, 1995.

Menashri, D. (1990), *Iran: A Decade of War and Revolution* (New York: Holmes and Meier).

Miller, B. (2003), 'Conflict Management in the Middle East. Between the "Old" and the "New"', in Diehl, P. F. and Lepgoold, J., *Regional Conflict Management* (Rowman and Littlefield).

Morris, B. (1996), *Israel's Border Wars, 1949–1956: Arab Infiltration, Israeli Retaliation, and the Countdown to the Suez Crisis* (New York: Oxford University Press).

Morris, B. (2002), 'Camp David and After: An Interview with Ehud Barak', *New York Review of Books*, 13 June.

Morris, B. and Barak, E. (2002), 'Camp David and After—Continued', *New York Review of Books*, 27 June.

Morris, R. (1977), *Uncertain Greatness: Henry Kissinger and American Foreign Policy* (New York: Harper & Row).

Mosely, P. E. (1969), 'Soviet Search for Security' in Hurewitz, J. C. (ed.), *Soviet-American Rivalry in the Middle East* (New York: Praeger, for the Academy of Political Science, Columbia University).

Mufti, M. (1996), *Sovereign Creations: Pan-Arabism and Political Order in Syria and Iraq* (Ithaca: Cornell University Press).

Munson, H. (2003), 'Islam, Nationalism and Resentment of foreign Domination', *Middle East Policy*, 10/2: 40–53.

MURDEN, S. (2002), *Islam, the Middle East, and the New Global Hegemony* (Boulder, CO: Lynne Rienner Publishers).

MUTAWI, S. (1987), *Jordan in the 1967 War* (Cambridge: Cambridge University Press).

NEFF, D. (1984), *Warriors for Jerusalem: Six Days That Changed the Middle East* (New York: Simon & Schuster).

NEVAKIVI, J. (1969), *Britain, France and the Arab Middle East, 1914–1920* (London: The Athlone Press).

NIBLOCK, T. (1990), 'The Need for a New Arab Order', *Middle East International*, 12 October, 17–18.

NOBLE, P. (1991), 'The Arab System: Pressures, Constraints, and Opportunities' in Korany, B. and Hillal Dessouki, A. E., *The Foreign Policies of Arab States: the Challenge of Change* (Boulder CO: Westview Press).

NONNEHAM, G. (2001), 'Rentiers and Autocrats, Monarchs and Democrats, State and Society: the Middle East between Globalization, Human Agency and Europe', *International Affairs*, 77/1: 141–62.

NONNEMAN, G. (1986), *Iraq, the Gulf States and the War* (London: Ithaca Press).

NORTON, A. R. (1995), 'The Challenge of Inclusion in the Middle East', *Current History* (January): 1–6.

NORTON, A. R. (2002), *The New Media, Civic Pluralism and the Struggle for Political Reform* (eds. Eickelman, D. F. and Anderson, J. W.) (Bloomington: University of Indiana Press).

NYE, J. (1968), *International Regionalism* (Boston: Little, Brown & Co).

NYE, J. (1971), *Peace in Parts* (Boston: Little Brown & Co).

NYE, J. (1997), *Understanding International Conflicts* (New York: Longman).

NYE, J. (2000), *Understanding International Conflicts. An Introduction to Theory and History.* (New York: Harper Collins).

NYE, J. (2003), 'US Power and Strategy after Iraq', *Foreign Affairs*, 82/4: 60–73.

NYE, J. S., Jr. (2004), *Soft Power: The Means to Success in World Politics* (New York: Public Affairs Press.

ORTEGA, M. (ed.) (2003), *The European Union and the Crisis in the Middle East*, Chaillot Papers No.62 (Paris: Institute for Security Studies).

OSTERHAMMEL, J. (1997), *Colonialism: a Theoretical Overview*, trs. Shelley L. Frisch (Princeton: Markus Wiener).

OWEN, R. (1981), *The Middle East in the World Economy, 1800–1914* (London: Methuen).

OWEN, R. (1999), 'Inter-Arab Economic Relations during the Twentieth Century: World Market versus Regional Market?' in Hudson (1999).

PARIS, T. J. (2003), *Britian, the Hashemites and Arab Rule, 1920–1925: The Sherifian Solution* (London: Frank Cass).

PARKER, R. (1992), 'The June 1967 War: Some Mysteries Explored', *The Middle East Journal*, 46/2: 177–97.

PARKER, R. (1993), *The Politics of Miscalculation in the Middle East* (Bloomington: Indiana University Press).

PARKER, R. (ed.) (1996), *The Six Day War: A Retrospective* (Gainsville, Florida: University of Florida Press).

PATTEN, C. (2003), 'Democracy Doesn't Flow From the Barrel of a Gun', *Foreign Policy*, 138 (September/October): 40–4.

PENNELL, C. R. (2000), *Morocco since 1830* (London: C. Hurst & Co).

PERES, S. WITH NOAR, A. (1993), *The New Middle East* (New York: Henry Holt and Co).

PERES, S. (1995), *Battling for Peace: Memoirs* (London: Weidenfeld and Nicolson).

PISCATORI, J. (1986), *Islam in a World of Nation-States* (Cambridge: Cambridge University Press).

POLLACK, K. N. (2003), 'Securing the Gulf', *Foreign Affairs*, 82/4: 2–16.

PRESSMAN, J. (2003), 'Visions in Collision: What Happened at Camp David and Taba?' *International Security*, 28/2: 5–43.

Project For the New American Century (1997), 'Statement of Principles', 3 June. http://www.newamericancentury.org/statementofprinciples.htm.

Project For the New American Century (1998), 'Letter to President Clinton', 26 January. http://wwwrense.com/general35/warmem.htm.

PUGH, M. (2002), 'Maintaining Peace and Security' in Held, D. and McGrew, T. (ed.), *Governing Globalization* (Cambridge: Polity Press).

QUANDT, W. (1986), *Camp David: Peacemaking and Politics* (Washington, D.C.: Brookings Institution Press).

QUANDT, W. (1992), 'Lyndon Johnson and the June 1967 War: What Color Was the Light?' *The Middle East Journal* 46, 2: 198–228.

QUANDT, W. B. (1993), *Peace Process: American Diplomacy and the Arab-Israeli Conflict Since 1967* (Washington, D.C.: The Brookings Institution and Berkeley: University of California Press).

RAMAZANI, R. K. (1986), *Revolutionary Iran: Challenge and Response in the Middle East* (Baltimore: Johns Hopkins University Press).

REICH, B. (ed.) (1987), *The Powers in the Middle East: the Ultimate Strategic Arena* (New York: Praeger).

REISER, S. (1984), 'Islam, Pan-Arabism and Palestine: An Attitude Survey', *Journal of Arab Affairs*, 3/2: 189–204.

RICE, C. (2003), Remarks Delivered at the National Association of Black Journalists Convention, 7 August 2003. www.washingtonpost.com/ac2/wp-dyn/A30602-2003Aug7.

RICHARDS, A. and WATERBURY, J. (1998), *A Political Economy of the Middle East* 2nd edn. (London & Boulder: Westview Press).

ROBERTS, A. and KINGSBURY, B. (1993), United Nations Divided World 2nd edn. (Oxford: Oxford University Press).

ROBERSON, B. (1998), *The Middle East and Europe. The Power Deficit* (London: Routledge).

ROGAN, E. (1998), 'Instant Communication: The Impact of the Telegraph in Ottoman Syria' in Philipp, T. and Schaebler, B., *The Syrian Land: Processes of Integration and Fragmentation in Bilad al-Sham from the 18th to the 20th Century* (Stuttgart: Franz Steiner Verlag).

ROGAN, E. (1999), *Frontiers of the State in the Late Ottoman Empire: Transjordan, 1850–1921* (Cambridge: Cambridge University Press).

ROGAN, E. and SHLAIM, A. (eds.) (2001), *The War for Palestine: Rewriting the History of 1948* (Cambridge: Cambridge University Press).

ROOSEVELT, K. (1948), 'The Partition of Palestine: A Lesson in Pressure Politics', *The Middle East Journal*, 2/1: 1–20.

ROSS, D. (2001), 'Camp David—An Exchange', *New York Review of Books*, 20 September.

RUBIN, B. (1981), *Paved With Good Intentions: the American Experience and Iran* (London: Penguin).

RUGGIE, J. G. (2000), *Constructing the World Policy. Essays on International Institutionalization* (London: Routledge).

RUGMAN, A. (2000), *The End of Globalization: a New and Radical Analysis of Glob and What it means for Business*, (New York: Random House).

RUSTOW, D. (1970), Transitions to Democracy, *Comparative Politics*, 2/3, 337–63.

SADAT, A. (1977), *In Search of Identity: An Autobiography* (New York: Harper & Row).

SAFRAN, N. (1969), *From War to War: The Arab-Israeli Confrontation, 1948–1967* (New York: Pegasus).

SAFRAN, N. (1986), *Saudi Arabia: The Ceaseless Quest for Security* (Cambridge: Harvard University Press).

SAID, E. (1995), *Peace and its Discontents: Gaza-Jericho, 1993–1995* (London: Vintage).

SAIDEMAN, S. (2002), 'Thinking theoretically about identity and foreign policy' in Telhami and Barnett (2002).

SALAME, G. (1988), 'Integration in the Arab World: The Institutional Framework', in Luciani and Salame (1988).

SALIBI, K. S. (1977), *The Modern History of Lebanon* (New York: Caravan Books).

SALIBI, K. (1998), *The Modern History of Jordan* (London and New York: I. B. Tauris).

SAYIGH, Y. (1991), *Armed Struggle and the Search for a State: A History of the Palestinian National Movement, 1949–1993* (Oxford: Clarendon Press).

SAYIGH, Y. (1991), 'The Gulf Crisis: Why the Arab Regional Order Failed', *International Affairs*, 67/3: 487–507.

SAYIGH, Y. (2000), 'Globalization Manque. Regional Fragmentation and Authoritarian-Liberalism in the Middle East' in Fawcett, L. and Sayigh Y., *Third World Beyond the Cold War* (Oxford: Oxford University Press).

SCHIFF, Z. and YA'ARI, E. (1984), *Israel's Lebanon War* (New York: Simon & Schuster).

SCHÖLCH, A. (1981), *Egypt for the Egyptians! The socio-political crisis in Egypt 1878–82* (London: Ithaca Press).

SEGEV, T. (2000), *One Palestine, Complete: Jews and Arabs Under the British Mandate* (London: Abacus Books).

SELA, A. (1998), *The End of the Arab-Israeli Conflict: Middle East Politics and the Quest for Regional Order* (Albany, NY: State University of New York Press).

SHAMBAYATI, H. (1994), 'The Rentier State, Interest Groups, and the Paradox of Autonomy: State and Business in Turkey and Iran', *Comparative Politics*, 26/3, 307–31.

SHAPLAND, G. (1997), *Rivers of Discord: International Water Disputes in the Middle East* (New York: St. Martin's Press).

SHAW, S. and SHAW, E.K. (1978), *History of the Ottoman Empire and Modern Turkey, Volume II: Reform, Revolution and Republic* (Cambridge: Cambridge University Press).

SHAZLI, S. (1980), *The Crossing of the Suez* (San Francisco: American Mideast Research).

SHEIKH, N. S. (2003), *The New Politics of Islam: Pan-Islamic Foreign Policy in a World of States* (London and New York: Routledge-Curzon).

SHLAIM, A. (1988), *Collusion Across the Jordan: King Abdullah, the Zionist Movement, and the Partition of Palestine* (New York: Columbia University Press).

SHLAIM, A. and TANTER, R. (1978), 'Decision Process, Choice, and Consequences: Israel's Deep Penetration Bombing in Egypt, 1970', *World Politics* 30/4: 493–96.

SHUEFTAN, D. (1989), *Attrition: Egypt's Post War Political Strategy, 1967–1970* (Tel Aviv: Ministry of Defense Publication).

SINGERMAN, D. (1995), *Avenues of Participation: Family, Politics, and Networks in Urban Quarters of Cairo* (Princeton, NJ: Princeton University Press).

SITKIN, S. B. (1992), 'Learning Through Failure: The Strategy of Small Losses', *Research in Organizational Behavior* 14: 231–66.

SLUGLETT, P. (1986), 'The Kurds', in CARDRI (ed.), *Saddam's Iraq: Revolution or Reaction?*, (London: Zed Press).

SLUGLETT, P. (2002), 'The Pan-Arab Movement and the Influence of Cairo and Moscow', in Louis, W. R. and Owen, R. (eds.), *A Revolutionary Year: the Middle East in 1958* (London and Washington, D.C.: I. B. Tauris and Woodrow Wilson Center Press).

SLUGGLET, P. (2002), "As on a darkling plain": British, German, Ottoman and Russian intervention in Iran, 1914–1919' (unpublished paper, Tufts University).

SMITH, N. (2003), *American Empire: Roosevelt's Geographer and the Prelude to Globalization* (Berkeley: The University of California Press).

SOMEL, S. A. (2001), *The Modernization of Public Education in the Ottoman Empire, 1839–1908* (Leiden: Brill).

STEIN, J. G. (1985a), 'Calculation, Miscalculation, and Conventional Deterrence I: The View from Cairo' in Jervis, R., Lebow, R. N. and Stein J. G., *Psychology and Deterrence* (Baltimore: Johns Hopkins University Press).

STEIN, J. G. (1985b), 'Calculation, Miscalculation, and Conventional Deterrence II: The View from Jerusalem', in Jervis, R., Lebow R. N. and Stein, J. G., *Psychology and Deterrence* (Baltimore: Johns Hopkins University Press).

STEIN, J. G. (1993), 'The Political Economy of Strategic Agreements: The Linked Costs of Failure at Camp David' in Evans, P., Jacobsen, H. and Putnam, R. (eds.), *Double-Edged Diplomacy: International Bargaining and Domestic Politics* (Berkeley: University of California Press).

STEIN, J. G. (1994), 'Cognitive Psychology and Political Learning: Gorbachev as an Uncommitted Thinker and Motivated Learner', in *International Organization*, 48/2: 155–84.

STOCKING, G. W. (1970), *Middle East Oil* (Vanderbilt University Press).

STORK, J. (1975), *Middle East Oil and the Energy Crisis* (New York: Monthly Review Press).

TELHAMI, S. (1990), *Power and Leadership in International Bargaining* (New York: Columbia University Press).

TELHAMI, S. and BARNETT, M. (2002), *Identity and Foreign Policy in the Middle East* (Ithaca, NY and London: Cornell University Press).

TELHAMI, S. and HILL, F. (2002), 'Does Saudi Arabia Still Matter?' *Foreign Affairs* 81/6: 167–73.

TESSLER, M., NACHTWAY, J. and BANDA, A. (eds.) (1999), *Area Studies and Social Science: Stragies for Understanding Middle East Politics* (Indianapolis: Indiana University Press).

TIBI, B. (1998), *Conflict and War in the Middle East: from Interstate War to New Security* (New York: St Martin's Press).

TILLMAN, S. P. (1982), *The United States in the Middle East: Interests and Obstacles* (Bloomington, IN: Indiana University Press).

TIVNAN, E. (1987), *The Lobby: Jewish Political Power and American Foreign Policy* (New York: Simon and Schuster).

TRIPP, C. (1995), 'Regional Organizations in the Arab Middle East' in Fawcett and Hurrell (1995).

TRIPP, C. (2000), *A History of Iraq* (Cambridge: Cambridge University Press).

The White House (September 2002), 'The National Security Strategy of the United States of America', http://usinfo. state.gov/topical/pol/terror/secstrat.htm.

TYLER, P. E. (1992), 'Pentagon drops goal of blocking new superpowers', *The New York Times*, 23 May 1992: http://www.yale.edu/strattech/92dpg.html (5 Oct. 2002).

United Nations, Economic and Social Commission for West Asia (ESCWA) (2001), *Globalization and Labour Markets in the ESCWA Region*, (New York: United Nations) 23 August.

United Nations, Economic and Social Commission for Western Asia (2002), *Annual Review of Developments in Globalization and Regional Integration in the Countries of the ESCWA Region: Summary*, (New York: United Nations) 10 December.

United Nations Development Programme, *Arab Human Development Report* (2002, 2003, 2004). Sponsored by the United Nations Development Fund and the Arab Fund for Economic and Social Development. New York: United Nations. http://www.undp.org/rbas/ahdr/english. html (5 October 2002).

United Nations Development Programme, *Programme on Governance in the Arab Region*: http://www.pogar.org.

UNDPKO (2004), http://www.un.org/Depts/dpko.

VATIKIOTIS, P. J. (1987), *Islam and the State* (London: Routledge).

VEST, J. (2002), 'The Men from JINSA and CSP', *The Nation*, 2 September.

WALT, S. (1987), *The Origin of Alliances* (Ithaca, NY: Cornell University Press).

WALTZ, K. N. (1979), *Theory of International Politics* (New York: McGraw Hill).

WATSON, A. (1984), 'European International Society and its Expansion', in Bull and Watson (1984).

WEULERSSE, J. (1946), *Paysans de Syrie et du Proche-Orient* (Paris: Gallimard).

WHITE, J. B. (2002), *Islamist Mobilization in Turkey: A Study of Vernacular Politics* (Seattle: University of Washington Press).

WILEY, J. R. (1992), *The Islamic Movement of Iraqi Shi'as* (Boulder, CO: Lynne Rienner).

WILSON, M. C. (1987), *King Abdullah, Britain and the making of Jordan* (Cambridge: Cambridge University Press).

World Bank, *World Development Report 1997: The State in a Changing World* (New York: Oxford University Press).

World Bank (2000), *Basic Development Report* (Washington D.C.).

XENAKSIS, D. and CHRYSSOCHOOU, D. (2001), *The Emerging Euro-Mediterranean System* (Manchester and New York: Manchester University Press).

YERGIN, D. (1991), *Prize: The Epic Quest for Oil, Money and Power* (New York: Simon and Schuster).

ZIMMERN, A. (1945), *The League of Nations and the Rule of Law* (London: MacMillan).

Zogby International (2003), 'Saudis Reject Bin Laden and Terrorims', report of a July 2003 poll, http://www.zogby.com/news/ReadNews.dbm?ID=725.

ZOGBY, J. (2002), April 11 The Ten Nation Impressions of America Poll, Washington, D.C.: Zogby International.

ZUBAIDA, S. (1989), *Islam, the People and the State. Political Ideas and Movements in the Middle East* (London. I. B. Tauris).

INDEX